# AUSTIN K. GRAY

# TERESA

## The Story of
## Byron's Last Mistress

*with eight plates in half-tone*

## GEORGE G. HARRAP AND COMPANY LTD
LONDON   SYDNEY   TORONTO   BOMBAY

FOR
CHRISTINE

*First published* 1948
*by* GEORGE G. HARRAP & CO. LTD.
182 High Holborn, London, W.C.1

*Copyright.    All rights reserved*

THIS BOOK IS PRODUCED IN
COMPLETE CONFORMITY WITH THE
AUTHORIZED ECONOMY STANDARDS

*Composed in Fournier type and printed by Western Printing Services, Ltd., Bristol*
*Made in Great Britain*

# Preface

THIS is the story, not a biography, of Teresa, by birth Gamba-Ghiselli, by her first marriage Countess Guiccioli, and known to history as the last and most persistent *innamorata* of Byron. As a wise critic has said, women do not lend themselves to academic biography—not even Queen Victoria, or Cleopatra, or that engaging spinster Jane Austen. We want to know more about them than that.

Less than most women does Teresa Guiccioli lend herself to biography. Although she wrote poetry and one large book, although she was scholarly and studied theology, although she was an industrious correspondent in three languages—Italian, French, and English—she remains strangely inarticulate. She lives for us to-day in the tongues and the eyes of men and a very few women. The women (Mary Shelley, Lady Blessington, Princess Belgiojoso) were almost without exception malicious about her. Perhaps—Byron being Byron—they were jealous. In any case, Teresa was serenely indifferent to their malice—or their praise. Two men, however, who played a great part in her life—Byron and Henry Fox—were poignantly articulate, and she emerges from their comments an enigma—a flat contradiction. Byron says one minute that she was unprincipled, imperious, and *exigeante*—the typical mistress— and the next that she was unselfish, gentle, and docile—for him, the ideal wife. Henry Fox on first meeting her declared that she was gross, a fool, and a sham, but later he found her frank, sincere, and clever. Byron, it would seem, advanced to the attack like an eighteenth-century rake in a *liaison dangereuse*. The Countess Guiccioli was, so far as he knew, young, pretty, unhappily married, and easy of virtue like other women that he had met in Venice. Henry Fox, in the first shock of finding himself in love or, at any rate, loved, took her for a harlot. The waves closed over them both and they learned to be less cocksure and more reticent, but in word they still remained humorous (often now at their own expense)—and always articulate.

Her fate in Byron biography has wavered. The friends of Byron who count—Moore, Shelley, and Trelawny (if he be a friend)—were, on the whole, favourable to her, though their favour was qualified and they did not understand what her hold over Byron was. Her first appearance in print was in Medwin's *Conversations*. She disliked Medwin, and he returned the compliment by declaring that she was "the ugliest woman"

5

he knew. In his book, however, he simpers and patronizes her—she is "a lovely girl," interesting, melancholy, sensible—but "too much embonpoint." Then came Leigh Hunt's *Lord Byron and some of his Contemporaries*—a sorry book. Hunt was out to 'debunk' Byron—to show him up as mean, treacherous, and vain. His resolute spite against Byron is exuded over Teresa Guiccioli. She was barely handsome, he tells us; she was unintelligent, jealous, theatrical, a virago, plaintive about her lover's meanness in money matters; she lost her looks and only her vanity kept her faithful to Byron—whom she bored. At least one of these charges we know to be false—the nagging about Byron's niggardliness. That was Hunt's prerogative.

Teresa Guiccioli started, then, with a poor Press. Moore, in his *Life of Byron*, came to her rescue. He had met her at the crisis of her love affair at La Mira, when she was sick and frail. He had found her "not very pretty" and then "prettier." He had been sorry for her, liked her, and wished, all the time he was at Venice, that Byron would stop being "unromantic" in speech—about Teresa, about Allegra, about honeymoon and sunset. He was kind to Teresa in his *Life of Byron*, even a bit sentimental in spite of Henry Fox's warning that she was not the heroine of a French romance. He set the fashion for polite sentiment about her in Byron biography. Lady Blessington imitated him in so far as she veiled her malice in gush and platitude. But Byron's own letters about Teresa in the early stages of their love affair make thoroughgoing sentiment difficult. For a lover, he was, to say the least, clear-eyed and objective—or so he thought he was.

Then Teresa grew slowly older. She came to England as the Victorian age was setting in. "Byron's last mistress" was not a respectable person in London—and she stayed with Lady Blessington. People differed about her. She was beautiful, said Henry Reeve, amusing, kind, innocent; her manners were charming and she allowed people to "hoax" her with unfailing good humour. But almost at the same time William Archer Shee wrote her down for a "fubsy" woman, stupid, pretentious, and vulgar. She squalled at the piano and—most shocking offence of all—hiccuped in the drawing-room—and then laughed! Then in middle age she married a second time, an absurd millionaire, and was (apparently) happy and (certainly) engulfed in his absurdity.

Finally Victorian sentiment in England turned against Byron. Shelley was their angel, and so perforce—the Victorians liking strong contrast in moral matters—Byron became their devil. Shelley was a good husband (Mary Godwin); Byron was not (Annabella Milbanke). Shelley was a good father (Ianthe); Byron was not (Allegra). Shelley was chivalrous to women (?Harriet Westbrook); Byron was not (Claire Clairmont!); and so on all down the line to that moot point of squabbling—did Byron send that letter of Mary Shelley's to Mrs Hoppner? Of course not, shout the Shelley biographers in glee, and that proves that he was "base and treacherous." As Byron declined in favour, Teresa's Press grew worse and she was tainted with moral disapproval. Then came the sophisticates of the twentieth century, who were remotely amused by the antics of genius and took particular pains to express their own immunity from romance or sentiment. Teresa Guiccioli slumped again. She was still tainted with moral disapproval, but now she was absurd—if not a downright sham.

Yet more, she was an Italian—a foreigner—a trespasser on Anglo-Saxon preserves—and a successful trespasser, when we compare her with Caroline Lamb, Claire Clairmont, Annabella Milbanke, and other Anglo-Saxon types. But though she trespassed, she resolutely refused to fit æsthetically into the sombre Byronic scene. She was not a tragic type. She never learned to hate Byron as other women did. She did not go mad when he left her, or take to drink, go bankrupt, or take to sour philanthropics. She died unromantically rich—and happy, too, according to her own way of thought.

On the whole, the modern verdict on Teresa Guiccioli in Byron biography is faintly hostile. One writer says that she was stupid and tactless. Another finds her plaintive, pathetic, absurd. A third dismisses her as tough and coarse-grained.

## II

My 'story' really has resolved itself into a problem in romance and sentiment to which I don't know the answer.

The protagonists in a romance of real life are too often unconscious of what is expected of them—of the etiquette, if we may so call it, of romance. In that they are like soldiers in a battle. They should behave —I choose the word rather than 'act' designedly—in a certain way. Above all, they should talk in a certain way. And they don't.

I give the background of the romance. A more 'romantic' background we could not hope for—Italy at the beginning of the nineteenth century—so theatrical, so violent, so tolerant, and—for its English visitors, at any rate—so grotesque, incomprehensible, unreal! Venice and the gondoliers singing at springtime! A gloomy palace! Dante's tomb! Forest, and the angelus ringing! A garden and a fountain! Flight to a lonely villa by a river! Hints of jealousy, of murder! A confidante, a duenna, a negro page! Plot and escape and a brawl in the street! Ubiquitous spies! And somewhere a tenor voice singing!

For Teresa the background of the Romagna landscape, the platonism of her beloved Italian poets, the stale and (I suspect) corrupt code of *cicisbeo* and *dama*.

For Byron his poetry—and "the nightmare of his own delinquencies."

But the stage once set, the characters emerge from the background. They behave and speak for themselves—not as I want them to behave and speak. The trouble is that they are real people—they once really lived. They are not puppets in a plot that I can control. They refuse to behave and speak according to a psychological scheme of my own choice—or invention—in which I know all the answers. I cannot hold them to a compact little thesis of mother-fixation or inferiority complex or anything else as profound. All I can say is: this is what happened; this is what my characters actually did and said; this is what a chorus of onlookers—all of them contradictory, not all of them truthful, nor all of them knowing all of the romance—did, and wrote, and said about the romance. All I can say is: there was sunset and autumn at La Mira, love and solitude and a strange elfin child; and Teresa told her husband that she was sick with piles there; and Byron sent her home—"with her linen," as he promised—and still the 'romance' went on. My plot has slipped beyond my control. My characters have jumped beyond my powers of analysis—beyond my omniscience as a story-teller—and my ability as moralist or psychologist to lay down the law. All those things I leave to my readers. I can only suggest what I guess—not what I know, for I don't know.

## III

Though this is a story, not academic biography, it is based on the facts as they are recorded in printed books and, to a much lesser extent, in unpublished manuscript. A bibliography of the printed material is provided.

On Byron's side, there are four outstanding works, all published by the house of John Murray—Moore's *Letters and Journals of Lord Byron*, *Poetry*, edited by E. H. Coleridge, *Letters and Journals of Lord Byron*, edited by Rowland E. Prothero (Lord Ernle), and *Lord Byron's Correspondence* (with Lady Melbourne, etc.), edited by John Murray. From these books come numerous letters of Byron's—to Hobhouse, Murray, Kinnaird, Hoppner, Augusta Leigh, Teresa Guiccioli, etc.

Further letters come from *Astarte*, by Lord Lovelace. The letters to Alexander Scott are in the Morgan Library in New York. They were published in part by Earl C. Smith (see Bibliography). Byron's letter to his sister, describing Teresa riding in the Pine Forest, is also in the Morgan Library. I do not think it has been printed before.

I have consulted unpublished letters of Byron, Augusta Leigh, and Teresa Guiccioli in other libraries—namely, the Huntington Library, the Clark Memorial Library (Los Angeles), and the library of the Historical Society of Pennsylvania. I have not used them for quotation purposes, but they threw a light on my story.

Of modern biographies of Byron I should like to express my gratitude in particular to five—*Byron*, by Ethel Colburn Mayne; *Byron: the Last Journey*, by Harold Nicolson; *Shelley and Bryon*, by Isabel Clarke; *The Pilgrim of Eternity*, by John Drinkwater; and *Byron in Italy*, by Peter Quennell.

On Teresa Guiccioli's side, I note first her own writings. She contributed a *storia* to Moore's *Life*. Another *storia*, mangled and falsified, appears spasmodically in Lamartine's *Vie de Byron*. It is said that at her death she left the materials, or manuscript, for a third *storia*, to be entitled *Byron en Italie*. No such work was ever published. Instead, Teresa published in 1868 a two-volume work in French—*Lord Byron jugé par les Témoins de sa Vie*. A tedious, disappointing book, because she always quotes other people and never draws upon her own experience and knowledge. The book was written as a protest against Lamartine's completely forgotten *Vie de Byron*, which had appeared three years earlier, and Teresa seeks to confound Lamartine—particularly on religious matters—by a vast horde of witnesses for the defence. Yet the book has its merits if you look for them. Teresa's opinions on Byron's religion have been appropriated by other biographers without acknowledgment. She shows shrewdness and insight about Shelley as a man and a poet. And there are distracting glimpses of what she might have told us—scraps of Byron's letters in Italian, the Romagna landscape in autumn, Allegra tumbling in the garden, Hobhouse entering on a tender scene, Byron laughing in the sunlight, Shelley pouring money at Mary's feet. I have used the original French in preference to the better-known English translation by Jerningham.

On the Italian side, *I Guiccioli—Memorie di una Famiglia patrizia*, by the Marchese Alessandro Guiccioli, has been of great help. The Marchese Guiccioli is commendably anxious to do justice to the memory of his grandfather, Count Guiccioli, but it must be admitted that the old gentleman emerges from his grandson's narrative still formidable and a bit mysterious. The Marchese Guiccioli is hostile to his step-grand-mother, Teresa Guiccioli.

Other Italian writers who shed a light on the story from the Italian angle include Giovanna Foa, Luigi Rava, Fulvio Cantoni, and E. Rodo-canachi (see Bibliography). From Luigi Rava's book on Byron and Shelley at Ravenna I have quoted Teresa's poem on Shelley and utilized another poem in describing Filetto. Fulvio Cantoni, in his *Byron e la Guiccioli a Bologna*, has given me the topography of the love-affair in Bologna, although on one or two points I am puzzled. The work of these Italian scholars has never been adequately recognized, and I wish to express my gratitude.

Of one work I have used—Lamartine's *Vie de Byron* (1865)—I must say a few words here. I have written at length about this compilation in an appendix. It must be used with discretion, but where Teresa's narrative can be disentangled from Lamartine's over-writing, his mistakes, misunderstandings, and falsifications, we have the core of truth. For example, from this source we may gather what, I am sure, were facts, such as the meeting with the Countess Benzoni at the inn in Padua, the flight from the Palazzo Guiccioli at Ravenna in the Papal Legate's coach, the house near the Campo Santo where Teresa first lived when she came to Pisa, etc. Another point. Teresa, in telling her story to Lamartine, mentioned the part that Alexander Scott played in her love-affair with Byron. That gentleman's presence in the story was suspected by Byron biographers but not made clear until Earl C. Smith printed the Byron-Scott correspondence in 1931. And a last point. Teresa's account to Lamartine of those days at La Mira tallies with the letters that she wrote from La Mira to her husband—not printed until 1935.

For Henry Fox, his journal, edited by the Earl of Ilchester (see Bibliography), is the first authority. Henry Fox was young and unhappy when he wrote this journal. He grew up into an honourable, public-spirited, lovable man, howbeit always a bit crotchety and queer. He is best remembered to-day for his friendship with G. F. Watts, the painter.

For Teresa's second husband the *Mémoires du Marquis de Boissy*, by Paul Breton, has been consulted. A very dull work in two volumes. But every now and then, when Teresa wasn't watching, M. Breton made sly jokes at the expense of the Marquis.

For Teresa's old age Miss Mary Rebecca Darby Smith, of Philadelphia (see Bibliography), is the first authority. Her book is a panegyric of Teresa and, says Miss Mayne, with more truth than charity, "the silliest book ever written." But for all its absurdities it gives a lively picture of Teresa as a rich, lonely, and always kind old woman, living in a vulgar palace in Paris. From others of her compilations I gather that Miss Smith was a 'lion-hunter,' and when she had caught her lion she fed it on incense. She cultivated impartially the acquaintance of John Howard Payne (of *Home, Sweet Home*); Jenny Lind; Abraham Lincoln; Phineas Barnum; Bulwer Lytton and his son, the author of *Lucile*; Martin Tupper (of the *Proverbial Philosophy*); Lady Wilde ("Speranza") and her son, Oscar Wilde; Archbishop Tait; Charles Spurgeon, the preacher; Count Waldeck, centenarian archæologist (whom in all kindness she recommended to Phineas Barnum as a possibility for his circus); and Princess Yourievska, mistress of the Tsar Alexander II of Russia.

In Sylva Norman's *After Shelley* there is an amusing glimpse of Teresa Guiccioli with Shelley's friend and biographer, Thomas Jefferson Hogg (see Appendix III). In *The Art Life of a XIXth Century Portrait Painter*, by Emma Fagnani, there is interesting detail about Teresa in her later Boissy period (see Appendix IV). In her life of her husband, Daniel Dunglas Home, his widow states that Teresa de Boissy corre-

sponded diligently with the medium, 1856–65, but I have, as yet, found
no trace of that correspondence.

## IV

I wish to make in all gratitude the following acknowledgments:

To Miss Belle da Costa Greene of the Morgan Library in New York,
for allowing me to consult the Byron-Guiccioli manuscript material in
her library; also for allowing me to quote Byron's letter to Augusta
Leigh about his rides with Teresa Guiccioli in the Pine Forest; and yet
again for allowing me to quote more fully from the Byron-Scott correspondence than Mr Earl C. Smith had done.

To the following libraries for allowing me to consult unpublished
manuscript material: the Huntington Library, the Clark Memorial
Library at Los Angeles, the library of the Historical Society of Pennsylvania. I have not quoted from this material, but I have found it
extremely helpful in solving conundrums. I wish in particular to thank
Miss Mary Isabel Fry of the Huntington Library for help and interest
in my researches.

To the New York Public Library and the Free Library of Phila-
delphia for unfailing courtesy and help. I wish to thank in particular
Mr J. G. Hartman of the New York Public Library staff and Miss Anna
Stringoski of the Free Library of Philadelphia staff (Ridgway Branch).

In New York, to the New York Society Library (in particular),
Columbia University Library, the Casa Paterno Library, the Metropolitan
Museum of Art, and the Frick Art Reference Library.

In Philadelphia, to the Library Company of Philadelphia, and in
Princeton to the University Library.

To Sir John Murray for being allowed to quote extensively from
*The Letters and Journals of Lord Byron* (ed. Lord Ernle) and *Lord
Byron's Correspondence*.

To Messrs Christophers for being allowed to quote extensively from
*Astarte*, by Lord Lovelace.

To Messrs Eyre and Spottiswoode for being allowed to quote extensively from the *Journal of Henry Fox* (ed. Lord Ilchester).

To Messrs Macmillan for allowing me to reproduce the portrait of
Henry Fox from *Holland House*, by Princess Marie Liechtenstein.

To the Huntington Library, San Marino, for being allowed to reproduce the drawing of Byron from their collections.

To the Frick Art Reference Library, of New York, for being allowed
to reproduce the portrait of Lamartine (by Chassériau).

To Messrs J. B. Lippincott and Sons, of Philadelphia, for being
allowed to reproduce the portrait of Teresa Guiccioli from Miss M. R. D.
Smith's book *Two Distinguished Persons*.

# *Contents*

13

# *Illustrations*

"If these gentlemen ... discover my weak side, *viz.*, a propensity to be governed, and were to set a pretty woman or a clever woman, about me ... why, they would make a fool of me. But ... I left my heart in Italy."

BYRON TO BARRY, *from Cephalonia,*
*September* 1823

# Prologue in Ravenna

THE grand *salone* in the Casa Gamba-Ghiselli in Ravenna was a large room, damp and shadowy. The plaster was flaking down from the ceiling, the gold about the cornices was tarnished, the mirrors were clouded, the walls stained and blotched. The furniture in its day had been splendid with all the glory of Pompadour and Versailles, but now it was dingy and threadbare. The portraits along the walls were faces only, staring in pale alarm out of a blank fog. On the hearth a log fire crackled and smouldered in blue clouds of smoke up the chimney. The only other light came from two silver candlesticks set widely apart upon a long table in the centre of the room.

Count Ruggiero Gamba and his wife were receiving company. Their guest was seated opposite them in a chair by the fire. He sat bolt upright, a lean, robust old gentleman dressed in the sombre black of a husband mourning a wife recently dead. He was a handsome old man with ginger-coloured hair and slight whiskers. His face was long and pale, his nose straight and sharp as an icicle, and the eyes above it were a cold-steel blue. His lips were thin and ironic with an impatient droop at the corners, as though his life had been spent in brushing aside the arguments of simpletons and knaves.

He was speaking with his hosts in the sharp tone of a man who had a bargain to drive and meant to have his way. Count Ruggiero leaned forward in his chair with the deference of a younger man listening to an older man. His wife said nothing, but showed her concern in a tense, unchanging smile.

At the far end of the room a door opened and a girl stood for a moment alone on its threshold. She came slowly down the room, and the old gentleman stopped talking and gazed at her steadily with the screwed-up eyes of a short-sighted man. She emerged out of shadow into candle- and fire-light and swept a curtsy, first to her father, then to her mother, then a deeper reverence yet to the old gentleman in the chair by the fire. Count Ruggiero and his wife smiled upon their daughter and glanced anxiously at their guest.

He was still gazing at the girl, shading his eyes from the light with his hand. Without a word he rose and picked up one of the candlesticks from the table. He advanced upon the girl and, holding the candlestick high, stared down into her face. . . .

19

A young face tilted up towards his in a frank and fearless smile—a face throbbing with youth and health—not pale and Italian nor framed in dark hair, but a bright northern face with clear white, blue-veined skin and rosy cheeks. The eyes were dark blue under dark-brown lashes, but in the candlelight they had a sombre violet look. A straight nose and scarlet lips that, parted on their smile, revealed small and beautiful white teeth. But the crowning beauty of the face was the hair that fell round it in curls upon ivory-white shoulders. In sunlight there must have been a deep auburn glow to it, like veiled lightning asleep, but under the gleam of the candle it was shining gold. . . .

The old gentleman stared down with narrowed eyes into the radiant young face. He stepped back, holding the candlestick above his head, still staring. His lips were set in a grim, sardonic smile. He said not one word. With catlike tread he walked slowly round the girl, examining her closely as though she were a valuable piece of furniture. Then, without a word, he strode back to the table and put the candlestick down. Slowly and stiffly he sat down again in his chair by the fire. He nodded his head.

The Countess Gamba fluttered her hand nervously. The girl curtsied to the old man, her father, her mother, withdrew into shadow again, and vanished quietly from the room.

A few days later the Count and Countess Gamba were receiving congratulations at evening parties upon the fine marriage their daughter Teresa was making.

Count Ruggiero Gamba was a man nearing fifty with hair prematurely white. He was handsome in the straight-nosed Italian way, and his manners were exquisite and a trifle formal in the style of eighteenth-century Court life. In the patriarchal society of Ravenna he ranked as a young man, for his father was alive and ruled the Casa Gamba. But poverty and disappointment had aged him before his time and in company he was taciturn. His wife in her day had been a beauty—far more beautiful than her daughter—and her hair was still golden. But she had borne Count Ruggiero many children—some were dead, others, alas, were girls, and the last child was not born yet—and the Countess was tired.

But even they melted under the warm trickle of congratulation, for at last a stroke of good luck had come their way. One of their more pressing cares had been the problem of finding husbands for their daughters with whom they could give only small dowries. Faustina, the eldest—a pretty girl, mild and religious, who painted pictures of flowers —had made a poor marriage with Signor Rampi-Geminiani, a middle-aged lawyer in the small town of Faenza. But Count Guiccioli was rich and nobly born. True it was that he was nearly sixty—ten years older than Count Ruggiero and over forty years older than Teresa. He had been married before and had recently buried his second wife. People said the poor woman—she was nobody in particular by birth—had not been happy in her marriage. There was a good deal of gossip about Count Alessandro. He was called Brunello because his hair was the colour of ginger, and his hug, said men, was fatal—he had made his money in wicked ways—and the Count and Countess Gamba had heard all the stories. But they were poor, had daughters to marry, and could see only the virtues of their prospective son-in-law. He was an old political crony of Grandfather Gamba, but was still a hale and hearty man who looked younger than his years—indeed, with his tall, erect bearing and his trim ginger-coloured whiskers he looked younger than the white-haired Count Ruggiero, who stooped a little in the shoulder. His manner towards Teresa as a suitor was a blend of old-world gallantry and paternal solicitude. He had first seen her through the grille on a chance visit to her convent in Faenza. That glimpse had made him "forget his years," said the Gambas complacently—forget, too, the wife whom he had just laid away with lugubrious ceremony in her tomb. Then and there he had made up his mind to marry again.

He refurnished the Palazzo degli Osi in Ravenna in gorgeous style. He tricked out his lackeys and postilions in fresh blue-and-white liveries with plumes in their hats to match, and a negro boy was imported from Venice to serve as page. The blue-and-white coach with the Guiccioli arms on its panels was repainted, and six black horses were bought to draw it. A brand new harpsichord was installed in the grand *salone*. Then there came a general house-cleaning. His sons the Count packed off to the monastic school for young nobles in Ravenna, his daughters were sent to the fashionable convent of the Salesian Nuns of Santa Chiara, in Venice. The girls' governess, la Signora F——, of Treviso, was retained to serve as duenna. Then, with all practical arrangements made ahead of time, Count Guiccioli demanded the hand of the *Contessina* Teresa Gamba in marriage.

She had only to step into the Palazzo Guiccioli as a young and pampered bride. La Signora F—— would be there to give her advice and show her how Donna Angelica of pious memory had won the good graces of her husband. The Count would continue to manage his house as in the past with the help of stewards and secretaries. If Teresa had a favour to ask, she had only to ask it, or if she had a complaint to make, she had only to make it—and, be it favour or complaint, her husband would listen to what she had to say. On the matter of dowry he had been generosity itself. Any little hoard of *zecchini* that the Gamba family saw fit to give him, he assured them, would be invested at a high rate of interest and the income therefrom doled out monthly to their daughter as her allowance. She might spend it any way she chose—on flowers and sweetmeats, if she liked.

Teresa was included in the chorus of congratulation. Her parents had not consulted her about her marriage. They told her that Count Guiccioli had fallen in love with her and asked for her hand and they had given their consent. Teresa was "a good girl," as her brother Pietro said, she would obey her parents in all things until the day she was married, and most of all in marrying the husband they had chosen for her. Yet more, she would make any sacrifice to help her family. Here was a case of love at sight on Count Alessandro's part, and that was satisfactory from the point of view of sentiment—a requirement in marriage that neither the Count nor Countess Gamba was willing to forget. But this, too, they told her in their frank Latin way—Count Alessandro was, probably, the richest landowner in Romagna. He owned estates and villas all the way from Ancona to Bologna and from Bologna to Venice, and his income, said the gossips, was reckoned at one hundred and twenty thousand crowns a year. She would never know want or insecurity if she married him, and he had promised that when he died she would be left a widow with a rich jointure. She must make a sacrifice now in the hope of happiness later in life with a husband of her own choosing. She must marry Count Guiccioli and, like Lydia Bennet, find husbands for her sisters.

Teresa accepted the situation for her family's sake with a radiant smile. She was grateful to Count Alessandro for falling in love with her and taking her away from the convent. She was ready to love him in her turn and show her gratitude in kindness and affection. She was proud, too, that she, with no fortune of her own, had borne away, from under the noses of ambitious matrons with daughters to marry, the richest man in Ravenna.

Count Alessandro knew well how to woo a girl. His thin lips unlocked in protective smiles, he was deferential and full of insinuating courtesies, he flattered her with flowers and pretty trinkets such as a young man brings his beloved. When he chose, he would converse in the most amusing fashion, although there was always in his talk an undercurrent of sarcasm. He had known famous people in his life, and she listened eagerly to his stories of the Emperor Napoleon and Alfieri, the poet. If she turned from Alfieri to other poets and to her own favourite, Dante, he spoke with knowledge about Beatrice or the doctrine of platonic love in *La Vita Nuova*. When she was his wife, he told her, she would have jewels and fine clothes, villas and *palazzi* everywhere to live in, and servants galore to wait upon her, horses to ride or draw her coach. He meant to buy a palace in Venice one day, and he would take her to Rome and Florence and, if she were good, to Paris. And, last of all, said the Count, wagging his head wisely as one who knows that youth will have its way, after he had trained her in wifely duties, she should have her *amico*. He would choose one carefully—a sprightly young *abbé* or a handsome cavalier from Venice—to carry her fan, to sit with her in her box at the opera, to give her his arm at balls and pay her those delicate attentions and whisper those sweet nothings from which husbands are absolved after the honeymoon of marriage is over.

It was as pretty a wedding of January with May, said every one, as might be seen on a fine spring day, and took place on a cold, damp day in January of the year 1818. All the nobility and fashion of Ravenna attended the ceremony, which was carried out with ostentatious pomp, as everything was in the outward life of Count Guiccioli. Teresa was flushed and excited and proud. But, as her bridegroom handed her into the blue-and-white coach, she heard in the polite murmur all round her words of tenderness and compassion. The coach rattled away through the streets of Ravenna out upon the road to Bologna; and as she gazed from its windows at the faces of poor folk in the city, they looked mournful and perplexed. Somehow she felt amid all her excitement that every one was sorry for her.

# BOOK ONE

# Matrimony

CHAPTER I

## Bride and Bridegroom

EVERY ONE liked the Gamba family—they were impecunious, happy-go-lucky folk—good-looking, amiable, and well bred, on visiting-terms with the best families in Romagna—the Cavallis, the Capponis, and the Ercolanis of Bologna. They belonged to the 'sacred forty' who had the privilege of dressing their footmen in the Papal green-and-blue. But, as Gambas, they could not boast of remote ancestry. They had emerged into the holy green-and-blue about 1660, and that—in Romagna, where most families claimed Gothic kings and Roman emperors for their ancestors—was nothing to boast about. Their importance, their wealth, and most of their ancestry came when a Gamba married the heiress of the old house of Ghiselli. Teresa's mother had brought as her dowry golden hair and pink cheeks from her own family of Machirelli-Giordani, which had migrated from Northern Italy to Vienna. All her life Teresa was proud of her noble descent. Was not her great-uncle, Count Cobentzel, once leading Minister of the Holy Roman Empire under the Emperor Joseph? Were not the Esterhazys and the Erdödis of Hungary her cousins? People who were not cousins of the Erdödis of Hungary or the Ercolanis of Romagna she tolerated, as she would the peasants and brute beasts of the field—they, too, were God's creatures.

By 1800 the Ghiselli fortune was a noble memory. It had vanished because the Gamba family was too improvident to hold it. As a breed they had a knack of putting their money on the wrong political horse or, if by chance they backed a horse that proved a winner, they backed it for the wrong race. Grandfather Paolo Gamba had welcomed General Bonaparte as a precursor of Italian independence, but he lived to regret his choice and retired in disgust from politics. His son, Ruggiero, was an ardent believer in the French Revolution, and in 1797 he was captain of the National Guard of Romagna. But when the Emperor Napoleon abolished the Cisalpine Republic in favour of a vice-royalty under Eugène de Beauharnais, he left Romagna as a voluntary exile and did not return to live there until after the battle of Marengo. He continued in disgrace with the powers-that-be and did not mend the family fortunes by marrying a beautiful but penniless woman and breeding a large family. By the time that Teresa was fifteen the Gamba palace in Ravenna was mouldering and the family lived there only in the winter. So soon as spring came they harnessed their oxen to a wagon—the family coach and horses had long since disappeared—and transported themselves—children, servants, and all—to their country house at Filetto, fifteen miles away. Here they lived healthily and happily all through summer-time and harvest, until the first cold wind from the Appenines drove them back to the damp house in Ravenna.

Filetto was home for Teresa. It was a ramshackle place, neither villa nor *castello*, and, like everything that belonged to the Gambas, the house was falling into picturesque decay. It stood upon a hill overlooking the Pine Forest and its sleepy lagoons with the blue-grey Adriatic in the distance. Down the hillside a vineyard sprawled in festoons of leaves, and at its foot were fields of nodding corn. Round the house, to shield it from the mountain winds, was a grove of plane-trees, and every winter a tree fell and lay rotting on the ground. A former Gamba had imported shrubs and trees from the Indies, East and West, to give him shade by day and a drowsy fragrance by night. Acacias huddled in untidy confusion against catalpas and sweet-smelling 'Ailanti' trees. In the once-trim garden the terrace steps were broken and grass and weeds sprouted between the flag-stones. The rose-bushes bloomed from winter to autumn and trailed along the ground without a gardener's care. One touch only of romance was wanting—as in all gardens forlorn, the hoot-owls had driven out the nightingales generations ago.

Within Filetto was full of rooms, sparsely furnished with huge old beds and antique furniture in varying stages of shabbiness. A long gallery ran the length of the house, with bedroom doors opening out upon it. In summer, when the nights were hot, all doors were left open, and laughter and talk rippled back and forth across the gallery between the Gambas, their children, and their guests. The Pine Forest was full of game—snipe and quail and partridge—and the Gamba men rose early to go out shooting. Their dogs were ancient, and their guns were old flintlocks dating from the eighteenth century. What with the produce of the flintlocks, with wheat from the cornfields, wine from the vineyard, olives and plums and apples from the orchard, and milk and cheese from a herd of goats, there was farm-house plenty at the Filetto dinner-table, and it was cheaper and more comfortable living there than in Ravenna.

Grandfather Gamba and his son Ruggiero were republicans and disapproved of the Church as a political power. But they were good Catholics, for all that, and a domestic chaplain ruled the roast at Filetto. He was a Spaniard and answered blithely to the name of Don Juan. His duties were as much agricultural as spiritual, for he was steward of the estate as well as priest. He talked crops with the *contadini* and always had a kind word and kinder eye for a pretty peasant girl. At the dinner-table he set the conversational tone, whether on goats or gossip, and, like all good priests, could find his way in his sleep to the fireside cupboard where the wine-jug was kept. But his spiritual duties were not neglected. He told his beads and read his breviary under the acacias in his hours of leisure. Once a week he summoned the elder Gambas to confession and repentance, and by daily exhortation set the young folk trotting down the path of religion and morality.

In her time the Countess Gamba bore her husband fourteen children. Five were laid away in small graves, and nine grew to years of qualified discretion: three boys—Pietro, Vincenzo, and Ippolito—and six girls, Faustina first, then Teresa, then, many years younger, Vittoria, Olimpia, Giulia, and Laura. As a group they were handsome in a northern rather than Italian way—with blonde or red hair, blue eyes, white skins, and apple-red cheeks. With their northern colouring they inherited sentimental souls—a delight in simple pleasures and a gentle pining for a litter of rose-leaves by day and a noise of nightingales at night. But they were Italian in their gaiety and their sense of drama. Domestic care and political disappointment might have made Count Ruggiero taciturn and left his wife resigned, but laughter was the note at Filetto. Now and then, in a rare moment of bad temper or depression, a young Gamba coughed and spat blood and then, with a return of the smile, would remark that there was an old legend of consumption in the family. Consumption, like gout, was a picturesque malady that afflicted only the nobly born. The peasants in the marshes of Romagna and poor folk in small houses in Ravenna also coughed and spat blood, but they were a sallow-faced crew and their sickness was fen-fever—a matter of tripes, not lungs.

At an early age Teresa was removed from the teachings of Don Juan and lodged in a convent school at Faenza, on the farther side of Ravenna. Convents in those days were not schools in the modern sense. They were genteel dormitories in which well-born maidens were kept until their parents had procured husbands for them or, for want of husband, told them to take the veil. The staple of education was polite accomplishments which would be useful in holding a husband, yet not altogether wasted on a nun. Teresa learnt to speak Italian correctly, with a lavish use of superlatives, and musically, in a deep, bell-like voice that in a whisper could be heard at the far end of a crowded room—with a strong Romagna accent for added charm. She learnt to write letters as a lady should from the *Academy of Compliments*—with such success that in later life she found it difficult to express any idea in her letters save polite interest in her correspondent. She learnt to read, write, and speak French, to play on the harpsichord, to sing, to embroider; she was given a patch of her own in the convent garden and grew flowers there and watered

them and arranged them tastefully in jugs. The good sisters soon discovered that she was not the stuff of which saints are made, so they led
her gently through legends of the Madonna and Her *Bambino* to a curt-
sying acquaintance with God. Teresa left her convent a gentlewoman
with a dutiful belief in the Catholic faith. In later years she was to
penetrate deep into new worlds of science unearthed by the nineteenth
century—into worlds that bordered perilously on black magic—palm-
istry, table-rapping, and spiritualism—but she never doubted that her
final home was with the angels in Paradise.

At Faenza Teresa acquired little beyond religion and accomplishments, for in convent schools the nuns did not believe in unsettling young
girls' minds with odd notions from history or literature. But in her own
home she was taught to love books and reading, and that interest lasted
all her life. With their love of field-sports the Gambas combined a sincere regard for learning and letters. Authors and scholars were guests at
Filetto in the summer, and from her father's friends Teresa heard talk of
politics and dreams of Italian freedom. One visitor opened her mind to
the riches of Italian poetry; that was Paolo Costa, a professor at the
University of Bologna. He read with her Dante and Boccaccio and
Petrarch and taught her to be proud of her country's poets as the cham-
pions of its national spirit. He led her on to French poets—to Ronsard
and the Pléiade—to the tragedies of Corneille and Racine and Voltaire
and the comedies of Molière—and she made acquaintance with the works
of that barbarous English genius, Shakespeare, in a French translation.
From poets and writers of plays she made her way to thinkers—Pascal,
Montaigne, La Rochefoucauld. But, strangest taste of all, he taught her
to read—with interest and intelligence—a vast amount of controversial
theology.

As a girl her passion was all for poetry and plays, and she learnt
whole pages of *Hamlet* by heart. Dante was her god and the *Divine
Comedy* her gospel, for had not Dante lived in exile in Ravenna, written
there, died and been buried there? Was it not, while walking in the Pine
Forest, that he had seen the vision of his dead Beatrice and realized that
our bitterest pain in life is to remember in an hour of sadness the time
when we were glad? Her brothers shared her love of poetry, and when
they came riding by her convent they brought her their favourite, Tasso,
to read. At sixteen she was a young lady, ripe for marriage, and faced life
serenely with a mind steeped in poetry. Her saints were the great poets
and the ladies of the poets—Beatrice and Laura. Francesca da Rimini
and Paolo, Romeo and Juliet of Verona, were for her real people and
models of right conduct in worldly matters. One day, she knew, she
would have a husband and, after that, an *amico*, but her *amico* must be
a poet, able to turn a sonnet in her praise, printed, in the high Italian
fashion, on a pink silk handkerchief drenched in scent.

The air round her was filled with disembodied poetry. Romagna was a state that had long lain outside the beaten track of history. Ravenna was a provincial city of crumbling churches and battered palaces, slipping like a wrecked ship down a dreary plain to the sea that had left it a thousand years ago. Filetto overlooked a waste of swamp and forest. But this forgotten corner of the world was a land of old, unhappy, far-off things and tales of long ago. On every side were remnants of vanished empire in the churches with their Byzantine mosaics and the tombs of Roman emperors. History always crept slowly back there from Charlemagne and King Pepin to Odoacer the Goth, and backward yet to the Emperor Honorius and to Cæsar Augustus and the days when Roman galleys rode at anchor by wharves that long ago had vanished amid woodland and marsh. Ravenna was the old Raven town of the *Nibelungenlied*—a city of legend and magic—of memorials—to the lovely Roman empress Galla Placidia, to the Emperor Theodosius and Theodoric the Goth and Gaston de Foix, the boy chevalier from France who died in the hour of victory outside its walls. At Rimini hard by Francesca had read the tale of Lancelot with her Paolo, and in the Pine Forest every night the Wild Huntsman rode. Teresa remained a child of Romagna all her life and breathed in tales of love and death with her native fog.

Count Guiccioli came of the same breed as the Gambas, but of incontestably nobler ancestry, as Teresa was soon to hear. His main preoccupation in life was the accumulation of wealth, and he made it his duty to hold his money out of reach of other people—wives, poor relations, priests, and the rest of the locust tribe. He had been born to the possession of estates and by one means and another added to his patrimony, so that in old age he was owner of land and palace all the length of the Adriatic coast from Romagna to Venice. Country life was not for him, as it was for the Gambas, a matter of shooting snipe all day and dozing by a log fire in the evening. Land was an investment that could be made to pay. Everywhere he had stewards and agents whom he drove remorselessly to their task of making money for him. Peasants might spin yarns about rheumatism and taxes, and he listened blandly and gave them as much attention as he thought they deserved. Apart from money-making he had one intellectual passion—the theatre—whether in the form of play or opera, ballet or wandering puppet-show. In his young days he had been a friend of the poet Alfieri, and at one time conceived a grandiose scheme of building a theatre, equipped with every modern device of acoustics and stage machinery, in which great Italian plays, old and new, should be acted to large audiences all the year round.

He was better educated in modern learning than most Italians of his class. As a young man he studied history and political economy; as an old man he still liked to have books of that type read aloud to him.

Outwardly he complied with the demands of the Church in religious observance, but at heart he was a *philosophe* of the eighteenth century in belief and a Whig aristocrat in politics. He admired the English way of life, with its land-owning nobility who never were too proud to make money—by trade or political jobbery or by marrying the daughters of rich merchants. Romagna since the Middle Ages had been a Papal state, ruled under a legate by the Pope from Rome. It was a backward state with bad roads, mouldering towns, and a dwindling population. The country people were savages at feud with one another like clansmen in the hills. The soil, which was rich for cultivation, was relapsing into forest in one place and treeless and arid in another. 'Rule by theocracy' had no merits in Count Guiccioli's eyes—it was stultifying in both the religious and the material sense—and he was an enemy of Papal government. What Romagna needed—and he would add, all Italy for that matter—was a Whig aristocracy, as in England, and a House of Lords.

His political theories were rudely jolted when General Bonaparte and the republican army of France swarmed over the Alps into Northern Italy. "People of Italy," announced Bonaparte, "the French Army comes to break your chains. . . . Let the people rest assured we are the friends of the people. To re-establish the Capitol, to awaken the Roman people from centuries of servitude—such will be the rewards of our victory." The Italians welcomed this horde of military ragamuffins as heralds of liberty, not invaders, and a new spirit filled the souls of poets and shop-keepers and peasants alike, and even beggars in the streets shouted "Long Live Italy!" as they showed their sores. The people! Who were the people? An illiterate herd of savages, the progeny of slaves from Cæsar's day, born to be commanded by their betters! Count Guiccioli despised the people and detested the levelling doctrines of the French Revolution, but he wasted no time in useless repining. "To-day," he said sarcastically, "there are only two alternatives left to a gentleman—to have his head cut off by the *canaille* or to make himself their head. I prefer the second alternative." He came to terms with Bonaparte and was sent to Paris as deputy for the commune of Ferrara. In Paris he pitted his wits against Fouché and Barras and made acquaintance with that master of intrigue Talleyrand. He put little trust in French promises of Italian independence, but returned to Milan determined to be on the winning side. For a while he held office in the Cisalpine Republic; when that state was merged in the Napoleonic empire, in recognition of his services he received a personal invitation to attend the coronation of the Emperor Napoleon at Milan. Unfortunately it was Count Guiccioli's weakness to intrigue, and he lost the favour of the Emperor, but he still paid court to Eugène de Beauharnais, the Viceroy of Italy. As he was shut out from politics he turned to his old pastime of making money. The Papal 'theocracy' in Romagna was overthrown, and he bought up Church lands cheap.

Alessandro Guiccioli emerged from the Napoleonic Wars a very rich man when other men had grown poorer. Napoleon's defeat left him in a difficult position. Romagna once more passed under Papal rule, but he was able to keep the lands that he had taken from the Church. For that he was in ill repute with the Pope and the priests in Romagna. At the same time, as a prominent Bonapartist in his day, he was identified with the cause of Italian independence. Secret societies, like the *Carbonari*, looked to him for support; and, in so far as the *Carbonari* were opponents of Papal rule in Romagna, Count Guiccioli was ready to support them. But he had no great faith in the political common sense of Italian Liberals and frankly despised the *Carbonari* as a pack of picturesque young fools. His aid to them was dilatory and uncertain and not much more than he could not well avoid. The *Carbonari* grew impatient and threatened raid and arson on his properties, so what he would not do for love Count Guiccioli then did for blackmail. But his dealings with the *Carbonari* roused the suspicion of the Austrian Government in Northern Italy, and to his mortification he found that on his tours round his estates he was being watched by spies. In the end all he wanted was a government that would guarantee him possession of his lands, and for that end he would play *Carbonari* against Pope and Austrians against *Carbonari*. He lived in a web of complicated intrigue in which he trusted no one and every one suspected him. In this dilemma he looked for support against Pope and *Carbonari* and Austrians alike from some government outside Italy. England was now the richest and most powerful country in Europe—England, then, must be induced to take him under her wing—and he sought the society of any member of his beloved House of Lords who came to Italy.

A war profiteer, in disgrace with conservatives and revolutionaries alike, cannot hope to be popular; and to do Count Guiccioli justice, he had a sturdy contempt for the opinion of his neighbours. There were wild stories about his murderous temper. He had killed two men with the help of hired ruffians, said old ladies in Ravenna with a shudder, and one of them was a *priest*! More placidly they added that he had poisoned one wife and murdered another wife's lover. So far as his wives were concerned it was true; he had been married twice, and both women died comparatively young. His first wife, the Countess Placida Zinanni, of Ravenna, he married in early life. It had been the usual alliance between two noble houses, arranged by parents, and the lady died without giving him children, and no one remembered her save that once she lived and now she was dead. He waited until he was forty to marry again and then chose a young woman of twenty—Angelica Galliani, of Budrio. She came of bourgeois stock and brought him a dowry of one hundred thousand lire. Donna Angelica was said by her descendants to be a woman of affectionate disposition and uncommon good sense. She

## CHAPTER II

# Brunello's Wife

DONNA ANGELICA, black-eyed and pale, died and the golden-haired Teresa took her place. For a while marriage was blue days at sea and green days on shore. Count Alessandro assuredly did not regret his speculation in a young wife. Teresa was affectionate and dutiful. She read aloud to him in the evening. She filled his gloomy houses with laughter and song and flowers—only he must drop a hint to Signora F—— that the best time for practising music was during his *siesta*. It pleased him to pose as the willing slave of a young wife. She had only to lay her behests upon him in public for him to wag a playful finger at her, and soon every one was saying that the Countess Teresa had her ogre well in hand. Count Guiccioli had reason to suppose that, for the first time in his life, he was in love with somebody other than himself.

Three days after their wedding the Count and Countess Guiccioli were in Venice and called in the evening upon the Countess Albrizzi. There Teresa noticed that her husband spoke for a few minutes with a foreign gentleman, but she was too busy receiving congratulations as a *spaʒina* (bride) from middle-aged matrons and young men to look at the stranger a second time. When they left Count Alessandro told her that he had been speaking with an Englishman who was reckoned a fine poet in his own country. Teresa laughed lightly. No doubt an Englishman, like a Laplander, could write poetry, but, as she neither read nor spoke English, she wasn't interested, and, in any case, she had eyes only for her *caro sposo* in a crowd. The Count said gravely that this Englishman was a milord and supposed to be very rich and he might be useful. He desired Teresa to pay him marked attention the next time they met.

Teresa found her husband, for all his years, as impetuous and exacting as a young man. He was restless and for ever on the move, travelling from one large house to another to manage his estates. He loved society despite his unpopularity and paraded his pretty *spaʒina* round the countryside from Pesaro to Venice. He was up betimes in the morning and expected Teresa to rise with him. All day long he was prying into household matters and lecturing her on her domestic duties. The words *ordine* and *economia* ran like a refrain through his talk. Teresa's first instinct was always to give pleasure, and she did her best to make herself a good housewife. She was popular with the servants, who called her

C                              33

their "smiling Countess," and went smiling about their duties. Signora F—— was friendly and a rich store of counsel. She had been Donna Angelica's confidante, perhaps, rather than the Count's, and if she warned Teresa of infirmities in her husband's temper and devised ways of rounding that shoal by simple cunning, no woman may blame her. She took her to see the *bambini* in the convent at Venice and watched her heap affectionate diminutives on their young, unbending heads. Carluccio and Ignazio were brought from school to meet their new mother. Carluccio, who was a year or two younger than Teresa, greeted her with the sullen hostility of a stepson and ignored her endearments, but with Ignazio she had better luck. He was a lively, excitable boy of twelve, who liked poetry and plays, hated school, and gave his father a great deal of trouble. He and Teresa quickly became allies.

"*Mio adorabile Sposo ed Amico*," wrote Teresa to her husband when he was away, "*tu sei tutta l'anima mia, sei il più gran bene che io abbia al Mondo, e sento che senza di te non potrei vivere. L' Amore dei Parenti si e fatto nullo per me dopo che tu sei divenuto mio Sposo. Questa tua lontananza me l' ha vivamente dimostrato.*" It is a shame to translate her raptures into a language like English, but we make the attempt. "My adorable husband and friend, thou art all my soul, thou art the very best thing I have in the world, and I feel that without thee I could not live. Love of family means nothing to me now thou art become my husband. Thy absence has shown me that vividly." The day he left her, she goes on to say, she wanted to cry, her heart was so heavy. She couldn't say good-bye to Carluccio when he went back to school. The opera begins on Sunday and the fair the day after, but she is too sad to go out—she only sees Grandmother and Uncle Paolo. "The evenings pass so dismally here—a little outing and then talk with old folks and priests. I've still got the five *scudi* thou gavest me for a present, and I hope when thou art home again thou wilt be pleased with my economy. My cough is gone and no need of medicine. And, O my dear, take care of the *scirocco* at Rimini and the heat and the night air on thy way home. . . . Go on loving me and be sure thou couldst not have a bride more loving and sincere than thy Teresa."

This wasn't all polite letter-writing according to the *Academy of Compliments*. Teresa was a passionate young thing, but she meant to play fair. Her husband loved her, and she wanted to love her husband. If words could do the trick, she loved. But there is an ominous note in this letter—the Gamba cough has returned, and it only went away when Count Alessandro was out of sight.

For the first few months married life had its compensations. Fresh from the harum-scarum poverty of Filetto Teresa enjoyed the luxury with which her husband surrounded her. Alessandro had many houses— at Ravenna, at Bologna, at Ca' Zen, on the Isola d'Ariano, in the lagoon at the mouth of the Po—and they were all richly upholstered. Hosts of well-trained servants waited on her, and life was organized on a stately ritual. Meals, toilet, pastime—everything went by elaborate protocol, and she lived like the Queen of France in Versailles, a spoilt young queen who had only to smile to be obeyed—within the limits of the protocol. Then there had been the honeymoon visit to Venice and the round of theatres and fashionable *salons*. Old ladies caressed her and chanted hymns to her beauty. Young men flattered her and were only waiting until the time came to offer their services as *amico* to the pretty young wife of a nobleman so rich as Count Guiccioli. Alessandro was proud of his *spazina's* beauty and took her everywhere to be stared at and admired. He stood paternally behind her chair and beamed through his short-sighted eyes at cooing dowagers and ogling cavaliers with the fatuous smile of possession. To enhance her beauty he allowed her, as a special favour, to wear the jewels that he had accumulated for Donna Angelica.

After Venice there was the excitement of travel and making yet more amusing acquaintances. Count Guiccioli was sedulous in courting foreigners of wealth who lived or travelled in Italy. His bride must be presented to Napoleon's wife, the Empress Marie Louise, and to the *amica* of his old friend Alfieri, the Countess of Albany. At Pesaro they were neighbours of that cheerful vulgarian Caroline of Brunswick, Princess of Wales, and Teresa, as became a newly married wife, was prim in word and glance about the Baron Bergami. That the princess should have an *amico* she understood, but to choose a courier of all creatures for *amico* —that she could not forgive.

But after a while Alessandro preferred to travel alone, and Teresa was left behind in the palace at Ravenna under the watchful eyes of Grandmother Gamba. The time went drearily by—only the duenna for company and now and then Carluccio and Ignazio from school, only priests and old ladies and Uncle Paolo—no horses to ride nor young people to romp with. Nor was life any brighter when the Count returned. He was closeted with his stewards, always talking of business troubles, and, if Teresa yawned, he rebuked her for having a flighty mind. Then he began to find fault, to nose out derelictions from the path of *ordine* and *economia* during his absence. The chairs and tables in the *salone* had been shifted from their right place, flowers and trinkets were left lying about, clothes were heaped pell-mell into trunks and wardrobes. Teresa could never find anything at a moment's notice, and she gave orders to the servants without consulting him. He was an old man, he reminded her, and needed not only order in his house, but all her care and attention. It was time she stopped being a spoilt beauty on whom every one waited, she must take her place as his subaltern, ready to receive his orders and see that he was obeyed by servants and children. Carluccio was not to be trusted about money, Ignazio was in perpetual scrapes at school; Teresa was old enough now to play the part of step-mother—let her play it, then! She must stop asking for favours like a child. A little prattle in a young wife was a pretty thing, but when business was going badly silence was better still. Above all, in the presence of servants or children, more modesty, if you please! She must curb her tongue and call him *'signore'* and not argue when he said to her, as husbands daily must—NO!

Count Alessandro nodded and dozed by the fire. Teresa read to him from a heavy folio of history. Carluccio sulked and yawned behind his hand and fell a-dozing like his father. The Count snored and Teresa pushed her book aside and, with a grimace at Carluccio, tip-toed from the room. Carluccio glared at her crossly as she stole away.

A sound of music from the neighbouring room and a young voice rose defiantly in song. The Count woke up and told Carluccio to go and bring his *mammina* back. Carluccio ran to give his orders and returned with a scared look. The young voice still went on singing, then stopped sharply. A breath of wind fluttered the curtains, and the Count shivered impatiently in his furred dressing-gown. Carluccio peeped through the doorway into the next room. The window was open and his stepmother was leaning with her hands crossed upon the iron balustrade, gazing dreamily at the stars. . . .

When the second year of marriage started on its way Teresa was with child. Count Alessandro showed his sympathy as a would-be father, not by redoubling his attentions, but by issuing a new set of commandments—no riding, no visitors, no lying late in bed nor splashing in the bath, no more coughs and no more loss of temper, if you please. She must think less about her own pleasure and more about her duties to her child. A change had come over the scene, and Teresa was nervous and restless now. She had learnt that Count Alessandro, for all his protestations of affection, never did anything for anyone unless he wanted to. She had seen him in a rage several times, and then he roared and clenched his fist; but more formidable than his rages were his grins and silences. Unfortunately for his peace of mind he had married one of the few women in Romagna who would not be frightened by him. Teresa stuck resolutely to her guns and would be humoured as the mother of a prospective son. She wanted a horse, she said, a maid, more pocket-money than a beggarly five *scudi* every now and then. He must stop treating her like a child, and, she must tell him frankly, she could not manage his house if the servants were allowed to ignore her. The 'thou' of intimate affection dropped from her letters for the more respectful 'you,' and her husband was now only her *Caro Alessandro*. "My dear Alessandro," she wrote him on the matter of the servants, "from now on I shan't take the risk of interfering in household matters unless you give me the sign . . . feeling sure that it is all one to you whether I'm about or not."

On the evening of April the First—All Fools' Day—they were in Venice once more. Teresa had been going out night after night to please her husband, and now she was tired and cross. Count Guiccioli wished her to come with him to the Countess Benzoni's. Teresa begged to be excused, but the Count insisted. The English milord, of whom he had spoken to her last year, would be there, and he wished her to meet him. Teresa pouted and protested, but finally she consented to go—but for five minutes only or a quarter of an hour at most—and the Count promised to bring her home at the end of that time.

There was spring even in the salt-sea air of Venice as they were rowed down the Grand Canal and the gondoliers were singing. But this feeling of spring only exasperated Teresa, and suddenly she burst into tears like an angry child. The Count patted her hand and whispered words of encouragement in her ear, but she turned away from him with a sob. The tears were still wet upon her cheeks as they went up the steps into the Countess Benzoni's palace.

## CHAPTER III

# Enter Childe Harold

THE *salone* was in all but darkness when the Count and Countess Guiccioli entered. One light only from a crystal lamp shed a glimmer round the room. To Teresa's eyes, still half blinded with tears, there was no one there save her hostess sitting alone by the fire. The Countess Benzoni came forward to greet her guests with cordial words of welcome. Count Alessandro was an acquaintance of long standing. She congratulated him gracefully on his marriage, then, turning to Teresa, embraced her in motherly arms and drew her to a chair by the fire while the Count walked away down the room. The Countess Benzoni chatted briskly with Teresa, talked of her parents and praised her beauty, while every now and then she glanced with the frank, inquisitive eyes of a matron at the young *spazina's* waistline. Under her kind chatter Teresa returned the smile, but she said little in response to her hostess's flow of compliments. Sleepily she listened to the waves lapping against the walls of the palace outside and the cheerful song of the gondoliers. Then a murmur of voices struck upon her ear from the far end of the room—a merry masculine laugh—the steady tap of a foot drumming on the floor. She raised her eyes quickly and looked.

Her husband was standing by a sofa on which two gentlemen lounged together in idle talk. It was a dark corner there, and for a moment she saw nothing clearly. Then she caught a glimpse of a young face raised to the light of the lantern, alert and humorous. In dreams that face came back to her with eyes for ever laughing, only because it hung in the darkness beside another face that, waking or dreaming, she was never to forget. That other face! It, too, was young, but it was tired and listless and set in a moody frown. Her eyes lingered on it, and all her life she tried to remember it as she saw it then, tried to find words to describe it as she saw it then, only to lose herself in the unavailing platitudes of a love-sick schoolgirl—"That noble and exquisitely beautiful countenance! That sublime brow! Those eyes so infinitely and intensely soft! Those nostrils of the Belvedere Apollo! Those lips made for tenderness and disdain!" He sat there, dressed sombrely in black, with his arm resting on the back of the sofa and his chin propped on his hand. His companion was rallying him and tried to call his attention to the Count, for he was silent and morose, and his foot beat absently on the carpet as though it were keeping time with his thoughts.

All this the Countess Guiccioli saw as in a swift flash before she lowered her eyes.

The Countess Benzoni had followed her glance into the shadows. "It is time," she said with a laugh, "that I stopped the *signori* whispering in the dark there." She rose from her chair and bore down upon the sofa. Teresa sat alone by the fire, gazing into the flames.

The conversation from the corner reached her ears as a babble of words with little meaning, like something heard far away through an open window at night. She heard what they said, yet she could only remember a word here and a word there. Afterwards she asked one of the speakers to tell her what they had said and tried to write it down, but it would not come. When she was old and every one who had played a part in that conversation dead or vanished from her life, she gave her notes to an elderly French poet and begged him to conjure back the words as they had been spoken. This is what he told her—it was not their words exactly but it was the spirit of them, perhaps, and she had to be content.

"Come, I beg of you," said the Countess Benzoni to the young man in black, "you must let me present you to this delightful *spaȝina*."

The young man looked mutinous. "No, I implore you, don't insist. All the *spaȝine* in Venice, however pretty they are, mean no more to me than the head of the Cenci there, looking at us out of that canvas on the wall. The world of women, except for a few friends like you, doesn't exist for me any more. It was my ruin; don't drag a poor wretch back who doesn't want to tempt fortune there again."

"Bah!" said the Countess. "Your age and your face give the lie to your stoicism. A few polite words to a bride of yesterday won't hurt your genius or your sleep. I ask you a favour for myself, not for you. I won't have this pretty *spaȝina* think my empty *salon* is a place where only shadows talk."

"No," insisted the young man; "it's my turn to beg. In the name of friendship, don't exact this drawing-room duty of me, as if I were a famous man to be shown to strangers like a prize bit of furniture, when all I want is to hide myself from the world." He sat up on the sofa and continued with a smile half mocking, half mournful—"What do you want me to say to your delightful *spaȝina*, who doesn't know my name even, and, instead of a rattle, has been given a husband"—Count Alessandro bowed politely, but the young man went on recklessly—"old and jealous, no doubt, who parades her round one palace after another. I have an invincible desire not to leave my lazy browsing here with Scott in this dark corner of your *salon*. Why be so rough with me for my shyness and natural coldness? What have I to gain from this silly presentation to a newly wed child to whom I've nothing to say? Either she'll bore me with the meanness of her mind—and in my day I've had

enough boredom from insipid women to give them a wide berth—or
she'll lay a spell on me by the mere charm of youth which her face
shows under her embarrassment, and then I shall go mad with love and
despair. Either way I shall only lose—either my time or my heart. For
heaven's sake, leave me where I am."

The Countess Benzoni laughed in polite vexation at this tirade.
"Really, you're selfish and unkind with me. Come," she said, turning
to the other young man, "Signor Scott, help me to obtain this favour
from your friend. Don't you see, all this whispering of yours has made
the poor little *spazina* blush, all by herself there at the other end of the
room—of course she thinks we're talking about her."

Signor Scott looked at his friend with a mischievous grin. "The
Countess is right," he said; "I don't understand you to-night. Anyone
would say she was asking a sacrifice of you beyond a man's power, when
it's only a matter of crossing the room to say a few polite words to the
loveliest little creature we've seen yet in Venice. Frankly I think you go
beyond the bounds of decent melancholy with our kind friend, who has
put up with enough ill-humour and moodiness from you for the sake of
that godlike genius of yours."

With a laugh he laid hold of his friend's hand. The Countess seized
the other, and together they dragged him from the sofa. Teresa dared not
look as they approached her.

"This," said the Countess, "is Lord Byron, one of my best friends—
a lowering young man sometimes, like the sky in his own country. But a
look from you will light him up, just as the morning wind clears away
the clouds in our Dalmatia. Talk with him while I go and chatter politics
with Scott and your husband in the other corner there."

Teresa looked up timidly, and Lord Byron's frown changed to a
polite grimace. His face was pale, it sagged under the jaw, there were
dark lines under his eyes and a peevish droop at the corner of his mouth.
He looked cross, dilapidated, and ill. He was fat, his hands were small
and white and plump, and he limped. But she saw nothing of all that.
She saw only his small, well-shaped head—with the curling hair—that
nose, those eyes, those lips—the beauty of feature and expression that lay
behind a tired and dissipated face.

He sat down beside her wearily. It was a warm spring night, he said
in a bored tone, and his voice was low-pitched and melodious. She
answered shyly that it was a warm spring night. Slowly they pushed
off from shore and floated into conversation. Suddenly she laughed,
noisily and happily. He looked up from under his eyelids with a startled
smile. A moment later they were both laughing. Then with a return of
shyness she said something about Dante—spoke of Beatrice, mentioned
Francesca da Rimini and stumbled into silence. Again he glanced at her
in surprise—this little fool, he seemed to be thinking, is no such fool,

after all—she can laugh and she talks intelligently about poetry. He took up her topic and tossed it back to her, and there they sat for an hour, talking eagerly about Dante and Petrarch and Boccaccio.

Two negro boys in turbans and tunics had lit the candles round the room. Other guests arrived as the theatres emptied, and there was light and chatter all around them. No one ventured to break up their conversation. Lord Byron's low, soft voice flowed steadily on, and every now and then it was swallowed up in the deep organ-tones of the *spazina*. Lord Chesterfield said that there is no more disgusting sound in good society than audible laughter, but the *spazina's* laugh rang out frankly across the room. The other guests looked at the pair with sidelong eyes and smiled at one another. They cared nothing about poets or poetry; they only knew that this nobleman from England had amused and shocked them for two years past by his squalid love-affairs. The *spazina* with the flashing white teeth and the laugh a thought too loud was, it appeared, the latest wife of that sinister old man Count Guiccioli, who was slowly groping his way to the fireplace. . . .

Lord Byron slipped a scrap of paper into her hand. She stared a moment like a puzzled child, then hid it in her nosegay. They both rose, full of affable speeches, to greet the Count as he stood blinking before them.

"I perceive," he said with a polite smirk to his wife, "that your *quarter of an hour* has passed quickly and"—he bowed to Lord Byron —"pleasantly."

Teresa placed her hand in her husband's arm. Affectionately she piloted him down the room, for every day he was getting more short-sighted and needed her help in crowds.

In the gondola she burst into tears again—tears of excitement and sheer happiness. Count Alessandro screwed up his eyes and stared at her curiously, then leaned back and gazed into the water.

## CHAPTER IV

# *Platonic Love*

IN Italy, in the early nineteenth century, an ill-assorted marriage could not be broken by divorce. Yet another complication full of dramatic possibilities—young people were not allowed to choose their husbands or wives for themselves. Marriage was a sacrament of the Church. It was also a business contract involving outlay of money in the form of dowry and jointure—the only commercial transaction that had achieved the dignity of sacrament. A business contract might, with infinite difficulty, be dissolved by law, but a religious sacrament was indissoluble. A girl was ordered to marry a man whom, as often as not, she had seen only once before her wedding-day; the lawyers tied them up in settlements and the priest bound them together in bonds of holy wedlock, and there they were united until death did them part. They might detest each other at sight, the husband flog the wife or the wife breed bastards on the husband, but their union must not be annulled. It was not surprising, therefore, since husbands and wives were brought together by decree of parents and held together by force of religion, that marriage was looked on as an unnatural institution and some way of relieving the situation had to be found.

Every country has its own methods of easing the strain on marriage —the *amant* in France, the little woman in England, and mental cruelty in America. The Italians—at any rate those in what is called good society—had discovered a palliative all their own. It was taken for granted that marriage had nothing to do with love. It was a chain that men must drag, a cross that women must bear, if legitimate heirs to the family estates were to be procreated. Young men of family should be married, while they were yet full of youthful sap, to girls carefully selected for their birth and dowries. If a girl was poor she were best married to an old man, for old men are often rich and have a trick of leaving their wives rich widows. A husband, once he had procreated his species, was entitled to the 'vices'—that is, infidelities of the more spectacular kind in the right quarter—with an actress, for example, a *prima donna*, or, if his fortune ran to it, a courtesan who by her extravagance would advertise his good nature. The Italians, being a gallant people, accorded their wives at least the appearance of the same licence, and it was often entered in the marriage articles that the bride should be allowed a *cavalier servente* after the purpose of marriage was fulfilled.

A *cavalier servente* was a respectable gigolo, with this difference from his modern counterpart: he was accepted as an honourable pillar of society, a necessary prop to matrimony, and served—in theory and even in practice—for love and not for profit. He went by the name of *cicisbeo* or *amico*. The lady he served was called his *dama* or *amica*, and their association was termed an *amicizia* or *relazione*. Not only was the *amico* 'friend' to the wife, he was 'friend' to the husband, too—in fact, sometimes the husband selected him for the post—and the *dama's* own family treated him as a son-in-law. Usually he was a younger son of good family but little means. *Abbés*, however, were a favourite choice on account of their vows of celibacy. But a married man with a family sometimes qualified for the post of *cavalier*, and an ambitious wife appointed herself *amica* to a cardinal.

An *amicizia* was entered upon for life. The *amico* undertook those responsibilities from which the husband had willingly abdicated. He must know how to carry a fan and double a shawl and must always be available for the opera-box. Unlike the husband, he was vowed to eternal constancy. He must never love another woman in his *dama's* lifetime, for that would be flagrant infidelity. He was not allowed to enter even into so loveless a contract as marriage while she lived—at any rate, not in the strictest circles. He could not hope—in the strictest circles—to marry his *dama* when her husband died, for marriage between *dama* and *amico* would suggest adultery in the husband's lifetime, and in polite circles in Italy it was assumed that adultery must not, and therefore did not, exist. No gentleman was ever jealous about his wife. If he were so foolish as to make a scene about her *amico*, he was laughed out of decent society. How far an *amico* might go beyond the limits of polite attention and meek fidelity depended upon circumstances—the temper of his *dama*, the blindness of her husband, his own initiative, or a combination of all three. In theory an *amicizia* was platonic, although well-bred people benevolently assumed the reverse.

The Italians were proud of their system of *serventismo*. It had the merit of being gallant where the ladies were concerned. It preserved the outward decencies of morality, or, if there were any suspicion of impropriety, it was embalmed decorously in sentiment. It was a civilized arrangement, said the Italians, and had this advantage over codes in other countries for hushing up the truth about marriage: it was open, frank, free of all taint of subterfuge or hypocrisy. They liked to point out to foreigners, as proof of their superior civilization, a knock-kneed old *cicisbeo* driving round the town with his ancient *dama* and standing outside the confessional box with her fan while she confessed her sins. Sometimes foreigners asked questions about the nature of the *dama's* sins or the extent of her confessions while she kept her *cicisbeo* waiting. But the Italians only smiled and gave them to understand that to such questions there was no answer. If the foreigners were English, they were apt to denounce arranged marriages as unnatural and the whole business of *cavalier servente* as a graceless compound of immorality and hypocrisy. Then the Italians smiled yet more tolerantly and explained that under their system, at least, they did not have Gretna Green escapades, nor marriage-markets in Smithfield, nor elopement of married folks with duels for a result, nor, least of all, scandalous divorce-suits in which, all too often, the price of a husband's honour was vulgarly assessed in the amount of damages which he could wring from the seducer of his wife.

Such was the world into which Teresa was ushered on her wedding-day. She had taken the first step along the right road by marrying a man old enough to be her grandfather, but in her artless fashion she lingered on the way by trying to fall in love with her husband. But now she was ripe for a *cavalier servente*, and, with her husband's leave, she meant to have one. By rights she ought to have consulted with him and her parents and followed their wishes in the choice of cavalier, but she was wilful and had chosen for herself. This English poet—Lord Byron—must be her *amico*.

There was little time to lose, for before the month was out the Count would carry her back to Ravenna. She and Lord Byron met every day. She told him all her life—about Filetto and her brothers, about Ravenna, about Paolo Costa and far-off days in the convent, and then her tale was told. The moral tone in Ravenna, she assured him with a matronly shake of the head, was bad—worse than anything in Venice. From the morals of Ravenna she glanced to her favourite topic, poetry, and once more the story of Paolo and Francesca was debated; yet, with all her love of poetry, she cared not for the moment that her *amico* was a poet in his own country. In a few days' time she was lecturing him upon his duties. He must not laugh when he carried her fan, he must try to look less like a fiddler with his smooth-shaven face, and she ordered him to grow whiskers like a man. Their relations, she insisted, must be platonic—she would be his Beatrice and he must be her Dante—and when he came to Ravenna, as come he must, she would lead him to Dante's tomb and there they would pray together—for grace or what you will. As her *amico*, she told him, he must treat her husband with the greatest deference in public and speak of him everywhere as though they were bound together by the ties of closest *amicizia*. Her father would greet him as a member of the family and her brothers call him their *cognato*, or brother-in-law. He must vow eternal fidelity to her, must never love another woman in his life, never leave Italy; and then, when they were old folks, oncoming generations would point them out to strangers as a miracle of constancy and faith.

Teresa laughed because she was happy. Lord Byron laughed because he was amused. He had thought to do all the love-making himself, yet never in his life had he been so frankly and so shyly wooed. There were conventions in this game upon which, in an idle moment, he had embarked, but he was too lazy, or too indifferent, to learn them. Teresa might lecture him upon his *serventismo*, but she was too young and headstrong to observe the rules and a great deal too much in love. She wanted to belong to her *amico* body, heart, and soul, and cared not if all the world should know it.

Lord Byron had given Venice plenty to talk about. Every one knew that he was a poet in his own country, but in Italy poetry was not a trade for men of birth and breeding. Every one knew that he had a wife in England, but the marriage had broken down in a black cloud of rumour and he left home in disgrace. He had done nothing in Venice to belie the evil fame in which he had arrived. It would seem that he took a perverse pleasure in rolling in the mud and slime of the canals. He chose his mistresses from the *fazziole*—the kerchief-wearers or women of the slums and back alleys of the town. First there had been the tailor's wife on the Frezzeria, Marianna Segati, with her great black eyes, who cheated him, deceived him, and made him jealous scenes. Marianna had been routed in a battle of words by 'La Fornarina,' the baker's wife—Margarita Cogni—a vigorous slut with large eyes flashing and hair streaming in the moonlight. The Palazzo Mocenigo on the Grand Canal echoed to her voice as she roared at servants or drove out rivals with her bare fists. There were stories worse yet of orgies with nine cheap drabs (one for every Muse) in a *casino* in a side-street. Finally, to make the scene yet more disreputable, he had imported into his palace a tiny bastard child by some unknown woman in England and left her to the care of his Fornarina.

The Venetians watched him with sharp, mocking eyes. He was an Englishman, they said, and naturally had a taste for low life. His English friends in Venice were angry and disgusted. The British Consul took his baby daughter away from the palace on the Grand Canal. Then the doctors intervened. He was killing himself, they told him, with his stupid debauchery. La Fornarina was ejected by force from the Palazzo Mocenigo. There were yells and shrieks of rage, oaths and threats of suicide, a splash in the canal; then in the water the lady changed her mind and went back to the baker's shop.

A farcical ending to a poet's love-affair! Lord Byron turned hermit and lived alone in his palace, nursing the remnants of his health. But the demon in him was not dead yet. A noble family in Venice was warned by neighbours that this English daredevil had been seen by night climbing up to their daughter's bedroom window. Angelina was the girl's name, and she was barely eighteen. She was madly in love and wanted to marry her midnight suitor though she knew that he had a wife alive in England. Her parents locked her up behind a grated window on a diet of prayers and bread and water until they could find a respectable Italian husband to take her off their hands. A commissary of police and a priest called upon Lord Byron in his palace, and a treaty of good behaviour was ratified over a cup of coffee.

The Venetians had sneered at La Fornarina and the *casino* drabs, but they were frankly shocked when Lord Byron carried his depredations into decent society. Once more he withdrew into the seclusion of his palace, and months passed without scandal. On the few occasions that he appeared in the *salons* he declared that he had outlived all emotion and never wanted to meet a woman again. People had begun to think he meant what he said, when suddenly here he was wooing the young wife of Count Guiccioli. Well, at any rate, they said, now his lordship has met his match. Count Guiccioli was a jealous husband, he was unscrupulous, and he had a short way of dealing with the lovers of his wives.

Yet the Count seemed strangely blind to what was happening under his nose. Apparently he accepted Lord Byron as a *cicisbeo* for his wife without a twinge of jealousy and cultivated his friendship. His young wife, no doubt, was trying her hand out on this Englishman before she settled down to a more formal *amicizia* with an Italian who knew the decencies of the game. Then something happened to set tongues in Venice wagging more viciously than ever.

A new comedy was performed at the theatre one evening, and the boxes were crowded with a fashionable audience. But the play on the stage was soon forgotten for a shocking *sbaglio* (blunder) that was being enacted in Lord Byron's box on the first tier. For there sat his limping English lordship, nonchalant as Mephisto, and by him sat the Countess Guiccioli with her hair falling in dishevelled ringlets on her gleaming white shoulders—and, what was stranger yet, there sat old Count Guiccioli, too, peering through his *lorgnon* at the actors in the play.

The *cavalieri serventi* in other boxes gaped and stared at the sight, some in frowning disapproval, others in cynical amusement. Their *damas* clucked and pursed their lips disdainfully and whispered behind their fans. A buzz of virtuous astonishment filled the theatre and enveloped even the actors on the stage and well-nigh threw them from their parts. Lord Byron, presumably, had been playing for the post of *amico* to the Countess Guiccioli these past few days and her husband had accepted him for the part, but never had there been so public a flouting of the rules of *serventismo*! An *amico* sat in his *dama's* box at the theatre and, if he liked, the husband might attend as a gesture of good will— but never did a *dama* (and even less her husband) sit in the *amico's* box! Lord Byron was a foreigner and doubtless knew no better. The Countess

Guiccioli was young and didn't seem to care, but didn't she know that by sitting in her *amico's* box she had as good as proclaimed herself his mistress, like an actress or woman of the town? But Count Guiccioli bore the brunt of general displeasure. He was not a foreigner, he was not young, he knew the rules—surely, or so it was argued, his moral sense had been blunted and his manners ruined by his graceless English friend.

Old ladies in Venice said sourly to their grizzled *cicisbei* that the young Countess Guiccioli was behaving like a chambermaid. This time a year ago she had been a sweet, modest child and they had been sorry for her because she was married to that grim old Brunello. But now she seemed bent on calling attention to herself in every way. No doubt she was pretty but, *mio caro*, have you noticed her legs—short like a peasant's, with a clod-hopping foot to match! Why did she wear red satin shoes when she walked in the *piazza*? Why did she let her hair fall in ringlets and curls on her shoulders, as though she had just been roused from sleep? She had a pretty bust, it was true, and a beautiful white throat like a column, but she had no right to expose them to the public gaze in the theatre—like an Englishwoman, clacked the old ladies, as they pulled their draperies more snugly round their own lean necks and bosoms. No doubt her husband was old, but she was a great deal too free in her remarks about the indignities of old age, particularly with ladies who had not yet given up their failing battle against time. She whispered "*Mio Bairon*" the whole length of a crowded *salon* when her *amico* entered, and all conversation died away at the sound, like a breeze lost in a garret. She was a young baggage—and old Brunello had gone the way of all husbands or there was no wisdom in old ladies' tongues. She would snare this barbarian in her charms and parade him as her lover for a while; then she would throw him over for a civilized Italian who knew the game of *cicisbeo*—or, at any rate, for decency's sake, it was to be hoped she would!

All this cackle reached the ears of Byron's friends in Italy. Henri Stendhal, the novelist, heard the gossip as far away as Milan and regaled his correspondents with tales of Lord Byron's latest Venetian trull—a gross and blowsy creature (he was told) with yellow hair and heavy, naked bosom—"*une* wife," in short, in the English style of beauty, with venal husband in the background. Nearer home in Venice Mr Belgrave Hoppner, the British Consul, picked up the chatter of the *salons* and, being a conscientious man, decided that at the proper moment he would drop a word in Lord Byron's ear and let him know that he was making a fool of himself again—this time about a minx.

Only eleven days, but they were eleven days of dreams come true, of life reopening and springtime blowing through the windows of the beauty sleeping in the wood. Lord Byron was pleased and a little touched by the frankness with which his advances had been met. He sent her a brooch set with brilliants. But she sent it back to him with a note. She begged him not to take her refusal as an affront, but she must not accept from him a gift of so much value. She hoped he would not think its value impaired by the enclosure. He looked at his rejected bauble more carefully and saw that she had twined a lock of her own hair in it. Sentimentally he strung the brooch on a gold chain and wore it near his heart. He laughed and caressed her with his voice and gently tried to woo her from her chatter about Dante and platonic love. But she was firm. No, she stammered, no, not—and then, seeing his lower lip pouting like a hurt schoolboy's, she added—*yet*.

According to plan Count Guiccioli carried his wife away from Venice to his house on the Isola d' Ariano at the mouth of the Po—*Ca' Zen*, it was called, *Cavanelle di Po*. All his houses had a prison-like atmosphere despite their luxury, and Ca' Zen was the gloomiest of them all. Ariano was a desolate spot, a flat, marshy district that had once been an island, looking out across a dull, flat sea. Neighbours there were none, and Teresa chafed at her solitude. She lay about the house, languidly reading books, and her husband rebuked her for indolence. She put down her book with a sigh and took up her embroidery. The Count was sorry for himself because she never tried to entertain him in the evening now. She tossed away her embroidery and went to her harpsichord and sang. Then he worried about his unborn child, scolded her for moping, and told her she should take more exercise. She teased a horse out of him and went for long, solitary rides, but now the Count was dissatisfied because he was sure that riding on horseback would displace her womb and kill the child. Teresa was obstinate and only rode harder and more often. Then, to his relief, she grew cheerful again. She took an interest in housekeeping, read aloud to him, and played his favourite tunes.

All this while she was writing to her *amico* in Venice. For his sake, she told him, she had learnt to love solitude. She read books, she embroidered and was busy about the house, she played music, she went out riding, and—she "would," she assured him, "be everything he wanted her to be."

She "would be everything he wanted her to be." To so humble an appeal Lord Byron needs must answer and take her at her word. He had not wished to meet her, he told her, deliberately he had meant to guard himself against all emotion for the rest of his life; but she had put his resolution to flight, he was now wholly hers, and he, in his turn, "would be everything she wanted *him* to be." "I may be happy in your love, *ma tranquillo mai più* [but tranquil never more]." He closed his letter with a pretty little jingle from Guarini:

Che giova a te, cor mio, l'esser amato,
Che giova a me l'aver si cara Amante!
Se tu, crudo Destino, ne dividi
Ciò che Amor ne stringe![1]

A charming letter, written by a master in the craft of love. She wrote more openly, lamenting the difficulties that have beset love from the days of Francesca and Paolo to the present time—and why did he think that in loving her he would lose his peace of mind? Lord Byron's answer was noble, melancholy, no answer at all. "What we have to suffer is the commonplace of life and we must bear it as others have, for true love is never happy. We two shall suffer the more because ours is a case not like any others'."

This was not the language he had used in wooing her in Venice. There he had been mischievous and playful, with that sudden glance of mockery up from under his eyelids, and often she rebuked him for uttering heresies against love and poetry. But behind his gaiety it would seem there was a deep sadness. He looked upon himself as a man foredoomed to tragedy. Somehow, said she to herself, I must save him from that! She was fond of poetry, but she was not a fatalist, nor was sad love-longing her favourite mood.

It was now time to leave Ca' Zen and return to Ravenna. Three times on the first day of the journey Teresa fainted. The Count fussed and fumed about his unborn child. When at last they reached Ravenna she took to her bed. She was coughing and spitting blood now. Her face was mottled, feverish, ugly. Desperate letters reached Lord Byron in Venice.

[1] *Translation.* "What joy for thee, my heart, to be beloved, what joy for me to have so dear a mistress! If only, cruel Fate, thou dost not sunder that which Love hath bound!"

# BOOK TWO

# Romance

## CHAPTER I

## Pilgrim's Progress

BYRON must always have an audience. He played Childe Harold for the Countess Benzoni with all the weariness and disdain for women that the part called for, and the Countess Benzoni broke the performance with a laugh. For that wise old woman Lady Melbourne, in years gone by of London fame, he had acted the comedy of conquering Harlequin and the frail Columbine. From hour to hour he told her in his letters of his midnight wooing of that wistful beauty, Lady Frances Webster. Lady Melbourne followed the performance with ironical amusement. More greatly daring, he told her the story of hysterical scene and wailing letter into which his love-affair with Caro Lamb had broken down. Lady Melbourne's son was Caro Lamb's husband, but still the old lady was amused by the aftermath to romance. Neither by temper nor experience was she romantic, and she despised those people who were, and most of all her daughter-in-law, who, in her opinion, was a tiresome egotist. But when Byron in his turn grew romantic and hinted in his letters at mysterious delinquencies of another nature, she pounced on him like a hawk. He must never act a tragic rôle, she warned him, for that would lead to his damnation in this world (about which Lady Melbourne knew everything worth knowing) and in the next world, too (though for that world Lady Melbourne would not speak with the same authority). The sooner he married and settled down the better. So Byron married Lady Melbourne's niece. He ignored his kind aunt's warning on his honeymoon and acted the part of his own corsair, with dark hints of inexpiable sin and inevitable doom that would engulf both him and his bride. His audience shuddered and responded to the performance only too tragically, and Lady Melbourne was proved right. In this world in England Byron was hissed off the stage as the villain in one of his own poems.

In exile in Italy he sought refuge in comedy once more and made his correspondents his audience. Back home there was Tom Moore, the poet, to write to, and his Cambridge friend, John Hobhouse, his publisher, John Murray, and his banker, Douglas Kinnaird. Now and then his sister, Augusta Leigh, was favoured with a letter of graceless confidence and, very rarely, his wife, Annabella, was tickled with the whip. In Italy he had an audience in Belgrave Hoppner, the British Consul at Venice, and Alexander Scott (from Chisholm, in Roxburgh), who served as secretary to the consulate. In England Hobhouse and Murray and the others passed his letters round, as Byron meant them to, and there was hearty laughter over the "dear fellow's" escapades among those "damned immoral foreigners." But in Venice his friends, who watched from near at hand, were distressed and did their best to wean him from this exhausting life of harlotry into which he had fallen. As His Britannic Majesty's representative in the city Hoppner was ashamed that an Englishman should make such a sad exhibition of himself and tried to steer him into grace by solemn admonition. Scott, more skilfully, plied him with sarcasm.

Since the expulsion of La Fornarina he had purged himself and made a sober effort to live cleanly like a gentleman. Reformation had not come quickly nor all at once. There had been the episode of the pretty Angelina, but she was now locked out of love's way behind her grated window, and for several months he lived quietly and alone in the Palazzo Mocenigo. It was high time, too, that he took a rest, for his nerves and health were in a dangerous way.

Debauchery was not the sole cause of his poor health, nor was it even the ultimate cause. He had arrived in Venice miserable and angry and flaunted his amours in the eyes of all the town, and of England, too, in his letters to his friends, out of sheer defiance. But besides the lust of the flesh there had been the toil of the mind to make him sick. Poetry is a hard trade to follow, and all his time at Venice he had been "sweating poems"—*Childe Harold*, *Manfred*, *Beppo*. It was like somnambulism—this "poeshie" of his, the dream of sleeping passions, and he found the dream yet more exhausting than the actuality. His brain was as tired as his body.

With the purging of his physical life had come a catharsis in his mental life. He was weary of the tinsel and sentiment of *Childe Harold* and *Lara* and *The Corsair*. For God's sake, let him stop posing on mountainsides or brooding among ruins; let him be the rogue he was and stand upon his head for a while and laugh at life between his legs! He set to work upon his longest and greatest poem, *Don Juan*, and away went the first canto to his publisher. John Murray was disturbed. There was a market for *Childe Harold* and *The Corsair*, but this poem was a flat negation of all he had written before. It was cynical, it was indecent, it was full of coarse attacks—on his wife, on Lord Castlereagh, on Bob Southey, the Poet Laureate. Murray called in Hobhouse and Kinnaird, and together they expostulated with the sinful poet. If the poem were published there must be wholesale changes and excisions.

Better still not to publish it at all. Why didn't the "dear fellow" retire into private life for seven years and write an epic poem in the manner of *Paradise Lost*—something that a young girl might read without a blush? The proposal stirred Byron to ironic merriment. God help us, he replied, where shall we all be this day seven years? And who would read his blameless epic? It were better to be a farm-labourer than slog away at "poeshie" like a learned dunce. He wrote a second canto of *Don Juan* and sent it off to Murray two days after meeting Teresa Guiccioli.

He was alone now and bored in the Palazzo Mocenigo. The golden-haired countess with the rounded bosom and milk-white throat was gone, and time alone would decide what came of that business. He had meant what he said when he declared he did not want to meet her nor wish to have anything more to do with women. *Don Juan* was done with, too, for the time, and he waited idly for remonstrance from London. Let them turn his cantos into a 'Book of Canticles' if they could! He went riding with Hoppner on the Lido and called on Mrs Hoppner to look at his daughter, Allegra. Mrs Hoppner was a kind, simple-hearted woman—a little prim, perhaps, and loquacious, but certainly not blind to Childe Harold's charm. What she would like best was for him to fall in love with a nice, sensible girl who would look after him and keep him away from those Venetian harpies. In spite of warning looks from her husband she encouraged him to talk about the Countess Guiccioli and told him archly that he had better be careful—he showed every sign of love! As for Allegra, he was growing proud of that child. Mrs Hoppner worried like an ineffectual hen about her health, and Hoppner said gloomily that she wetted her bed o' nights and was not an attractive child. Certainly she had a spirit of her own and (Hoppner be damned!) for a baby had lovely limbs and delicate, clear-cut features. They said she looked like him, but, as he stared at her, he was puzzled by her likeness to—not her mother, God be thanked!—but Annabella, his wife!

This quiet life was monotonous, without love and without poetry to keep him busy. He yawned over books in his study and scolded his valet, Fletcher, for carrying on a *liaison* with a garlic-breathing countess. A faithful creature, Fletcher, with a wife in England, but he was always getting into scrapes in Venice and had grown monstrously fat in humble caricature of his master—damn his curly, flaxen poll! Then he bethought him of his friends in London. Pending their virtuous bleatings about *Don Juan* he might as well write and tell them about his latest adventure among the "feminie" in his best comedy vein.

A few days after his first meeting with Teresa Guiccioli he wrote to Hobhouse. For all his talk of respectability Hobhouse was heading for Newgate Gaol for indiscreet utterance in politics, and Byron gave him a prod on that point before he proceeded to the story of his latest affair. This time, Hobhouse was to understand, it was no Fornarina stuff. He had to deal now with a young woman, married and of good birth, whom he had met in the course of wandering through the best *salons* of Venice. Nothing sudden about the business—it had developed gradually—and he added a year or two to Teresa's age to convey the illusion that his love-affairs now were conducted on the old, worldly plane.

My dear Hobhouse,

I have not derived from the Scriptures of Rochefoucault that consolation which I expected "in the misfortunes of our best friends" . . . but like old "Curry-comb" you make "so handsome a corpse," that my wailing is changed into admiration.

I must write again in a few days, it being now past four in the morning; it is Passion week, and rather dull. I am dull too, for I have fallen in love with a Romagnola Countess from Ravenna, who is nineteen years old, and has a Count of fifty—whom she seems disposed to qualify, the first year of marriage being just over.

I knew her a little last year at her starting, but they always wait a year, at least generally. I met her first at the Albrizzis', and this spring at the Benzonas'—and I have hopes, sir—hopes, but she wants me to come to Ravenna, and then to Bologna. Now this would be all very well for certainties; but for mere hopes; if she should plant me, and I should make a 'fiasco,' never could I show my face on the Piazza. It is nothing that money can do, for the Conte is awfully rich, and would be so even in England—but he is fifty and odd; he has had two wives and children before, this is his third (a pretty fair-haired girl last year out of a convent; now making her second tour of the Venetian *conversazioni*) and does not seem so jealous this year as he did last—when he stuck close to her side—even at the Governor's.

She is pretty, but has no tact; answers aloud, when she should whisper —talks of age to old ladies who want to pass for young; and this blessed night horrified a correct company at the Benzonas' by calling out to me *"mio Byron"* in an audible key, during a dead silence of pause in the other prattlers, who stared and whispered their respective *serventi*.

One of her preliminaries is that I must never leave Italy. I have no desire to leave it, but I should not like to be frittered down into a regular *cicisbeo*.

What shall I do? I am in love, and tired of promiscuous concubinage, and have now an opportunity of settling for life.

Yours, B.

Hobhouse chuckled over this letter. He had a real, but terribly possessive, affection for Byron. The "dear fellow" had an infinite capacity for tumbling in and out of scrapes, and here he was riding for another fall. Playfully he sent his respects to "La Romagnuola—is that the way to spell it?" Then, in return for Byron's dig about Newgate, he hoped, unkindly, that the second canto of *Don Juan* was "decenter than the first, else were we all shamed."

By the same post Murray received a savage reply to his complaints of indelicacy in *Don Juan*. Byron mounted the high horse and gave him a taste of Childe Harold in his most scornful mood. He cared not a fig for the favour of the English people, if that was what Murray was worrying about. "They made me, without my search, a species of popular idol; they, without reason or judgment, beyond the caprice of their good pleasure, threw down the image from its pedestal; it was not broken with the fall and they would, it seems, again replace it—but they shall not." Then, because he would not end on a scolding note, "You ask me about my health," he added; "about the beginning of the year I was in a state of great exhaustion, attended by such debility of stomach that nothing remained on it; and I was obliged to reform my 'way of life,' which was conducting me from the 'yellow leaf' to the ground, with all deliberate speed. I am better in health and morals, and very much yours ever, Bn."

The Count carried his wife away to Ca' Zen and now—on April 24 —Byron wrote a bulletin of his affections to Kinnaird. He opened with a defiance about *Don Juan*, then passed on to an account of his affair from the financial point of view and added yet another year to Teresa's age.

DEAR DOUGLAS [he wrote],

I sent off on April 3rd the 2nd canto of *Don Juan* addressed to Murray, I hope it is arrived—by the Lord it is a Capo d' Opera, so "full of pastime and prodigality," but you shan't decimate nor mutilate, no—"rather than that, come critics into the list, and champion me to the uttermost." . . .

I have fallen in love, within the last month, with a Romagnuola Countess from Ravenna, the spouse of a year of Count Guiccioli, who is sixty—the girl twenty.

She is as fair as sunrise, and warm as noon, but she is young, and was not content with what she had done, unless it was to be turned to the advantage of the public, so she made an *éclat*, which rather astonished even the Venetians, and electrified the *conversazioni* of the Benzona, the Albrizzi, and the Michelli, and made her husband look embarrassed.

They have been gone back to Ravenna some time, but they return in the winter. She is the queerest woman I ever met with, for in general they cost one something one way or the other, whereas by an odd combination of circumstances, I have proved an expense to HER, which is not *my* custom, but an accident; however it don't matter.

She is a sort of Italian Caroline Lamb, except that she is much prettier, and not so savage. But she has the same red-hot head, the same noble disdain of public opinion, with the superstructure of all that Italy can add to such natural dispositions.

She is also of the Ravenna *noblesse*, educated in a convent, sacrificed to wealth, filial duty, and all that.

I am damnably in love, but they are gone, for many months—and nothing but hope keeps me alive *seriously*.

Yours ever, B.

April vanished into May, and humble letters came from Ca' Zen, then desperate and unhappy letters from Ravenna. There it was all over again—the girl was in love with him—why couldn't the women leave him alone? Why couldn't love be a little fun now and then? What was this green-sick child to him? Should he obey the call and go? Bleakly he remembered love-affairs dead and gone. This girl with her red-gold hair and her reckless disregard of public opinion reminded him of Caro Lamb years ago—and what a business that had been! Reproaches, scenes, tears, quick disgust, and lasting disillusionment! Innocently, too, Teresa had led his thoughts to dwell on Paolo's love for his brother's wife, Francesca, and their eternal punishment in hell. He turned in a gush of despairing tenderness to his sister, parted from him by sea and mountain far away in England. For Teresa reminded him, too, of Augusta, with her laughter and her quick response and love of baby names. Yet somehow with Augusta, for all their love of folly, comedy had turned to tragedy. When he had last spoken with her he was angry and embittered and without hope, and in his exile he had teased her with letters about those other women—Allegra's mother and the tailor's wife in Venice and La Fornarina. Yet now he could not bring himself to mention Teresa Guiccioli, could only hint that she existed. Somehow she was an infidelity—and for that he blamed Augusta. He wrote to her —on May 17—passionately and reproachfully.

My DEAREST LOVE,

I have been negligent in not writing, but what can I say? Three years' absence—and the total change of scene and habit make such a difference— and that we have now nothing in common but our affections and our relationship.

But I have never ceased nor can cease to feel for a moment that perfect and boundless attachment which bound and binds me to you—which renders me utterly incapable of *real* love for any other human being—for what could they be to me after *you*? My own—we may have been very wrong—but I repent of nothing save that cursed marriage—and your refusing to love me as you had loved me—I can neither forget nor *quite forgive* you for that precious piece of reformation—but I can never be other than I have been —and whenever I love anything it is because it reminds me in some way or other of yourself—for instance I not long ago attached myself to a Venetian for no earthly reason (although a very pretty woman) but because she was called ... and she often remarked (without knowing the reason) how fond I was of the name—It is heart-breaking to think of our long Separation—and I am sure more than punishment enough for all our sins —Dante is more humane in his "Hell" for he places his unfortunate lovers (Francesca of Rimini and Paolo, whose case fell a good deal short of *ours* though sufficiently naughty) in company—and though they suffer—it is at least together.—If ever I return to England—it will be to see *you*—and recollect that in all time—and place—and feelings—I have never ceased to

## CHAPTER II

# Sentimental Journey

MEN are unaccountable creatures. Teresa Guiccioli had made him homesick for Augusta. He sealed up his letter and addressed it to the Hon. Mrs Leigh, care of John Murray. A few hours later he wrote to Murray, and the two letters arrived together in London. Murray forwarded the letter to Augusta and opened the letter to himself. Hobhouse had told him about "the Romagnuola Countess," and he looked for some amusing naughtiness about that lady. There was not a word about her in this letter . . . She was forgotten! Byron was picking up the threads of an affair with another woman, and Murray was gravely perturbed by what he read.

> I wrote [write?] to you in haste and at past two in the morning, having besides had an accident. In going, about an hour and a half ago, to a Venetian girl (unmarried and the daughter of one of their nobles), I tumbled into the Grand Canal, and, not choosing to miss my appointment by the delays of changing, I have been perched in a balcony with my wet clothes on ever since, till this minute that on my return I have slipped into my dressing-gown. My foot slipped in getting into my gondola to set out (owing to the cursed slippery steps of their palaces), and in I flounced like a carp, and went dripping like a triton to my sea-nymph and had to scramble up to a grated window—
>
>> Fenced with iron within and without
>> Lest the Lover get in or the Lady get out.

Angelina had sent him a message. Father was ill, Brother was away at Milan, Mother was asleep, the servants were on the side of love, and there was no moon at midnight. Wickedly Byron went on to tell what they talked about through the window.

> She proposed to me to divorce my mathematical wife, and I told her that in England we can't divorce except for *female* infidelity. "And pray (said she), how do you know what she may have been doing these last three years?" I answered that I could not tell, but that the [here Moore in printing the letter relapsed into a row of stars] was not quite so flourishing in Great Britain as with us here. "But," she said, "can't you get rid of her?" "Not more than is done already (I answered): You would not have me poison her?" Would you believe it? She made *no answer*. Is not that a true and odd national trait? It spoke more than a thousand words, and yet this is a little, pretty, sweet-tempered, quiet feminine being, as ever you saw, but

the passions of a sunny soil are paramount to all other considerations. An unmarried girl naturally wishes to be married: if she can marry and love at the same time it is well, but at any rate she must love. I am not sure that my pretty paramour was fully aware of the inference to be drawn from her dead silence, but even the unconsciousness of this latent idea was striking to an observer of the passions.

Really, said Tom Moore, when he saw this letter, this is *too gross*. Byron hoped to shock his friends in England with his Venetian love-affairs. Therein he had failed with his tales of Marianna, the tailor's wife, and the Fornarina, but with this story of midnight wooing on a balcony in dripping clothes at last he had succeeded. In his closing paragraph he said airily, "Tell Augusta that I wrote to her by yesterday's post, addressed to your care." John Murray could only hope that the letter to his sister was less gross than this letter to him, but he wouldn't trust him for that. Byron told his sister everything, as well he knew.

Casually, on the top of his account of Angelina, he had written, "In a few days I leave Venice for Romagna," but Murray was too shocked to note the significance of that line. But two weeks later the rascal had really left Venice and was on his way to Ravenna. Now it was the turn of friends in Venice to get a letter, and he wrote to the British Consul.

Hoppner was a fussy, self-important little man, who was proud of his friendship with a nobleman who wrote poetry and was talked of all round the world. Like Hobhouse and Tom Moore and every friend that Byron ever made, he was possessive. He took great pains about him, kept his accounts, hired horses for him, and rented houses. On their rides together on the Lido he remonstrated with him about his vicious life and told him to go back home to England. Yet more than that—he had taken Allegra into his house to be brought up with his own boy, Rizzo, judging rightly that the Palazzo Mocenigo with the terrific Fornarina was no place for a delicate English baby of two. Byron was grateful to him and to his wife, too, for their kindness; but there it was—Hoppner was solemn, and he couldn't help fooling with him when he wrote.

Hoppner had great powers of disapproval, as became an Englishman who for official purposes had to reside among the Italians. He disapproved of Venice, Italy, Byron, Allegra, and most of the friends that Byron had made in Italy. At this moment his disapproval was focused on the Countess Guiccioli, and if this journey to Ravenna had any connexion with her, sooner or later he would have to speak his mind. Unfortunately he was a gossip, and a great source of his disapproval was the chatter of old women in *salons* or the mendacious indiscretions of gondoliers and discharged servants. Byron knew his friend's weakness for gossip and disapproval. He was also aware that the Countess Guiccioli was not one of his favourites, for some reason unknown. In writing to him, therefore, he dangled him on the end of a hook and kept him gasping. He boasted of his delinquencies, exaggerated them, and hinted always at a little bit more than the truth. It was fun to watch Hoppner's long, doubtful face when next he met him.

"My dear Hoppner," he wrote on June 2 from Padua on the mainland,

I am just setting off for Ferrara . . . I am proceeding in no very good humour, for La G[uiccioli]'s instructions are rather calculated to produce an *éclat*—and perhaps a scene—than any decent iniquity. I had a letter from her on Monday, which merely repeated the directions she had given me before, with the addition of something about her own house.

Now to go to cuckold a Papal Count, who, like Candide, has already been "the death of two men one of whom was a priest," in his own house is rather too much for my modesty, when there are several other places at least as good for the purpose. She says they must go to Bologna in the middle of June, and why the devil then drag me to Ravenna? However, I shall determine nothing till I get to Bologna, and probably take some time to decide when I am there, so that, the Gods willing, you may probably see me again soon. The Charmer forgets that a man may be whistled anywhere *before*, but that *after*—a journey in an Italian June is a conscription, and therefore she should have been less liberal in Venice, or less exigent at Ravenna.

If I was not the most constant of men, I should now be swimming from the Lido, instead of smoking in the dust of Padua . . . Believe me, ever your disconsolate and affectionate, B.

Hoppner shook his head over this letter—he would gladly see Byron leave Venice for his own good, yet he could not trust him out of his sight—and, for all his faults, he really was fond of the unaccountable creature.

When Byron saw an hour of decision bending over him he grew pensive and flirted dreamily with the thought of death. Like Romeo, he had bought poison from a lean apothecary, and at Bologna he went for a stroll in the Certosa graveyard, outside the city walls. There he fell into conversation with the sexton—a worthy after his own mood at the moment—the gravedigger playing to him as Hamlet, seated in his black cloak upon a tombstone, chin propped upon his hand. This man of bones told him that he had planted all the cypresses in the cemetery, and he seemed really to love his dead people. He showed him the tomb of a young and beautiful girl, dead two hundred years ago, and, said he, when they opened her grave a short while since, her hair still was "yellow as gold." And here, he said, picking up a skull, "this was Brother Desiderio Berro, who died at forty—one of my best friends. I begged his head of his brethren after his decease, and they gave it me. I put it in lime and then boiled it. Here it is, teeth and all, in excellent preservation. He was the merriest, cleverest fellow I ever knew. Wherever he went, he brought joy, and when anyone was melancholy, the sight of him was enough to make him cheerful again. He walked so actively, you might have taken him for a dancer—he joked—he laughed—oh, he was such a *frate* as I never saw before, nor ever shall again!"

Alas, poor Yorick! Hoppner must be told of the visit to the Certosa graveyard.

I found, too [he wrote] such a pretty epitaph, or rather two: one was—

Martini Luigi
Implora pace;

the other,

Lucrezia Picini
Implora eterna quiete.

That was all; but it appears to me that these two and three words comprise and compress all that can be said on the subject—and then, in Italian, they are absolute music. They contain doubt, hope, and humility; nothing can be more pathetic than the *implora* and the modesty of the request;—they have had enough of life—they want nothing but rest—they implore it, and *eterna quiete*. It is like a Greek inscription in some good old heathen "City of the Dead." Pray, if I am shovelled into the Lido churchyard in your time, let me have the *implora pace*, and nothing else, for my epitaph.

Hoppner was reassured. These meditations among the tombs betokened a serious state of mind. No mention anywhere of the Countess in Ravenna. Better still, he closed by writing, "I will thank you . . . to prepare for my return. I shall go back to Venice before I village on the Brenta. I shall stay but a few days at Bologna. I am just going to see sights. . . . After that I shall return to Venice, where you may expect me about the eleventh, or perhaps sooner . . . my respects to the Consuless, and to Mr Scott. I hope my daughter is well. Ever yours, and truly, B."

On the outside was a postscript. Hoppner glanced at it suspiciously. Byron had kept the letter two days before sending it. "I am just setting off for Ravenna, June 8, 1819. I changed my mind this morning, and decided to go on."

At Ferrara he walked moodily beside the river Po. As he watched it flow past him, he saw in its waves a symbol of Fate, bearing its victims relentlessly out to sea, and as he journeyed on slowly to Ravenna he found time to write a poem.

River, that rollest by the ancient walls,
Where dwells the lady of my love, when she
Walks by thy brink, and there perchance recalls
A faint and fleeting memory of me—

True, the river Po doesn't run anywhere near Ravenna, but it doesn't matter—let the verses flow—Ca' Zen, on the isle of Ariano, where a lady dwelt a few weeks ago, lies at the mouth of the Po.

> Borne on our old unchanged career, we move;
> Thou tendest wildly, onwards to the main,
> And I—to loving one I should not love. . . .
>
> The wave that bears my tears returns no more:
> Will she return by whom that wave shall sweep?
> Both tread thy banks, both wander on thy shore,
> I by thy source, she by the dark-blue deep.

Fate again had won—and "poeshie"—why fight against ourselves?

> A stranger loves the lady of the land,
> Born far beyond the mountains, but his blood
> Is all meridian, as if never fanned
> By the black wind that chills the polar flood.
>
> My blood is all meridian; were it not,
> I had not left my clime, nor should I be
> In spite of tortures ne'er to be forgot,
> A slave again of love—at least of thee.

Back—back to the Certosa graveyard and dreams of easeful death—

> 'Tis vain to struggle—let me perish young—
> Live as I lived, and love as I have loved;
> To dust if I return, from dust I sprung,
> And then, at least, my heart can ne'er be moved.

All this while Alexander Scott had been forgotten in Venice. If any man were to blame for this latest *imbroglio*, it was Scott. Hadn't he forced Byron to speak to the Countess Guiccioli against his will and judgment? But Scott was a humorist, and with him Byron dared not play the fool. It was better to drop the mask and let the truth out. Scott, too, was sympathetic about the Countess Guiccioli. He thought her a simple, unaffected child, passionate, perhaps, and reckless, but she was undoubtedly a lady, she seemed very much in love. She would be good for his friend and keep him out of mischief.

"My dear Scott," wrote Byron from Ravenna in a hasty scrawl on June 10,

the moment you get this letter, let *Augustine* be dispatched off to Bologna to wait for me at the Inn *Pelegrino* with the remaining carriage—the carriage horses—and the two Grey saddle horses—let him bring my letters and perhaps he will apply to Mr Hoppner or to Siri for money—but pray let him set off immediately and wait for me according to the above directions for Bologna bringing with him the saddles—harness etc. he can hire a man to lead the saddle horses if necessary. The point setting off no time for a word more. Pray answer me by return of the same yrs ever Byron.

The meat of the letter lay in the postscript. "The G[uiccioli] has been very ill—still in bed but better—I have seen her—and she is as usual —I am in love with her—more in my next."

For three weeks the letters rattled out of Ravenna to Hoppner and Scott in Venice, to Hobhouse and Murray in London—each man played according to his temper.

> I don't like to say much by post [he told Scott] but all goes very well here. The lady does whatever she pleases with me and luckily the same things please both. She had really been very ill and is a good deal thinner. *She* is very popular here with the inhabitants—who seem good-natured people. But at present I shall enter no further in detail though there has been comedy enough for a long narrative. *He* is the wealthiest of the district —and not so much liked—but they all—even the women—speak well of her.

Later in the same letter was another hasty scrawl: "The G[uiccioli] is better—and will get well with prudence. Our amatory business goes on *well* and *daily*."

With Hoppner he was more mischievous. A letter bragging about his prowess, and the stage was set for cheerful melodrama.

> I find my situation very agreeable, but want my horses very much, there being good riding in the environs. I can fix no time for my return to Venice —it may be soon or late—it all depends on the *Dama*, whom I found very seriously in *bed* with a cough and spitting of blood, etc. all of which has subsided, and something else has recommenced . . . I found all the people here firmly persuaded that she would never recover; they were mistaken, however . . . *She* manages very well . . . but if I come away with a stiletto in my gizzard some fine afternoon, I shall not be astonished.

His "unlawful love" went gaily forward and everything was going the way Mrs Hoppner had guessed it would and—"do pray—send off Augustine—and carriage—and cattle to Bologna without fail or delay —or I shall lose my remaining shred of senses."

To Murray in London he announced that he was in Ravenna now with his *amica*. She was, he said (as though he had never mentioned Angelina), the Countess Guiccioli—twenty years old, married to a rich old man, perpetual cough, intermittent fever, but bears up *gallantly*, etc. He joked Murray about "meridian" morality and closed on a mocking note of Childe Harold heroics.

> I see my *Dama* every day at the proper (and improper) hours; but I feel seriously uneasy about her health, which seems very precarious. In losing her, I should lose a being who has run great risks on my account, and whom I have every reason to love—but I must not think this possible. I do not know what I *should* do if she died, but I ought to blow my brains out—and I hope that I should.

Hoppner, the shabby fellow, had answered only one of his letters, in a purely business tone, and was distractingly slow in sending horses. He wrote to him again to prod him into action or disapproval, one way or the other. He once more played the pensive tune of the Certosa grave-yard. "I greatly fear," he wrote, "that the Guiccioli is going into a con-sumption, to which her constitution tends. Thus it is with every thing and every body for whom I feel a real attachment—'War, death or discord doth lay siege to them. . . .' I never even could keep alive a dog that I liked or that liked me." He sent a message to Mrs Hoppner in his postscript. "If anything happens to my present *Amica*, I have done with the passion for ever—it is my *last* love. As to libertinism, I have sickened myself of that, as was natural in the way I went on, and I have at least derived that advantage from vice, to *love* in the better sense of the word. *This* will be my last adventure—I can hope no more to inspire attachment, and I trust never again to feel it."

Hoppner sneered as he read this letter. He tossed it over to his wife and glared at her crossly while she lingered over the postscript. The moment had come for plain speaking, and he wrote to Lord Byron at length.

"Human nature is such," he said in the sad, superior tone of a man who suffers not from that weakness, "that our greatest pleasures are derived from and depend upon illusions, and," he added, warming to his task, "it is the more cruel in anyone who attempts to destroy those which make others happy. . . . Perhaps," he continued, as he raised the birch to strike, "you will think I am taking an unwarrantable liberty with you—it is your own fault, you have had repeated proof of the frankness of my disposition." He ought not to—and would not—say harsh things of a lady who was ill, and he hoped—and was confident—that she would recover. But it *was* his duty to state with all possible clarity that "La Guiccioli" was unworthy of affection. He would not interfere with the *pleasures* of a friend, but he must tell his lordship that once more he was making himself absurd. "La Guiccioli" did not, as he had good reason to know, return his affection. *Avowedly* she had en-trapped him in her net from vanity, and, when she was *sure of him*, she would *leave him in the lurch* and boast of her betrayal. "If I am not right in my opinion of the fair Guiccioli," wrote Hoppner, closing the topic with all the authority of a judge reaching for the black cap, "I have been grossly deceived by what is said of her here."

Having dealt roundly with the Countess Guiccioli, he proceeded to bring his correspondent to book on another matter—his daughter, Allegra. The child was ailing and tiresome, and "no one will be troubled with her" among the servants. Her "*mademoiselle*"—one Elise—had been discharged on the day Byron left Venice, apparently at his own desire. Hoppner was sorry that his friend would not subscribe to his plans for the child. She was not made for the warm air of Italy and should be sent to colder northern climes. In the meantime he was setting off on a journey to Switzerland, so he had sent Allegra to La Mira, on the mainland, to stay with Mrs Martens, the wife of the Danish Consul. A change of air from the fetid summer heat of Venice was essential, he said, for the child.

One other point, and Hoppner was done with his charges to his lordship. His friends—the Shelleys. They had come to Venice last September, as Byron remembered, and their child, Clara, had died there. Mrs Shelley's stepsister, Miss Claire Clairmont, had joined them at their villa in the Euganean Hills. Now Hoppner had to inform him that the Shelleys had lost their son, too, "which has left them childless and in deep despair. The lady, however," added Hoppner coldly, "is about to replace the loss." From reporting ill news of the Shelleys, he fell to dark insinuations against Miss Clairmont. "I do not know whether Miss Claire is gone quite crazy or not; but it is certain that both Mrs Hoppner and I would willingly ascribe what we must otherwise attribute to innate wickedness in her, to folly." All in all, the British Consul had boiled up for his friend a goodly cauldron of mysterious delinquency and grim disapproval, in which the Countess Guiccioli, Miss Clairmont, and Allegra companionably simmered together.

That letter went by return of post straight back to Venice to Alexander Scott. With it came a furious letter from the lover, written backward and forward across the sheet with postscript chasing postscript until they emerged on the cover and Byron's opinion of Hoppner was plain to all the world. "I will never forgive him for his gratuitous, officious, *bilious* intermeddling. He might at least have waited till asked."

"My dear Scott," the letter opened explosively,

> . . . all his amiable bile is *gratis*—and *unasked*—now I ask you—and whatever you say on the subject disagreeable will not be your fault but mine. I never supposed that the G[uiccioli] was to be a despairing shepherdess—nor did I search very nicely into her motives—all I know is that *she* sought *me*—and that I have had have [?] *there and here and everywhere*—so that if there is any fool-making on the occasion—I humbly suspect *two* can play at that—and that hitherto the parties have at least an equal chance. I have no hesitation in repeating that I *love* her—but I have also *self-love* enough to be cured by the least change or trick on her part when I know it—Pride is one's best friend on such occasions— As to her "vanity" (I wish it were, there is no passion so strange) in getting me, as Hoppner says,—that might be very well in an English woman but I don't see how *English* poetical celebrity is to operate on an *Italian*. . . . Will you tell me to what Gossip he alludes—at any rate you will tell it me without *mystery* and *hints* and without *bile*—so pray do—I forgive whatever may be unpleasant in the intelligence and it may be of use to me. . . . What does he mean by "avowedly"? Does he think that a woman is to go and "avow" her likings in the piazza? . . .

TERESA, COUNTESS GAMBA-GUICCIOLI
At the age of eighteen.

BYRON IN 1816

As his wife and Claire Clairmont remembered him, with the pugnacious lower lip.

*From a rough sketch* (1816) *by G. H. Harlow*

65

P.S. What does he mean by "when she is sure of me"? how sure? when a man has been for sometime in the habit of keying a female—methinks it is his own fault if the being "left in the lurch" greatly incommodes him . . . unless he be a sighing swain . . . if the lady takes another caprice—*Ebbene?* can't one match her in that too, think you? Then let her boast of betraying . . . hitherto I am faithful—but the slightest dereliction (at least when aware of it) will give me liberty . . .

[P.S.] There has been no public exhibition for I never go out with her—except twice or thrice—in the Carriage—but I am *not in waiting* [*i.e.*, not a *cicisbeo*]. Give me but proof . . . and I will rejoin you directly and we will village at The Mira—There's a bribe for you . . . remember you and I can say and hear anything from one another—it is in *our line* . . . but I never gave him the right of *hinting* and teasing one out of temper.

[P.S.] You will think me a damned fool—but when she was supposed to be in danger—I was really and truly on the point of poisoning myself—and have got the drug still in my drawer.

[P.S.] All this you may say to Hoppner from me—with my sentiments on his conduct into the bargain— He really is *intolerable*. . . .

[P.S.] You may imagine her answer—of course she would be at no loss for that—none of them are— She volunteered an elopement saying "Then instead of being at my mercy—I shall be at yours—for you have my letters in which I have not only exposed my feelings but my name— You have every proof that a man can have of my being in earnest—and if you desire more try me." Besides what do they know of me in Venice? You should judge by what they say of me here—if you like *hearsay* better than *experience*.

[P.S.] If Hoppner is not gone, ask him in a friendly way from *me* what he means—but don't show him this letter.

Scott wrote back a soothing letter. He gave the gist of the talk in Venice, but advised Byron to pay no attention to it. Then, fearing that the same fate might befall his letter with all its *rechauffé* of ill-natured gossip, he rebuked his friend for showing Hoppner's letter to Teresa. But Byron would have none of it—he read Scott's letter to Teresa, mercifully omitting only the sentences in which her critics in Venice had mocked at her for being "ridiculous." As for Hoppner, he declared with engaging frankness, what he resented most in his letter was not his slander against Teresa but the insult to his own vanity. If Hoppner had accused *her* of being dull or stupid, naturally he would never have shown her the letter, but, as it was, Teresa's feelings were in no way hurt by the knowledge that Hoppner thought her astute. You may, he wrote, tell a man that he is thought libertine—profligate—a villain "but *not* that his nose wants blowing."

Peace, however, descended. Scott received a letter from the pretty little countess in Ravenna. Her feelings were in no way hurt by what Hoppner insinuated, or Venice asserted, about her. She wrote in a spirit of composure that almost touched smugness. Her letter was brief, but written in a steady copy-book hand on lines carefully ruled, and there

## CHAPTER III

# Angelus in the Forest

IT was Corpus Christi Day when Byron arrived in Ravenna, and the town was making holiday. He was greeted with the sound of church-bells ringing from steeple and *campanile*. Carpets and tapestries were flung over balconies and in the streets the priests were leading processions of children chanting hymns in shrill staccato. He drove through their midst to a battered little inn standing over the way from Dante's tomb. It was proudly named the Imperial Hotel, in the hope of luring travellers to this forgotten city of Ravenna.

The innkeeper waved his arms wildly in the air when the carriage drove to his door and pointed to his throat with a dramatic gesture to indicate that he had that minute been interrupted in the act of suicide. His wife was in tears, and the servants were chattering in loud voices in the street outside. There were bailiffs in the house, and the innkeeper was about to be led away to gaol. The English milord descended from his carriage, ordered the best rooms of the inn, and summoned the bailiffs into his presence. This was his house, he told them, and they disfigured it with their ugly mugs—how much did the innkeeper owe? The bailiffs shouted in a cataract of conflicting figures, and Milord disdainfully flung a purse upon the table—let them help themselves and begone! The bailiffs swooped upon the purse with shrieks of joy and tumbled, all fighting and squabbling, downstairs. The innkeeper fell upon his knees and kissed Milord's hand. His wife, more passionately, hugged him in her arms and kissed him a dozen times on both cheeks. The servants outside heard the news and incontinently fell upon the bailiffs with broomstick and dishcloth and in a fit of feudal loyalty drove them down the street. Then they ran back and gazed up with dancing eyes at the windows of Milord's room.

In the privacy of his room Byron stormed—there it was again—why couldn't people leave him alone? All he wanted was peace and eternal quiet, and here was all Ravenna gaping at his windows! The common people—God knows he liked them!—they were just like the women—he might shrink shyly into the darkness he craved—but they dragged him out into the light of day and made love to him! They wouldn't even let him into this town of theirs without setting all the church-bells pealing!

When he saw Teresa he was stricken with remorse. He found her in bed—a very sick child indeed. He was ashamed of himself for playing with the affections of a girl beating her wings helplessly against a gilded cage. She was thin and haggard, and her eyes were feverish. She was coughing and spitting blood, and every one round her shook his head and talked of the consumption in the Gamba family and all those tiny graves. But she smiled when she saw Byron and flung her arms round his neck in the presence of her husband, who cried out anxiously to her to have a care. He drew the visitor aside and told him with a solemn face that his wife had suffered a grievous disappointment—she had had a dangerous miscarriage and all hope of the boy was gone. . . . Teresa whispered in his ear that she was glad she had miscarried of her husband's child, because now—she could be everything—but Byron loosed her arms from his neck.

He was chastened and perturbed. He unpacked his medical books and hovered round her bed, proffering advice. He insisted on her taking Peruvian bark—a noxious medicine that he would not swallow himself —and meekly Teresa swallowed it and held out her cup for more. Then he bustled away to Count Guiccioli and Count Gamba and told them that they were wrong in their treatment of their patient. He wrote to Scott in Venice, begging him to persuade Dr Aglietti to come to Ravenna—he would pay all expenses for the journey and the prescription—and Dr Aglietti came.

The doctor was a good friend of Byron and, like Hoppner, was anxious to get him out of Venice for his health's sake. He held Teresa's pulse and looked at his watch wisely. At the end of his diagnosis he was able to reassure every one. He counselled Byron not to take this coughing and spitting of blood too much to heart—with care and, he would suggest, consideration, it would disappear. To Count Guiccioli he spoke in terms of highest praise for the treatment he was following with his young wife—it was sensible, humane—with time it would lead to a certain cure. If she liked drinking Peruvian bark, she might.

The doctor spent two days in Ravenna, and when he left he told Count Guiccioli and Lord Byron that he had come solely in the spirit of friendship and really hadn't the face to charge a fee for the advice he had given. In fact, between them all in Ravenna, they had found the right treatment for his patient without his help.

People at Ravenna were good-natured and polite. The Cavallis and the Capponis and the rest of the local gentry called at the Imperial Hotel and invited Byron into their houses. The poor people in the streets doffed their hats as he rode by and looked in at the inn to inquire after his health. The Vice-Legate invited him to his palace and beamed upon him through his spectacles. He was a scholarly old gentleman who had lived carnally with his housekeeper for forty years and passed for a moral liver in his diocese. The priests called upon this affable foreigner to show him their churches, and one obliging *abate* offered to carry any letters that he did not wish to send through the post.

For months past Byron had lived in seclusion in Venice and had not gone out in society, except now and then to call on the Countess Benzoni. But he expanded under the kind hospitality of these people. He mustn't go back to Venice, they said, and he didn't want to! He took rooms in the Strada di Sisi, went about and saw people, and was gay and cheerful. A priest came to him about a new organ in his church, and gladly he paid for it. A poor man called at the inn with a tale of bad luck, and he gave him money and bade him tell no one. Ravenna's great man was Count Rasponi. He had married a daughter of Joachim Murat, King of Naples, and was reckoned a liberal as a consequence. With him Byron heard talk of Italian politics and began to take interest in a people whom hitherto he had looked upon only as ministers to his comfort and pleasure as a tourist. But he remembered Teresa's instructions. All these people were kind, but he felt that, for all their simplicity, they looked at him curiously and with ironical eyes. Surely, said they, he had put himself to great trouble and expense to come to their poor town and stay so long there—they appreciated the honour he had paid them and marvelled at it. Byron replied that he had come to see their churches and Dante's tomb and the mausoleum of Theodoric the Goth, and any expense that he had been put to was amply repaid by the *amicizia* with which Count Guiccioli had distinguished him.

Only the Gamba family held aloof. Count Ruggiero received him with grave courtesy, but somehow Byron felt that he was looked upon as an intruder—as an unwanted son-in-law who had forced himself upon the family. Teresa's brother, Pietro, was away in Rome, where he had met many English people. He wrote to say that his sister must give up this foreigner as her *amico*—he was a brute, a savage who had locked up a young wife, beautiful and innocent, in his *castello* in England.

Within the Palazzo Guiccioli everything was strange and mysterious. The old porter glowered at him, but the negro page welcomed him every morning with a grin that showed all his white teeth. La Signora F——, the duenna, was a sphinx, sitting with folded hands and downcast eyes in the background, yet there was a suspicion of a smile in every curve of her drooping, plump shoulders. Carluccio was home from school, scowling at his stepmother all day long—he was watching, surely, and running like a young sneak to his father with stories. But at any rate he was a boy, and Byron had a way with boys when he chose. He took Carluccio out for rides, laughed with him one minute and listened with admirable seriousness the next, as years ago he had done with little lame Harry Fox, Lord Holland's son. Carluccio continued to scowl upon his stepmother, but capitulated to her *amico* and chattered away with him gaily on their rides. He wasn't happy at home, he confessed; his father was nagging and suspicious. A ring, a chain, and an odd handful of *quattrini* belonging to the Signora F—— had been stolen, and Count Guiccioli accused him of the theft. Byron, who had given Count Guiccioli advice upon the treatment of his wife, next took up the cudgels for his son and told him he was all wrong about Carluccio. By his kindness he won for himself the affection of at least one male in the house.

But Count Guiccioli was the darkest enigma in this puzzling house. Husbands can be formidable to their wives' *amici*, as Byron knew to his shame—and sometimes to his cost. James Webster was fussy and talkative, suspicious out of season—and asked him for a thousand pounds —a loan which Byron had made, demurely wondering. Caroline Lamb's husband was handsome, humorous, nonchalant, with a strange, sensitive charm, kind and understanding—just the man with whom he could have made friends for life. But in William Lamb's eyes, as they lazily met his, he had seen an expression that was at once contemptuous and sad. Now here was Count Guiccioli towering above him from his six foot of height. His eyes were half closed as though he were bored, and his mouth was drawn down at the corners in a disdainful pucker. His politeness was majestic, as of an emperor talking etiquette with a chamberlain. He listened urbanely when Byron discussed his wife's health; the treatment was wrong, and the Count bent his head—might he send for Dr Aglietti? —the Count bowed again—at his own expense?—and the Count smiled. He called on Byron at his inn; he begged him to visit the Palazzo Guiccioli daily, for his company was balm to his wife and set her on the road to health. "I can't make him out at all," Byron wrote in exasperation to Hoppner before the "bilious" letter came; "he visits me frequently and takes me out (like Whittington, the Lord Mayor) in a coach and *six* horses. The fact appears to be, that he is completely *governed* by her—for that matter, so am I. The people here don't know what to make of us, as he had a character of jealousy with all his wives —this is the third." The "people here," perhaps, were not frank with their wild intruder from England. They might have told him that an Italian gentleman always paid these delicate attentions to the *amico* of his wife.

Teresa's health took a quick turn for the better. She laughed at the sight of her poet spilling medical books on the bedclothes. She laughed again when Pietro's letter came telling of the wife locked up in England and showed it to Byron, who laughed more wryly. The coughing and the blood-spitting vanished. Soon she was out of bed, and in a few days she was riding with her *amico* in the Pine Forest and bathing in the Adriatic. "It is a fine forest," wrote Byron cheerfully to Hobhouse on July 30; "so full of pastime and prodigality, and I have persuaded my *Contessa* to put a side-saddle upon a pony of her *sposo's*, and we ride together—

she in a hat shaped like Punch's and the merry Mrs Ford's of Windsor, and a sky-blue tiffany riding-habit, like the ghost of Prologue's grandmother." Sometimes, when they came to a fallen tree or a stream, Byron held the reins and they jumped their horses together, and Teresa laughed for joy. Sometimes she tumbled off her horse, and they laughed again. And sometimes Byron tumbled off his horse and didn't laugh, and her eyes were full of pretty ruth. As they rode she told him the stories of the forest, of the ships that once had moored there, the armies that had fought there, and the 'wild huntsman' who rode every night with his pack of baying hounds, for ever pursuing the phantom of a lady who had been too proud to love. They rode out to Filetto and sat under the acacias and chatted with Don Juan, whom Byron greeted with a humorous eye on account of his name—he must get to work on that poem again. And thence away to the seashore, where they watched the gold-and-copper sails of the fishing-boats billowing in the summer breeze. Teresa was ruddy and sunburnt, the sweat ran down her pretty nose, and she smelt of warm, clean flesh and saddle-leather. The fat jowls fell from Byron's face, revealing once more the beauty of his features and, *O mia carissima*, his paunch was folding up! He, too, was feeling better, and there was a flush of colour in his cheeks. Every day, in obedience to his *dama*, whiskers sprouted more luxuriantly round his jaw and throat in the rich and manly growth of Sir Mulberry Hawk.

The duties of sentiment were not forgotten in the quest for health. One day the Guiccioli coach drove at a slow pace to Dante's tomb while the people in the streets stood reverently by. Arrayed in cocked hat and brocaded coat, with sword hitched uncomfortably to his hip, Byron laid copies of his works—*Childe Harold, Lara, The Bride of Abydos*—on the tomb of the poet of *The Divine Comedy*. Teresa knelt and told her rosary and her lips moved in prayer, while her *amico* stood leaning against a pillar and watched her with folded arms and melancholy frown. From Dante's tomb they went to the church where the Polentani family had their tombs, and once more Teresa prayed for the soul's rest of Francesca da Rimini and her lover, while Byron brooded like a disconsolate heretic in the background.

That evening Teresa laid her commands upon her *amico*. He had written a poem in honour of Tasso, the poet of Ferrara; now he must write a poem about her poet—Dante of Ravenna—in the *terza rima* of *The Divine Comedy*. Any woman, said the patient Fletcher admiringly, could do what she liked with his lordship—except My Lady. Byron set to work upon his task, and in quick time produced two cantos of his *Prophecy of Dante*.

"Lady! if for the cold and cloudy clime,"

he wrote in a dedicatory sonnet—

> Where I was born, but where I would not die,
>     Of the great Poet-Sire of Italy
> I dare to build the imitative rhyme,
> Harsh Runic copy of the South's sublime,
>     Thou art the cause; and howsoever I
>     Fall short of his immortal harmony,
> Thy gentle heart will pardon me the crime.
> Thou, in the pride of Beauty and of Youth,
>     Spakest; and for thee to speak and be obey'd
> Are one; but only in the sunny South
>     Such sounds are uttered, and such charms display'd,
> So sweet a language from so fair a mouth—
>     Ah! to what effort would it not persuade?

Teresa loved that sonnet. With all her heart she admired *The Prophecy of Dante*, though she could not understand a word of it until Byron translated it into Italian prose. For she neither spoke nor understood English yet, and he wouldn't have her speak it with its flat vowels and cackling sibilance of hissing geese—let her always talk with him in her own dear Italian undersong with her cowbell voice and deep Romagna tones. Humbly she obeyed him and never in his lifetime spoke English nor read his poems save in French translation.

She would have liked him to speak only of Beatrice when he wrote about Dante—how love of her had been his guiding force through life and revealed to him the love of heaven that passes understanding. But no, said Byron, *our* Dante is the exile and the rebel whom tyrants might banish but never enslave. He played on Teresa's other enthusiasm—her love of Italy, her longing for its freedom and its union as one of the great states of the world. *Our* Dante, said Byron, shall speak from his tomb here in Ravenna; he shall prophesy harsh days of wolf and vulture, of tramping armies and perpetual invasion, but he shall see beyond those troublous times to the hour when Freedom shall dawn.

> I may not overleap the eternal bar
> Built up between us, and will die alone,
>     Beholding with the dark eye of a seer
> The evil days to gifted souls foreshown,
>     Foretelling them to those who will not hear,
> As in the old time, till the hour be come
>     When Truth shall strike their eyes through many a tear,
> And make them own the Prophet in his tomb.

She had turned him back to "poeshie," and he took up *Don Juan* for a third canto. He felt less ribald now, less anxious to shock Murray with his dread of falling sales or Hobhouse with his growing itch for decency. Juan had been washed up on the shores of a Greek island in the last canto, and there Haidee found him and nursed him back to life.

Onward with the tale now into a quiet backwater of love and dusk and sleep! The "lady and her lover were alone"—in a forest. The sun was dropping behind the mountains, and from a distant city church-bells rang the *Angelus*—"Ave Maria; blessed be the hour!" Did they ring for Haidee and for Juan on their pagan island? . . . Teresa reined in her horse and bent her head and crossed her breast. Her *amico*, too, was silent for a while. Far away the faint dying day-hymn stole aloft—

> And not a breath crept through the rosy air,
> And yet the forest leaves seemed stirred with prayer.

Round them were the pines tipped with dying fire; the shrill cicadas making their eternal summer song; the wind carrying the burden of the chime; and, faintly, the dull murmur of the sea upon the shore. The last note was blown away. Suddenly twilight swooped. . . . The horses whinnied impatiently. . . . With a laugh Teresa dropped the reins and threw back her head for her lover to kiss her throat—pulsing, tremulous with a voice that tried to speak, and spoke . . . not one word.

CHAPTER IV

# Juliet in Ravenna

WITH this child he was happy for the moment as he had never been since he was a boy. The days of first love had returned, and she reminded him no longer of his sister. She was Mary Chaworth now, with whom he had gone riding in Sherwood Forest long ago—poor Mary, who had scorned him and tried to call him back, had been unhappy and lost her mind.

But a truce to such sad memories—he was happy again in the Pine Forest with its drowsy, reed-fringed pools where herons brooded, its long glades carpeted with moss, and the sea glittering in the sunlight at the end. He was happy in Ravenna, yet more silent for all its cobbled streets than Venice with its canals. He had prayed for peace and eternal quiet in the Certosa graveyard as he came, not hoping to find them this side of death, but weren't they here, waiting for him in loving ambush —here in this desolate old town from which all life seemed to have ebbed away with the sea a thousand years ago? What the devil did that slobbering poetaster Leigh Hunt mean by prating about its "clear-shewn towers"? It lay so low in its flat plain that you were close upon it before you saw it at all—a city of squat towers and melancholy *campanili*, like an old town in an illuminated breviary, and you had to climb a steeple to get a comprehensive view. Its ramparts were covered with moss and crumbling into their moat under the weight of brambles. Its streets were silent and grass-grown with prison-like houses toppling over them from either side. Its churches were deserted, and their pillars sinking into the bog below them. The mosaics on their walls were faded as though for centuries they had lain at the bottom of the vanished sea. Wind and mist were the only true inhabitants of this "good old city of the Dead." You could walk for an hour through little clouds of dust and tinkling, dry leaves of last year's autumn and meet no one in its streets, and then you turned the corner suddenly and saw a gallows with corpses dangling from it and under it the bored Papal Guards eating their midday meal. Now and then a black-coated priest hurried across the square carrying the Holy Wafer to a dying sinner. Pale faces with smouldering eyes looked out from dark doorways. Yet always there hovered that sound of subdued gaiety that fills the air in all Italian cities, but in Ravenna it was for ever round the corner—the sharp, clear sound of children's voices. . . . Here in this quiet old town a man might doze away his life very comfortably to the murmur of the wind among the trees and the cracked chimes counting the hours slowly one by one.

His lameness and his poetry had left him weary. Like other men born crippled, he hankered after an athletic life—for boxing, for riding, and—one sport where his damned foot made no difference—for swimming. He craved, too, the active life of other men of his rank in England —the hustings, the noisy election mob, the give-and-take of political life and parliamentary debate. Above all, he wanted the society of men. He had a quick gift of friendship, and his friendships endured time and absence; from friends he suffered criticism gladly and gave them as good as he got. But, for his sins, he had written a poem that ran like wildfire all the length of England. Neck and crop he was tossed into the laps of women, and he found he needed them, too—as an interlude to friendship. They flattered him, they sympathized, they were devoted, but, being women, they never understood. Always they mistook him for the man he wasn't—the sombre hero of his own poems—not, as he tried to explain in impatience, "a very facetious personage." Consumptive spinsters and lovelorn housemaids wrote him letters. Strange young women burst into his rooms—voluble, tremulous, excited—and left, offended by his warmth or his coldness, to write him yet more letters, blistered with their tears. Caro Lamb—who, at least, was a well-born lady and might have known the rules of the game—had inveigled him into a love-affair on the high romantic plane—and there she came, tapping at his door, disguised as a page. A few days of happiness, and months of tears and recrimination! He had grown to hate her choir-boy face, her slender body, her tumbled golden curls, her everlasting lisp and drawl.

Marriage—preferably a loveless marriage—was his only refuge from the depredations of womankind. He chose Miss Annabella Milbanke because, when first he saw her in Caro's drawing-room, he thought she was the governess. This serious-minded girl was an heiress, but that mattered little to him. She had intellectual yearnings and a soul above fashionable life, she was good and pious and had piqued his curiosity by refusing his first offer of marriage. But she was the stuff of which wives are made. You could see from her face she had great powers of devotion and would manage him for his own good.

Annabella's one vice was that she loved Byron and was fascinated by him against her will. Honeymoon and marriage with her had been a horrible dream ending in a thunderclap. Furious tirades and pained bewilderment, raving recoil of physical repulsion and clumsy attempts at pity, gibes and sneers and "sermons and sentiments." Out of this nightmare a child had been born—Ada—and then he told his wife to leave him and go back to her mother. Annabella obeyed and took Ada with her. For a few days letters came to him, full of pitiful jokes about "being good" and water-closets and the damnable trade of versifying, and then, suddenly, he learned that neither Annabella nor Ada would ever come back.

He was shocked, angry, remorseful. "Weren't you ever *once* happy with me?" he wrote to Annabella. And again, like a naughty schoolboy, craving pardon but too proud to own his fault, "Dearest Pip, I wish you would make it up. I am dreadfully sick of all this." But Annabella had hardened her heart against the wayward Byron charm. She had left him because he was a *"wicked"* man, she told him, because he meant to break her heart—and damn her soul and their daughter's too. She talked learnedly of "principles" and "derelictions." "I have," she wrote virtuously and reproachfully—"I have *consistently* fulfilled my duty as your wife," and then the woman breaking through the schoolmarm, "it was too dear to be resigned until it became hopeless. Now my resolution cannot be changed."

Annabella's heart, in truth, was broken. She emerged from her year of marriage a woman in whom the spring of life had snapped. There was nothing left her now but long years of malignant charity and dreary brooding. Husband died, and daughter—both alienated from her—for somehow her affection killed where it grappled. She went to her grave, a grim, silent woman, shrinking from the glare marriage had brought upon her and hugging her bitter secret to herself—that she had failed Byron through her own hurt pride. Many years after his death she met Chopin, and something in this frail musician, so near to dying, appealed to the pent-up devotion within her. But "Oh," said Chopin ungratefully, "I know she bored Lord Byron—when I'm with her, I feel like a sucking-pig being catechized by a goose."

The British public was passing through one of its truculent moods of chivalry when Annabella left Byron. In a few years' time it was to clasp Queen Caroline to its rugged heart; now, for Annabella's sake, it hissed an unoffending actress off the stage for breaking up a decent home. The great world called Society was wiser yet; and at one persistent rumour of sin, shocked countesses rustled away with protesting shoulder-blades from Byron and his sister at a ball.

He left England for three years of wandering and tormented thought and ceaseless poetry—the sombre note gradually melting into defiant ribaldry. There had been months of peace when he talked poetry and philosophy with a new friend, Shelley, at Geneva. Then he crossed the Alps and set up house in Venice and there plunged into a life of stupid vice. He was done with ladies—with Caros and Annabellas—and took his pleasure with the daughters of the game. With their animalism, their savage affection, their shouts of *"Can' della Madonna!"* they amused him, and what else were women meant for but his laughter? But in the end they filled his fastidious soul with a profound disgust.

He was not made for high romantic love, nor for domestic life, even less for rank debauchery. Perhaps with this girl, in this game of *cavalier* with his *dama*, he might find something like repose.

"I should not like to be frittered down into a regular *cicisbeo*," he told Hobhouse. Perhaps he understood his own temper little when he expressed that fear—it was not likely that he would be content with carrying fans and doubling shawls for long. Certainly he understood Teresa not at all.

There was nothing sensitive in the face she turned to him. It was resolute and bold, it was bright and candid, it was irradiated with a dauntless innocence, a joy that knew no fear. It was never clouded, but it flashed lightning sometimes when he made fun of love or looked at another woman. But there was devotion in it, strong and earnest, and in the deep-blue eyes, turned up to his so frankly under their dark-brown lashes, there was nothing but kindness—startled kindness, eager kindness, holding out its hands! She could never keep a thought from her face nor hide it from him nor anyone else nor, least of all, herself. Nature had made her happy, and happiness she must have, and when she had found it the world must know. She was Juliet, crying like a hungry child to love-performing night, "Give me my Romeo!" and she leaped to his arms by daylight like the wilful runaway she was! The pity of it was their love-making was so furtive—yet so open; ring-time in the woods, where the birds sang hey-ding-a-ding, or clasped hands and strangled, blind kisses at noon in the darkened house, while the Count dozed in the chimney-corner—oh, for a day, a night, a week of nights, alone together, far away from watchful faces, and voices whispering round them, and curious eyes, smiling and asking questions on the morrow!

Why was it, when the bells rang at evening and he listened at Teresa's side, that sometimes his mind harked back to a dark, snowbound house in England and honeymoon with his wife?

Since he left England he had written to her once or twice, scornfully or bitterly, to gibe or torment, or coldly on matters of business. But now from Ravenna he wrote her a long letter.

His excuse was some verses that a German poetess had sent him upon his domestic affairs, with a request that they be forwarded to his wife in the hope that her heart would soften when she read them. Doubtless, he wrote to Annabella, "you will smile" (oh, that insufferable smile of hers!) at the simplicity of the poor lady's appeal, and "perhaps it may not offend you" to realize that the Byron marriage was being discussed in every language in Europe, "to as little purpose as in our own." But this was not his reason for writing. Fletcher had told him that she refused to give his wife a character as a lady's maid on account of (in good Annabellese) "doubts of her veracity." Presumably the trouble was about some testimony that Mrs Fletcher had given at the time of their separation. What that testimony was he knew not, or if he had ever known he had forgotten, and whether it were true was for Annabella to judge; but he would recommend her to consult her sense of justice before she deprived a woman of the means of earning her bread. But that wasn't his reason for writing either. She must know that he was in Ravenna now. It was a city "out of the way of travellers and armies and thus they have retained more of their originality. They make love a good deal and assassinate a little." Hard by was the Pine Forest—doubtless she had heard of it—a great place for *love*, celebrated in the works of Dryden and Boccaccio. "I am just going to take a Canter (for I have resumed my Tartar habits since I left England) in the cool of the Evening, and in the shadow of the forest 'till the Ave Maria. . . . I have not heard of Ada for many months but they say 'no news is good news.' . . . You must let her be taught Italian as soon as she can be taught any language but her own. . . . I presume that Italian being a language of *mine* will not prevent you from recollecting my request at the proper time. I am, B."

What was the good of writing to Annabella? She never answered. He folded up the letter and threw it to one side. Some weeks later he sent it off. He added a postscript saying he didn't need an answer—let her notify him through his sister that the letter had reached her. "I should like to have a picture of Miss Byron, when she can conveniently sit to Holmes or any other painter. *Addio*."

And Augusta, his sister? She was behaving meanly towards him. She wrote him nothing but "damned crinkum-crankum" these days, hinting vaguely at sorrow—was it heartache or toothache that tormented her? Almost, one might suppose, the virtuous Annabella were looking over her shoulder while she wrote! Was it possible she showed his letters to her to that damned woman! If that were the way Annabella gleaned her news, let the poor spy take it full in the face! But Augusta, too, must be punished for her shuffling. She had not replied to his letter from Venice—not really—had put him off with sad chatter about "a pain in her side." He had only hinted at the existence of Teresa in writing to her; now he would add the Countess Guiccioli to his catalogue of frail Italian ladies. But, though he would tease Augusta with a new love, he would not be too unkind. Here was nothing but a worldly *liaison* with a married woman—and distractions on the side. The business had been going on for a year and more, and—well, the lady had miscarried of a child in May. Augusta might try conclusions for herself and guess who had been father of that vanished child.

Two weeks had gone by since he wrote ferociously to Scott, declaring that he *loved* Teresa and had meditated suicide if she were to die. But Teresa was better now. "My dearest Augusta," he wrote on July 26,

I am at too great a distance to scold you—but I *will* ask you—whether your letter of the 1st July *is an answer* to the letter I wrote you before I quitted Venice?—What, is it come to *this?*—Have you no memory? or no heart? You *had* both—and I *have* both—at least for *you*.

I write this presuming that you received *that* letter—is it that you fear? do not be afraid of the past—the world has its affairs without thinking of *ours* and you may write safely—if you do—address as usual to Venice. . . . Shall I come to *you*—or would a warm climate do you good?—if so say the word, and I will provide you and your whole family, including that precious luggage your husband, with the means of making an agreeable journey— you need not fear about *me*—I am much altered and should be little trouble to you—nor would I give you more of my company than you like—I con- fess after three years and a half—and *such years!*—and *such a year* as preceded those three years—It would be a relief to me to see you again—and if it would be so to you—I will come to you.

Pray—answer me—and recollect that I will do as you like in everything —even to returning to England. . . .

But here in Ravenna England was receding far away—he was too tired to make the stroke now that would lift him out of the waters that were closing over him. Proudly Teresa had shown her poet a sonnet that she had written a long time ago when she was a *spaʒina* and, she hoped, married to a kind husband. The poem was addressed to her cousin, Teresa Cavalli, on the occasion of her marriage to Count Sassi. As a young matron the Countess Guiccioli referred to her own happy mar- riage and her *eternal* devotion to her husband. Byron enclosed the poor little poem in his letter to his sister. Against the opening lines of devotion to husband he had scribbled, "Ask Hobhouse to translate this to you —and tell him the reason." . . . Augusta dropped the verses—who was this poetess, this Countess Gamba-Guiccioli who loved her husband? . . . the letter roamed on . . . and the "reason" came. . . .

I write from Ravenna—I came here on account of a Countess Guiccioli —a girl of . . . [he had crossed out the word "twenty" on second thoughts and had written again in its place] twenty married to a very rich old man of sixty—about a year ago; with [*whom* crossed out in favour of] her I had *liaison* according to the good Italian custom . . . [now her rogue of a brother was floating off in his nonchalant, naughty strain . . . ] she miscarried in May—and sent for me here—and here I have been these two months.

Augusta laid the letter down with a wry little cackle of laughter. . . . O Baby B . . . then she frowned—and sighed—and picked up the letter again. . . .

She is pretty—a great coquette—extremely vain—excessively affected—clever enough—without the smallest principle—with a good deal of imagination and some passion. . . . [Augusta smiled as she read] . . . She had set her heart on carrying me off from Venice out of vanity—and succeeded . . . [Augusta laughed outright—O dear, darling, fatuous B!] . . . and having made herself the subject of general conversation has greatly contributed to her recovery. Her husband is one of the richest nobles of Ravenna—three score year of age—this is his third wife. You may suppose what *esteem* I entertain for *her*—perhaps it is about equal on both sides.

And now for a canter at twilight—

There is good riding in the forest—and with (my horses) . . . and the sea—and my books—and the lady—the time passes—I am very fond of riding and always *was* out of England—but I hate your Hyde Park—and your turnpike roads—I must have forests—downs—or deserts to expatiate in. I detest *knowing* the road—one is to go—and being interrupted by your damned finger-posts, or a blackguard roaring for twopence at a turnpike.

Augusta smiled again—so like her Baby B not to want to know the road he was travelling—what kind of road was he riding down now? Then, in a moment, she was laughing out loud and merrily—because he told her to.

I send you a sonnet which this faithful Lady had made . . . in which she swears the most alarming constancy to her husband—is not this good? You may suppose my *face* when she shewed it to me—I could not help laughing—one of *our* laughs— All this is very absurd—but you see that I have good morals at bottom.

She is an equestrian too but a bore in her rides—for she can't guide her horse—and he runs after mine—and tries to bite him—and then she begins screaming in a high hat and sky-blue riding habit—making a most absurd figure—and embarrassing me and both our grooms—who have the devil's own work to keep her from tumbling—and having her cloathes torn off by the trees and thickets of the Pine Forest.

Augusta could almost love this funny little Italian countess—and, O Baby B, who are you to put on airs about horseback-riding—you, the clumsiest rider in the world! . . . But here was more naughtiness.

I fell a little in love with her intimate friend—a certain Geltruda—(that is, Gertrude) who is very young and seems very well disposed to be perfidious —but alas! *her* husband is jealous—and the G. detected me in an illicit squeezing of hands—the consequence of which the friend was whisked off to Bologna for a few days—and since her return I have never been able to see her but twice—with a dragon of a mother-in-law—and a barbarous husband by her side—besides my own dear precious *Amica*—who hates all flirting but her own— But I have a priest who befriends me—and the Gertrude says a good deal with her great black eyes, so that perhaps—but alas! I mean to give up these things altogether . . .

BYRON IN VENICE, 1819

Teresa's favourite portrait. It shows Byron as she thought he looked at their first meeting.

*From the miniature by Prepiani*

TERESA, COUNTESS GUICCIOLI, AGED THIRTY

Nobody looking at this portrait, said Teresa, would forgive her her sins.

*Engraved from the drawing by W. Brockedon*

"Write to me—love me—" he wrote at the end, then a postscript—
"This affair is not in the least expensive—being all in the wealthy line
—but troublesome—for the lady is imperious and *exigeante*—however
there are hopes we may quarrel—when we do you shall hear."

Augusta folded up the letter and sat pondering. No need now to
answer that letter from Venice. Her brother was busy—and happy.

With his friends in England he kept up a brave show of comedy. He
painted in the scene for them. Ravenna—a sleepy little town, full of
ghosts and memorials of ancient time. Round about it the Pine Forest,
haunted, like the town, by phantom riders and old dreams of love. In the
distance, the sea with its perpetual murmur and its fishing-boats plying
to and fro. Then his lady in her prison-like palace—with himself round
the corner in poor lodgings and Dante's tomb across the way. The lovers
held the stage with a grim old pantaloon for husband, reputed jealous
and prone to murder. Then a priest, a chambermaid, and a negro page
to run to and fro with letters and warnings. In charge of the ministers
of love was Teresa's confidante, Signora Gertrude Vicari of the great
black eyes, arrayed in white linen like Tilburina's crony. She was yet
more unhappily married than Teresa. Count Guiccioli was old and rich,
but Gertrude's husband was a—theologian. In the background the
watchful Gamba family, worrying about its unmarried daughters,
and the placid *duenna* with the crooked smile and that scowling young
Carluccio.

There was the devil of a business one day about doors—"which like a
goose had been locked, and then afterwards forgotten to be reopened,"
so that the Count "knocked his horns against the doors of his own
drawing-room." What manner of husband was this Count, anyhow?
Was he simple? Was he merely resigned to the knowledge that his wife
was young? Or was he meditating some roguery? According to his
mood, or his correspondent, Byron rang the changes on the tune of
*il marito*. *Carpe diem*—gather ye rosebuds while ye may—all things must
have an end—one day *il marito* would wake up. Would he present a bill
for damages like an honest English husband? Or—who knows?—one
fine day the merry *amico* might be found in a secluded copse in the Pine
Forest with a dagger between his shoulder-blades!

His "business" was going well. He saw his *dama* daily, "at the
proper (and improper) hours," but his friends mustn't suppose that his
heart was deeply involved. She had a leaning towards scenes and kept
him in order. There were "the usual *excerpta* of some *gelosie*" but that
was "the fault of the climate, and of the conjunction of two such capricious people as the Guiccioli and the *Inglese*, but here hath been no
stabbing nor drugging of possets." He had still a truant eye and was
looking over the manor for game. He had exchanged smiles at a window

with an affianced bride—"Ursula—something, one of the prettiest
creatures I ever saw." Her barbarous mother had caught the wink and
locked the pretty creature up till the wedding-day was over—then, of
course, Ursula would be free for love, and Mother would look the
other way. In the meantime his obliging *abate* had smuggled in letters
to the captive. By the end of July the elegiac note had vanished from his
letters. No more talk of love or consumption, of pistols and spilled
brains or drugs in a drawer. The time was passing "viciously and agreeably." Teresa was devoted, the Count polite, the people kind, all was
midsummer fooling, merry as a wedding-bell, with now and then a
jangle to break the monotony of fun.

Count Rasponi remarked to his neighbours that the Palazzo Guiccioli
seemed to have more charms for Lord Byron than Dante's *Rotonda* or
the tomb of Theodoric the Goth. Signor Valtancoli, the spy, who
reported on political naughtiness to the Pope's *Buon Governo* in Romagna,
was disturbed by the constant visits of this "*stravagante Inglese*" at
Count Guiccioli's house. The Count had dealings with the *Carbonari*,
and Lord Byron's political views were, no doubt, as corrupt as his morals.
Between them they were assuredly up to no good.

That sound of children's voices—for ever round the corner in
Ravenna—singing a song of—

> Il vecchio falcon fatto cucu,
> E i rimedi che il Lord venire fa
> Da Venezia, da Londra, e dal Peru.[1]

July slipped into August, and the days grew shorter and the nights
were hotter. The shadow of the pines lengthened and fell like darkness
across Teresa's face, as she leaned against a tree-trunk and he gazed at
her with his back to the setting sun. The sand whirled up beneath their
feet as they loitered back to their horses in dry clouds of dust. The sea
sounded louder in their ears as the quick twilight dropped.

The Count called on Byron and told him that he was leaving with
his wife for Bologna. He politely hoped that his departure would not
close their delightful *amicizia*. They would go to Forli first to see a new
play—might they have the pleasure of his lordship's company there? In
any case, my Lord Byron must honour their poor house, the Palazzo
Savioli, in Bologna, with a visit. They expected to be there by August
the 9th.

Teresa still looked frail, but with happiness health was returning to
her face. Her *amico* needn't come to Forli for duty in her box if he

1 "The old falcon turned cuckoo,
　　　And the cures the Lord had brought
　　　From Venice from London and Peru."

didn't want to, but imperiously she ordered him to follow her to Bologna within twenty-four hours of her setting out.

A tiredness dropped with all the weight of destiny upon him. He hated the sweat and bother of packing. It had taken a lot of resolution to leave Venice and come all this way to Ravenna—must he now uproot himself and travel the road back to Bologna, and thence in the winter to Venice? After two months of love-making here and galloping through the Pine Forest he hated the very thought of Venice, and his damp and dreary palace there, the stench and chatter of its canals, the memory of his own follies. Of all towns he had known in Italy Ravenna contented him most, and, superstitiously, he believed that if he left it it would only be to find unhappiness awaiting him in the world outside. Perhaps it would be the end of his love-affair with Teresa. Sourly he looked upon the present moment and found himself dissatisfied. This business of stolen kisses and hidden meetings, with its theatrical paraphernalia of negro page and confidante, was not a man's life. If the business were to continue, if he must leave Ravenna, were it not better to bring matters to a head? Come what might, he would not trail round Italy after Teresa and the Count. He sat down at his table and wrote her a letter, asking her to leave her husband and fly with him.

When Hoppner's letter came Teresa had been the first to propose elopement as the bravest answer to the cackle of old hags and their snuffling *cicisbei* in Venice. But a change had come over the spirit of their dream since that day. She had given every proof of love, and it was her turn now to demand proofs from Byron. He was her *amico*, and a loyal *amico* followed his lady wheresoever she ordered him. His demand now for elopement filled her with perplexity and alarm. For all her disdain of public opinion she was a well-bred Italian lady, a good Catholic, and she wished to play the game of *cavalier serventismo* according to the rules. Under her code a wife might (under certain conditions) deceive her husband, openly (for choice) or in secret, but never must she run away with her lover; that was an idea too monstrous to be conceived in good health or sanity, an outrage on the laws of courtesy and the teaching of the Church. She must, too, think of others besides herself—the honour of her husband, of her own family's honour, of her sisters, too, depending upon her good conduct for marriage. It was distracting that her *amico*, this Protestant from the land of Gretna Green, where you made or unmade marriages by running away in a coach, could not realize the moral duties of a *cicisbeo*. But he was an *amico* unlike all others in the world, and if he wanted her to run away with him, a fig for the honour of Guiccioli—go she must!

Her quick Italian wits went to work upon the problem. Her lover was an Englishman and a poet. So, too, had Shakespeare been English and a poet, and he understood the Italian temper and love as one to the manner born. She pulled down her French translation of Shakespeare from the bookshelf and with its help sketched out a plan for elopement on paper and sent it to Byron by the negro page.

Let her lover procure some powerful drug that, when swallowed, threw the drinker into a lifeless trance that looked like death. She would drink it one night before she fell asleep, and in the morning her husband and parents would find her, to all appearance, dead. They would bury her in the tomb of the Guicciolis and leave her there alone. But an accommodating friar would be close at hand, and the sexton, and Gertrude, the theologian's wife. Her lover would come to the tomb with his valet, Fletcher, carrying spades and shovels. Together they would exhume her and revive her with a cordial. Then she would fly with him over the Alps and far away—to Geneva, if he wished, or England, or Venezuela, and there they would be married—if need be—and live respectably ever afterwards. Thus happiness would be won, honour saved, and the Church would be none the wiser for its knowledge.

The negro boy, who, no doubt, had already been rehearsed in his part for the exhumation scene by the theologian's wife, brought this document to the house round the corner and handed it to Byron with a happy grin.

## CHAPTER V

# Garden in Bologna

I WRITE in haste"—wrote Byron to John Murray on August 9, 1819, "to-morrow I set off for Bologna—I write to you with thunder, lightning, etc., and all the winds of heaven whistling through my hair, and the racket of preparation to boot. My 'mistress dear,' who hath 'fed my heart upon smiles and wine' for the last two months, set off for Bologna with her husband this morning, and it seems that I follow him at three to-morrow morning."

He had left Venice in a bad temper to join Teresa at Ravenna. He was leaving Ravenna now in a thunderstorm to follow her husband back to Venice.

"I cannot tell," he told Murray, "how our romance will end, but it hath gone on hitherto most erotically—such perils and escapes—Juan's are a child's play in comparison. The fools think that all my *poeshie* is allusive to my *own* adventures: I have had at one time better and more extraordinary and perilous and pleasant than these, any day of the week, if I might tell them; but that must never be."

He rolled into Bologna on the heels of his thunderstorm and put up at the Pellegrino Inn. Teresa was reckless and exultant and went to call upon him in the full state of coach and horses. An inn, she declared, was no place for her *amico*. He must find some other place to live while he was in Bologna—less public, more worthy of his station in life. He answered crossly that he must be getting on his way back to Venice, and immediately went and inspected rooms in the Palazzo Merendoni close by the Palazzo Savioli. From the windows of the palace he looked down into a garden with a fountain. There was a gardener there, looping up his grape-vine, with a wife and a son, and the son had a pretty wife.

Count Guiccioli called at the Pellegrino Inn. Once more he was profuse in offers of *amicizia* and hospitality. An inn, he declared, was no place for his lordship to live. He begged—nay, he would take no denial —his wife added her entreaties—Milord must stay with them at the Palazzo Savioli until he returned to Venice.

Byron looked blank at this invitation. He scanned the old gentleman's face inquisitively. It was set in a polite simper, and those bright blue eyes stared back at his with steady and disarming candour. He sighed and acquiesced—this was the will of God.

Bologna was the 'city of sausages'—a bourgeois town of merchants, the seat of an old university, more formal and suburban than Ravenna. There was no Pine Forest near by—only Byron's old haunt, the Certosa graveyard. Somehow he felt a constraint here that he had not known in Ravenna. Teresa, too, was different. She was a woman of the world now, and more demanding of *cicisbeo* duties than ever she had been before. He was nervous, impatient, out of humour.

The night after his arrival she insisted that he sit with her in her box at the theatre. The play was a tragedy by Count Guiccioli's old friend Alfieri—the story of Mirrha and her incestuous love for her father. Teresa watched her lover's face with more attention than the play. It had been surly when he came to sit beside her, but now it was turned upon the actors on the stage with a deep and brooding interest. Suddenly his body quivered and grew taut. His face was pale, his hand went to his brow. Harshly, in broken spasms—with infinite difficulty and pain—as though he were racked by intolerable memories—he was crying. In sheer sympathy she burst into a flood of tears.

He wrote to Murray the next morning—one of his teasing letters. Casually he told him about the play. "The two last acts . . . threw me into convulsions. I do not mean by that a lady's hysterics, but the agony of reluctant tears, and the choking shudder, which I do not often undergo for fiction. . . . The worst was, that the *dama*, in whose box I was, went off in the same way, I really believe more from fright than any other sympathy—at least with the players: but she has been ill, and I have been ill, and we are all languid and pathetic this morning, with great expenditure of sal volatile."

A truce, however, to sentiment. He was writing one of his letters of business and badinage. He threw out a word about "Donny Johnny"— a poem which still made Murray unhappy. He had no plans, he said, but hinted that another canto was on the way, full of "pastime and prodigality" and the very stuff of life. From "Donny Johnny" he flitted to Tom Moore, to the Prince Regent and the attainder on Lord Edward Fitzgerald, a dash of verse and—"Will you get a favour done for me?" asked suddenly.

*You* can, by your Government friends, Croker, Canning, or my old School-fellow Peel, and I can't. Here it is. Will you ask them to appoint (*without salary or emolument*) a noble Italian (whom I will name afterwards) Consul or Vice-Consul for Ravenna? He is a man of very large property—noble, too; but he wishes to have a British protection, in case of changes. Ravenna is near the sea. He wants *no emolument* whatever: that his office might be useful, I know; as I lately sent off from Ravenna to Trieste a poor devil of an English sailor, who had remained there sick, sorry, and penniless (having been set ashore in 1814), from the want of any accredited agent able or willing to help him homewards. Will you get this done? It will be the greatest favour to me. If you do, I will then send his name and condition, subject, of course, to rejection, if *not* approved when known.

Murray read between the lines of this letter. He knew well enough that Ravenna was "near the sea" and in the days of the Emperor Augustus had boasted a busy seaport where swamp and forest now spread. The story of the English sailor stranded in this pine-tree haven did not surprise him. Sailors were like that—God bless their stupid souls! Byron's life was sprinkled with kindly actions, but he preferred to do them by stealth. Only some ulterior motive would bring him to avow them—the need, for example, for a British Consul at Ravenna Port. That morning he had fallen into the dumps and needed sal volatile. The Count, presumably, had taken his opportunity to talk prose.

Yet Count Guiccioli had his poetic moments, too. Teresa was better in health now, kinder, more cheerful, diligent about the house, cleaning and routing out old furniture from the attics, and in the evenings she could not read enough, nor play enough, to please him. In Ravenna she had been too tired to sleep with him, but now with the return of health he would woo her again. He told her that he wished to make her a present, and it was to be a gold ring. Teresa wouldn't accept it, but Count Guiccioli, once his mind was made up, was not to be foiled in a generous action. He insisted, and Teresa was driven to a compromise. She would accept his ring—as an earnest of his affection—and Lord Byron should choose it.

The Count's face clouded, and for a moment it seemed that he would recall his gift. Gravely and austerely, with infinite kindness, he told her that the matter must be left in his hands—he could not possibly spend more than one hundred *scudi* on his gift. Teresa burst into peals of merry laughter and told him that Lord Byron was the meanest man she knew—he was English and could be trusted not to spend too much. Still shaking his head dubiously, the Count gave permission for Lord Byron to visit the jeweller's shop. Milord returned with the most amusing little bauble in the world, and Count Guiccioli remarked politely, as he paid down the money, that he could scarcely believe that it had been procured for so small a sum as one hundred *scudi*. Lord Byron took the compliment with a smile and a bow—the ring had cost him three hundred and fifty *scudi*, but he never told the price to anyone. The Count slipped the little love-token on Teresa's finger and kissed her hand with a courtier's gallantry; she curtsied to him modestly and away she ran to her *amico* to show him her ring. Gratefully she threw her arms round his neck and kissed him.

The Palazzo Savioli was the gayest of Count Guiccioli's many homes. It stood upon the Via Galleria (No. 567), a long, stately building with an arcade upon the street. It had once been the property of a poet,

Lodovico Savioli, author of sundry volumes of amorous verse. He had furnished his palace gloriously within as a temple of Ovid. The rooms were resplendent with gilded cornice and bright, painted ceilings, and on the walls hung numerous landscapes of love among the shepherds at spirited noon or reflective sunset. Behind the house lay a garden crossed by a canalized rivulet, and beyond the rivulet was a trim, painted folly and a miniature waterfall, gracefully plashing over rocks in a grotto. Tucked in a nook between the Savioli Palace and its neighbour, the deserted Palazzo Merendoni, was a small house (No. 567² Via Galleria) with a garden behind it. This was the garden that Byron had seen from the windows of the Palazzo Merendoni, with fountain and grape-vine, and here dwelt the elderly Luigi Poletti, who served Count Guiccioli as porter and gardener, with his middle-aged wife and his son and his pretty daughter-in-law, Anna.

Byron took an apartment in the Palazzo Merendoni, and Fletcher and his Italian groom scoured the shops of Bologna for tables and beds and curtains. A comfortable nest for a bachelor who needed solitude for writing poetry was furnished in the vast, almost empty palace. But the poet never moved into his nest, and the "learned" Fletcher dwelt there, not alone, but supreme. His master accepted the Count's invitation to stay at the Palazzo Savioli (or Guiccioli, as we must now call it) and only came to his rooms in the Palazzo Merendoni by day to collect his mail or meet strangers who wished to know him in Bologna. His rooms in the Guiccioli Palace were on the ground floor, and the quest for furniture started again, and now an old family servant of Teresa's joined the band of pilgrims.

There was a flutter of excitement in academic circles when it was learned that the author of *Childe Harold* was living in Bologna. Professor Cardinali called at the bachelor nest in the Palazzo Merendoni with the manuscript of a great work that he proposed dedicating to the famous English poet—in return for the usual patron's fee. The Abbé Machiavelli was all agog to meet him, and so was the Abbé Mezzofanti, Librarian of the Institute, and the poet Michele Leoni, who had translated the fourth canto of *Childe Harold*. But Byron was surly and aloof. He did not wish to meet people in Bologna. He rose late and lounged about his rooms in the Palazzo Guiccioli, and in the afternoon he sat with Teresa by the fountain in Luigi Poletti's garden. So the day whiled away until sunset and darkness, and at midnight strayed revellers in the Via Galleria saw the poet's lamp light in his study and gleam steadily into the morning.

There was a gentleman of Ferrara residing in Bologna at that time —Count Francesco Rangone, a friend of Count Guiccioli—who undertook to serve as intermediary between this elusive English poet and aspiring scholars in Bologna. He petitioned Alessandro to allow him to see his guest, and Alessandro answered with a polite assurance of interest in his ambition. He wrote to Teresa, telling her that the great Michele Leoni was pining to meet his English *confrère*, and Teresa replied effusively that nothing would please her better in life than such a reunion of choice spirits. Count Rangone still clamoured and wrote, and at length a meeting was arranged. But alas, when the hour came, Count Rangone had to send his lordship his heartbroken, contrite excuses—he was prostrate on his bed with a tragic constipation.

The lovers went their quiet way without intrusion of visitors in the dead poet's palace or in Luigi Poletti's garden. But sharp eyes were watching them all the time.

The *Buon Governo* in Ravenna had scored a black mark against Count Guiccioli's name. He was a crafty, intriguing man, very rich, avaricious, arrogant, with a grim reputation for murder. It was common talk that he had the 'famous Manzoni' picked off with a stiletto one evening at the theatre doors for being so rash as to outwit him in a lawsuit. But, apart from his murderous propensities, he was a robber of Church lands, had once been a friend of that arch fiend Bonaparte, and now it was almost certain that he had dealings with the *Carbonari*. And then this foreigner, Lord Byron, with whom he was so intimately associated— there were stories of intrigue and political heresy in his own island! The Ravenna police recommended the police in Bologna to keep a vigilant eye upon comings and goings at the Palazzo Guiccioli. In particular they would do well to watch Lord Byron carefully. In Ravenna people said his only business just now was "planting antlers in Count Guiccioli's head"—but still—who knows? There were probably things more sinister taking place in the Palazzo Guiccioli than that ancient roguery.

Prince Colonna-Sciarra, the Director of Police in Bologna, was disturbed. There were rumours that a new revolutionary society had been formed called the *Roma Antica*, or *Romantica*. Its moving spirit was a lawyer of Milan, Pellegrino Rossi by name, and it was his policy to enlist the sympathy of English intellectuals and noblemen in the cause of sedition and rebellion. Lord Kinnaird, for example, was living at Forli with a *ballerina*. It was a well-known fact that he had once fired off a pistol at the Duke of Wellington, and it was a pretty sure thing that, through the blandishments of Rossi, he had now become a *Romantico*. Then there was Lady Morgan, travelling in Italy with her husband. She had written a novel with the suspicious title of *The Wild Irish Girl*, and she and her husband talked out loud about "constitutions." Lady Morgan was fairly certainly a *Romantica*. Was this secretive English nobleman Lord Byron in touch with Rossi—was he, too, a *Romantico*? Prince Colonna took the hint from Ravenna. He set his watchdogs to work upon that suspicious trio in the Palazzo Guiccioli—the old Count, his pretty wife, and the nobleman from England.

Day by day and week by week the reports came in. This milord was "an Englishman in the fullest meaning of the term, he was mad." He was lustful, insolent, mad with a desire to rob, to destroy property, to shed the blood of quiet citizens. No woman's virtue was safe from his onslaught, even in a crowd of her own sex. The Cardinal had given a *conversazione* in his honour at Ravenna, but declined to be present himself for fear that people would say that he had served as a decoy to the ladies. He openly used such terms as 'Manchester' and 'Salford' in his conversation—terms that stood for revolution in England. All day long he sat within doors in the Palazzo Guiccioli scribbling in cipher, and his steward in Venice—a clever young rascal—then distributed the offensive documents among the ungodly. He was on terms of intimacy with Professor Cardinali, and "men of that type, as Your Excellency knows, are never friends of good government." Another ominous fact was that Lord Byron frequented Masi's bookshop. He bought books there, and it was reported that he read them. Books, as the police pointed out to Prince Colonna, were dangerous commodities. They were full of ideas. Authors and poets and scholars—of whom many thronged Masi's bookshop—were more responsible than any other group of men for the ill-regulated fancies that were confounding 'theocracy' in Romagna. It was certain that Pellegrino Rossi lay at the back of this lunatic lord's visit to Bologna. Certainly he was a *Romantico*. The police were hot upon the trail of a manuscript that he had left behind at Faenza—a list of rules and regulations for the *Romantici* to which he had given the curious name of *The Statutes of the Funny Fellows*. Pending the discovery of that document they were studying another of Lord Byron's works— *Childe Harold, Canto IV*—in Michele Leoni's translation—a sinister work.

Lord Byron's movements were perplexing in the extreme. Ostensibly he had come to Bologna in pursuit of a lady called Vissoli. The young 'Marchesa' Guiccioli called daily at his inn. Then it was discovered that he was planning to abduct a girl from a convent. When he first arrived he had said that he was going on to Venice. Then he took rooms in the Palazzo Merendoni, and his servants went about town buying furniture. But when the rooms were furnished he still remained sulkily in the Pellegrino Inn. In the afternoons he sat by the fountain in a small garden lying between the Palazzo Merendoni and the Palazzo Guiccioli, and there he chatted with the old gardener and his daughter-in-law. The young Countess Guiccioli joined him, and they sat together by the fountain and talked in a confidential manner. Sometimes the spies, peering through the windows of the Palazzo Merendoni above them, observed that Lord Byron read aloud to the Countess in a low voice from scraps of paper in his hand. The Countess listened with uplifted face and hands clasped upon her knee.

Prince Colonna ordered the police to intercept all letters that passed between Lord Byron and the Count, or Countess, Guiccioli. But some one must have warned his lordship, for he foiled all attempts at tampering with his correspondence by taking up his residence on the ground floor of the Palazzo Guiccioli. The disconcerting fact about this move was that Count Guiccioli himself had suggested it. Surely he would not have made that suggestion if—as they said in Ravenna—Lord Byron were conducting an intrigue with his wife. More and more the Bologna police began to doubt those amorous yarns from Ravenna.

Two weeks went by, and at last the police had hopeful news to report. Count Guiccioli had left his palace in Bologna and gone to stay at a small house of his—Alberino—near Molinella, in the country. The Countess Guiccioli had accompanied him, and Lord Byron was now living all by himself in the Palazzo Guiccioli. What might be inferred from this development? That the Count had discovered the business between his wife and his English visitor and taken her out of harm's way? That seemed unlikely, for Lord Byron, at the Count's request, still made the Palazzo Guiccioli his home. Apparently, too, Count, Countess, and Milord had taken leave of one another with mutual protestations of *amicizia* and the hope of a quick reunion. The Count declared that he was making a tour of inspection among his farm properties, but the police were not deceived by that flimsy pretence. The Count was a secretive man and had a habit of vanishing on those so-called tours of his estates.

But now those letters, so long desired, must surely pass between the English lord in the Palazzo Guiccioli and the Count (or Countess) in the country. Patiently the police mounted guard in the arcade of the Palazzo Guiccioli and waited for messengers to come and go. They dipped into the mailbags to look for incriminating letters. But they found no letters, and no messenger came or went along the road to Molinella. Once more, the police realized, that old rascal of a Brunello and this crazy foreigner had fooled them.

It was a pity that, in the absence of the Countess, they kept slack watch on the garden with the fountain. Lord Byron still went there every day and talked with the gardener and his son's wife. One afternoon he sat by the fountain alone—reading. He closed his book and let it fall listlessly to the ground. He sat for a while, chin propped in his hand, frowning at thought. Then he rose to his feet and, with a slow, backward glance, left the garden. . . .

A young and pretty woman stood in a dark archway, looking impatiently down the street. A negro boy, with a turban on his head and a silver-mounted pistol stuck in his red sash, came sauntering lazily towards her. His mouth was wide open in a mischievous smile, but his

eyes were turned up to the roof-tops in far-away day-dream. He strolled
past the pretty woman in the archway, lost in elaborate reverie. She
leaned forward and tapped him on the shoulder. She drew open her
cloak, their hands clasped a moment in secret, she stepped back, a finger
at her lips. One glance of unutterable complicity, a white, flashing smile,
a joyful gurgle, and, with a turn on his heel, he was gone. . . .

That worthy theologian, Count Vicari, had come—much to his
surprise—to Bologna to pursue his studies, and, with every display of
unwillingness, his young wife had come with him. The negro boy beat
on the door of their house and was admitted. . . . An hour later a horse-
man in the Vicari livery was galloping down the road to Molinella.

For a while Lord Byron remained all by himself in the Palazzo
Guiccioli. In the late afternoon he mounted his horse and rode out to
the Certosa graveyard. There he sat in the cloister and talked with the
sexton, Germano Sabaud. Germano's daughter was, by common acclaim,
the prettiest girl in Bologna, and sometimes, too, Milord talked with
her. He gazed very attentively into her face as he spoke, and the spies
of Prince Colonna, as they strolled with obtrusive laziness among the
tombs, noted that his stare was mournful. Try as they would, they could
not make out what he talked about with Germano Sabaud. And his
daughter? Did this mad, lustful Englishman mean to seduce her? There
were rumours that already she had become his mistress. . . . His lordship mounted his horse and rode slowly back to the Palazzo Guiccioli.
His face was sombre as he rode.

Then there came a curious development. One hot evening of dust
and sunshine a carriage drove up to the Palazzo Merendoni. Lord Byron
was standing there waiting by the entrance door. Out of the carriage
the servants lifted a tiny girl with red-gold hair, milk-white skin, cheeks
like rose-petals, and a dimple in her chin. Long ago the police had
noted that Lord Byron, too, had a dimple in his chin. He took the child
in his arms and kissed her. "*Bon dì, Papa,*" cooed the little stranger as
she nestled against his shoulder. . . . The listening spies were dumb-
founded. This child, then, was Lord Byron's daughter! She looked so
unutterably English, yet she spoke Italian like a gondolier's child! They
pondered the phenomenon and wrote to Venice for information. Yes,
the Venetian police replied, the child was certainly Lord Byron's daughter
—a bastard by some nameless trull in England.

The little bastard was lodged with her nurse and servants of her own
in his lordship's bachelor-nest in the Palazzo Merendoni. In the afternoon the nurse led her charge down into the garden with the fountain,
and there her father watched her play. Then, suddenly, the erratic
creature changed his residence again. He left the Palazzo Guiccioli and
went back to the Pellegrino Inn. . . . Still those mysterious jaunts to

the Certosa graveyard . . . still those melancholy broodings in the garden as he watched the child play. . . .

Professor Cardinali called at the Palazzo Merendoni . . . and the Abbé Mezzofanti. . . . A lieutenant of dragoons from Parma—a man of invidious reputation but politically without offence—called several times on his lordship at the Pellegrino Inn and remained closeted with him in serious talk. The police kept a wary eye on the doubtful dragoon from Parma.

One afternoon loud screams of "Help! Murder! Help!" issued from the inn. A crowd gathered before its doors. The lieutenant from Parma staggered out into the street, white of face, his hair on end with terror, and fainted dead away on the pavement.

No sign came from the inn of his English lordship. The incident petered out disappointingly. The lieutenant of dragoons had sold Lord Byron a bad horse—that was all.

Count Rangone had recovered from his constipation, and in the absence of the Count and Countess Guiccioli he managed to scrape acquaintance with Lord Byron. He called upon him at the Pellegrino Inn every afternoon at three o'clock. Michele Leoni had gone from Bologna, but he presented the Abbé Machiavelli and the Abbé Mezzofanti to his lordship. Byron was amiable but absent-minded in receiving them. The police decided that Count Rangone must be watched. They opened his letters to Lord Byron and found them disappointing. They were mostly petitions to the poet to meet his friends.

Count Rangone, too, noted that Lord Byron was gloomy. He ate and drank little and went on melancholy excursions to the cemetery. He sat in the garden at the back of the Palazzo Guiccioli and watched his child play—and a prettier, more delightful child Count Rangone had never seen in his life—oh, she was of an "*amabilità*" altogether "*particolare*." Lord Byron dined late and worked from midnight to dawn. But there were hours of daylight when he was nowhere to be found.

The police had discovered where those hidden hours were spent. Every afternoon about five he called at the Palazzo Guiccioli and was admitted by the servants. The police made smiling inquiries of the negro boy and chambermaids and lackeys—what did Lord Byron do when he came to the Palazzo Guiccioli? With answering smiles the servants replied that he sat all by himself in the library—or sometimes in the Contessa's room—reading. And what else? asked the spies. Sometimes, said the servants, he wrote in the books and put them back on the shelf. But what did he *write* in the books? The negro boy shook his head. He couldn't read.

·            ·            ·

Yet even negro pages are curious. One day he found a book lying on the table in the Contessa's room, and on its fly-leaf the English lord had written a few lines. With frustrated eyes he scanned them and showed the book to the chambermaid. She called on the steward for interpretation. That dignitary announced that the book's name was *Jacopo Ortis*, and it had been written by a famous man called Ugo Foscolo. The first few words that the Signor had written were Latin, and the steward benignly copied them out. The rest was in English, a language he deigned not to know.

The negro page laid the book reverently back in the wrong place on the shelf.

When the kindly old priest with the military walk next waylaid him in the arcade, he showed him his scrap of paper with a triumphant leer —this was what the Englishman wrote in the books—just Latin—just something out of the church service. There was no harm in showing it, and negro boys like to oblige when they can—without harm to their friends.

The kindly old priest stared at the words with a frown. *Coelum, non animam, mutant qui trans mare currunt*—"sky but never the soul they change who cross the sea." This was not Scripture. What on earth did this perplexing Englishman mean by writing that? Whom was he warning? And of what?

But the negro boy had other—and better—news to tell. With a face shining with happiness he told the kind priest that—unexpectedly— Count Guiccioli had come home last night. And his "pretty, smiling Contessa" had come back with him, too—with a smile more radiant than ever!

Once more the conspirators had fooled the police.

## CHAPTER VI

# *Flight from Brunello*

REFLECTION is a good thing for a lover. Count Guiccioli, in announcing his departure, had expressed the hope, politely, that Lord Byron might not be gone to Venice when he returned. Until the day came when he must go home, Milord must look upon the Palazzo Guiccioli as his own house. The Count once more expressed his deep sense of obligation for all that Milord had done in the matter of the consulship at Ravenna. Might they not expect a favourable answer by the time Milord was settled in Venice again?

Byron was left alone now—without husband and without lady. Reflection made him surly, and from surliness he dropped to melancholy. He must have company in his solitude, and he sent for Allegra from La Mira to distract him with her baby ways. In the Certosa graveyard he brooded luxuriously over the emptiness of life and the nothingness of love. The sexton's daughter was young and fair as noonday, but in his mournful state of mind, with her father chattering skulls and corpses in his ear, she stirred no emotion in him save a gloomy sense of sad mortality—of death, and death again—of physical death with all its ugliness and worms. "I amuse myself," he wrote to Murray,

> with contrasting her beautiful and innocent face of fifteen with the skulls with which he [her father] has peopled several cells, and particularly with that of one skull dated 1766, which was once covered (the tradition goes) by the most lovely features of Bologna—noble and rich. When I look at these, and at this girl—when I think of what *they were*, and what *she* must be—why, then, my dear Murray, I won't shock you by saying what I think. It is little matter what becomes of us "bearded men," but I don't like the notion of a beautiful woman's lasting less than a beautiful tree—than her own picture—than her own shadow, which won't change so to the sun as her face to the mirror.

From the thought of death he dropped with a sigh into life and brooded on death's precursor—age. The sunlight fell across the cypress trees in a harsh, revealing glare, and here he sat, biting his nails and frowning moodily at a sculptured death's-head—old, tired, and thirty—with hair turning grey and blemished teeth and, for all his riding in the Pine Forest, a belly that threw its shadow across the grass as noonday lengthened into dusk. What had he done with his life but age and fatten and grow loveless? He was an outcast, an exile, without home, without wife or child, without love or ambition—no journey's end, no hope. He had been a sluggard on the way, and he wrote gloomily to Hobhouse.

> I have to do with a woman rendered perfectly disinterested by her situation in life, and young and amiable and pretty; in short as good, and at least as attentive as anything of the sex can be, with all the advantages and disadvantages of being scarcely twenty years old, and only two out of her Romagnuolo convent at Faenza.
>
> But I feel—and I feel it bitterly—that a man should not consume his life at the side and on the bosom of a woman, and a stranger; that even the recompense, and it is much, is not enough, and that this Cicisbean existence is to be condemned.
>
> But I have neither the strength of mind to break my chain, nor the insensibility which would deaden its weight. I cannot tell what will become of me—to leave, or to be left would at present drive me quite out of my senses; and yet to what have I conducted myself?
>
> I have, luckily, or unluckily, no ambition left; it would be better if I had, it would at least awake me; whereas at present I merely start in my sleep.

He deserted the Palazzo Guiccioli for the Pellegrino Inn and settled down there to solitude. But he did not forget the Count's invitation to make the Casa Guiccioli his own. He went back there every day. The servants welcomed him home with ready smiles and that air of gay sympathy that only Italians can give to a man who, they think, should be in love. The negro page led him to Teresa's room, unlocked the door, and left him there alone. A book covered in purple velvet was lying on the table where she had left it—*Fragments des Pensées de Corinne*—the novel written by his friend, Mme de Staël. But his thoughts were not kind about Teresa in that moment. Did she really love him? Hadn't she, after all, left him in the lurch, as Hoppner said she would? He picked the book up and fingered its pages with a contemptuous smile—he had always thought *Corinne* a silly book—it had taught more young women to talk bombastic nonsense about love than any work he knew! He carried it away to their garden, and there he sat under a purple canopy of grapes beside the fountain and talked with the gardener of his toils which seemed greater than Adam's, and with his wife, and with his son's wife, who was the youngest of the party and, he thought, talked the best of the three.

Yet somehow utter loneliness made his heart soft. Even in the solitude of No. 13 Piccadilly Terrace, when his household gods lay shivered around him and his trunks were packed and ready to accompany him on his voyage into exile on the morrow, he thought for a moment of Annabella kindly and wrote her a poem of farewell. He was not a good hand at writing love-letters. There was nothing for a man to say in them but "I love you" over and over again, and if you varied the theme with laugh or quip the women said you weren't being serious, and love, apparently, for them was no laughing matter. Yet without knowing why he picked up *Corinne* and on its fly-leaf wrote a letter—in English, which she couldn't understand—to Teresa.

MY DEAR TERESA,

I have read this book in your garden; my love, you were absent, or else I could not have read it. It is a favourite book of yours, and the writer was a friend of mine. You will not understand these English words, and *others* will not understand them—which is the reason I have not scrawled them in Italian. But you will recognize the handwriting of him who passionately loved you, and you will divine that, over a book which was yours, he could only think of love. In that word, beautiful in all languages, but most so in yours—*Amor mio*—is comprised my existence here and hereafter. I feel I exist here, and I feel that I shall exist hereafter—to *what* purpose you will decide; my destiny rests with you, and you are a woman, seventeen years of age, and two out of a convent. I wish that you had stayed there with all my heart, or, at least that I had never met you in your married state.

But all this is too late. I love you, and you love me—at least, you *say so*, and *act* as if you *did* so, which last [oh, that Byron laugh that never would be silenced!] is a great consolation in all events. But *I* more than love you, and cannot cease to love you.

Think of me, sometimes, when the Alps and the ocean divide us—but they never will, unless you *wish* it.

BYRON

The gardener's son's wife found the book lying by the fountain and gave it with her high-priestess look to the negro boy, who ran with it to the theologian's wife. Gertrude's eye fell on the words *Amor mio*, and she dashed for the dictionary. *Corinne* was in Teresa's hands that night with a translation of the letter folded in its leaves.

She came back with a husband bewildered by his change in plans. She was wild with happiness over the letter in *Corinne*—it was beautiful, the first real love-letter that her laughing cavalier had ever written her. "I loved you" and "I love you"—at last he had said it—and "I more than love you and cannot cease to love you"—all the infinite variety of love's anthem, like softest music in attending ears! He was sad when she was not there—and wished he had never met her—and doubted that she loved him—O *Amor mio! Amor mio!*—alone there in our garden! But she wasn't so young that she wasn't a woman. There was a note of renunciation in this letter—a dying, farewell sound. "Think of me, sometimes, when the Alps and the ocean divide us—but they never will, unless you *wish* it." "I don't wish it," she said stormily; "so it shan't be!"

She had unwittingly put his loyalty to a test too severe. He couldn't understand that, though she no longer cared for her husband, she would still be an obedient wife—in everything that didn't matter! But love transcended the duties of a wife—love was Heaven—and Heaven was

G

the Madonna—and Beatrice in the Seventh Heaven—the realm of the eternal feminine leading men upward and on. Husbands, no doubt, would find a place in Heaven, but a woman's true reward there was in the everlasting company of her lover upon earth. Good-bye, *caro Alessandro*! She whistled him down the wind. She was her lover's now —and for ever—on earth or in Heaven—always his!

She lured him back to the Palazzo Guiccioli. She suffered his mournful sarcasms and sulky looks with delighted meekness. Her smile was kinder and more radiant than ever as they sat by the fountain in their garden. She held Allegra in her arms and murmured pretty Italian nothings into her hair as she gazed over her head at her lover. There was a dimple in Allegra's chin just like the dimple in his chin—she was all his child—nothing of that other woman in her! Allegra shook off her embracing arms impatiently and staggered across the grass to her father's side. He snatched her up from the ground and stood her on his knees and gazed with a frown up into her frowning little face. She was his—all that he had left of England now! Teresa laughed as she watched the two together—they were so alike. . . .

Count Guiccioli was cursing because he had come home with his tour of inspection unfinished. He told Teresa that they must start out again on a journey, this time to Ravenna. She laid the book down that she was reading to him and modestly made a suggestion. She still felt tired from her illness in the spring and would be no company for him upon his travels. A skin complaint of long standing—that cough—she laid her hand lightly across her heart—and she greatly feared that in her miscarriage her uterus had slipped. While he went to Ravenna, why should she not go on to Venice and await him there? She wished to consult a doctor, and she recommended to her husband's notice that kind Dr Aglietti who had been so wise in his prescription in July. The Count replied benevolently that without doubt her ailments were more imaginary than real, and much was to be blamed on her love of cold baths and galloping about on horseback in the woods. But that story of the slipped uterus touched him. He was anxious and annoyed—by all means she should go to Venice and consult with Dr Aglietti. He would take lodgings for her there, the Signora F—— would go with her, she might take one maid, and she would be good enough to call at the Convent of Santa Chiara and see how the *bambini* were faring.

Teresa thanked him and made another suggestion. Her *caro sposo*, she said, as she gazed modestly down at the gold ring on her finger, could not, for business reasons, accompany her to Venice, but she ought not to travel without an escort. Lord Byron was leaving in a few days for Venice—the Count lifted his eyes hopefully at the news, and Teresa's eyes demurely met them as she went on—why shouldn't Lord Byron squire her on her way? The Count closed his eyes and pondered, then opened them wearily and said—a little ungraciously—that he "saw nothing amiss" (*n'y voyait aucun inconvénient*) in that arrangement. Teresa sighed and picked up her book and ran her finger across the page to find the word on which she had stopped reading.

Count Guiccioli sent for Signora F—— and told her of the trip to Venice and the 'arrangement' that had been made. That honest duenna —very meekly and in a faltering voice—hinted that, perhaps, some people might think it odd if Lord Byron went with the Countess alone to Venice. But—as Signora F—— had learnt many years ago—it was enough to tell the Count what 'some people' thought, or might presume to think, about his actions for him to insist upon going his own way. He eyed her sourly and told her that he had every confidence in Lord Byron's sense of honour and good intentions. Signora F—— curtsied deep with head bent lowly under the rebuke and rejoined Teresa in her room, where an excited chambermaid was dragging clothes and slippers out of closets and pleading noisily that her *Contessa* would need every one of them.

The Director of Police still had found no proof that Lord Byron was a *Romantico*, but he had a startling development to report to the Director-General of Police in Rome. "To my very great astonishment," he wrote on September 15, 1819, "Lord Byron left Bologna on the 12th for *Venice*, in company with the Marchesa Guiccioli. Three days *before*, the Marchese, her husband, left for *Ravenna*."

Signora F—— was right. Some people thought that Count Guiccioli's 'arrangements' were odd beyond the bounds of probability.

Alone at last! Three days of blissful journey—alone for hours with her lover! In the long years to come she looked back upon that journey as the climax of her happiness. She travelled, like Cinderella going to the ball, in the family coach with the six black horses and the lackeys and postilions in their blue-and-white plumes. Signora F—— and her maid sat with her in the coach. Byron rode on horseback beside it, and Fletcher ambled along in the dust behind. Every now and then the coach would stop and Byron dismounted from his horse. Then the pair walked away—slowly, because of his foot—alone—over the hill, down by the stream, into the woods. The mellow light of autumn was settling over the landscape, bringing with it a sombre note of winter and leafless trees; but as Teresa walked by the side of the man she loved, familiar scenes were transfigured in a fresh beauty—they were edged with the sharp, clear light of utter joy—vivid and serene as in springtime yet throbbing in the heat of summer.

At night, as she huddled in her lover's arms by the window of their inn, she saw beyond his shoulder brooding starlight and harvest moon, and for once she couldn't speak. They turned aside to Arquà to visit Petrarch's tomb and signed the pilgrims' book together. At Ferrara she knelt upon the cold stones of Tasso's grave and prayed in sheer thankfulness for grace received. The sun was setting when they arrived at the inn in Padua, their last sleeping-place on the way to Venice.

The Countess Benzoni was staying at the inn with her elderly *cicisbeo*, Count Rangone. They threw up their hands in consternation when they set eyes on this incorrigible pair. There had been gossip enough about them in Venice in the spring, then they had vanished and gone their lonely ways and been forgotten for later themes, and now—here they were together at a public inn with Count Guiccioli nowhere in sight. The Countess Benzoni gaped at the coach, the postilions, the duenna looking demure, the smiling chambermaid, the dusty, sweating Fletcher, and then her glance rested in horrified fascination on Teresa's happy face and Byron's laughing eyes! Was anything more shameless—these two together—with the husband's servants in the husband's coach—three nights on the road—going where? She cried out that this was elopement in the English style and turned to look into the frowning eyes of her *cicisbeo*.

Byron hastily explained that the Countess Guiccioli was returning to Venice and he was acting only as her escort. The Countess Benzoni received his explanation kindly but with less than her usual equability. She turned to Teresa and, as an elder woman respectably connected with a *cicisbeo*, gave herself the privilege of lecturing her on the unseemliness of her conduct. When Teresa protested that all was done with her husband's sanction, Count Rangone added his admonitions to those of the Countess Benzoni. Did she not know—did Lord Byron not know— that Count Guiccioli was one of the astutest men in Italy—that he was notorious for his clever tricks and long-range plots? He surely was meditating mischief by this complaisance. The Countess, knowing her Teresa, quoted a verse written years ago by the poet Monti against her husband—

> Quel
> Si di frodi perito che Brunello
> Saria con esso un.

Byron was impressed by the arguments of the Countess Benzoni and her *cicisbeo*. But Teresa didn't believe a word of this legend of her husband's deep-plotted villainy—he was egotistical, arrogant, capricious, cared not a fig for other people's feelings or opinions—that was all. Byron drew her aside and counselled prudence for her own sake. She answered impatiently that rather than bear this indecision she would take the Countess Benzoni at her word and run away with him for good —to-night. It was Byron's turn now to hesitate. She was only seventeen, he reminded her, and he an aging man of thirty—she must think of her family, her sisters—he recited all those arguments that Teresa had turned over in her own mind when he had proposed elopement—it were best they went on to Venice—to-night. Teresa reflected bitterly that this was the third time that her *amico* had rejected her offer of elopement. She acquiesced with a burst of tears, like a child cheated of a promised joy. But, she added, why go back to Venice? Why not continue their journey slowly, night by night, to Lago Maggiore, to Como and other hills and other forests yet? Again Byron reasoned tenderly with her—let them go back to Venice now, then later she could write and ask for her husband's leave to make a trip to the Italian lakes.

They left Padua that night and crossed the lagoon to Venice. Teresa went with her duenna to her lodgings. Byron returned to the Palazzo Mocenigo, on the Grand Canal, which he now hated.

## CHAPTER VII

# *Dream at La Mira*

THE morning after she arrived at her lodgings in Venice—September 15—Teresa wrote to her *caro Alessandro* at Ravenna:

> I reached Venice last night in fine condition, for the two days on the road have done me more good than any medicine. . . . This morning Aglietti came to see me, and, after inquiring about the state of my health, he didn't prescribe medicine, but recommends another journey for change of air. Your business certainly wouldn't allow you to come with me. So Byron offers to take me with him to the Lakes of Garda and Como, a good trip for this time of year, which he means to take, as he is rather discontented with Venice. I ask your permission therefore and I am waiting for it with the utmost anxiety in the world. . . . Since I've got to Venice, I haven't left the house. I shall go out only to see the children.
>
> Byron sends his greetings and charges me to tell you that his friend in England, to whom he wrote about the Vice-Consulate, etc., has answered that he will make the request at once, the way you suggested. . . .
>
> I beg you, answer me quickly. Give my best love to Papa and all our friends and relatives, and, believe me,
>
> Your very affectionate consort,
>
> TERESA

Byron's counsels of prudence—backed by the warnings of the Countess Benzoni and her *cicisbeo*—had evidently borne fruit with Teresa. She did not believe half what Count Rangone told her about old Brunello, but, to reassure her lover, she would get permission from her husband to continue their journey to the Italian lakes.

Five days went by. A letter came by express from Count Gamba begging Teresa to give up the trip to the Italian lakes—for her sisters' sake. But old Brunello said nothing. Teresa wrote to him again.

> . . . I am not at Venice but La Mira, a lovely place where I've come on Aglietti's advice. . . . I am still looking after my health under orders of Aglietti and the surgeon Campana, having suffered great inconvenience the last few days from an attack of piles, from which I'm not yet completely recovered. He has reassured me, however, on the point that worried me most, that is, the slipping of my womb, so my mind is more at rest. Byron, who overwhelms me with attentions, sends you hearty messages.
>
> Good-bye, my Alessandro, let me have your news and be sure I'm your very affectionate consort,
>
> TERESA

Alessandro wrote to say that he was glad to hear that she had recovered her health. Teresa had been now twelve days at La Mira. She wrote again to her husband, telling him that he mustn't be too hopeful because she made light of her ailments in her letters. Piles was a distressing malady, and though they were gone, she now had headaches and her cough had returned. Dr Aglietti recommended another journey, but she would have to think that matter over.

I am still here at La Mira, a most delightful spot, where one can live—as I do—in the utmost seclusion without being at all bored. I cannot tell you how kind Mylord is! He has had a piano brought here for me, and music, and no end of books. Then there is his company, which is more precious than all the rest together; if only I was well I shouldn't have anything left to wish for! Byron sends his greetings and is distressed that in your last letter there wasn't a word for him. I am grieved to hear you have so many worries.

A few days later she wrote a letter of affectionate expostulation to the Count.

I hear from a letter of Papa's that you are vexed with me for leaving the lodgings. . . . I don't know whether you say that for appearance's sake or some other reason. But in any case, my Alessandro, you should have made your complaints to me, and—if they had seemed reasonable—I should have done my best to please you. But either you don't write at all—or only two lines—about my health, or things of no importance, or your business. So who is most to blame?

But this was not all the fault that she had to find with Alessandro. He had written that business detained him and he would reach Venice ten days later than he had hoped. Teresa must now tell him that a "consort's" patience was not eternal.

You won't rejoin me till All Saints' Day! This isn't what you promised when you left me! What am I to do in the meantime? I'm in a pretty fix, I can tell you. I needed a man and an *amico* like Byron to cheer me up a little, the way things are with me, and I must tell you, if from now on I judge all men by him—the only person with whom I can live—I shall always be dissatisfied with them. I couldn't wish for a better *amico*.

I am coming, wrote Alessandro. As the day of his return drew near Teresa moved for a few days into the lodgings in Venice, but duty and affection called her back to La Mira. On October 23 she dispatched a last letter to her husband.

I go on always improving in health. I hope you will find me all right in that respect as in others . . . which is why I tell you to get rid of any idea that makes it look as though you weren't sure. Byron begs to remind you of his friendship, and we both look forward to seeing you again.

La Mira stood upon the banks of the river Brenta, not far from Padua
—on the mainland. It was Byron's summer residence, and he had
'villaged' there with the tailor's wife in days gone by. It was, as Teresa
told her husband, a delightful spot. Once the villa had been a convent,
and over one of its arches was an inscription in Latin:

HIC SAEPE LICEBIT
NUNC VETERUM LIBRIS
NUNC SOMNO ET INCERTIBUS HORIS
DUCERE SOLLICITAE
IUCUNDA OBLIVIA VITAE

In this house the happy dwellers might find, in old books and sleep and
timeless hours, a sweet oblivion from life and all its cares. Elm-trees
sighed and whispered round it, and from its windows you watched the
sun set beyond the hills while the river that ran by the trailing rose-
bushes at the garden's edge turned slowly to molten red and gold.

But Teresa shall tell us in her own words how Beauty found her way
to Prince Charming's home amid the elms.

"When I arrived in Venice," she told Thomas Moore years later,
"the physicians ordered that I should try the country air, and Lord
Byron, having a villa at La Mira, gave it up to me, and came to reside
there with me. There we spent the autumn, and there," she reminded
Moore with friendly Italian courtesy, "I had the pleasure of making
your acquaintance."

When she was an old lady, she looked back on those weeks at the
villa on the Brenta as a dream—a curious but happy dream—about
something that had happened to some one else. Like all happy dreams
it was filled with suspense—an Armida's palace suspended in mid-
heaven by a single hair—and when she woke up she was crying. But
there it was—a dream about a child whom she had never known. She
told it all one day to her friend Lamartine, and declared that the whole
episode seemed "improbable" to her in old age and she could hardly
believe that it had happened! And, she supposed, other people wouldn't
believe it was true; for aught she knew, M. Lamartine would tell her she
had dreamed the whole thing—he was a poet, he must know.

There were few neighbours at La Mira—an ancient *hidalgo* from
Mexico across the road, and an ancient Frenchman who had known
Voltaire in the next-door house—and they troubled the lovers little.
There were few visitors to the house. Nothing but books and timeless
hours and sleep.

Byron was busy writing—more *Don Juan*, more *Prophecy of Dante*.
She noticed that he wrote quickly and on odd scraps of paper—the backs

of envelopes, old theatre programmes, and the like. Usually he did not start writing until after midnight, and then he wrote steadily into sunrise. All poets need inspiration while they write, and his was an English concoction called gin and water. . . . He came to her bedside, pale and exhausted, and dropped down there among the pillows and fell into a troubled sleep. She drew his head closer to her heart and, leaning on her elbow, gazed down into his face.

. . . Oblivion fell at last for both and, when she woke, the noonday sun slanted between the window curtains in a strong shaft of light across her bed. From without came the lonely note of birds among autumnal trees, a dog barking in the garden, the rumour of the countryside—wagons rumbling down the road, the sharp crack of a whip, and cheerful shouts. . . . He was prowling round the room, humming a tune quietly to himself . . . she nestled back into the pillows, feeling happy and at rest. . . .

If ever she felt that his "poeshie" was a rival, she fought the idea down. It was his life, and she must help him—and somehow she would stop him drinking gin. In the afternoon he limped into her room, bubbling with laughter, and translated from the scraps of paper in his hand. Gladly she dropped her book to listen.

She knew nothing about the first cantos of *Don Juan*—nothing about the caricature of Annabella in Juan's mother, Donna Inez—nothing about Donna Julia and her *roulade* of outraged virtue and the discovery of Juan in her bed. Byron told her that, after an unfortunate love-affair in Spain, Juan had been sent to sea, had been shipwrecked, nearly died of starvation, and then at last was washed up on the shore of a lonely Greek island where Haidée found him. By a strange coincidence Haidée was seventeen years old and her hair was auburn, like Teresa's in bright sunshine. Yet another resemblance of fiction to real life. Haidée was not married, but she had for father a sinister old man—a pirate who had fished in the troubled waters of tyranny and revolt and grown rich and yet, for all his wealth, objected strongly to "the inflammation of his weekly bills." All this, however, must be looked upon as the prophetic soul of poetry dreaming on things to come—for Byron had not met Teresa when first he conjured up the picture of Haidée. And in one respect Haidée was not Teresa. She was tall and her eyes were dark, whereas Teresa's eyes were bright blue in daylight and she was short and inclined to plumpness, when she wasn't sick.

Sometimes she listened with a puzzled frown, sometimes with a look of genuine distress—why did he say things he didn't mean? When he said that all that Dante had deified in Beatrice was mathematics she protested noisily. But, said Byron wickedly, my wife is a mathematician —"my mathematical Medea" he called her. She was not disarmed—she

saw no connexion between Beatrice and Lady Byron and declared that
he paid his wife too much honour in linking her in thought with Dante's
*innamorata*. Mercifully he did not read his stanza about *liaisons* with
married women, for he knew by now that, whatever else Teresa lacked,
she had a strong moral sense—fiercer in its kind than Annabella's. But,
being Byron, he read her the lines about woman and love and watched
her face mischievously as he read—

> In her first passion woman loves her lover,
> In all the others all she loves is love,
> Which grows a habit she can ne'er get over,
> And fits her loosely—like an easy glove.

With all her training in theology Teresa never could understand what
woman was, but from poetry she had learnt much upon the more con-
crete subject of love. She confounded his cynical theories with an
avalanche of poetic logic in which Beatrice fought for pride of place
with Mistress Millamant—love, of course, was greater than the lover
—it ennobled him—and what is a lover, anyhow? If a woman doesn't
want his love he simply doesn't exist—and so on through the age-old
argument that leaves us all cold to-day. But Byron went on reading.

> Men grow ashamed of being so very fond;
> They sometimes also get a little tired
> (But that, of course, is rare), and then despond.

Now Teresa was angry, and her anger made her silent. Hastily he
explained that the lines referred to husbands only. Her face cleared.

As the story went on she was happy and excited. Haidée had fallen
in love with Juan, and Juan loved Haidée. What mattered theories
about love? All was well. She saw herself as Haidée, and he was Juan.
And Lambro, the old pirate, must surely be Alessandro—with his exquisite breeding, his dangerous smile, his passion for *ordine* and *economia*
in his household:

> . . . the mildest manner'd man
> That ever scuttled ship or cut a throat.

He "lay coil'd like the boa in the wood."

> His angry word once o'er, he shed no blood,
> But in his silence there was much to rue,
> And his *one* blow left little work for *two*.

She shivered in apprehension for the poor young lovers, but in her heart
she thought that for Alessandro the portrait was overcharged. Yet her
lover had caught one side of Alessandro—one sympathy that, fitfully,
had bound her to him—his hope for the independence of Italy. Unfortunately Alessandro's love for Italy had been corrupted, like old Lambro's

love for Greece, by years of political servitude, by intrigue and self-seeking and the pursuit of material wealth.

Suddenly the poem shifted its mood, and there came a pæan and a dirge for liberty—"The Isles of Greece"—the song that was sung—or ought to have been, or possibly was, sung—at the love-feast of Haidée and Juan by a poor creature of a poet who, for the moment, had been stirred out of moral torpor into genuine feeling.

> Place me on Sunium's marbled steep
> Where nothing, save the waves and I,
> May hear our mutual murmurs sweep;
> There, swan-like, let me sing and die:
> A land of slaves shall ne'er be mine—
> Dash down yon cup of Samian wine!

The daughter of the *Carbonari* grew excited as she listened to Childe Harold's song. For Greece think Italy, and the story was the same. In imagination she saw her lover setting out to fight for freedom—the freedom of her own dear Italy—or the freedom of Greece which he loved so well. Never would she hold him back from such a battle, even though it meant death for him and widowhood for her!

From cynical reflections on life the poem had carried her, as she listened, to love, to romance and revelry, and thence again to dreams of liberty. Suddenly again, without warning, it dropped into pensive twilight—the Pine Forest at sunset, the angelus ringing from distant city towers, two lovers alone.

> Ave Maria! 'tis the hour of prayer!
> Ave Maria! 'tis the hour of love!
> Ave Maria! may our spirits dare
> Look up to thine and to thy Son's above!
> Ave Maria! oh that face so fair!
> Those downcast eyes beneath the Almighty dove—
> What though 'tis but a pictured image—strike—
> That painting is no idol—'tis too like.

Teresa bent her head once more, as her lover read, and crossed her heart. *Don Juan* was her poem. More than ever she was sure that she was Haidée. And Juan? And Juan, she told her lover, Juan was an *"aimable enfant"*—a nice boy!

## CHAPTER VIII

# *Little Pilgrim*

ALLEGRA joined them at La Mira. Teresa often wondered, as she drew the child into her arms and gazed into its face. An odd, elfin child —a changeling, kindled in sunrise and dew, a little pagan sprite without a soul, her head too large for her frail shoulders—a solemn little face with a line between the brows, curling golden hair, and dark violet eyes under dark upturned lashes.

For the most part she was a quiet child. For hours she would sit without speaking, like a little old witch beside the fire, or she would nestle in the crook of her father's elbow and watch him eat his *petits pois.* Yet she had a spirit of her own, too. She gave herself airs like a spoilt beauty, she was mutinous sometimes beyond all bearing, she flew into tantrums and tore her clothes. When she was naughty all the household adored her and she ran naked about the garden, pursued by excited, chattering servants.

Teresa had scarcely a maternal thought in her mind, but she was kind and couldn't help being sorry for this baby. She petted her and tried to tame her into a good little, self-possessed Italian girl. Privately she thought that the child would do better in a convent in the hills—she was delicate, high-strung, and, in her silence as in her mutiny, in every way intractable, and here the servants alternately neglected and spoiled her. But her lover's attitude towards his child puzzled her. He was fond of her, proud of her beauty, and laughed when she greeted him with her "*Bon dì, Papa,*" or preened herself and trailed a shawl before the mirror. Yet he would talk about her with careless disdain, as though she were a funny little gutter-child, and harshly called her his "bastard." He seemed indifferent about her health, and then in a fury a servant was dismissed for not reporting a tumble and a bruise. Sometimes he would sit for hours watching her play in the garden, then another time, when Teresa brought her to his room, he turned away, as though he really detested the sight of the child, and shouted angrily, "Take her away! She's too like her mother!"

Who was this child's mother? Sometimes Teresa felt a sharp pang of envy for this unknown woman, and then she wished Allegra were out of the house. Byron said she had been named after a beautiful woman in Venice, but Teresa waited patiently for the truth. Then he told her the whole story.

Just before he left England, when he was living alone in Piccadilly Terrace, with his wife and his daughter, Ada, gone for good, a letter was handed in to him signed "E. Trefusis." He knew those letters of old and read this one with contemptuous amusement. It was written in a clear, educated hand, and the writer told him that she had loved him for years and wished to "place her happiness in his hands." Another letter came, and the lady—she called herself G.C.B. now—said that she wished to see him that evening on business of "peculiar importance." Why he knew not, but he allowed her at last to come in.

Her real name was Claire Clairmont, and she was not pretty. Her hair was raven-black, her eyes so black they seemed to have no iris. But she had an interesting face—dark olive and lively—with a glimpse of mockery behind it. And, ye gods! how she talked—in a sharp, brittle tone—about free love, about atheism and liberty and a young poet called Shelley whom, she said, she "loved." She came again and again, urging all reasons but the real one—she thought of going on the stage and needed his advice—she was writing a novel and would he look it over? And there she sat at his feet and wouldn't go. Sometimes he scolded her, and, when she flared up resentfully, he called her "a little fiend," but still she wouldn't go. One evening she brought with her a pretty girl with reddish hair, a soft voice, and keen grey eyes who could scarcely speak to him for awe. This was 'Madam Claire's' step-sister, Mary Godwin— daughter of the 'philosopher,' William Godwin—and she, too, it appeared, "loved" this young poet Shelley, whom Claire was for ever quoting, and lived with him as his mistress. Finally, a few days before he left England, Claire wrote to him and insisted like a housemaid on the spree that he should leave town with her for a house she had chosen— just for one night—she had made every arrangement—no one need know. Like a fool he went.

When, several weeks later, he arrived in Geneva, there she was waiting for him with Shelley and Mary. She had scrambled across the Alps, he said angrily, to continue her game of 'unphilosophizing' him. He had, at least, to thank her for the gift of knowing Shelley—and, Teresa noted, his eye always kindled pleasantly when he spoke of Shelley—but as for 'Madam Claire'—she pestered him to death with her inroads on his privacy, and when he showed his boredom she turned shrewish and made ill-natured jokes to hurt his pride or she snivelled and whined. After months of her intrusion he sent her back to England to have her brat alone. Then she came to Italy with the Shelleys and sent the child to him at Venice. He hadn't wanted it—a baby was sadly in the way in the Fornarina's household—but Claire said that with him it would have "worldly advantages," so he took the child on the express condition that her mother resigned all her rights. "The woman always disgusted me," he told Teresa, and he refused ever to set eyes on her again. Now she was trapesing round Italy somewhere with the Shelleys and wrote him nagging letters about Allegra, but he never had written her a word in reply—not one word.

About his wife he said little, but that little was contemptuous and bitter. Annabella "deceived herself learnedly," he said; she was always painting imaginary portraits of him, and none of them were like. Teresa was an honest soul; as Byron told Hobhouse, she had no tact, and when she thought, she must speak. "You loved her—at least a bit," she said. "You still think of her—you're sorry for what you said to her." He glowered at her, but she went on fearlessly, "You were cruel to her, you were a difficult husband, you treated her badly—any woman will tell you that." "But what have I told?" he protested. "You've told me all I need to know," Teresa answered firmly.

He talked about his mother. He was sorry when she died. He talked about his other daughter, Ada—"little Miss Legitimacy," he called her. She was scarcely a month old when he said good-bye to her. "Ada, sole daughter of my house and heart!" "When shall we three meet again?" he said sarcastically to Annabella when they parted, and she answered piously "In heaven"—a reply that should have warned him of what "that fiend" intended. As a son and a father Teresa was sure that her lover was perfect.

But when he spoke of his sister his face lighted up. Augusta had every virtue that he admired in a woman—Augusta could make him laugh—they had little secrets together and a baby-language all their own —only Augusta understood him. Then his face clouded, and he looked sad. "Oh, yes," he said, "I *loved* Augusta!"

Teresa ran to the writing-table and dipped a pen in the inkwell. She must write a letter at once to Augusta, giving her news of her brother and telling her how perfect he was as man and friend. But with a laugh Byron held her hand. He could see his sister's face bending over one of Teresa's *carissima* effusions, like a good dunce's, wrestling with a problem in arithmetic. Besides, he didn't want his sister to know of this, his latest scrape.

Teresa looked thoughtful. "*Loved* Augusta!"—everything he said about England was always past tense. She gathered all Augusta's letters in a heap by themselves and tied them together with a silk ribbon. When another letter came she reverently added it to the package. Augusta's letters were sacred—they must not be allowed to lie side by side with other letters from England.

Thus cosily and tranquilly the weeks slipped by at La Mira. Teresa read aloud in the evenings in her deep, musical voice, scanning all the superlatives in the solid work of divinity she had picked from the book-shelf as though they were so much "poeshie." Byron yawned behind his hand and fell asleep. A gust of fresh air woke him up, and he shivered impatiently. The window was wide open, and Teresa stood there with her hands crossed before her on the iron balustrade, gazing dreamily at the stars. "Oh, shut that window," he said morosely. But Teresa neither turned to him nor spoke. She went on looking at the stars. . . . He sighed and fell asleep again.

September faded into October, and the leaves began to fall among the elms. With the first days of November a cold wind blew from the mountains, prophesying storm.

All this while Teresa never once supposed that she was conducting her life with anything less than the most delicate regard for worldly convention. Her doctors had recommended country air. Lord Byron, ever kindly and considerate, had given up his villa that she might live there in quiet and seclusion and recover her health. Here she was— mistress in her own house, waiting till Alessandro rejoined her. In the solitude to which her husband's whims and her own poor health condemned her, she needed cheering up. Her *amico* had come to stay with her, as a good *amico* should.

In Venice, however, the moralists were shocked again, and there was a fine clatter of women's tongues. Virtue had been insulted and good taste besides, and it was hard to decide whom to blame more—the young Countess or the English milord. The Countess Benzoni was in despair. She had been infinitely patient with Lord Byron in the past, had even taken La Fornarina under her wing and tried to get her into good society. But now she broke with him. "You really must scold your friend," she told Tom Moore; "until this unfortunate affair he had behaved so well!" The Countess Albrizzi, who held the rival *salon*, visited her displeasure on the young Countess. It was disgraceful enough that a *dama* should run away from her husband with her *amico*, but to run away in broad daylight—and in the husband's coach! Night was the time for elopement and a public diligence the proper vehicle, and the Countess Guiccioli should have had the decency to don boy's clothes, and Lord Byron ought to have disguised himself as a Hungarian cavalry officer or a monk, and they should have run away to Rome or Naples— anywhere but Venice! Lord Byron, said gossip, had been living in Count Guiccioli's house in Bologna—well, that was Count Guiccioli's affair—an *amico*, after all, might stay in the house of his *dama* in given circumstances, but for the Countess Guiccioli to live openly in the house of her *amico*—that was too much! The Countess Albrizzi spoke for every honest *dama* and decent *cicisbeo* in Venice. Until Count Guiccioli returned and regulated the situation, his wife was out of bounds.

Count Gamba wrote many letters to his daughter, affectionate but severe. He begged her to think of her good name, of her own peace of mind, of the happiness of those who loved her and depended on her for their own happiness—of everything and every one, in a word, but her husband. He had been alarmed, he told her, when Count Guiccioli came back to Ravenna without her. He visited his son-in-law and was shocked to learn that she had gone off alone with Lord Byron to Venice. There had been angry words. He told Count Guiccioli that he was exposing his wife to slander and suspicion. Count Guiccioli replied that he had every confidence in the good will of his friend, Lord Byron. Count Gamba then told his son-in-law that he must go straight to Venice and rejoin his wife. But Count Guiccioli would take no orders, and Count Gamba left him saying that he himself would go to Venice to mount guard over his daughter. The money for the journey, alas, was not forthcoming. In the meantime he implored Teresa to give up all thought of going to Lake Como with Lord Byron.

Teresa was a loving daughter, and to please her father she gave up the trip to the Italian lakes. She went to the villa on the Brenta instead. Count Gamba wrote to her in more distress than ever. He abandoned expostulation as being of no use now, and his fears took a different flight. He had seen his son-in-law again and couldn't understand his silence in the face of this latest intelligence from Venice. He was sure that he was plotting mischief. Perhaps, he wrote, it would be best if Teresa ran away outright with Lord Byron—over the Alps and across the sea— rather than remain in the toils of a man so dangerous as her husband. Teresa would gladly have followed this advice, but Byron had declared against elopement, nor did she herself think it necessary in the present circumstances—at any rate, not for the reason her father gave. Count Gamba wrote again. He would do his best to come to Venice, but in the meantime, he warned her, Count Guiccioli was on his way there and would probably arrive before him. For God's sake she must leave La Mira and go back to the lodgings in Venice. She must write to her husband from there, and when he arrived she must greet him with kindness and cordiality.

Teresa sighed as an *amica*, but obeyed as a daughter. She returned to Venice, and when Count Guiccioli wrote her that he would be ten days late she answered with a brisk, wifely letter, scolding him for keeping her waiting so long. Then bad news came from La Mira. Byron had gone out riding in a thunderstorm and got wet through, and now he was sick of a tertian fever. She hurried back across the lagoon to Fusina and took the public coach to La Mira. She found her *amico* raving and delirious on his bed. All day long he spouted poetry and ordered Fletcher to write it down. He glared at Teresa with haggard eyes, shook his clenched fist at her, called her strange and ugly names in English. He howled at Fletcher and told him to throw that horrible woman out of the window. But Fletcher quietened him and whispered to Teresa in a mournful aside that in his delirium his lordship had mistaken her for his mother-in-law.

Byron woke from his fever one morning to find his *dama* and his valet sobbing on either side of his bed. He laughed weakly at their woe-begone faces. Dr Aglietti called and, with a smile to Teresa, prescribed Peruvian bark, but Byron shook his head and called for cold water—nothing but cold water. Fletcher gave him the sheets of paper on which he had taken down the poetry that his lordship had dictated when he was good enough to be out of his senses. Byron scanned the sheets lazily—much better stuff, he declared, than anything he wrote when he was sane—and told Fletcher to tear them up. Slowly he convalesced. Allegrina nestled in the counterpane and watched him grow well with solemn eyes. Day and night Teresa hovered round his bed and nursed him with glad devotion. She was still at La Mira when her husband arrived in Venice.

## CHAPTER IX

# *Pilgrim's Post*

ALL eyes were now turned towards the villa on the Brenta. Prince Colonna-Sciarra at Bologna was more sure than ever that Count Guiccioli was up to no good. These perpetual journeys round Romagna and back and forth from Ancona to Venice were cleverly masked as tours of his estates, but Prince Colonna had his suspicions. The Count, too, was in the habit of something more than blind intimacy with this English lord who was never away from the Guiccioli palace, at Ravenna or Bologna. Then Byron and the Countess Guiccioli had gone one way to Venice and the Count another way to Ravenna, and now, it appeared, all three were to meet somewhere near Venice. What manner of man was this Englishman? In his perplexity the Prince wrote to Signor Carlo Lancetti in Venice.

The military Governor of Venice, too—the Count von Goetz—had his eye on Byron and Count Guiccioli. Wasn't Count Guiccioli one of those so-called Italian 'patriots' of Bonaparte days? And wasn't his friend Byron mixed up in some revolutionary movement in England? It was currently said that he was a member of the new Italian secret society called *Roma Antica* and had been placed under temporary arrest at Bologna. And why had the Countess Guiccioli come to Venice without her husband? What were she and Lord Byron doing at La Mira? Count von Goetz also had recourse to Signor Lancetti for an answer to these conundrums.

Carlo Lancetti was what is politely called 'a government agent.' It was his business to keep his ear close to the keyhole and report to his superiors all that he heard from that source of information. In Venice it was an old profession, once plied by the excellent Casanova, and it was a fairly easy one. There were gondoliers to help, and keepers of gambling-hells and other haunts of pleasure, and servants. A brisk tour of the fashionable *salons* filled in rumour with more established fact, and thus a fair amount of mischief brewing in Venice was brought to light—and some of it was by no means political, as the police learned, no doubt, to their surprise. Carlo Lancetti set to work upon the assignment from Count von Goetz, but to Prince Colonna he was able to report at once.

Lord Byron, he said, had been reserved in expressing his political opinions in Venice. He was said to be a poet and certainly spent a great

114

deal of time writing in his palace. The results were pronounced by those who had seen them to be poetry—nothing worse. Sometimes in the fervour of poetic composition he had been heard to express ideas that might be described as 'anti-patriotic'—from the point of view of the Austrian government. But his main preoccupation in Venice had been what was generally called 'the fair sex.' His expedition to Bologna was confidently stated to have been made in connexion with some affair of gallantry.

In working for the Count von Goetz Lancetti was able to fill in his picture. In view of his past career there could be no doubt that Count Guiccioli was one of those political hotheads who were plotting secretly for the independence of Italy. It was not true, however, that Lord Byron was a member of the *Roma Antica*. He was a poet who wrote in a new style which was called *romantica* in England—hence the mistake. There was a political movement in England known as 'reform' which Lord Byron was said to favour, and the rumour was that he would shortly leave for England to help in 'reforming' that island. The Countess Guiccioli had come to Venice to be treated for a skin-disease. Lord Byron had met her at 'Lady Benson's' house and paid her court. Now, to the general stupor of Venice, the lady had joined the poet at La Mira. Having arrived thus far in his inquiries, Lancetti withheld his report. Count Guiccioli, said every one in the best houses, was on his way back to Venice, and it would be interesting to know what happened when he arrived there.

So much for politics in Italy as they touched upon the idyll at La Mira. Now we turn to politics far away in England. Murray sent the letter about the consulship to John Wilson Croker, who answered in his most hopeful and helpful fashion. Croker, for his sins, earned the ill-will of two masters of invective, Thackeray and Disraeli, and to-day he is remembered mainly as the pander of the self-seeking Rigby in *Coningsby*. He certainly had a jaunty manner in handing out other people's patronage. We Tories are placable folk, he told Murray—always ready to do a good turn for one of your Whigs. A full consulship at Ravenna was out of the question, as there was already a Consul-General at Venice, but a Vice-Consulate could be managed. My Lord Castlereagh made the appointment for Consul-Generalships, but for a Vice-Consulate they took the recommendation of the fellow on the spot. All Lord Byron had to do was to send in the name of his Italian to the Consul-General at Venice—by the way, he was Hoppner—Gifford's man (you know)—so Hoppner could write to Gifford, and Gifford could write to my Lord Castlereagh, and Murray could write to my Lord Byron, and my Lord Byron could write to Croker, and Croker was sure the business would be done. He'd been having a good laugh over *Don Juan*, by the way—hadn't shocked him a bit. Tell Lord Byron he'd be glad to have a young

Croker grow up like Don Juan. Hoppner was the man for his business—whatever the Italian fellow's name was.

After writing that "bilious" letter Hoppner had left for a holiday in Switzerland with his wife's relatives. Towards the end of October he returned to Venice to be greeted by the news that the Countess Guiccioli was living in free grace with Byron at his villa on the Brenta. Mrs Hoppner did not make matters better by laughing at her husband and reminding him that she had always said that Lord Byron was in love with the Countess. Scott, too, told him of Byron's fury over his well-meant letter of warning. Hoppner felt foolish, and there was nothing left but to apologize or, at any rate, explain. Byron was under many obligations to Hoppner and his wife for kindness and patience in the past. The quarrel, if there were any, was instantly closed. He blamed Hoppner only for not speaking like a man and quoting his own judgment or his own knowledge. As it was, he had quoted others and based his charge against Teresa solely on the tittle-tattle of Venice.

"Your letter," he wrote kindly but severely,

> displeased me very much—not that it might not be true in its statement and kind in its intention, but you have lived long enough to know how useless all such representations ever are, and must be, in cases where the passions are concerned. To reason with men in such a situation is like reasoning with a drunkard in his cups—the only answer you will get from him is, that he is sober, and you are drunk. Upon that subject we will (if you like) be silent.

Hoppner "did not like" and wrote to say more, but Byron closed the topic peremptorily. "How is your little boy? and how are you?" He was sorry that he was tied to La Mira for the moment, but he would be in Venice soon, and then, he added wickedly, "we will be bilious together. I hate the place and all that it inherits." Wisely he did not broach the subject of Count Guiccioli as Vice-Consul for the port of Ravenna.

Hoppner, on his side, realized that his friend was 'sensitive' on the subject of the Countess. Tacitly he yielded Byron the point that Teresa loved him, but he did not forgive her for putting him in the wrong. Elsewhere—and in particular with Mrs Hoppner—he insisted that Byron did not care the toss of a halfpenny about Teresa.

Soon he and Byron were writing one another letters again. Hoppner —not without malice—regaled Byron with the stories that were going the rounds about him in Venice—that he had become a *Carbonaro*, been arrested in Bologna, run away with a girl in a convent, etc. Byron was on guard in replying. He dreaded Hoppner's powers of talking and, where Teresa was concerned, would not expose himself to a second discomfiture. Both for the *Carbonari* and his love-affair he answered on a note of humorous detachment.

The Ferrara story [he wrote] is of a piece with all the rest of the Venetian manufacture; you may judge. I only changed horses there since I wrote to you after my visit in June last. "Convent"—and "carry off," quotha! and "girl"—I should like to know *who* has been carried off—except poor dear *me*. I have been more ravished myself than anybody since the Trojan war; but as to the arrest and its causes—one is as true as the other, and I can account for the invention of neither. I suppose it is some confusion of the tale of the F[ornarina]—and of Me. Guiccioli—and half a dozen more—but it is useless to unravel the web, when one has only to brush it away.

With friends in England he had been unwontedly silent ever since he left Bologna. Murray had written in concern in answer to his letter of brooding in the Certosa graveyard—it was not like his friend to think only of a grinning skull when he was looking into a pretty girl's face—was he well? Byron replied shortly that he had suffered from a bad head and nerves, owing to heat and exhaustion, "and plague with the illness of another person" in Bologna. He was right again now in health but in low spirits—and folly. Kinnaird scolded him for running up his expenses during the past months and suggested that he was misbehaving again with his Venetian harem. He answered wearily that his increased expenses were due to frequent journeys, to buying furniture—and books —and a horse or two, but otherwise he was faithful to his "honest *liaison*" with the Countess from Romagna, and again he repeated to his banker, "I can assure you that *She* has never cost me, directly or indirectly, a sixpence."

Tom Moore was travelling in Italy, and he stopped on his way to call on Byron at La Mira in the opening week of October.

Byron was hungry for England—for the sound of an English voice, the grasp of an English hand—though Moore was careful to say that he was Irish—in thought and feeling. Of all friends he had made in London Moore was, perhaps, the dearest—because he, too, was a poet. He might laugh at 'Tommy's' innocent enthusiasm for lords, but he was a man without malice or envy, genial, helpful, full of fun, and in time of trouble he had proved himself a staunch and understanding friend.

It was two o'clock in the afternoon when Moore arrived at La Mira, and Byron was still in his bath. He hastened downstairs and grasped his friend by both hands and rallied him for looking so "fresh and poetical ... this comes of marriage and being settled in the country." Moore, on his side, was disagreeably shocked. Byron was fat—in body as in face. He had lost that spiritual look of Childe Harold days. To please his *dama* he had grown whiskers round cheek and jawbone, and his hair was long, untidy, hung down at the back on his coat-collar. Altogether he had an odd, un-English look. But with affectionate loyalty Moore still found him the handsomest man he knew. What his face had lost in romance it had gained in humour. As he stood drinking tea by the mantel-piece and chattering, a lady entered and Byron introduced her as the Countess Guiccioli. Moore had heard of the "Romagnuola" Countess, and as he bowed politely before her he looked at her with scrutinizing eye. She was very young—almost a girl, he observed, and, for an Italian, surprisingly fair. She looked delicate, a little tired and frail, and, with some disappointment he added to himself, she was not "very pretty." Teresa welcomed him with the graceful courtesy of an Italian lady and hoped that she might see him again in her villa, when, perhaps, she would have the pleasure of introducing him to her husband. When she spoke Moore felt that she was kind and intelligent, but he was not allowed to talk with her for long. Byron whirled him away to the carriage. Teresa had granted him leave of absence for the evening on condition that he was home by midnight. Off the two poets drove to Venice and embarked on their gondola just as the sun began to set across the lagoon in a long gold haze and the snow upon the distant mountains was red.

Byron insisted that Moore should make the Palazzo Mocenigo his headquarters while he stayed in Venice. "Keep clear of the dog," he shouted, as they groped their way through the unlighted hall, and "Take care, or that monkey will fly at you!" as they climbed the stairs. He shouted for the servants and sent them flying in different directions—one to fetch dinner from the *tratteria*, another to bid Alexander Scott come to dinner, a third to order his steward into his presence. The key to his own rooms was lost, so he kicked the door open with humorous male-dictions, and in a trice Moore was standing on the balcony, gazing at the last reflection of sunset on the canal. He had got as far as the words "peculiar rosy hue" when Byron clapped a hand over his mouth and said, "Come, damn it, Tom, don't be poetical!" Dinner arrived, and with it Alexander Scott, and they were gay and tipsy together. At nine Byron, with a mutinous grimace, left them drinking and was rowed back across the lagoon.

He was in Venice again the next evening and for two evenings more. He was in tearing spirits, like a boy out of school, and his conversation was ludicrous and "anything but romantic," said Moore, who now and then would have liked to muse over setting suns and palaces sleeping in moonshine. Byron talked of old days and friends in London, about *Don Juan*, about his plans for settling in Venezuela. Only for a moment was he serious—when he talked about his wife. He admitted that he had been difficult with Annabella, had spoken to her with bitterness at times, had been angry and rude. But he laughed to scorn all charges of brutality and declared that he had been too rigorously punished for what, after all, were faults of temper, inevitable in a man shut up alone with a woman on a "treacle-moon." On his way to Italy Moore had written him hoping that they might travel together from Venice to Rome, and Byron was all for making the trip. But Moore was thinking now of the delicate, "not very pretty" girl in the villa on the Brenta, and he protested vigorously that his friend had no right to leave the Countess Guiccioli —that would be unkind and place her in a most equivocal position. Byron fumed and fretted and gave in, but, at least, he pleaded, let them go as far as Arqua together—two poets worshipping at the tomb of Petrarch —the Countess surely would not object to that? But Moore insisted that his friend had a duty at La Mira, and again Byron gave in with a naughty-boy grimace.

Teresa gave her *amico* a whole day off for Moore's last day in Venice, and Byron did not leave him until the small hours of the morning. In the afternoon Moore was ferried over the lagoon and drove to La Mira, where he took three-o'clock dinner with Byron and Teresa. As he crossed the hall with his host Allegra came in from a walk. Moore was struck by the child's beauty, but Byron remarked with elaborate casualness that he wasn't a family man and didn't know what it felt like to be a father. At his suggestion Teresa gave Moore a letter to her brother in Rome. Moore never met Pietro in Rome and later opened the letter and read it. The Countess had evidently been homesick for her own kin at La Mira. She rallied her brother on his story of the young wife languishing in a dungeon in England and told him that Signor Moore would be able to give him more reliable news about her *amico* than the gossips of Rome. "My dear Pietro," she said at the end, "whenever you feel inclined to laugh, do send two lines of answer to your sister, who loves and ever will love you with the greatest tenderness."

Moore liked Teresa and was disturbed on her account. His friend's talk of Venezuela, his light-hearted proposal of a journey to Rome—all this didn't sound as though his feelings for this girl with the heavy ringlets were profound or serious. He looked at her steadily a second time and noted in his diary that night that she "looked prettier than the first time." As he drove away from La Mira he pondered. Of all the men he knew he believed that Byron was the greatest poet, and he sometimes felt humble in his presence. He was proud of his friendship and felt sure that Byron was his friend, too. Byron had been by turns jovial and bitter about the horrors of being married; but here, at La Mira, with this golden-haired Italian girl and this pretty violet-eyed baby, hadn't he—on unconventional lines, it is true—built around himself something perilously like domestic life? Teresa was very young and, he would judge, innocent, but she was amiable, devoted, certainly a great deal prettier than Annabella. Ada, people said, was a plump child with something of her father's looks, but Allegra showed every sign of growing into dangerous beauty. It was all poetical, worthy of Childe Harold, and, he supposed, Italian; but how long would the pilgrim stay at home?

There had been one unromantic incident that had distressed the sentimental soul of Moore. While he was in Venice Count Guiccioli had
addressed a letter longer than usual to his wife. Teresa opened it in
trepidation, expecting notice of his instant arrival or, at the least, a
scolding and orders to leave La Mira at once. She drew a happy sigh,
however, when she found that the letter was written on a dull matter
of business. Alessandro had often rebuked her in time past for her indifference to money and lack of interest in his business worries. He now
requested her influence to obtain from Lord Byron the sum of one
thousand pounds, which, as he happened to know, lay to his lordship's
credit in the bank at Ravenna. He did not ask for the money as a gift,
as that, she would understand, would be an *avilimento*, unworthy of an
Italian gentleman. He would give security and meant to invest the sum
in a manner which would be advantageous to both parties—but especially
to Lord Byron. Teresa was never to have patience for money matters.
She gave the letter to Byron and forgot about it. Byron showed it to
Scott and Moore. Scott remarked philosophically that a man had to pay
for his pleasures. Moore was shocked but counselled payment, too.
Byron, however, had a streak of avarice in him. He could be generous
with his money, but he preferred to be generous on his own terms. He
bet Scott that he would keep the lady—and his money, too.

He had never felt well since that night when he burst into tears over
Alfieri's tragedy. In Bologna he had been gloomy and quarrelsome and
had challenged that swindling dragoon from Parma to a duel. At La
Mira he was restless and, between bouts of writing poetry, worried about
business matters in England and read the newspapers and began to think
of emigrating to America. The Anglo-Americans were too coarse for
him and their climate too cold. But Bolivar had caught his imagination,
and he would go to South America—they were a fine primitive people
there, fierce like their earthquakes and volcanoes. He would soon grapple
with the Spanish language. He sent Hobhouse clippings gleaned from
the newspapers about offers held out to settlers in Venezuela. He would
take Allegra with him there and pitch his tent for good and all.

I am not tired of Italy, but a man must be a *cicisbeo* and a singer in duets,
and a connoisseur of operas—or nothing—here. I have made some progress
in all these accomplishments, but I can't say that I don't feel the degradation.
Better be an unskilful planter, an awkward settler—better be a hunter, or
anything, than a flatterer of fiddlers and fan-carrier of a woman. I like
women—God He knows—but the more their system here develops upon
me, the worse it seems, after Turkey too; here the *polygamy* is all on the
female side. I have been an intriguer, a husband, a whoremonger, and now
I am a *cavalier servente*—by the holy! it is a strange sensation. . . . You must
not talk to me of England, that is out of the question. I had a house and
lands, and a wife and child, and a name there—once—but all these things

are transmuted or sequestered. . . . I feel no love for the soil after the treatment I received before leaving it for the last time. . . . Yet I want a country,
and a home, and—if possible—a free one. I am not yet thirty-two years
of age. I might still be a decent citizen, and found a house, and a family as
good—or better—than the former. I could at all events occupy myself
rationally, my hopes are not high, nor my ambition extensive, and when
tens of thousands of our countrymen are colonizing (like the Greeks of old
in Sicily and Italy) from so many causes, does my notion seem visionary or
irrational? There is no freedom in Europe—that's certain; it is besides a
worn-out portion of the globe. . . . Do not laugh at me; you will, but I
assure you I am quite in earnest.

That letter was written to Hobhouse on October 3, four days before
Moore's arrival. On October 11 Moore left La Mira. On October 25 a
Government agent reported to Cardinal Consalvi at Rome that the business at La Mira was over; Lord Byron had left for a pleasant rural retreat
on the Borromean Islands, where he was enjoying the hospitality of his
august *amica*, Caroline, Princess of Wales. If Hoppner had heard this
report, he was forestalled a few days later by another letter from La Mira.

Count G. comes to Venice next week and I am requested to consign his
wife to him, which shall be done—with all her linen.

What you say of the long evenings at the Mira, or Venice, reminds me of
what *Curran* said to Moore—"so—I hear—you have married a pretty
woman—and a very good creature too—an excellent creature—pray—um—
*how do you pass your evenings?*" It is a devil of a question that, and perhaps
as easy to answer with a wife as a mistress; but surely they are no longer
than the nights. I am all for morality now, and shall confine myself hence-
forward to the strictest adultery, which you will please to recollect is all that
that virtuous wife of mine has left me.

## CHAPTER X

# Brunello returns

COUNT GUICCIOLI arrived at Venice on November 6. Count Gamba followed hard upon his heels, and the two men quarrelled bitterly. Count Guiccioli had intercepted Count Gamba's letter to his daughter, advising her to greet her husband with a display of affection, and charged him with treachery. Count Gamba replied angrily that his son-in-law had brought his troubles on his head by his own inconceivable carelessness.

After consultation with his lawyers and a cross-examination of Signora F—— Count Guiccioli proceeded to La Mira. He was calm but displeased. He was in no mood for affection. He had come with an ultimatum to his wife. She must make her choice, once and for all, between husband and *amico*. He had no reason to doubt the answer. Not even Teresa would be so perverse as to leave her husband for her *amico*, for that would mean social ruin for her throughout Italy. Because he felt sure of victory, he had brought with him a document to which he desired her agreement before he took her back into his house—a table of articles for the management of his domestic life—which all husbands must read with awe.

This document went into the greatest detail, covering matters of clothes, pocket-money, and general demeanour, and we quote only the more outstanding of the Count's demands. It opened on the note of domestic duty and proceeded by degrees to conjugal fidelity, as thus:

1. She shall not get out of bed late, or loiter over dressing herself up or be fussy about lacing and washing, and thereby run the risk of harming her health.
2. She shall forthwith busy herself with such household matters as come within her competence and so arrange as to obtain the greatest cleanliness and the best order. Until she shall have acquired the experience that comes with practice . . . she may offer suggestions, or ask advice, but she shall not give orders. . . . She shall reflect that inasmuch as she neglects the care of business and house, so much the more I shall neglect her. Inasmuch as she despises practical matters, so much the more I shall despise, disrelish, and abominate her, who, while she is served by all, serves none, and who, while she adds to my worries and responsibilities, refuses to bear any of them herself.

3. After midday she shall spend the time till dinner with me, in conversation and reading aloud, and shall bear her share therein with my son.

4. After dinner, while I am resting, shall be her stated time for music.

5. After driving out with me in the early part of the evening there shall be reading aloud, as before dinner, then she shall go with me to the theatre, then there shall be conversation, and so to supper and to bed with me.

6. She shall not be conceited or impatient, for one can learn only with time, experience, and much thought. . . .

7. . . . She shall be content with her allowance of twelve *zecchini* a month, which is one hundred and forty-four *zecchini* a year and all the interest on her dowry . . . I might possibly, in the event of finding myself abounding in money, provide something more, but at most not more than two hundred *zecchini* a year. I must be spared the regret of refusing useless requests.

8. She shall be satisfied with the rooms and furniture as they now are, and shall not argue about that or fuss about details.

9. *She shall receive as few visitors as possible.*

10. She shall be always ready to stay, leave, or return to the place that best suits her husband's convenience, and shall therefore keep her things in order, and shall give up this desire for travel, or for living in places that do not suit her husband's, or her family's, convenience.

11. She shall be absolutely docile with her husband, and then only may she ask him that orders and complaints that in any way affect her shall be communicated direct to her and not to others.

12. She may, however, sweetly, modestly, and with proper hesitation submit her own ideas and opinions, and may even reply a second time to such arguments as I shall offer her. If, however, they fail to convince her, she shall nevertheless cease to insist and give obedience with good will and good temper.

13. She shall take constant and preventive care of her health, which she has harmed by her carelessness, empty-headedness, vanity, and caprice, and shall cease to fear complaints which a wise diagnosis will show do not exist.

14. She shall never cause trouble between her husband and her father or anyone else. . . . She shall consider [her husband] as her father, her husband, her *amico*, and her constant and faithful companion, and to him shall she prefer nobody else.

15. If she feel an inclination so to do [*i.e.*, prefer somebody else] she shall forthwith bring such a relationship to a close and never again have confidence in herself; otherwise she will stand condemned in the opinion of her husband as also in that of a prudent society.

After that last stipulation came one couched in language more plaintive than imperative, which leaves us wondering about the Count: was
he speaking as a moralist, or were the old man's feelings genuinely hurt?

16. How can she be completely frank with her husband with this
    gnawing at her heart? And when people cannot be completely open
    and frank, how can they be happy together?

The document closed on a note of menace. If she refused to obey
him, she would cease to be mistress in his house; his servants would take
over; his children would despise her; she would have no money of her
own, and he would give her none; and after his death, he assured her,
she would have great difficulty in finding another husband—if, with her
memory of life with him, she should look for matrimony a second time.

It was not unusual in those days, in drawing up terms of agreement
for a marriage, to include articles regulating the conduct of the wife, for
Italian husbands agreed with Dr Johnson that the advantages given to
women by nature were better for being tempered by law. But such
articles were signed, not by the bride, but by her parents. If the husband
attempted to enforce them, at least father and mother could reply to his
recriminations that they had broken their daughter in well and should
not be held to blame for his folly or his failure in attempting to administer
the rules. Count Guiccioli had generously waived this legal preliminary
in the calm assurance that he, who had managed and buried two wives,
would have no trouble in taming a child of sixteen. But surely now it
was too late to demand the rigour of the game in wifely obedience.
A wise woman would have signed the document at once and handed it
back to the Count with a curtsy and a smile. But Teresa was not a wise
woman, and she was in love.

Four days the battle raged. At first the Count was rigid, imperturb-
able, austere. Then he smiled and snarled and showed his teeth. Then
he raged and threatened and banged the table with his first. Teresa faced
him with eyes shining with hatred and unutterable scorn. Her first
answer to his ultimatum was woman-like—she would keep both her
husband and her *amico*. "Am I to be the only wife in Romagna," she
inquired in angry disdain, "who is not to be allowed her *amico*!" And
a pretty encouragement to go back to his house were these articles of
agreement—an insult to an honest woman! She picked up the document and turned its pages with a sarcastic sniff. Oh, yes, she would agree
to every one of his hundred-and-one stipulations, if he thought it would
do any good, and then and there she noted down the ones that she defied
him to enforce.

1. I'll get up when I choose to.
2. I won't discuss my *toilette*.

3. In domestic matters I'll be absolute mistress of all that is in a lady's province.
4. I don't refuse to read aloud to you, and I don't care whether your son is present or not.
5. I'll dine with you, but I'll spend your hour of rest the way I want to, even if it were in pulling the donkey's tail.
6. Driving out together, theatre, bed, supper, etc.—any way you like.

But none of this would be any good for a peaceful life if he refused her the following:

1. *A horse, with everything according, to go out riding.*
2. *The right to receive any visitor who comes.*

Also she must have a maid of her own, furniture that she liked, and a regular allowance.

The Count refused every one of her stipulations and demanded instant and absolute compliance with his own. Teresa laughed scornfully. He then went back to his original ultimatum and demanded that she make her choice—her husband or her *amico*. "*Ebbene*," cried Teresa, "I choose my *amico*," and flounced out of the room, ringlets all flying and nose in the air.

She refused to leave La Mira. Every evening Count Guiccioli toiled down the road to Fusina and was rowed over the lagoon to Venice. There he took Signora F—— to the theatre and brooded over his troubles in the box. The next morning, after consultation with his lawyers, he made the weary journey back to La Mira to renew the battle. It is a sad thing to relate, but his carriage sometimes passed Byron's on the road from Fusina. For Byron had decided that it was best that he should remain out of sight while the battle raged, and now and then he took refuge in the Palazzo Mocenigo. He was, by a strange chance, there when the Count arrived in Venice. But in the evening he was back at La Mira, and when Teresa came to him exhausted with victory and tears, he took her in his arms and comforted her in her hour of woman's triumph.

To Murray he must write and regale him with the glorious Punch-and-Judy farce playing under his roof—with him sitting by as disinterested spectator. *Don Juan* had arrived in book form, and he amused himself by reading it. One evening he came to stanza 137 of the first canto, where Donna Julia's maid bursts in on her love-making with Juan, shouting, "For God's sake, Madam—Madam—here's my master!" Teresa was leaning over his shoulder and asked what those words meant in Italian. "Nothing," he replied with emphasis, "but your 'husband is coming!'" "Oh, my God," shrieked Teresa, "is *he* coming!" "You may suppose," Byron wrote to Murray with studied nonchalance, "we laughed when she found out the mistake. You will be amused, as I was; it happened not three hours ago."

This pose of detachment was well enough for his friends in London, who took the tone that their "dear fellow" was a sentimental mountebank and would laugh him out of court if he owned to the "tender passion" in earnest. But in his heart he was not amused. He had got the "poor girl" into a scrape, he confessed to Murray, forgetting with noble condescension Teresa's infinitely greater talent for scrape-making, and he must help her, if he could. If she didn't make it up with her husband, he supposed that he would have to change his name and take her away to America and live a quiet provincial life. "Neither her birth," he said in all desperate seriousness, "nor her rank, nor her connexions by birth or marriage are inferior to mine." A lover's diffidence unaccountably took hold of him, and he added lamely, "Besides, she is a very pretty woman—ask Moore."

Count Guiccioli was appalled by his wife's undisguised hatred. He gave up the battle and went to Byron in tears and begged him to plead with Teresa to come back home. Byron stared in comic distress at this tall, stately man with the tears running down his ginger-coloured whiskers and dripping off his chin. Where now were the stilettos and stabs in the back, the demands for consulates or loans of a thousand pounds? Did the old man really care for his young wife? Or was he weeping only for property stolen and strayed? And what a pickle he had got himself into —with the husband crying in one room and the wife pacing another, sobbing and tearing her handkerchief to shreds! He was still weak from his tertian fever. Should he burst into tears, too, and then they might all sit down together with their grief, forlornly hiccuping and mopping eyes? Or should he sit back and laugh at himself ruefully for a "damned fool"? He bit his nails angrily and glowered at the Count, then pulled himself together with a frown. A faint blush overspread his white face. Heigho, now was the time for that virtue so admired of foreigners— English common sense.

Very well, he told the Count, he would speak with Teresa. "But," he added fiercely, "if you abandon your wife, I will take her undoubtedly. It is my duty—it is also my inclination—in case of such extremity. But if, as you say, you are really disposed to live with her and like her as before, I will not only not carry further disturbance into your family, but even repass the Alps, for I have no hesitation in saying that Italy will be now to me insupportable."

Lord Byron's hand fell with a melancholy flap on the mantelpiece, overturning the clock on to the floor, and there he stood with bowed head—like Dejection on a monument. The Count dried his tears. He could not be too grateful to his lordship for his generosity nor admire the nobility of his sentiments too much—he had always placed his trust in them—he agreed with everything that Milord had said—would promise everything he wished.

Byron hobbled slowly and reluctantly from the room to plead with Teresa.

Carlo Lancetti completed his report and sent it in to Count von Goetz with apologies for delay and the disappointing results of his quest. Count Guiccioli had arrived in Venice on November 6, 1819, and had thence proceeded to Lord Byron's villa on the Brenta. He had been in close confabulation there for four days, and on November 10 left for Ravenna, taking the Countess Guiccioli with him. In parting with Lord Byron Lancetti begged to state that the Countess had "given vent to transports of love." Lord Byron had promised to see her again, but as a matter of fact, he would shortly cross the Alps and sail for England to take part in the Reform movement there. His departure had been delayed by the illness of his natural daughter, who, Signor Lancetti had the honour to report, had been "procreated" in Switzerland. The mischief at La Mira might now be considered at an end.

# BOOK THREE

# Tragi-comedy

## CHAPTER I

# Winter in Venice

IT was Annabella's failing that she analysed too much. She analysed herself and all her motives, and she analysed other people, too, in the light of her own wisdom; then she brooded and came deliberately to a conclusion. As often as not her conclusions were wrong; but, a conclusion once formed, Annabella never changed her mind, and further brooding only hardened her in the belief that she was right. But now and then she used a wife's privilege of hitting the nail on the head and driving it home into her husband's hide with a thump. "It is unhappily your disposition"—she was always using that phrase to every one with whom she disagreed—"it is unhappily your disposition," she wrote to him at the time of their separation, "to consider what you have as worthless—what you have lost as invaluable." Byron might well have retorted that the charge was true, but wherein did he differ there from other men—or Annabella, for that matter?

He left La Mira after Teresa had gone and returned to the Palazzo Mocenigo. But now he hated Venice and all that it inherited—it was a haunt of enervating pleasure, degenerate and mouldering in its own ooze and slime, "a Gehenna of the waters," an "empty oyster-shell." Never had he felt more alone in Italy, more homesick, more an outcast, than now in his damp palace on the Grand Canal. He was bitter in his diatribes against the city and its people with Hoppner as they rode once more on the Lido—so bitter that Hoppner, who had little love for Venice, was driven to defend it. But he was a good fellow, was Hoppner. He knew that his companion was feeling sick and sorry about the business at La Mira and did his best to wean his mind from it by pointing out, as they rode along the sands, the play of light and shadow on sea and mountain and the towers and domes of the hated city across the flat expanse of water. Considerately he said nothing about Teresa, though in his heart he still believed that Byron's affections had not been greatly involved in that affair. But, with all his prejudice against her, he was fain to admit one thing—Teresa had rescued her lover from the life of foolish love-mongering that had distressed his friends in Venice.

Byron couldn't help thinking of Teresa—critically always, yet always with sharp regret. Thank God, she could laugh—therein she was like Aunt Sophy, and Augusta, and all the Byrons—they could always make fun of the *ridicules* in the people with whom they had to live. But, for all her laughter, she had no sense of humour; she couldn't make fun of herself, and she would have died sooner than make fun of him. Nor, strange to say, had she that smiling irony of an Italian woman who sees life as a sprightly comedy of principle at war with practice. Her laughter only meant that she was happy. And yet—wasn't it something to know a woman who, unlike Annabella or Caro Lamb or Mary Chaworth —those phantoms of the past—had no vocation for sorrow? And yet— she could be deadly serious at times, and when she was serious she was resolute. She was one of those happy diplomatists—they are said to be more often women than men—who always manage to get what they want—though how to get it, or why they want it, or what it is they want, they never know. She had volunteered elopement, then balked for worldly considerations; then, before he knew what was happening, she had run away with him in the eyes of all Venice. She had a *penchant* for scenes—and yet her scenes were exhilarating. There was no malice in them, they were like something in a play, and they shifted, like an English April, from shower to rainbow in the clouds. He deplored her tendency to make what he called an *éclat*, yet wasn't it her natural frankness that drove her to *éclat*—a pride, too, not in herself, but in him?

Why had he slipped that scrap of paper into her hand at their first meeting? Was it, as Hoppner believed, merely for his own amusement? For Teresa their affair had been an exalted dream of love that must last till death on earth and live for ever under the approving smile of the Madonna in Paradise. For him it had been but one more *liaison* with a married woman, and he had grown tired—of the scandal it had caused, the bewilderment, the distressing scenes with weeping husband and sobbing wife—and then, those long evenings at La Mira! He wrote to Hobhouse and his friends in England that he had sacrificed himself to save Teresa, but hadn't that pretty piece of renunciation been more wise than noble? To what a life had he surrendered Teresa! In the end she must pay the bill for his nobility. There she was now in Ravenna, reading drearily to her old husband noon and night. . . .

He had told his sister nothing of his latest escapade in Italy save to imply that it was a pastime. But eighteen days after Teresa had gone home—on November 28—he wrote to Augusta, enclosing a letter to show how serious a business it had been—for Teresa.

My dearest Augusta,

. . . since I wrote to you last I have had with all my household and family a sharp tertian fever. I have got well, but Allegra is still laid up though

I

convalescent; and her nurse—and half my ragamuffins—gondoliers, nurses —cook—footmen, etc. I cured myself without bark, but all the others are taking it like trees. I have also had another hot crater, in the shape of a scene with Count Guiccioli, who quarrelled with his wife, who refused to go back to him, and wanted to stay with me—and elope—and be as good as married. At last they made it up—but there was a dreadful scene; if I had not loved her better than myself, I could not have resisted her wish, but at thirty-one years, as I have, and such years as they have been—you may be sure—knowing the world that I would rather sacrifice myself ten times over—than the girl, who did not know the extent of the step she was so eager to take. He behaved well enough, saying "take your lover or retain me—but you shan't have both," the lady would have taken her lover as in duty bound—not to do—but on representing to her the destruction it would bring on her own family (five unmarried sisters) and all the probable consequences—she had the reluctant good grace to acquiesce and return with him to Ravenna. But this business has rendered Italy hateful to me, and as I left England on account of my own wife, I leave Italy because of another's.

You need not be frightened—there was no fighting—nobody fights here—they sometimes assassinate, but generally by proxy—and as to intrigue, it is the only employment; but elopements and separations are still more serious than even with us, being so uncommon, and indeed needless; as excepting an occasionally jealous old gentleman—everybody lets their spouses have a man or two—provided he be taken with decency. But the Guiccioli was romantic and had read *Corinna*—in short she was a kind of Italian Caroline Lamb—but very pretty and gentle, at least to me; for I never knew so docile a creature so far as we lived together, except that she had a great desire to leave her husband who is sixty years old—and not pleasant. There was the deuce—for her father's family (a very noble one of Ravenna), were furious against the *husband*—(not against me) for his unreasonable ways. You must not dislike her, for she was a great admirer of you, and used to collect and seal up all your letters to me as they came that they might not be lost or mixed with other papers; and she was a very amiable and accomplished woman, with however some of the drawbacks of the Italian character now corrupted for ages.

All this—and my fever—have made me low and ill; but the moment Allegra is better we shall set out over the Tyrolese Alps, and find our way to England as we can, to the great solace of Mr Fletcher . . . I cannot fix any day for departure—so much depending on circumstances—but we are to be in voyage as soon as it can be undertaken with safety to the child's health. As to the Countess G[uiccioli], if I had been single and could have married her by getting her divorced, she would probably have been of the party; but this being out of the question—though *she* was as "all for love or the world well lost"—I, who know what 'love' and 'the world' both are, persuaded her to keep her station in society.

Pray let Ada's picture be portable as I am likely to see more of the portrait than the original. Excuse this scrawl. Think that within this month I have had a *fever—an Italian husband and wife quarrelling;*—a sick family—and the *preparation for a December journey over the mountains of the Tyrol* all brewing at once in my cauldron. Yours.

P.S. I enclose *her* last letter to me by which you may judge for yourself —that it was a serious business—I have felt it such, but—it was my duty to do as I did as her husband offered to forgive everything if she would return with him to Ravenna and give up her *liaison.*

So, reflected Augusta, as she read this letter, my baby Byron has been in and out of mischief again with somebody else's wife, but he has behaved wisely, and this poor little woman from Ravenna is dead so far as he is concerned. By Christmas he will be home—then God help me— what shall I do? What will Annabella say?

His tertian fever, Byron told his friends in England, had left him feeling dull and unintellectual. But gradually he returned to his old task of "poeshie"—the "poeshie" that Teresa had inspired. He took up *The Prophecy of Dante* and spun it out for two cantos more. As he wrote, he began to identify himself more and more with Dante. He, too, was a poet and an exile, and his wife, like Gemma Donati, was a "cold partner who hath brought destruction for a dowry." By inference he exalted Teresa to the height of Beatrice, which was what Teresa wanted him to feel about their love.

He toiled away at the third canto of *Don Juan.* The grim old pirate, Lambro, had returned to his Grecian isle, and farewell now the love of Juan and Haidée! Juan was put on board ship and sold into slavery at Constantinople, and so drifted into the presence of the imperious Gulbayez in the Sultan's harem. Haidée went mad and died of a broken heart. Then he found that the canto was too long, so he divided it in two. The third canto ended where Teresa had left it—at angelus time and twilight falling on the Pine Forest. His friends and well-wishers should know—and the stupid British public and Annabella, for aught he cared—that in Canto I Donna Inez with her prudish airs was meant for his wife, but in Canto III with Haidée he told the broken story of illicit love. And if it were comfort to Annabella, he regretted now this love that he had thrown away.

With Teresa gone his passion for Venezuela collapsed. His friends had never been seriously alarmed by that hare-brained scheme. "Our poet is too good for a planter," Hobhouse told Murray. He would soon grow tired of camp-fires made of mares' legs and beef without salt or bread, of 'yellow jack' and plague and famine—in short, "no toothbrushes, no corn-rubbers, no *Quarterly Reviews* . . . plenty of all he abominates, and nothing of all he loves." But the restlessness remained —a homesick longing now. Why should he not come back to England and lead 'a charge of horse' for political reform—it would be fun to head a revolutionary committee in Leicestershire and furnish the 'patriots' with a faithful account of his mother-in-law's cattle, corn, and coach-horses.

By the end of November he was packing, and his friends in England were told they must expect to hear from him any day at Calais. Then he reopened his letter to Hobhouse to say that Dr Aglietti had just told him that Allegra had the "*droppa terzana,*" so the journey had to be postponed—"alas! here I am in a gloomy Venetian palace, never *more* alone than when alone—unhappy in the retrospect, and at least so much so in the prospect; and at the moment when I trusted to set out—taken aback by this indisposition of my child, which, however, thank God, as far as I can learn, is not dangerous; but very tiresome and tedious . . . all my plans . . . are lulled upon the feverish pillow of a sick infant."

November gave way to December, and the Alps were now lost in cold grey clouds, and with keen wind and icicles Christmas drew nearer. Allegra recovered, and the day for setting out upon their journey came at last. All the baggage had been carried downstairs and loaded on the gondolas, and Allegra was safely stowed away on board. The servants stood waiting. Byron was ready, dressed for the journey, with his gloves and cap on and riding-cane in his hand. And then—once more—in an hour of decision he said, "Let Fate decide, not me." His swords and pistols and ammunition were not yet on board. If the clock struck one before the gondola was fully loaded, he wouldn't set out that day. He went upstairs to his study. Fletcher looked like an offended deity, and the servants ran chattering about the palace, looking for what they wouldn't find. The clock struck one, and they lifted Allegra joyfully out of the boat and carried her upstairs to Byron's room to announce the will of God.

Douglas Kinnaird received a brief and gloomy letter, dated December 10. The journey home was postponed—"perhaps to the Greek Calends." Allegra was better; the last part of his new canto of *Don Juan* was "very *decent,* but dull—damned dull." But he must leave Venice. "I shall go again to Ravenna; anything better than England. It is better to be with a woman I love, at the risk of assassination, than in a country where I neither like, nor am liked. . . . But for all that, we shall or may meet in the spring."

To Murray he wrote on the same day with a peevish note added to his profound self-pity. The journey to England was definitely off, and no reason was given save his dislike for the island.

Perhaps I may take a journey to you in the spring; but I *have* been ill, and *am* indolent and indecisive, because few things interest me . . . I have got such a cold and headache that I can hardly see what I scrawl; the winters here are as sharp as needles. Some time ago, I wrote to you rather fully about my Italian affairs; at present I can say no more, except that you shall know further by and bye.

At this point Don Juan laid his pen down to wipe his streaming eyes —and blow his nose. Then he took up the pen again and continued resentfully on another topic.

Your Blackwood accuses me of treating women harshly; it may be so, but I have been their martyr. My whole life has been sacrificed *to* them and *by* them. I mean to leave Venice in a few days, but you will address your letters *here* as usual. When I fix elsewhere, you shall know.

P.S. Pray let my sister be informed that I am not coming as I intended: I have not the courage to tell her so myself, at least as yet; but I will soon, *with the reasons*. Pray tell her so.

Murray and Kinnaird were not anxious for his return to England—for many reasons that were kind and sensible. They received the news of his change of plan with equanimity and without surprise. They were sorry for his cold and his headache and his low spirits, but in the spring he would be writing blithely about another affair of gallantry among those easy-going Venetians. Murray sent the news to Augusta with his best respects.

Three or four days before Christmas Hoppner received a hasty, undated scrawl.

MY DEAR HOPPNER,

Partings are but bitter work at best, so that I shall not venture on a second with you. Pray make my respects to Mrs Hoppner, and assure her of my unalterable reverence for the singular goodness of her disposition, which is not without its reward even in this world. . . . Make, too, what excuses you can for my omission of the ceremony of leave-taking. If we all meet again, I will make my humblest apology; if not, recollect that I wished you all well; and, if you can, forget that I have given you a great deal of trouble.

In the end Augusta must be told the news direct. She received a brief and matter-of-fact letter, dated December 23, 1819. It came from Bologna.

The health of my daughter Allegra, the cold season, and the length of the journey induce me to postpone for some time a purpose (never very willing on my part) to re-visit Great Britain. You can address to me at Venice as usual. Wherever I may be in Italy, the letter will be forwarded. . . . In a letter to Murray, I requested him to apprize you that my journey was postponed; but here, there, and everywhere, know me,

Yours ever and very truly, B.

Augusta sighed when she laid her letter down. So he wasn't coming home, after all. Murray had told her that the reasons for this change would reach her in due time. Now she read them she was disappointed. It was not like her brother to alter his plans for anything so commonplace as a child's sickness or the coldness of the winter. She was a good-natured woman who never thought back very much and scarcely ever thought forward at all. As long as things were going comfortably for the moment she was contented. Byron was not coming home—that was well, and she was mildly sorry—and unutterably relieved. He wrote to her from Bologna, but that told her nothing—not even that he was going to Ravenna, where that funny little countess lived.

Hoppner whistled over his letter and tossed it with a scowl to his wife —who sighed, too, and doubtless shed a sentimental tear. She was kind—and gullible—and Swiss—and understood these things.

## CHAPTER II

# The Pilgrim returns

ALL this while Teresa was crying for the moon in Ravenna, and now the moon must come.

"My heart sank," she wrote, "while I watched the campaniles of Venice sink beneath the sea." Signora F—— was no longer with her, for Count Guiccioli had dismissed her in high displeasure from the post of duenna to his wife. But her maid sat with her in the coach and scowled bleakly at the Count. She found opportunity, when he was not by, to whisper in Teresa's ear, between sobs and sniffs, that everything was over—Milord Byron would never come to Ravenna—he had promised the Count not to—he was going away over the mountains to his own country—if he came to Ravenna the Count would have him murdered for sure—and Teresa's heart sank deeper yet. When they reached Ravenna she took to her bed and was delirious for a few days. Then she began to cough and spit blood. She grew thin and languid. Her soul, she wrote, was now only a mirror and an echo.

The Count, having won a victory with Byron's help, could afford not to insist too rigorously upon the terms of his bond. But he was arbitrary by nature and impatient and gradually asserted his rights as a husband. The everlasting readings were resumed, and now Teresa had no horse or companion to go riding with in the Pine Forest. But the Gamba family was up in arms. Teresa had taught them one thing—not to be frightened of her husband. Count Ruggiero roundly declared that Count Guiccioli was killing his young wife by harsh treatment. Grandfather Gamba took up the cry, and so did Uncle Cavalli, the leader of social life in Ravenna. The Vice-Legate was sympathetic. Upon their souls, they all declared, what sort of man was this Count Guiccioli to rob his wife of her *amico*—heretic and foreigner though he be! He had brought shame upon his order by an unworthy display of jealousy! And then to take his wife back by making an appeal to the *amico* whom he had banished from her graces! Surely he was a very credulous old man, too, and ladies whispered behind their fans that never had he poisoned wife nor stilettoed *amico* in all his days, but, as sure as Lent must come, he would be the death of his pretty little Gamba wife. Count Alessandro, despite his wealth, had lost prestige.

Against all orders Teresa wrote letters every day to her *amico*. His answers were melancholy and undecided. He said nothing about going to England, but protested sadly against her reproaches of desertion. He had acted for the best, he said. The mail service was not enough for Teresa. She sent him special messengers bearing letters by hand, with orders that he must send his answer by return. Nor was the Papal Government alone in employing agents to watch Byron's comings and goings in Venice. Gertrude Vicari and her sister-in-law Betti, a pretty, black-eyed *spazina* of Teresa's age, ran backward and forward with bulletin and message. Signora F—— remained behind in Venice and plied her trade of duenna, for love now and not for pay. She it was who reported the loading of the gondolas at the Palazzo Mocenigo, the clock striking one, and the sudden change in Byron's plans. Teresa's heart rose at the news, for in the closing days of November she had received a terrible letter from Venice, written in Italian, so that every word fell like a weight of lead.

You are, and will ever be, my first thought. But at this moment I am in a terrible state, not knowing which way to decide;—fearing, on the one hand, to compromise you for ever if I return to Ravenna, with all the consequences that must follow; and, on the other, to lose you, and myself, too, and all that I have known or tasted of happiness, if I nevermore may see you. I beg you, I implore you, calm your mind and believe I can only give up loving you with life itself.

I am going away, to save you, and I leave a country that has become unendurable to me without you. Your letters to F—— and to myself do wrong to my motives; but with time you will see how unjust you are. You talk of sorrow—I feel it, but words fail me. It is not enough that I must leave you—for motives that ere long you will be convinced were right—it is not enough that I go away from Italy with a wounded heart, after passing every day since you went away in loneliness, sick in body and soul—but I must bear your reproaches, without answering them and without deserving them. Farewell! In that word dies my happiness.

When Teresa read this letter she was in despair. Her heart went out in anguish to her lover, alone in his palace, sick of mind and sick in body from his fever. She rained down a thousand angry words upon her own head for reproaching him—she had thought only of herself—always he had been patient and kind and noble. But, most desperate thought of all, she would never see him again! That night the Count asked her to read to him, but as she read she burst out crying and the tears fell down upon her book. The Count raised his eyebrows and asked her what was the matter. In the past he had complained that she wasn't frank with him, but frankness was surely the first of Teresa's virtues and had given him trouble enough ere now. She blurted out the whole story—Lord Byron was leaving Italy, he wouldn't come to Ravenna because of his promise to the Count, and she would never see him again.

The Count muttered and frowned and called her a fool for her pains.

"*Dio mio!*" he exclaimed impatiently. "If your feeling for him is only friendship and the admiration he deserves, I don't say 'no' to his coming back."

Teresa wrote at once to Venice and sent the letter to the watchful Signora F—— by special courier. A few days later her father was in Ravenna, and she confided in him. Count Ruggiero told her to say to her *amico* that he desired his instant return—nay, more than that, he promised to write himself and beg Lord Byron to come—his daughter's health and happiness—the happiness of them all—depended upon his return. The first courier had come back with the news that Lord Byron was nowhere to be found. Away went a second, bearing two letters this time. In a few days he brought an answer back.

La F—— must have told you, *with her usual sublimity*, that Love has won. I couldn't find the strength of mind to leave the country where you are without seeing you at least once more; on *you* it must depend whether I ever leave you again. About the rest we will speak. You must know by now which will best help your well-being—my presence or my absence. I am a citizen of the world—all countries are alike to me. Ever since we knew each other you have been *the sole object of my thoughts*. I thought the best course for your peace of mind, and for your family's peace of mind, was for me to leave and go far, far away; for to be near you and not to go near you would have been impossible for me. But you have decided that I must come back to Ravenna. I shall come back—and I shall do—and I shall be—everything you wish. I can say no more.

So, sighing and laughing a little ruefully and blaming all things on Teresa, the Pilgrim of Eternity came riding back to Ravenna. It was Christmas Day when he returned, and the church-bells were pealing under leaden skies. But Teresa was happy again. The moon was shining now—hadn't she always known it would?

CHAPTER III

# Sing, Cuckoo!

THE first time that Byron came to Ravenna he came as a stranger. The provincial gentry greeted him politely and hospitably, but there had been a smiling reserve in their welcome, a great deal of curiosity and a spice of malice. Their visitor was English, and he arrived in their midst with a reputation for eccentricity and murky love-making. It was soon apparent that he had not come to Ravenna to look at the churches or lay books on Dante's tomb. Count Guiccioli's pretty wife was his attraction to the city. It was amusing, and not a little thrilling, to watch how he paid court to his *amica*. Obviously he knew nothing of the rules of the game of *cicisbeo* and even less about the temper of Count Guiccioli, who had never yet suffered an intruder gladly. If he flouted their conventions of love-making by galloping about the Pine Forest with his *amica* at Ave-Maria time, the ladies and gentlemen of Ravenna returned the compliment by dropping gentle hints of murder in the dusk.

But when he came the second time he arrived as an old friend and popular favourite. Whatever Count Guiccioli had decided, Ravenna society welcomed him as the acknowledged *cavalier servente* of the Countess Guiccioli. He was more than an old friend; he was now member of a large clan and everybody else's cousin. For the first time in his existence he had struck family life. The only child of a widowed mother, he had never known what brothers or cousins meant. Annabella, too, had been an only child and brought him little else but elderly parents-in-law. But now Count Gamba greeted him with open arms, as though he were his favourite son-in-law. He could not be too grateful for his chivalry where his daughter was concerned. His beautiful manners evaporated into charming *bonhomie*, and Byron found, much to his surprise, that behind the mask of Greek-nosed silence and old-world courtesy there lay a simple-minded country squire who, in the bosom of his family, was kindly and loquacious—in fact, not unlike Annabella's father—rosy, prosy Sir Ralph Milbanke. In Count Gamba's wake followed all the clan of Gamba from grandfather to grandchild, all the uncles and aunts and cousins, all the Cavallis and Capponis and Machiavellis, holding out their hands and haling him into their houses. Only Count Guiccioli preserved his former attitude of dignified politeness. He had recovered from his fit of weeping at La Mira and was his old inscrutable self.

138

The first impact with family life was exhilarating. Byron's spirits shot again into the welkin like a skylark; he ceased to be sorry for himself, and in a week's time his cold was gone and his humour had returned. He felt less of an exile and domestic outcast and thought of giving up his gypsy life. But the business of settling down must not be made too serious, and by the New Year his friends in England and Venice were regaled with the old gay letters, telling them the story of a well-regulated love-affair and life in a small provincial town.

The truth was that he liked the people in this mouldering little city that had dropped out of history long ago. They reminded him of Nottingham in his boyhood with their gossip, their candle-lighted card-parties, their tea-drinking and quadrilles—with this difference, that these people were not lawyers and parsons but noble folk of Gothic antiquity. They lived in large, gloomy palaces, and all had titles of some kind; their manners were stately in the old minuet way, and the ladies at evening parties were weighed down with ancient heirloom jewellery. It was Nottingham on a stately scale, if you will—an Italian Nottingham with its theatre and opera, its fairs and carnival and saintly festivals, which called for church-bells ringing and a general dressing-up.

It amused him to write to his friends in the manner of the vicar's daughter in the provinces writing to her cousins in town. You big people in London or Venice, he slyly insinuated, may think us little folks here quiet country mice, but we have our own notions of fun. True, there's not much to write about but the usual round of love and death, and even there the times are degenerate. The young men no longer twang guitars and serenade under windows with the voice and spirit of their fathers, nor do the local Capulets and Montagues pepper each other round street-corners in broad noonday with the careless audacity of old time. Alas, young people nowadays are solemn; they talk of nothing but horseflesh and liberty and are more apt to shoot a Papal *gendarme* than a rival under the balcony, as a lad of mettle should. In fact, the winter season had been dull—no new *liaisons* formed, no stabbing at theatre doors, nor any murder committed that was worth the name.

In Ravenna there was more rejoicing over one lover that returned to duty than for a thousand that lived in blameless sin. A party must be given, at which Byron and Teresa should be the guests of honour. The night after the poet's arrival the Marchese Cavalli opened the doors of his *palazzo* to the *beau monde* of Ravenna, and between two and three hundred of the best families attended the reception. There were music and dancing and cards, the old ladies wore their diamonds, and the Vice-Legate attended with the official clergy to shed the light of Papal benediction on the affair. Byron was obliged to put on knee-breeches, silk stockings, and brocaded coat, to gird on an old sword and carry a cocked-hat in his hand. Thus uncomfortably arrayed, he took Teresa under his arm and together they paraded, bowing and smirking like royalty, among the guests. Nobody seemed to think there was anything strange in the ceremony, and the women were all smiles and congratulations. Somehow, Byron realized, he had 'arrived' socially. Ravenna had adopted him, and his status was settled—he was cavalier to the Marchese Cavalli's niece. Nothing, in fact, could be more paternal than the attitude of the Marchese and his wife, the Donna Clelia, or more friendly than the welcome accorded him by his Cavalli cousins.

His last letter to Hoppner had been melancholy in tone. But on New Year's Eve he wrote him again, giving him a slightly wondering account of the Cavalli party. For youth and beauty and diamonds, he would have Hoppner know, the ladies of Ravenna put all your painted harridans in Venice to shame. "The G[uiccioli]'s object appeared to be," he wrote, with his studied lack of gallantry when he told Hoppner anything about Teresa,

> to parade her foreign lover as much as possible and, faith, if she seemed to glory in the scandal, it was not for me to be ashamed of it . . . I can understand nothing of all this; but it seems as if the G. had been presumed to be *planted*, and was determined to show that she was not—*plantation*, in this hemisphere, being the greatest moral misfortune. But [he added, with a return to contrition] this is mere conjecture, for I know nothing about it—except that everybody are very kind to her, and not discourteous to me. Fathers, and all relations, quite agreeable.

Whatever she wanted, Teresa had got it, and all Ravenna helped her to keep it. Hands were waved and fingers kissed as she drove home with her *amico* in the coach-and-six, and Byron respectfully took leave of her at her husband's door.

Three weeks later he was able to furnish Hoppner with a clearer report upon the situation—and his own state of mind, which once more was irresolute. Let another rule his life for him; he was past all care.

> I have not decided anything about remaining at Ravenna [he wrote]. I may stay a day, a week, a year, all my life; but this depends on what I can neither see nor foresee. I came because I was called, and will go the moment that I perceive what may render my departure proper. My attachment has neither the blindness of the beginning, nor the microscopic accuracy of the close of such *liaisons*; but "time and the hour" must decide upon what I do.

Of all women in his life, curiously, Teresa reminded him now most of Annabella. Sometimes, as he gazed on her eager, animated face, he slipped into a day-dream about his "Pippin" with her eyes turned up to his and drawn together in a puzzled frown. Like Annabella, Teresa had a touch of the blue-stocking about her; she loved poetry, she was pious and terribly in earnest. If anything, her sense of what was respectable was stronger even than Annabella's. But Annabella, he remembered with remorse, was sensitive, whereas Teresa was tough and could take a lot of punishment. Now she was doing for him what Annabella ought to have done—weaving his life into a domestic crazy-quilt. Remorse gave way to malice, and as the bells were ringing in the New Year, with its crop of good resolutions, he took up his pen and gave Annabella another flick.

His excuse for writing now was his *Memoirs*. He wished Annabella to see them and mark what she pleased for deletion. "You will perhaps say *why* write my life? Alas! I say so too, but they who have traduced it and blasted it, and branded me, should know—that it is they, and not I—are the cause." But, after all these years, with her in England and him in Italy, at least they could be "gentle" with each other.

I speak to you from another country, and as it were from another world, for this city of Italy is out of the track of armies and travellers, and is more of the old time. That I think of you is but too obvious, for three hours have not passed, since in society where I ought not to think of you, though Italian customs and Italian, perhaps even English, passions attach more importance and duty to such *liaisons* than to any nuptial engagement, the principal person concerned, said to me—"*Tu pensi a tua moglie*" ["You're thinking of your wife"]—it was so right a conjecture that I started and said, "Why do you think so?" The answer was—"because you are so serious— and she is the woman *tu ami la più ed amerài sempre*" ["you love most and always will love"]. If this had been said in a moment of anger or playfulness, I should have thought it the consequence of ill-humour or curiosity, but it was said without any such prologue, in a time of indifferent things and much good company, Countesses and Marchionesses and all the noble blood of the descendants of Guido di Polenta's co-temporaries with names eloquent of the middle ages.

Count Guiccioli was a proud man and rich and would not be outdone in courtesy by his wife's relations. He called at the *locanda* and insisted that Milord should take up his residence in the Palazzo Guiccioli—he would resign to him the whole second floor—dining-room, library, and all. The Count knew well how to deal with an Englishman. He was business-like and took care not to insult his lordship's insular conceptions of good form. Lord Byron should have his own servants and his own coach and horses while he stayed at the Palazzo Guiccioli, run his household the way he wished, order his own meals, and pay his own bills. In return for these concessions the Count would charge a sum which, paid monthly and spread over the years, would amply recoup him for the thousand pounds he had failed to obtain in the autumn, and, he assured his lordship, the sense of obligation would be all on his side. So Byron duly found himself living in a spacious set of apartments in his *dama's* house. He was comfortable but mystified. There had been the deuce of a racket in Venice when Teresa stayed in his house—why was it right now for him to live in her house at Ravenna? Did husbands rank as chaperons in their own homes in this crazy game of love upon which he was embarked? He gave the problem up. All Ravenna nodded and smiled upon him, as though nothing that hurt their sense of decorum had been done.

Lega Zambelli, the Secretary, came from Venice, and Tita, the bearded gondolier, and Agostino and Vincenzo and all the host of 'ragamuffins.' Gaps in their ranks were filled by recruiting yet wilder 'ragamuffins' from the hovels of Ravenna. Arrayed in the Byron livery they circulated through the Guiccioli palace and round the streets and squares. As luck would have it, their uniform was the same colour as that of the Papal Guard, and the Vice-Legate entered a protest on behalf of the Vatican. But Byron answered, haughtily and untruthfully, that such had been the colours of the Byron retainers ever since the battle of Hastings and ordered his ragamuffins, if they met with impudence from the Papal mercenaries, to draw their knives and fight for their livery. The bulldogs came from Venice, and the monkey, and the falcon, and the crow. Allegra came from Venice with her nurse and her own staff of servants. Then guns and firearms and ammunition came from Venice and were stowed away on the ground floor of the palace. Furniture was shifted round, pictures were taken down, and in due time a new fresco was painted on the walls of the main *salon*.

At the fashionable hour for driving in the Corso the blue-and-white coach went out and Allegra sat beside Teresa among the cushions as they drove. Byron joined the party, with Carluccio on horseback. Ravenna accepted the situation with tender equanimity. There, said every one, goes the young Countess Guiccioli with her English *amico* riding by her carriage. The boy on horseback is the old Count's son by a former wife, and the little girl is the *amico's* bastard child from England—don't they make a delightful group together! Byron was proud of the effect that his daughter's beauty made in Ravenna—she was a great favourite, he told Hoppner, and "shines among their dusky children like the milky way." Teresa was absorbed in her *amico* and would have gladly done without Allegra—like Carluccio, she was an intruder on her enjoyment. But Allegra's health improved under kindness and a little care. She was more clean and lively and called Teresa her "*mammina*." She grew vainer every day, and no one fought her baby will.

Count Guiccioli was often away upon those never-ending tours of his estates, and now his travels carried him as far away as Rome. When he returned to his house in Ravenna he must have felt like the owl that had invited the cuckoo to share his nest. Servants in a strange livery greeted him at his door and brawled with his own servants in the courtyard. Bulldogs growled at him as he climbed the stairs. A monkey gibbered at him from a doorway. A small child with a dimple in her chin welcomed him home with all the airs of a little princess, chattered in broad Venetian dialect, and held up her hand imperiously for him to kiss. Carluccio bowed before him gravely and ran downstairs, flourishing a fine new English riding-crop. He glanced through a door, and there sat his wife at her desk, struggling with her *amico's* Italian correspondence. In the distance a voice quavered upward into sharp and broken song that haunted all the palace with a cheerful note of ownership—the voice of the *amico*, trolling an air from Rossini in his bath.

The snow had been piled several feet high against the palace walls when Byron returned to Ravenna. Spring came, and he was plucking violets by the roadside with Teresa. King George III died in England. Byron wrote to Hobhouse that he would not return for the coronation. Let his "dearest duck," Annabella, waddle alone to that ceremony. He was contented where he was.

> I have settled into regular *serventismo*, and find it the happiest state of all. . . . I double a shawl with considerable alacrity; but have not yet arrived at the perfection of putting it on the right way; and I hand it in and out, and know my post in a *conversazione* and theatre; and play at cards as well as a man can do who of all the Italian pack can only distinguish *asso* and *re*, the rest for me are hieroglyphics. Luckily the play is limited to *papetti*, that is, pieces of four Pauls, somewhere in or about two shillings.

A quiet picture—Childe Harold playing cards with old dowagers. To Hoppner he admitted that quietness went hand in hand with dullness. Sometimes he varied the ritual of delivering the shawl by bringing away several shawls for Teresa's choice. Then there were wailing and confusion among the *serventi*, their ladies frowned, and Teresa was humiliated by her *amico's* stupidity. And Ravenna, he said, was

> a dreadfully moral place, for you must not look at anybody's wife except your neighbour's; if you go to the next door but one, you are scolded, and presumed to be perfidious. And then a *relazione* or an *amicizia* seems to be a regular affair of from five to fifteen years, at which period, if there occur a widowhood, it finishes by a *sposalizio*; and in the meantime it has so many rules of its own, that it is not much better.

In Ravenna, said Byron's friends in London, the "dear fellow" had surely "gone native." He lived with Italians and tried his best to behave, think, and even feel as an Italian. There were no English living in Ravenna, and few came to visit him there. His old friend William Bankes came in the winter, undeterred by Byron's warning that Ravenna was full of red hair. And in the spring Sir Humphry Davy, the scientist, drove over from Bologna on a visit to the Legate, a cleric with scientific tastes. He and Byron met several times, and Byron was all agog to go back with him to Bologna to pay his respects to Lady Davy. Sir Humphry could not help thinking that this eagerness to visit Bologna was inspired not so much by a wish to see Lady Davy as by a hope of giving his Contessa the slip. But he took a great liking to the city of Ravenna. With Byron he agreed that there was a fierce honesty about its people that was a welcome contrast to the refinement and corruption of Venice. Teresa was friendly and gracious with a compatriot of her *amico's*. "What do you call him?" she asked Byron. "A great chemist," quoth Byron. "What can he do?" asked Teresa. "Almost anything," said Byron. "Oh, then, *mio caro*, do pray beg him to give me something to dye my eyebrows black. I have tried a thousand things and the colours all come off; and besides, they don't grow; can't he invent something to make them grow?" Sir Humphry called upon Teresa and described at length his fourteenth ascent of Mount Vesuvius. Teresa was all interest and asked "if there was not a similar volcano in Ireland?" Sir Humphry looked puzzled, and Byron hastily interpolated the suggestion that she meant Mount Hekla, a volcano in Iceland. Teresa insisted upon her topography with the amiable pertinacity of "the feminie," and then conceded the point to the gentlemen with her usual triumphant smile.

Byron was abashed by the simplicity of his *amica*, for, whatever else he said about her, he always insisted that she was neither ignorant nor a fool. But there, he said, "they speak like children, when first out of their convents; and, after all, this is better than an English blue-stocking." He did not proffer Teresa's request to Sir Humphry to invent something for her eyebrows. Without shame she made the request herself, and the great chemist gave her a recipe at once.

Sir Humphry Davy found Teresa charming. He liked her—very much indeed. One day he would come back to Ravenna—delightful climate, and so friendly and quiet—there was game, too, in the forest worth a scientist's investigation—and when he came back, he hoped that the Countess Guiccioli would still be there. He was sure that, for all her prettiness, she was kind.

## CHAPTER IV

# Exit Brunello

BY the time that the violets had faded in the woods Count Guiccioli rebelled. A spiteful *abbé* had told him tales. He followed up the *abbé's* insinuations with inquiries of his own and came to the conclusion that all was not well in the Palazzo Guiccioli. He summoned Teresa into his presence and expostulated with her. He spoke in all seriousness to Lord Byron, who withdrew from his house in a huff. Teresa scolded her husband, and Byron returned, and then she scolded him. The Count and Byron greeted each other with cold politeness when they crossed on the stairs. In private the Count returned to his old game of snarling and banging on the table with his fist, but his wife bent her neck meekly under the storm and faded quietly from the room. Finally the Count took a leaf out of Byron's book and left the Palazzo Guiccioli in a huff. Then he came back to mount guard over the stable door.

He was a practical man and went the English way in procuring justice for himself against his wife and her English *amico*. He had, he declared, obtained the "services" of many "famous witnesses" to the act of adultery on his wife's part. With their evidence he laid his case before the courts at Rome. He was firm but, as surely all husbands must admit, reasonable in his demands. Once more he claimed that Teresa must choose between her husband and this English nobleman who dwelt on the second floor of the Palazzo Guiccioli. If she cast the vote in her husband's favour, he would forgive her infidelity and take her back into his house—or that part of it in Ravenna, at any rate, that was still his. If she refused his offer of a free pardon, he still insisted on his rights as a husband. Teresa must be parted from her lover and placed in a convent for the rest of her days. The Count was not a man to lay his plans hastily. Whichever way Teresa decided, he would not be the loser in a financial sense. He would keep her dowry, and Byron would, he hoped, continue to pay rent for the second floor of the Palazzo Guiccioli. He might be angry, but, as Count Rangone had told Teresa, old Brunello was a man who laid his plans carefully and well.

Ravenna rose in its wrath against the Count. Never for over a hundred years had there been such a rank case of 'husbandry' in their annals. The women were naturally louder in their exclamations of shocked virtue than the men, but even Byron's rivals among the local *cavalieri serventi* cried shame upon the Count, and where *dama* and *cavalier* were agreed, it was not for husbands to take an independent tone. But the common people of Ravenna, who loved Byron for his charities, were just as fierce on behalf of the lovers as were the ladies and their appendages. This kind of support, said Byron, meant nothing for the morals of the case, for women and the mob always take the side of wrongdoers in a conflict with the law—particularly when this popular passion called love enters into the picture. But even the lawyers of Bologna refused to plead Count Guiccioli's cause. They demanded from the "famous witnesses" more lively evidence of adultery than locked doors and tumbled beds. The nobility of Romagna were humiliated by such an abject admission of 'coronation' from one of their own order. Here was a man, they said, who accused his wife of adultery and then petitioned the Pope to discharge the paramour and send his wife home, as though nothing had been said—or done, for that matter—about adultery. He pleaded that Byron had always seemed to like him better than Teresa, and when he had discovered his mistake he had endured the affair until he could stand it no more. On the top of that confession of utter folly he boasted that he had watched the lovers carefully to find out in how "deep water" they were! He had suborned witnesses, too, to prove his case! Well, no doubt his hirelings had not spared his feelings in telling him how deep the water was! He had been warned in Venice that this Englishman was a dragon among the ladies. Either the old man was a fool or he was a rogue— a fool if he had only now discovered the *liaison*—a rogue if he had connived at it all this time for no better reason than eventually blabbing to the world for some bad purpose of his own.

When she was accused of adultery Teresa proudly refused to deny the charge. The Count was infuriated, and her friends were thrown into a fever of alarm. Injured innocence should have been her pose. Byron once more summoned common sense to his aid and advised her to come to terms with her husband. He pointed out the unfortunate state of a separated wife in Italy. He reminded her that the priests would not let lovers live together unless the husband sanctioned it, and that her husband refused to do. He indulged, as he told Tom Moore, "in the most exquisite moral reflections," but they did not help, as he knew they would not. There it was; the Count was old and obstinate, and Teresa was young and a woman, determined to sacrifice everything to her affections. She answered her lover's arguments with the old retort that had baffled Count Guiccioli at La Mira. "I will stay with him," she told Byron, "if he will let you remain with me. It is a hard thing that I should be the only woman in Romagna who is not to have her *amico*. But if not, I will not live with him, and as for the consequences, love, etc."— "you know how females reason on such occasions," quoth Byron to Moore.

In the past Byron had persuaded himself that he had made the greater sacrifice when he surrendered Teresa to her husband, but to-day he realized that he would not be allowed to practise that piece of nobility a second time. Teresa would not accept his sacrifice, would not allow him to suffer now as he had suffered then for her sake. Now it was her turn to make sacrifices, and gladly she gave up for him wealth and position, good name, rich jointure when she was a widow, and all prospects of a second marriage, and impulsively she declared, when he protested, that there was no merit in her sacrifice, for she was only doing what she wanted. Byron gave in to her argument, which he found unanswerable in truth or reason. He had told her when he returned to Ravenna that he would do all and be all that she wanted—very well, then, he would stand by, he would not quit the Palazzo Guiccioli nor leave Ravenna while the Church was meditating on her fate. He was kinder with Teresa than ever, and when she burst into his room with appeals for sympathy he threw down his pen and caressed her, and out again they went riding in the woods.

Towards Count Guiccioli he tried to conduct himself with dignified politeness with just a hint of commiseration thrown into his smile when they met. But it was the Count's ill fortune always to wound the pride of others. In his bill of complaint against his wife he had stated that her paramour's age was thirty-five. This charge rankled with Byron, and he so far dropped his philosophic pose as to write the Count a sarcastic letter. His age, he wished him to know, was a matter of public record, and the Count in his insolence had merely made himself ridiculous in the eyes of God and man—how would he like it if Byron were to speak of him as a man of seventy—though that were only adding a seventh to his real age! Byron, too, Count Guiccioli realized bitterly, was added to the host of men who disliked him.

Byron felt that he owed the Gambas some amends for the trouble that he had brought upon their daughter and talked of making settlements in money if Count Guiccioli should discard his wife. But the Gambas rejected his offer with indignant pride. Their quarrel was with old Brunello, and they pushed their attack with the greatest fury.

Pietro in Rome forgot his dislike of his sister's foreign *amico* and sprang instantly to their defence. With all the haughtiness of nineteen in its most belligerent mood of pained reason he wrote to Count Guiccioli, demanding an explanation of his incomprehensible conduct about Lord Byron. The Count replied as haughtily by sending him—without comment—a detailed list of his complaints against his wife and an *exposé* of the evidence of the "famous witnesses." Pietro returned to Ravenna, hugged his sister, and folded Byron in his arms. Count Gamba made no claims, like his son, to sweet reason. He sent two gentlemen to call upon his son-in-law and ask his choice in weapons and called him into the field.

Once more Count Guiccioli brought the scorn of Ravenna tumbling about his ears, for he declined his father-in-law's invitation on the score of respect for his white hairs. People don't fight in Romagna, said Byron cynically; they shoot, like Irishmen, round the corner. He was warned to be careful how he went riding in the forest, but he went out there just the same. Sometimes he invited a friend to accompany him. Byron whistled gaily as he rode, but the friend peered with an anxious eye into bush and undergrowth. There was really no need for alarm. The Count, said Byron, was too stingy to spend five *scudi*—the regulation price for a good, clean *bravo* in Ravenna.

The Gambas decided that Teresa must be rescued from the toils of an impossible husband. They had influence with the Vatican. Pope Pius VII—the gentle, courageous Chiaramonti—was an old friend of the family. He had been the officiating priest at the wedding of Teresa's parents. The old Marchesa Sacrati, Teresa's great-aunt, had been long years ago the *dama* of His Holiness, in so far as a young bishop was allowed to play the game of *serventismo*. Added to his pleasant memories of the Gamba family was a profound dislike of that robber of Church lands, Count Guiccioli. He lent a kindly ear to the Gambas' appeal for a separation of their daughter from her husband. He would not, he promised, allow this "madman of a Guiccioli" to shut up his young wife in a convent if he could help it.

For weeks Teresa's fate lay upon the knees of the Pope. No one looks for diplomacy in a government, yet here was a matter that required the deftest handling. Fortunately the Vatican is not as other powers; it is an old power and a spiritual one, and the Church rose like a dove from the ark over the troubled waters. In July Cardinal Rusconi notified Teresa that "His Holiness benignly condescends to allow you to leave your husband's house and return to the house of your father, Count Ruggiero Gamba, where you may live in that laudable manner that is proper in an honest and noble lady who is separated from her husband." Count Guiccioli, added the Cardinal with relish, had been instructed to make his wife an allowance of one hundred *scudi* a month. She might take from her husband's house "linen, clothes, and such other things as appertain to the decent adornment of a married woman." Jewellery, however, she must not carry away, nor, in the circumstances, any but the more worthless of her wedding presents. Count Gamba was instructed that he now, not Count Guiccioli, was guardian of his daughter's honour, and His Holiness looked to him for a strict accounting for his trust. Lord Byron was an Englishman, a heretic, and lay outside the paternal concern of His Holiness. His name was not mentioned in the rescript. Thus, with the customary benediction, the Pope closed the case of Count Guiccioli against his wife.

The Count awaited the sentence of the Pope in his house at Ravenna.

Once, through a messenger, he had politely suggested to Lord Byron that he should quit the house, but Byron replied as politely that he must decline to go, and the Count acquiesced. At least he would show his critics in Ravenna that it was not vulgar jealousy that had prompted his appeal to the courts at Rome. On the contrary, he wished only to regulate the sphere of influence of his lodger in his domestic life. Byron, on his side, felt himself bound by his promise to Teresa to stand by in her hour of trouble. So it came to pass that when Cardinal Rusconi's letter arrived, the Count and Teresa and Byron were living together under the same roof.

Count Gamba knew his duty. He must at once remove his daughter from her husband's house. She was not safe there for one good reason—and another. One noonday, while Count Guiccioli was taking his *siesta*, he arrived with Pietro at the Palazzo Guiccioli in the Papal Legate's coach with the Papal Legate's footmen. Pietro went in search of Byron, leaving Count Gamba to speak with his daughter alone. The carriage was waiting below, he whispered in her ear; she must come with him at once to Filetto, while her husband was still asleep. Darkly he hinted his reason for insisting that she come with him now. Her husband was unscrupulous. He might defy the Pope and spirit her away to one of his country houses and lock her up. He had another reason for not wishing her to stay a moment longer in the Palazzo Guiccioli, but if Teresa could not guess it her father was too kind to mention it.

Hastily Teresa packed a few belongings and crept downstairs past her sleeping husband's door. Byron was standing with Pietro by the carriage, looking thoughtful. She embraced him, there were a few hurried words, tears, promises of reunion. Count Gamba cried out impatiently, bidding her waste no time. She climbed into the carriage, slowly and reluctantly, with still a backward glance into her lover's brooding face. Pietro and Count Gamba climbed in after her, and with a loud crack of the coachman's whip away they drove to Filetto. Byron stood watching until the carriage rounded the corner of the street. Then he turned and went back slowly into the house.

Count Guiccioli woke from his *siesta*. With a grim smile he heard that his wife was gone. He gave orders that the coach be ready to carry him away, too, on the morrow.

Upstairs Byron sat at his desk with his chin propped on his fist, staring blankly through the window at the falling rain. Was this the end? He pulled forward a sheet of paper and wrote, "Dear Douglas." He paused, then rummaged in a drawer and pulled out several sheets of verses. He had written them a long time ago, when he was sick in Venice and Teresa had gone back home with her husband to Ravenna. Should he send a copy now to Kinnaird? Yes, he would, but he would tell him nothing of the turn that his love-affair had taken.

Could Love for ever
Run like a river,
And Time's endeavour
    Be tried in vain—
No other pleasure
With this could measure;
And as a treasure
    We'd hug the chain.
But since our sighing
Ends not in dying,
And, form'd for flying,
    Love plumes his wing;
Then for this reason,
Let's love a season
But let that season be only Spring.

When lovers parted
Feel broken-hearted,
And, all hopes thwarted,
    Expect to die;
A few years older,
Ah! how much colder
They might behold her
    For whom they sigh!
When link'd together,
Through every weather
We pluck Love's feather
    From out his wing—
He'll sadly shiver
And droop for ever,
Shorn of the plumage which sped his Spring.

Wait not, fond lover!
Till years are over,
And then recover
    As from a dream;
While each bewailing
The other's failing,
With wrath and railing,
    All hideous seem—
While first decreasing,
Yet not quite ceasing,
Wait not till teasing,
    All passion blight:
If once diminished
His reign is finished—
One last embrace, then—and bid good-night!

## CHAPTER V

# Rain and Drizzle

THE old Count vanished from the scene like a bad fairy. He drove away from Ravenna, still rigid and austere, in all the pride of armorial coach and six black horses. He was done for ever with 'theocracy' in Romagna. He would settle in Venice, where the Austrians, at any rate, would guarantee a Government that knew its own mind. The Pope one day, he reflected with a sardonic grin, would have cause to repent his leniency to the Gamba family. He was rid of that feckless breed now —rid of the *Carbonari*, too, and their exactions. He had failed to tame Teresa and, for his pains in fighting her, had been made a laughing-stock and scapegoat. But at the convent of Santa Chiara in Venice he had daughters, and in time they would feel the weight of a father's hand.

Byron was now master of the Palazzo Guiccioli. The Count's servants were withdrawn, and his own 'ragamuffins' and his dogs and birds and beasts spread through the house. Only the Count's porter stayed behind —to collect the rent and report on damage to the property. This fellow was a remnant of the feudal age. He was humiliated because the Count's marriage had broken down. He missed his stern and masterful overlord and mourned his "pretty, smiling Contessa" who had brought sunshine and laughter into the gloomy house. He despised this limping Englishman who lorded it now in his master's place. He kept a surly eye upon his movements and found him no better than a poet! What was to be said in favour of a nobleman who sat up all night, drinking gin and writing songs? When, in later years, sentimental pilgrims came to see the room where Byron had written poems, the old porter showed it with a sneer. This *Inglese* was a Punchinello and, like all his race, mad.

Byron sent away his verses and took stock of the situation. His comedy in Ravenna had taken a turn not authorized by the stage and come to an unexpected climax. The husband, for all his talk of jealousy and shooting, had wept on the lover's shoulder and begged for his wife, and home the wife had gone. Now the lover was left kicking his heels in the husband's house with wife lost in the wood and husband flown across the hill. A virtuous ending, no doubt, to a tale of mischief, but the laugh was on the lover. For, sombre thought, he must now shoulder the burden of making Teresa happy. He had promised her, against his better judgment, to stand by when the Count claimed his rights, and now, it would seem, he must stand by for ever and a day. The Gambas would take no monetary compensation for the trouble he had brought upon their daughter, but he told them that he felt in honour bound to marry her when Count Guiccioli died, though how that was to be done, with Annabella living in chaste seclusion in England, he did not know. Count Gamba was puzzled by his offer, but decided that Lord Byron was satisfying some incomprehensible English point of honour. Now that Teresa was a wife without a husband she was no longer entitled to an *amico*, and Byron henceforth could be nothing but a delightful acquaintance. Deep in his heart Count Gamba hoped that, when she married again, Teresa would give him an Italian for a son-in-law.

With Byron's promise Teresa was ready to play the game the English way. Italians would not understand, but now she was 'engaged' to Byron. True, from the English point of view she had confused the steps. She had jumped from 'falling in love' to 'honeymoon,' the 'proposal' had been omitted, and 'betrothal' came too late in the game for propriety. An island critic would add that in the lifetime of her husband a lady does not become 'engaged' to another man. But in old age Teresa insisted with English and American people that, when she left Count Guiccioli to live under her father's roof, she had become Lord Byron's affianced wife. She did not say this to placate the fondness of English-thinking races for modesty in matters of the flesh. She explained a situation that they would be sure to understand.

Every crisis in her love-affair found Teresa thinking swiftly and surely and ready to make concessions to her lover's English way of thought. As she was his affianced wife a certain reserve must now enter into their relationship. That, perhaps, was as well. Count Gamba was a man of honour. He had given his word to the Pope. He loved Teresa, was kind, wished Lord Byron well, and wrote a poem in his praise; but he was a stricter guardian than Count Guiccioli had been.

The poet sometimes shared the porter's regret that the old Count lived no more in Ravenna. With his departure a thrill of naughtiness was gone from the affair. Byron chafed against the gentle chains that Teresa laid upon him. Her father had carried her off to Filetto, fifteen miles away, and there she remained all the rest of summer till the verge of winter. It was ill work being constant to a woman who lived so far away. Once or twice he mounted his horse and rode out to Filetto. The family greeted him with open arms, and he sat there in the rose-garden, sunning himself in their affection. But if he rode with Teresa in the forest, Pietro or Vincenzo was only too glad to join the party. They blazed and banged away with their guns and woke the echoes with their hunting-cries, but they never strayed far out of sight. When the angelus rang, Count Gamba looked at his watch and worried about the dark falling—hadn't his friend Byron better be getting back to Ravenna?

Then the autumn came, and Count Gamba had his way. Equinoctial gales blew inland from the sea with a damp heavy sough and a far-off moan of screaming seagulls; a grey mist wound along the brakes, and for days and weeks the rain fell steadily. Bridle-path and woodland track vanished into bog, and Byron could go out riding no more. He moped at home beside the fire and played with Lion, the mastiff. Teresa wrote to him every day and sent him flowers from Filetto, but he dropped her letters with a yawn to the floor.

Because she wasn't there he was cross with her. Hadn't he sacrificed a great deal for her sake—followed her to Ravenna, lived under the same roof with her, stood by when her husband would have called her back? He made her jealous scenes through his letters. One day, he discovered, she had come to Ravenna for an hour on business of her own. She hadn't come to see him, hadn't told him she was coming or that she had come and gone. What right had she to hide anything from him? What business had she in Ravenna that he must know nothing about? He blamed his ill-temper on the weather. "This time of year," he wrote (September 28, 1820), "kills me with sadness—when I am thus sick in mind—it is better for every one else I keep away from them. I thank you from my heart for the roses. Love me. My soul is like the leaves that fall in autumn—quite yellow." Then the Byron laugh, and a lover's pinch for Teresa—"there's *poetry* for you!"

In the winter Count Gamba moved into the family house in Ravenna. Pietro came with him, and resolutely Teresa came, too. Her father would not allow her to visit the Palazzo Guiccioli, but she persuaded him that the Pope would surely have no objections to Byron visiting his bride in her father's house. The order went out to Byron, and every evening he donned his greatcoat and rode through the streets to the Casa Gamba. He read his poems to Teresa; she listened and criticized and gave counsel and encouragement. She played on the piano and sang old country tunes and songs to Indian airs in the loud, emphatic voice of a *prima donna*, so different from her voice in conversation. He thanked her, and she smiled, and he criticized her singing and her songs. They talked about religion, about people, about love considered as an abstract passion, and Teresa sighed, and Byron yawned. Count Gamba came in from the theatre, vacuous and kindly, and the talk dropped to weather, snow, slippery streets, church-bells ringing the hour, and the best way for his lordship to take in riding home. Then in came the "no less Count," Pietro, fresh from a political meeting, and the talk shifted to Italy and freedom. Towards midnight Byron rose, kissed Teresa's hand, and said good-night. Pietro accompanied him to the door and stood there for a moment, whispering and talking about "plots." Back he rode to the Palazzo Guiccioli to drink gin and write poetry with the snowbound night deepening all round him.

To while away his boredom he kept a diary. So little happened that

he chronicled his state of mind more often than his actions. "Mist—
thaw—slop—rain—" he wrote gloomily, and then again "Rain—mist—
snow—drizzle." He stayed at home all the morning and looked at the fire
and wondered when the post would come. Then he read the newspapers
and meditated on fame, tried on a new coat and fed the crow. Some
fool had stepped on its leg, and it had gone lame. The falcon was "pretty
brisk" and the cats were "large and noisy," but the monkeys were out
of sorts and the horses kicking their heels off in the stables. . . . He
took up Bacon's *Apophthegms* listlessly and read them for a while, then
shouted for Fletcher and showed him seven or eight passages marked
where the philosopher had committed blunders such as "a schoolboy
might detect." The "learned" Fletcher carried the book off to copy the
offending passages out with his lordship's corrections. . . . Dinner, with
plum pudding, but he would *not* eat the two apples that English bumpkin
Fletcher had laid shyly beside his plate as a Twelfth Night gift. . . .
"Clock strikes—going out to make love. Somewhat perilous, but not
disagreeable. . . . Heard a little music—like music. . . . Found there the
Countess Gertrude Vicari, Betti Vicari and her husband . . . Pretty
black-eyed woman *that*—*only* nineteen—same age as Teresa—who is
prettier, though." . . . On the way home "very high wind—lightning
—moonshine—solitary stragglers muffled in cloaks—women in masks
—white houses—clouds hurrying over the sky, like spilt milk blown out
of a pail—altogether very poetical. It is still blowing hard—the tiles
flying, and the house rocking—rain splashing—lightning flashing—
quite a fine Swiss Alpine evening, and the sea roaring in the distance."
. . . More moping by the fire. . . . "What I feel most growing upon me
are laziness and a disrelish more powerful than indifference. If I rouse,
it is into fury. . . . Oh! there is an organ playing in the street—a waltz,
too! I must leave off and listen . . . Music is a strange thing . . . Laziness,
is that the 'root of all evil'—no, the master of all passions? Who knows?
. . . What is the reason that I have been, all my lifetime, more or less
*ennuyé*? . . . I will go to bed, for I find that I grow cynical."

One evening in January—"deuced muggy," nothing but "slop and
rain"—he came back to his big, empty house from the Casa Gamba feeling "hopeless." Music, and then chatter with Pietro about an actress!
Why should he go there every night? Love—gallantry—politeness? He
jotted down a few sarcastic reflections on the "feminie" in his diary.
They were in this century of enlightenment a barbarous remnant of the
Dark Ages—of a dead and useless chivalry—artificial—unnatural in all
their emotions. Slaves, they make slaves of us all. Let them mind home
—and be well fed and clothed—but not mixed in society. "Well educated, too, in religion—but to read neither poetry nor politics—nothing
but books of piety and cookery. Music—drawing—dancing—also a little
gardening and ploughing now and then . . . I have seen them mending

the roads in Epirus with good success. Why not, as well as hay-making and milking?" From women he jumped without a conscious thought to *ennui*. Why was he so easily bored? Why did he wake in low spirits every morning? Violent passion stirred him sometimes, or a dose of salts. Just now he moped in quietness. "I . . . like being alone better than any company—except [he added remorsefully] the lady's whom I serve. But I feel a something which makes me think that, if I ever reach near to old age, like Swift, 'I shall die at top' first. Only I do not dread idiotism or madness so much as he did. On the contrary, I think some quieter stages of both preferable to much of what men think the possession of their senses."

To Murray he complained bitterly of the inroads that his love-affair made upon his work. He was writing *Marino Faliero* when Teresa's fight with her husband was reaching a crisis. "I never wrote nor copied an *entire scene of that play*," he said, "without being obliged to *break* off—to *break* a commandment, to obey a woman's, and to forget God's . . . The lady always apologized for the interruption, but you know the answer a *man* must make when and while he can." But he was not fair to Teresa. Of all his "feminie" she most respected his poetry, though she still could not read it in English. She loved to discuss his work with him, to listen to him translate, and if he were annoyed by unkind reviews she was distressed. She wished he wouldn't always gibe at all he wrote as "poeshie" and "versifying," as though he were ashamed of following in the footsteps of her other hero—Dante.

Byron relied on her sympathy, too. When a notice appeared in the *Milan Gazette* saying that *Marino Faliero* had been damned in perform-ance at London, he wrote to her reminding her of their days together when he was working on that play. How all men conspired against him! The tragedy had never been written for performance in the theatre, as well she knew, for "it was written at your side, and at a time certainly rather more *tragic* for me as a *man* than as an *author*—for *you* were in distress and danger." He went on to complain that people said that he had "given a reading of the play." Where, if you please? In Ravenna? And to whom? To that illustrious man of letters, Fletcher, he supposed. No woman could fail to respond to this appeal for sympathy, though Teresa sighed to think that her lover forgot an audience in Ravenna yet more admiring than his valet.

The proof that she did no harm to his work lies in the poetry that he produced in Ravenna days. In her honour he wrote his "Danticles," as he sportively called *The Prophecy of Dante*, and translated the story of Paolo and Francesca from the *Inferno*. He translated Pulci's *Morgante Maggiore* into "cramp English." He wrote three cantos of *Don Juan*—numbers three, four, and five—the best, perhaps, certainly the most popular, of the poem. He essayed drama in the Alfieri vein with *Marino*

*Faliero* and *The Two Foscari.* He turned from Venetian history and wrote the tragedy of *Sardanapalus.* Then he tried his hand at dramatizing the Old Testament in *Cain* and *Heaven and Earth.* Finally, before he left Ravenna for good, he started work upon *The Vision of Judgment.* Side by side with these greater works he wrote a vindication of Pope and minor poems such as *The Irish Avatar, Hints from Horace,* and *The Blues.*

More than ever Teresa looked upon herself as the Beatrice of her poet, inspiring him to write, encouraging him, always listening; and, as his Beatrice, she had the right to dictate now and then. Certainly she helped him in one practical way. She had saved him from debauchery in Venice, and somehow, through all the storms of Count Guiccioli's wrath, she steered him into tranquillity. He could mope now in quietness; he had a comfortable home all to himself in her husband's palace, an affectionate family life among the Gambas, and leisure to write. How much farther did her influence go? He wrote his "Danticles" to please her, also the Ave Maria lines in *Don Juan.* The old pirate, Lambro, in that poem, perhaps, owed something to Count Guiccioli. Did Haidée of the love-scenes owe anything to *her?* Was *she* the prototype of Mirrha in *Sardanapalus,* or of golden-haired Aurora Raby in the last cantos of *Don Juan?*

Teresa, no doubt, exaggerated her rôle, but she was not without shrewdness. Byron often talked about religion with her. So far as she was concerned there was nothing in that subject left to discuss. Everything had been settled by a good-natured Italian divinity several thousand years ago. She had no sense of sin. Like the old French *marquise* she was sure that God would never damn a man of quality. A woman's duty was to compass happiness here on earth, and after death she entered into the glory of the Lord. Sin, like poverty or sickness, was a cross that the human race must bear, but it counted nothing towards damnation at the Judgment Seat—cruelty, meanness, bad manners, would count there, but never sin. But, she observed, her lover was on his knees to an angry Jehovah and did not share her certain hope of being one of the Elect. He questioned, doubted, defied, and, in his tragedy *Cain,* gave voice to much that troubled him. Teresa neither doubted nor defied, but for her Cain, the doubter and rebel, was her lover, and she understood, and let him rave as a Protestant. All her life she defended the play against the charge of blasphemy. It revealed Byron as the man she knew, talking of religion beside her harpsichord in the evening—a Christian, troubled and groping blindly, but a believer in God—an honest heretic, slowly stumbling upward into Paradise.

If Cain were Byron the Calvinist, Sardanapalus was Byron the voluptuary, lotus-eating in Italy. As he saw his hero, here was a man who for one moment wrenched himself free of the thraldom of the senses to become a warrior and a leader of men. In such a play Woman must be little more than a symbol, a shadow in the background, typifying the very slavery from which Sardanapalus would fain escape. He drew up a list of *dramatis personæ*, sketched out the story, and went to the Casa Gamba to discuss the play. All the woman was now aroused in Teresa, and she understood everything but the point. Where is your heroine? she demanded in her best blue-stocking manner. And, with kindling eyes, Where is Love? A woman's love inspires a man to noble deeds. Besides, with a drop to reason, you can't write a tragedy without love in it—that's a truth in human nature. "She quarrelled with me," wrote Byron in his diary, "because I said that love was *not the loftiest theme* for true tragedy; and, having the advantage of her native language, and natural female eloquence, she overcame my fewer arguments. I believe she was right. I must put more love into *Sardanapalus* than I intended." So the Greek slave Mirrha entered into the tragedy to inspire Sardanapalus by talk of love and liberty. She is eloquent, artless, earnest, and ubiquitous. Sardanapalus fights and wins and fails, and fights again and falls, but Mirrha is always at hand to inspire or sympathize. Dare we say it, knowing that she owed her existence to Teresa?—she is a gentle little bore. But she is devoted unto death and dies with her lover in the end.

In *Sardanapalus* Teresa won a minor victory. Her fiercest battle was fought over *Don Juan*, and there, for a moment, she won a victory over her poet that no woman nor all his host of men friends had ever gained. Always the undercurrent of mockery in that poem had jarred upon her. In Juan she saw another phase of her lover and clung obstinately to her belief that he was "a nice boy," but why must her Byron always jeer at the things he most cared about? He only gave his enemies an opportunity to traduce him as a cynic and a profligate. She read the first two cantos in a French translation and was horrified. She scolded Byron for his caricature of Annabella and refused to listen to his protest that the likeness between Donna Inez and the English lady was one of type, not design. Yet more shocking was the virtuous tirade with which Donna Julia belaboured her husband when he was scouring her bedroom for her lover. When Juan vomited in sea-sickness over his *dama's* broken-hearted letter of farewell Teresa, like Francesca, "read no more that day." She tried to pardon this ribaldry by remembering that it had been written by Byron before he met her. But she was no happier with the way the story was going since Haidée died, for now Juan was fighting for a cause already lost with Dudu in the harem. For his own sake she begged Byron to stop writing the poem.

He protested ruefully that it was a better poem than *Childe Harold* and would live longer.

"Ah, but," cried Teresa, with shining eyes uplifted, "I would rather

have the fame of Childe Harold for three years than an immortality of
Don Juan!"

Byron threw up his hands in humorous despair. Oh, the absurd
"womenkind," always wanting him to be Childe Harold! They all hated
Juan. Augusta said his don was "odious," and even Harriette Wilson had
written and told him not to be "vulgar." Teresa was no better than the
rest. But he gave in. He promised to write no more *Don Juan*.

Teresa was proud of her victory but a little frightened and repentant.
Once more she had been unreasonable and Byron had been noble.
"Remember, *mio Byron*," she wrote to him, "the promise you have
made me. Never can I tell you the satisfaction that I feel—so great is
the feeling of happiness and confidence with which your sacrifice has
inspired me—all the more because words explain so little what is passing
in the soul! If you could have seen fully how it was with *mine* yesterday,
I am sure you would be in some way rewarded for your sacrifice! I kiss
you, *mio Byron*, 1000 times. *La tua amantissima in eterno*." Woman-
like she added a postscript, heaping maledictions on the cause of their
offence. "I'm only sorry D. Giovanni isn't still in Hell!"

Byron sent this note to Murray and told him that there would be no
more *Don Juan*. "The truth is," he declared, . . . "the women hate
everything which strips off the tinsel of *sentiment*; and they are right, as
it would rob them of their weapons."

CHAPTER VI

# *Conspiracy and Flight*

THE Gambas were an exasperating family—untidy, improvident, wrong-headed—but it must be confessed they existed likably. For Count Ruggiero Byron had a real affection, calling him 'Papa,' like a good son. Count Ruggiero had notions of honour, but was tranquil in enforcing them, and Byron could not but respect him for his independence in one thing—like his daughter, he would take no presents. An *amicizia* with a great English poet was for him a reward in itself. From 'Papa' Byron's affection spread to the rest of the family. Ippolito was but a boy to romp with, but Vincenzo was a youth of honest rustic tastes. He was fat, had missed the good looks of the family, and in company was silent like his father, but in the home he was as animated and theatrical as the rest. His devotion to his sister was dog-like, he fetched and carried for her all day long and gladly performed the same service for her *amico*. But with Pietro, the elder brother, Byron made a friendship that lasted all his life.

Pietro was twenty years old, fair of hair and skin like his sister, with a frail, consumptive look about his eager face. He had studied law at the University of Bologna and considered himself an *esprit fort*. He then travelled in Italy, and at Rome met Elizabeth Foster, Duchess of Devonshire, who knew Caro Lamb and something of the truth about Annabella. The other English in Rome filled in a dark portrait of Byron. Pietro conceived a sharp dislike for his sister's *amico* and wrote her stories about a wife imprisoned in far-off England. Teresa's letters did not disarm him of his disapproval. But when he came home to Ravenna all his suspicions melted in the sunshine of Byron's company. With that ready gift that Italians have for friendship, he instantly made Byron his friend and never swerved in his affection. Byron was for him a wise elder brother, and he loved him in his own fashion with all the devotion of his sister. For Teresa her lover was a poet and (in his way) a saint and a gallant cavalier. For Pietro, however, he was a hero and a leader of men.

Byron, with his zest for friendship, could not fail to respond to this artless adoration. Pietro took Carluccio's place as his companion on his rides in the Pine Forest, and they talked about religion as they rode. Pietro had none of his sister's piety nor her interest in theology. At the University of Bologna he had become an agnostic, and he aired his views

with the generous certainty of youth. To his surprise Byron called him
to order and defended the Bible and the tenets of the Church—more on
the grounds of common sense than for any mystical reason. Then it was
Pietro's turn to listen while Byron confessed that he was tired of a life
of "poeshie" and idle *serventismo*—it was not a man's life—action, he
wanted action! Teresa's brother understood and, with no thought of
disloyalty to his sister, sympathized with every word that his *cognato*
said. "*Povero* Byron!" he cried gaily, and confided in him that he, too,
was bitten by the itch to be up and doing—something—he cared not
what—for Italy!

He's a fine fellow, wrote Byron to his friends in England, a right
good 'liberty boy,' ingenuous and brave. And in Pietro's enthusiasms
he found escape from his own boredom.

While he lived in Venice he had taken little interest in the political
disturbances of Italy, but in Ravenna he found himself in a nest of conspiracy. From the Cavallis, from Count Rasponi, from Count Guiccioli,
he had learned of the aspirations of patriotic Italians for a strong, free
Italy, released from the clutches of the Austrians and their royal and
priestly satellites. He had got in touch with Pellegrino Rossi in Milan
and, in spite of Carlo Lancetti's assertions to the contrary, in Bologna he
joined the society of the *Roma Antica*. The first symptom of his association with the rebels was his quarrel with the lieutenant from Parma, and
ever afterwards the mere sight of a dragoon made him furious. The
ever-watchful police soon spied out his backsliding and toiled after him
from Bologna to La Mira and back again to Ravenna, seeking in vain to
fathom the motive of his constant journeying. They had not found evidence of his revolutionary activities for the good reason that for a long
while love kept him busy. But now Pietro introduced him to the
*Carbonari*, and he attended their meetings in a house outside the city gates
of Ravenna.

Count Gamba, as an old Jacobin, held a high place among the conspirators, though age and care had damped his ardour for the cause.
Pietro and his brother, Vincenzo, and their uncle, the Marchese Cavalli,
were outspoken opponents of Papal rule and fruitful in devising plots.
Pietro drew up plans of campaign beginning with the word *considerando*;
Vincenzo preferred an open-air life and vanished into the woods to carry
out his brother's plans; then something went wrong, and every one
blamed Pietro for having the *mal' occhio* ('evil eye'), and they started
work all over again. Filetto was a favourite place of meeting when
Ravenna grew too warm, and Byron was initiated into the order with all
the mummery of oath above the stiletto and hazel in the sleeve. Eventually he was chosen *Capo* (or 'Captain') of the *Americani*—the shock-
troops of the *Carbonari*, who drilled and chanted songs in the Pine Forest.
After his longing for Venezuela he was delighted to find himself an

*Americano*—it made him feel rugged and independent, although, he complained, his *Americani*, like their namesakes across the Atlantic, were all leaders and no led. As a final proof of devotion to the cause he allowed the *Carbonari* to store their guns and ammunition in the cellars of Count Guiccioli's palace.

The year 1820 was filled with rumour of revolution. In Spain King Ferdinand had been forced by insurrection to revive the constitution that he had annulled six years before. A fever of constitution-making then set in, and in Naples another King Ferdinand was forced to grant a constitution. The fever spread northward through the Papal States and the duchies beyond, and the King of Sardinia in his turn granted a constitution. The kings and dukes of Italy were in a flutter, and on the farther side of the Alps the Emperor of Austria took alarm. A conference of monarchs was summoned to Laybach to regulate the situation in Italy.

Byron's letters to England assumed a fine swashbuckling tone. He talked like Hotspur one moment, a brawling Capulet the next, then slipped into the dialect of the Waverley Novels, turned Dugald Dalgetty and sprinkled the page with Lowland Scots. For God's sake, he wrote to London, get Annabella's money out of the funds, for there was *that* brewing in Ravenna that would set all thrones toppling and send "your scoundrel Tories rolling in the mud." "The kiln's in the low," he cried, and there would be sparks and "fechting" and a fine "cutting of thrapples" and the Austrians would "get their paiks." He, for one, would not sit idly by "twirling his thumbs"; he would take service with his horse "on the savage side of the question"—aye, he would "wink and hold out his iron" and remember his "swashing blow." He was "skirring the country" and making friends with the "puir hill folk" —they'd got their bandoliers on, and soon there would be "unco bands of blue bonnets" over the border.

In Ravenna the walls were scribbled with "Down with the Pope!" and the Cardinal glared pale through all his purple. He prayed every day to St Apollinari for help, but the saint, like Baal, slept and heard him not. "*Evviva l'Italia!*" mocking children's voices chanted out of sight, and the Papal Guard scurried round the corner to find an empty street. There were angry shouts at night and scuffles between police and cavaliers twanging their guitars under ladies' windows. The Cardinal told Byron once more to strip his footmen of their livery, which made them look like Papal troops—in all kindness, for one day they might well be murdered in mistake by the rebels. But Byron chose to take offence and armed his 'ragamuffins' from his stores in the cellars of the Palazzo Guiccioli. Fletcher was arrested one night as he was sauntering home from some rendezvous, but he thrust the police disdainfully to the wall and continued on his way. All this and a great deal more Byron told his friends in England and apologized for his cryptic tone of writing.

L

He dared not speak out boldly nor avow his sympathies, for the "Huns," he knew, were opening his letters and reading them, and if there were one race yet more beastly than the English, he would have his correspondents know that it was the Austrians.

The Revolution, he wrote, was set for the summer. But May came, and he had only parochial gossip to report. There had been an alarming sound one night of pistols fired, and the whole town was in a tremor. Now, at last, they thought, the first blow has been struck for freedom. The next day the Countess Rasponi retired in well-merited confusion to the country. Two gentlemen had met under her balcony by an oversight in her arrangements and shown their displeasure by firing at each other. Luckily neither marksman had been hit, but in horror the lady's family sent post-haste for her *cavalier servente* to reason with her, and Count Rasponi announced his intention of thrashing her soundly, when he came home, for her inconstancy to her regular *cicisbeo*. May slipped into June, and the Gamba family was too busy waging war upon Count Guiccioli to attend to revolution. When Count Guiccioli had been routed Byron learned that the R— (as they called it) had been set to break out in October. But rains of autumn intervened, military ardour was damped, and the R— was postponed until the spring.

Revolt was heralded in the best style of melodrama. On the evening of December 9, 1820, Byron was putting on his greatcoat to go and pay his evening call on Teresa when he heard shots fired in the street outside. His 'ragamuffins' rushed out on the balcony and raised a howl that a man was being murdered. Good manners in Ravenna forbade them to interfere in other people's murders, but Byron called on Tita, the Venetian, and ran down into the street. There he found the Papal Commandant lying flat on his back with five bullet-wounds in his body. His lieutenant was crying over him like a child, a priest was sobbing a frightened prayer, a surgeon stood by without offering help, while all around a crowd wept and wrung its hands in helpless consternation. The man was a political opponent, but Byron would not leave him lying there, and with Tita he bore him into the house. There he forced the surgeon to examine his wounds, but the Commandant moaned "*O Dio!*" and "*Gesu!*" two or three times and died. Byron sent word to the Cardinal, and the lieutenant dried his tears, lit his pipe, and sat down philosophically to keep watch beside his commanding officer's corpse.

A queer people, this, said Byron—fierce, yet strangely timid. He ran great risk of being murdered for trying to help the dead man, but "he was a brave officer," he declared, "and I shall never be deterred from a duty of humanity by all the assassins of Italy, and that is a wide word." The Commandant's brother wrote from Rome to thank him for his help and kindness, and Teresa drafted a reply in the set phrase of Tuscany. It was a long letter, beautiful and dithyrambic, and Byron cut it down—

really there was too much in it about his own bravery for a modest man.

Christmas followed hard upon this murder, and the citizens of Ravenna abandoned themselves to peace on earth and good will towards men. But with the New Year (1821) the Emperor of Austria and his 'Barbarians' forced the pace, and from day to day Byron recorded in his diary the course of revolution.

On January 5 he went to pay his evening call upon Teresa. Pietro was there, and the talk fell upon Alfieri, Italy, freedom. From politics they proceeded to military matters, and the virtues of the Hungarian as against the Highland claymore were discussed. Pietro told Byron that the R— was to break out on March 7 or 8—"in which appointment I should trust," noted Byron, "had it not been settled that it was to have broken out in October." However, "it was all one to Ranger"—it did not do to be too particular, one must take rebellion in its way. He returned home and read Xenophon's *Anabasis* and went to bed.

Two nights later he was at a *conversazione* with his old friends Gertrude Vicari and Betti. Pietro arrived, looking young and important. He drew Byron aside and said that the R— would certainly break out that night. The patriots of Forli had sent word that the Cardinal intended to make wholesale arrests immediately. The Liberals had posted patrols in the streets to sound the alarm directly the arrests began—what did Byron think should be done? "Fight for it rather than be taken in detail," replied Byron shortly. He offered Count Guiccioli's house as an asylum for the Liberals—if necessary they could defend it, for they had arms and ammunition there. He went home, took out his pistols, made a round of the house to take stock of its military properties, sat down by the fire, and read a book. Gunshot might be heard from the street any minute, and the Liberals would pour into the house—he must not be found in bed. . . .

Pietro woke him up at noon and whispered in his ear that the advices from Forli were wrong—the Cardinal had issued no orders for arrest— so the R— was postponed. Byron advised Pietro to be prepared for arrest —why not attack now? Attack in detail, and in different parties, in different places (though at the same time), so as to divide the attention of the troops? Again he offered the Palazzo Guiccioli as a rendezvous. If it came to a fight, it was a "strongish post" with good walls, only approachable by a narrow street. Pietro said he would tell Vincenzo and withdrew arms and ammunition from the cellar and went off hunting with his father in the Pine Forest.

On January 9 came the news that the King of Naples had denounced his constitution. Pietro burst in upon Teresa and Byron in the evening and shouted that they meant to rise at once in Romagna. Byron felt doubtful, but "*Onward!*" he wrote in his diary. "It is now the time to act . . . It is . . . the spirit of liberty which must be spread. The waves which dash upon the shore are, one by one, broken, but yet the ocean conquers."

There was a lull in activity until the end of the month. The 'Barbarians' were building bridges across the Po. The *Carbonari* held meetings in the Pine Forest and withdrew more arms from the Palazzo Guiccioli. The Carnival arrived, and on January 24 Byron noted that they were masquerading in the streets as he rode to keep his evening tryst with Teresa. "*Vive la bagatelle!* The Germans are on the Po, the Barbarians at the gate . . . and lo! they dance and sing and make merry, 'for to-morrow they may die.' Who can say that the Arlequins are not right? . . . I rode on."

Teresa was alone. She told him that Pietro and the others had gone off (with arms and ammunition) for a shooting-party in the forest and wouldn't be back till Sunday. Byron exploded in a fury. A shooting-party! A snivelling, popping, small-shot, water-hen waste of powder, ammunition, and shot—for their own special amusement! A few days later he rode out to the Pine Forest to see for himself what was passing. There he met his *Americani*, armed and singing with all their might "*Sem tutti soldati per la libertà!*" ("We are all soldiers of liberty!") "They cheered me as I passed—I returned the salute and rode on. This may show the spirit of Italy at present."

On the last day of January Pietro returned from his outing in the forest and gave Byron the new passwords for February. They were — and —, the reply —, the rejoinder —, and — was changed to —, and there was a new word —. Byron's spirits rose. "Things seem fast coming to a crisis—*ça ira!*" The 'Barbarians' intended to cross the Po on February 15, by which time Romagna would be in a blaze of insurrection. The 'Barbarians' crossed the Po on February 7, and on February 11 there was a sound of firing at Commacchio. The scouts of revolution reported that it was the Emperor of Austria's birthday and the 'Barbarians' were firing off their cannon in honour of their "principal pig." On February 14 came news of fighting at Russi, a village not far from Ravenna—three persons killed, six wounded. But this, too, was a false alarm. Two gangs of peasants had met at a dance and pulled their knives on each other in the moonlight.

On the day of the battle of Russi the Cardinal issued a proclamation that all persons having arms or ammunition concealed on their premises would be liable to, etc., . . .

Two days later Pietro and his friends returned their arms and ammunition to the Palazzo Guiccioli.

Byron was annoyed. They hadn't notified him of their intention of returning arms. It was lucky that Lega, the steward, and Tita, the gondolier, were there to receive them—otherwise, with the wrong servants, the news would have been all round the town and he would have been in a fine scrape! He beat the crow angrily for stealing the falcon's water and took a moderate dose of water himself "mixed with other ingredients."

On February 18 he wrote that he had lost touch with his "*Carbonari* cronies." "In the meantime my lower apartments are full of their bayonets, fusils, cartridges, and what not. I suppose that they consider me as a depôt, to be sacrificed in case of accidents. It is no great matter," he added philosophically, "supposing that Italy could be liberated, who or what is sacrificed. It is a grand object—the very *poetry* of politics. Only think—a free Italy!"

On Feburary 20 his *Americani* invited him to a dinner in the forest, to which he went with the full intention of getting as tipsy and patriotic as possible. The next morning he was able to report "Business begins to thicken . . . nothing but the most decided success of the Barbarians can prevent a general and immediate rise of the whole nation." Three days later he was notified that "the *plan* had missed" and the R— was over.

"Scrub, bring me a dram! . . . Drank some Imola wine, and some punch." He went out to a ball, where there was a row. Three of the Cardinal's footmen had the impudence to attend, masked and without tickets, and were forcibly ejected by the enraged nobility. Two minutes more, and there would have been bloodshed, insurrection, and an angry mob in the streets, and the Cardinal would have had to flee the city.

The diary closed on February 27. The night before, Byron had dined at the Casa Gamba with Teresa and her father. Pietro joined the party, carefree as ever, and they partook of a dish of hot cockles diluted in Imola wine. "When I came home, apprehensive of the consequences, I swallowed three or four glasses of spirits. . . . All was pretty well till I got to bed, when I became somewhat swollen, and considerably vertiginous. I got up, and mixing some soda-powders, drank them off. This brought on temporary relief. I returned to bed; but grew sick and sorry once and again. Then took more soda-water. At last I fell into a dreary sleep. Woke, and was ill all day, till I had galloped a few miles. . . . Let us hope the best—it is the grand possession."

Thus ended the diary—and the Revolution.

"Foolish virgins! foolish virgins!" scoffed Byron, "locked without the gate!" This winter plot was only one of many that had failed. Always something rose to prevent success—the rains of autumn, the winter carnival, hunting in the woods, or the 'Barbarians' marched too soon. He did not blame Pietro. He blamed the *Carbonari* as a group. They were playing at revolution, letting 'I dare not' wait for ever upon 'I would.' They were impractical, exclusive—a handful of young men of good family and intellectuals from the law and universities. They made no attempt to win support from the *bourgeoisie*. Byron observed that all this while the 'merchants,' though they gave lip-service to liberal doctrine, were cornering the wheat-market—for "supplies to the armies," said they, and he noted the plural use of the word with sarcastic merriment—for purposes of profiteering the Austrian army, no doubt, was a safer bet than anything the *Carbonari* could raise. The country people of Romagna were a fine, wild race. Napoleon said they made the best soldiers in all Italy and, for a cause, would submit to iron discipline, but the *Carbonari* gave them no lead. They were no better now than hordes of Highland clansmen. Their stabbing and shooting round corners might be picturesque, but it helped no one. The hard fact was that there were too many people ready to plot and shoot and kill for Italy, but not enough to live and think and organize. It was difficult, he wrote in his diary, "to play amongst such a set of assassins and blockheads." He had learned his lesson—noble sentiment is not enough to win freedom.

As the January plot was fizzling out, a letter reached him from Lord Sidney Osborne. He was in some way a step-brother, for his father, the Duke of Leeds, had been the first husband of Augusta's mother, and Byron loved to respond to the call of kin, especially when it came from ducal heights. Lord Sidney was on his way to Ancona and would sail thence to Corfu—why shouldn't Byron join him there? Corfu—with Greece beyond, where men were really fighting and dying for their independence! "Why not?" he wrote in his diary. "Perhaps I may" —and then the old, old words—"next spring."

The seed had been planted, but for the moment it would not blossom. His chains still held him in Italy. He was fighting the battle of the Gamba family, father and sons, and trying by every means in his power to save them from the consequence of their share in abortive insurrection. He would not leave Romagna so long as they were there; and if they were exiled he would still stay and fight for them. Ancona might be a good place of refuge for Teresa and her father if trouble came. "My movements," he wrote resignedly in his diary, "will depend upon the lady's wishes—for myself it is much the same." But Corfu lay across the water from Ancona—and Greece! This much he knew—if he ever went there, he would go as a soldier and a man of affairs, not as a poet and a plotter.

Teresa knew nothing of this dream of Greece. She listened sadly to his sarcastic diatribes against "the Charcoal-burners." Her pride as an Italian woman was humbled, as a revolutionary she was in despair. "Alas," she said, as she sat at the harpsichord, "the Italians must now return to making operas." "I fear that and macaroni are their *forte*," said Byron, "and motley their only wear." But courage, *mia carissima*, "there are some high spirits among them still."

Now that rebellion had collapsed the Cardinal Legate and his priestly associates proceeded in leisurely fashion to mete out punishment. The Gambas had repaid the Pope for his tact in dealing with their daughter's domestic difficulties with nothing but conspiracy and revolt. Their friend Lord Byron had openly abetted them and, taking advantage of his immunity from foreign Governments as an Englishman and a lord, had turned Count Guiccioli's house into an arsenal for revolution. It was more important that he should be expelled from Romagna than the Gambas, for he was rich and popular with the common people. But at the bare hint that he might be expelled petitions on his behalf poured in upon the Legate, and—what complicated the business—the parish clergy were all his friends, too. The Church realized once more that it must use all its powers of persuasion, all its knowledge of human nature, to dislodge Lord Byron from Count Guiccioli's house and spirit him over the borders of the state.

It was not until summer came that the Cardinal proceeded to punishment. A proscription list, containing more than a thousand names, was drawn up—Ercolanis, Cavallis, all the great names, were included. The punishment was not death, but banishment, without trial, from Romagna. Pietro Gamba's name stood high on the list, and his brother Vincenzo's, too. The *Buon Governo* made short work of them. They were arrested and conducted with every courtesy across the borders into the more patient state of Tuscany, where they settled down in Florence under police supervision. Then Count Gamba was given a passport and notified that he had forty-eight hours in which to pack and follow his sons to Florence. Teresa now was alone at Filetto.

Count Guiccioli heard the news; and more, perhaps, to embarrass 'theocracy' than with any hope of recovering his wife, he petitioned that, since her father and guardian was gone, Teresa should be returned to his hands or shut up in a convent. The Cardinal gave Count Guiccioli's petition his polite attention and forwarded it to Rome. In the meantime he directed the police to furnish the Countess Guiccioli with a passport to leave the state and rejoin her father in Florence if and when she wished.

Here for a moment the Cardinal—God forgive him for a stupid old bachelor!—was at fault in his understanding of woman. Byron had not gone to see Teresa at Filetto when she was left there alone. She was in despair and refused to use the passport. She wrote to Byron instead, pleading for help and counsel—and him!

Help me, *caro Byron*, for I'm in the most terrible way and, without you, I can't make up my mind to anything. —— has just been with me . . . to tell me that I must leave Ravenna by next Tuesday, as my husband has had recourse to Rome for the purpose of forcing me to go back to him or else putting me in a convent, and the answer thence is expected in a few days.

## CHAPTER VII

## *"Shiloh comes"*

AT ten o'clock on the night of August 6, 1821, a post-chaise drove up to the Palazzo Guiccioli in Ravenna. Out of it leaped a tall, bareheaded man wrapped in a riding-cloak. He beat strenuously on the door. The old porter opened it slowly and admitted the stranger with a frown—another *Inglese*! With a swift movement, like a snake walking on the tip of its tail, the visitor glided through the door. Tita, the bearded gondolier, ran to meet him with a beaming countenance and kissed his hands rapturously. Together they mounted the stairs, the visitor bounding up two steps at a time with head bent forward like a battering-ram. The mastiffs growled sleepily, the monkey glared between its paws, and the crane turned its back with an air of scornful indifference. At the top of the stairs stood Fletcher, smiling agreeably under his flaxen hair. He shook hands with the visitor as with an old friend, and together they went to the library. Lord Byron was lounging on a sofa with a book on his knees and a glass of gin and water beside him. He struggled to his feet and held out both hands in welcome. His visitor seized them and, with a high, shrill laugh, pumped them vigorously. "Fletcher," cried Byron, "green tea, and plenty of it! You know Mr Shelley's tastes! Green tea—and dry biscuits!" But Fletcher nodded with his head towards the table. There stood the teapot, the caddy, and the biscuits, and Tita came striding back holding the hot water before him as though it were the Host.

Shelley held a place all his own among Byron's friends. There were his friends of Harrow, to whom he was bound by a deep, almost morbid, affection, his Cambridge friends—fellow-fighters in the game of intellect —and later friends of London days—boon companions in an hour of mirth. His boyhood friends—alas, so many of them were dead!—were creatures of another world—a memory rather than a fact—and when he met them now, he was oppressed with a painful sense of happiness for ever lost. With friends of Cambridge or London he was affectionate, humorous, and gay. He had a keen eye for their oddities, as they for his, but half the fun of knowing them lay in their casual imperfections. But Shelley brought with him no memory of happiness, nor was he a boon companion like Hobhouse or Moore. He had a baffling quality of earnestness and radiated a warm inner fire that somehow caught you in its glow. He dreamed great dreams, and you loved him for his dreams. You laughed at him and questioned him about his eccentricities, and Shelley listened with a gentle smile that had no humour in it. Of all the men Byron knew he was the greatest poet in word and thought and deed. He was more than that; to Byron's knowledge, he was the kindest, the bravest, the least selfish of men. He had made a sad confusion of life and brought unhappiness on others yet more than on himself, but through all his mistakes there shone a bright intellectual ardour, a restless desire for truth. Byron respected him, almost against his will, for a fighting quality that he lacked himself. Only this was wanting for absolute friendship. He suspected that he liked "Shiloh," as he called Shelley in sport, more than "Shiloh" liked him.

The rift in the lute was Allegra's mother. Claire Clairmont had been tricked into her brief *liaison* by vanity, and under Byron's indifference what little love she had felt was souring into hate. Byron had never pretended to love her, and in retrospect she aroused in him only shame and loathing. Like Annabella, she was a school-ma'am, but where Annabella dealt in big words from the dictionary or reproving silence, Claire was plaintive, and—what was worse—she argued. She touched a cruel streak in Byron, and malevolently he refused to let her see her child—thus avenging himself on his wife, who mounted guard over Ada as though she were a sacred cow. But Shelley was fond of Claire. Ever since that hot summer day when she had run off with him and Mary on their crazy elopement to France he had made himself responsible for her happiness. He was not blind to her faults and suffered at her hands more, perhaps, than Byron. "Oh, my dear girl," he once told her in a burst of frankness, "I shall always try to help and comfort you and, as you always tell me, with so *little* success!" But one day he would persuade her to be reasonable, and then he would be left to deal with Byron alone and would break down his obstinacy.

Allegra, frankly, had brought him to Ravenna. When Teresa fled from the Palazzo Guiccioli there was no one left there to keep an eye upon that baby. Teresa had been kind, she had played with Allegra and petted her, she had taken sensible precautions about her food and health, and the child whom the Hoppners found dirty and morose was now clean and lively. Teresa, too, was proud for Byron's sake of his daughter's beauty, but she was too preoccupied with her lover to spank a child of three or discipline its temper. Byron was amused when she was naughty, and Allegra grew up among servants who treated her like a little queen because they knew that pleased Milord her father. With Teresa gone Allegra grew wilder, vainer, more intractable than ever, and her father realized that now he had a spirited young animal, not a pretty plaything, on his hands. She no longer tore her clothes, but she laughed scornfully when they would make her say her prayers, and tossed the books on the floor when they tried to teach her to read. Byron made up his mind that she should be reared in Italy, as Miss *Biron*, to distinguish her from 'Little Legitimacy,' and be bred a Catholic. But there was no one in his household fit to bring the child up, so, at Teresa's suggestion, he decided to send her to a convent school. But he was indolent, or perhaps did not want to let the child go; anyhow, she remained for six months in the Palazzo Guiccioli after Teresa left. Only when the January conspiracy came did he realize that a house that any day might become a scene of fighting was no place for a baby. Lazily and reluctantly he made preparations to send Allegra away to the convent of the Capuchin nuns at Bagnacavallo.

All arrangements had been made by Teresa. Bagnacavallo was an old walled town in the hills and might be considered a more healthy spot than the plain. There a friend of her father's, Don Vincenzo Fabbri, had recently set up a convent for the Capuchin sisters in an old dissolved monastery. Don Vincenzo had seen Allegra for himself and was touched by her beauty and the story of her birth. He used his influence to have her taken into his convent under the usual age. It was not a rich institution, and its buildings were dark and partly in ruin. In point of fashion, too, the school had not yet arrived. But Byron had his own sense of propriety. He did not think it right that his illegitimate daughter by a woman of the *bourgeoisie* should be reared in the company of little aristocrats. The convent at Bagnacavallo was betwixt and between for social fitness—the middle classes patronized it, but some of Teresa's noble relatives sent their children to the school—there was her cousin, the little Marchesa Ghislieri, about Allegra's age, and a Contessa Loreta and a Donna Ippolita Biancoli, too!

But Teresa was not there in the house to see that the child was sent away. He forgot her for the excitement of conspiracy, and then he found that he still did not want her to go. On February 10 he wrote to Hoppner. Allegra was still with him, and she was as 'perverse' as ever—really it was high time that she was sent to a convent—when he had taken that step he would let Hoppner know. The conspiracy collapsed, and he was sick of his supper of hot cockles and Imola wine. Then at last he bethought him seriously of Allegra. On a cold spring day a carriage drove up to the door of the Palazzo Guiccioli. Allegra walked sedately down the stairs, holding her father's hand. Teresa stood by the carriage step, talking with a grave-looking gentleman. The servants were gathered round her, noisily chattering and showing every sign of grief.

Signor Pellegrino Chigi, the banker of Ravenna, had undertaken to drive Allegra out to Bagnacavallo. Her modest baggage was loaded into the carriage—bed, washstand, chest of drawers, two chairs, eighteen chemises, a black cloth gown, several dolls beautifully dressed, and— "*Bon dì Papa's*" present to the convent—the coronation robes of a Peer of the Realm. Wrapped in her little ermine coat to keep her

from the cold, Allegra said good-bye to the golden-haired lady who had
taken her out in the coach, and to Papa, and off she drove to Bagnacavallo.
She held out her hand to be kissed by the nuns when she arrived. "Walk
behind me," she said haughtily to the lay-sisters who would have led her
to the garden; "you are my servants." The Prioress spoke to her of God.
"Who is this Lord," she inquired disdainfully, "who is greater than me?"

"*Bon di Papa*" made no mention of his daughter's going in his diary.
He had fallen into a fit of depression and could think of no one but
himself. His thirty-third birthday had come and gone, and gloomily he
wrote an epitaph for his dead youth.

Here lies . . .
the Thirty-third Year
of an ill-spent Life,
which . . . expired
January 22, 1821,
Leaving a successor
Inconsolable
for the very loss which
occasioned its
Existence.

All the love of which Claire was capable was bound up in her child.
But, as her hatred for Byron grew under his contemptuous cruelty,
Allegra became something to fight about and to vex him with. When
she heard that he had sent the child away to a convent she wrote him
a long, intolerable letter of argument. He had broken his word, she told
him, for he had promised her that Allegra should never live away from
one or other of her parents. "Every traveller and writer" would tell him
that the convent schools of Italy were miserable places, and there was no
hope that a convent in a "secondary" town like Ravenna would be better
than the worst. All her frustrated motherhood, all her jealousy, flared
out against Teresa as she wrote—what were the women who came out
of those convents but "bad wives, most unnatural mothers, licentious,
ignorant, the dishonour of society! . . . How will Lady Byron . . . be
soothed, and rejoice in the honourable safety of herself and child, and
all the world be bolder to praise her prudence, my unhappy Allegra
furnishing the condemning evidence." If he would not listen to her, let
him take (said poor Claire, not knowing what she asked) Mrs Hoppner's
advice, and she would abide by the decision. Then, miserably contra-
dicting her opening argument, she begged that Allegra be sent to a
respectable boarding-school in England, "if the purity of your principles
does not allow you to cherish a natural child." And if, she added, he
did not want to spend that much on the education of a natural child, she
—by which she meant Shelley—would foot the bills!

Claire had said enough to infuriate Byron in every possible way. He sent her letter to Hoppner. "The moral part," he wrote in notice of the attack upon Teresa, "comes with an excellent grace from the writer now living with a *man* and his *wife*—and having planted a child in the F. Foundling." Hoppner would understand the allusion.

There the situation stood when Shelley arrived in Ravenna. Byron was obstinate and exasperated and declared bitterly that Claire was a "damned bitch," Claire was bickering and spiteful and called Byron "a damned brute." Shelley did not realize all the fury of ill-will that had accumulated over the unconscious head of Allegra, nor how deeply he had been involved himself in the ugly squabble. He came as a seraphic Pickwick to throw himself between the fire-shovel and the carpet-bag. He must visit Bagnacavallo, see Allegra, and report to Claire. Then he would talk to Byron and try to get him to leave Ravenna, bringing Allegra with him. He must be steered to some place where Claire could come without rousing suspicion—to stay with her step-sister, Mary, for example—and then—Claire and Allegra and Byron would be living close by one another, and eventually the pair would stop fighting about their child out of sheer proximity. It was a difficult task, but it did not daunt Shelley. He was accustomed to making people do what he wanted when he was on a good deed bent. He brought to the game not only the wisdom of the dove and the tenacity of a bulldog, but a serpent-like cunning that Machiavelli might have envied. And, a curious thing, when he was wooing people to do what he wanted, he had blinding attacks of humour and hilarity that never afflicted him at other times.

Byron was really glad to see Shelley once more. He kept him up until five in the morning. They talked of poetry and discussed each other's works. Shelley's admiration for *Don Juan* was unbounded, but he told Byron that his *Marino Faliero* was constructed on a wrong principle of tragedy. Byron was loud in praise of *Prometheus Unbound*, but declared that *The Cenci* was too painful for the stage. Shelley put in a word for the poems of John Keats, who had just died in Rome. Byron was sorry to hear of his death, but he would not allow that *Endymion* was anything more than a mawkish dream. Let us get back to "that great little man," Alexander Pope, he cried. But Shelley saw no radiance of "the Intense Inane" in the *Dunciad* or *The Rape of the Lock*.

From Pope and Keats the talk flung to politics, and Shelley was delighted to learn what Byron had done for revolution in Romagna. Talk of the *Carbonari* brought the conversation to Teresa Guiccioli, and Byron told the story of her 'escape' to Florence. He read out some of her letters, and Shelley felt sure that she was a clever, amiable woman. And so to Allegra, and the convent at Bagnacavallo, and thus to Claire, and Shelley's mission in Ravenna.

From Allegra Shelley steered adroitly to Hoppner and his wife. He had liked Mrs Hoppner—her eyes were like Mary's—and she and her husband had been kind to Allegra. They had been kind to Claire, too, when she came with him three years ago to Venice. Above all they had been kind then to poor Mary when she arrived in Venice, carrying her dying child in her arms. They had taken her into their house and given up several days of well-earned holiday in Switzerland to comfort and distract her from her grief. Shelley could not speak too highly of the Hoppners; anything that they had to say about Allegra, he was sure, was disinterested. Byron read him Hoppner's letters in which he spoke with harshness of Claire. Shelley was surprised, for he had hoped to use the Hoppners as advocates on his side. Then Byron could hold out no longer. He gave Shelley a letter that Hoppner had written him a year ago.

Byron had noticed that Hoppner, from liking "Shiloh," now spoke of him as though he had 'some notion' against him. Hoppner replied to Byron's inquiry with a full statement of his 'notion.' His authority was unimpeachable—Elise, Allegra's nurse—from Switzerland, like Mrs Hoppner. Elise had taken service with the Shelleys after leaving Venice, had married their Italian courier, Paolo Foggi, and thereafter with her husband had been dismissed. The tale she told the Hoppners was sordid and disgusting.

Claire had been pregnant by Shelley when they came to Venice in 1818 and had swallowed a lot of drugs to procure an abortion. At Naples a child had been born, and half an hour after its birth it was placed in the Pietà there. Poor Mary Shelley knew nothing of this disgraceful business, but "these beasts," wrote Hoppner wrathfully, then proceeded to treat her with the utmost brutality, and Claire did not scruple to tell her the sooner she were dead and out of other people's way the better. For Mrs Shelley's sake the story must not get abroad, and he trusted to Lord Byron to keep his mouth shut. But naturally he approved of Byron's unwillingness to have any further dealings with Claire, knowing, as he did, the creature she was. As for Shelley, if he chose to lecture Byron on Allegra's upbringing, his ideas might be dismissed with good, sound, Christian contempt.

Shelley was not taken by surprise by this story. In his day he had been accused of being Allegra's father because he loved the child and was kind to Claire. Elise, too, and her husband had given him trouble ere now. Paolo, who was a rogue, had seduced Elise, and the Shelleys, whose theories of free love did not apply to servants, forced him to marry her before they dismissed him for general dishonesty. Unfortunately there had been an incident that gave Paolo an opportunity for revenge. In one of his moments of higher lunacy Shelley had 'adopted' a foundling at Naples. The child died, but Paolo had been trying to collect blackmail on the episode ever since, and Shelley was obliged to set the lawyers on him. In dealing with Paolo he had been gravely handicapped by one thing. He had never dared to tell Mary all the silly story of the adoption of the child in Naples. Mary had just lost her own child Clara at that time and was greatly depressed. Yet more, he had registered his foundling as Mary's daughter. In retrospect Shelley was free to confess that this experiment in adoption was one of his less considerate actions.

What shocked him about the story Elise told was that the Hoppners, of all people, should believe it—the Hoppners, who had been kind to him, to Mary, to Claire, Allegra, Byron! It was not the charge that he had begotten a child on Claire that hurt him. If he and Claire 'loved' each other, under his code they were entitled to a child. But they would have had it in the light of day. This talk of drugs and attempted abortion and baby deserted in a Foundling Hospital—that hurt him sorely. But he realized that for Claire's sake the story must be scotched at once. Mary was not fond of Claire, but he could trust in her loyalty. He wrote to Mary. She must, he said, write to Mrs Hoppner and deny the story— he would not advise her how, but with cruel insight he begged her to do it "for my sake," not Claire's—and he could give the letter to Byron to send on.

Mary's letter, long in writing, took some days to reach Ravenna. It makes fine reading. Fearless love and furious anger are its only ingredients. "It is all a lie." Mary, in theory if not always in thought, was her husband's disciple. The story of the illegitimate child meant less to her than the charge of cruelty. You, Mrs Hoppner, you who know Shelley— you who saw his face—how dare you believe this story! "He is as incapable of cruelty as the softest woman." As for the rest of the miserable tale—it is false. Claire had no child, and "I am perfectly convinced in my own mind that Shelley never had an improper connexion with her . . . such a thing could not have passed unknown to me." Claire is timid, but "her heart is good, and if ever we quarrelled . . . it was I, and not she, that was harsh." You, Mrs Hoppner, "were kind to us, and I shall never forget it, but now I require justice"—bravo, Mary, justice for whom?—"you must believe me."

As he looked at Shelley's face—so lucid and angelic, yet so like a prize-fighter's—Byron knew that he had never believed the story, and so he told him and told him true. But in writing to Hoppner, though he pooh-poohed Elise as a witness, in his anger against Claire he had implied that he accepted her "pretty story" for a fact—"so like" Shelley, he said, meaning the "free love" and the "love-child," not the cruelty. Shelley handed him Mary's letter to forward to Mrs Hoppner. Mary received no answer to her appeal. Her letter was found among Byron's papers after his death with the seal broken—and what we are to guess from that God only knows.[1]

[1] Did Byron forward that letter? A disputed point in Byron-Shelley biography. I do not see any reason why Byron should not, and did not, forward it or Mrs Hoppner

This squall broke out the night that Shelley arrived. As the days went by and he waited for Mary's letter, he relapsed into mournful indifference to the slander—perhaps his sense of persecution had made him hasty in troubling Mary with the vile story. He bent his energies once more to achieving the purpose that had brought him to Ravenna. His task was difficult, for not only had he to fight with Byron's obstinacy—he must manage Mary, too, at the other end, who, for all her defence of her step-sister, did not love her nor want her in her house. But Byron, he observed, was remorseful about the Hoppner letter, so patiently he bided his time. He explored the antiquities of Ravenna and was not impressed; everything was mouldy and sinking into the earth, and the people were wild and spoke an abominable *patois*. In the morning he reported progress to Mary, then wandered about the dark "Circean" palace, watching the "unarbitrated quarrels" of falcon, crane, and crow. In the afternoon he went out riding with Byron in the Pine Forest and they shot at pumpkins. After dinner they sat up till sunrise talking poetry and politics, and slowly Shelley wound his way back to Allegra and the convent.

Teresa Guiccioli had been good for Byron, he wrote to Mary. His health, his nerves, his temper—even his political opinions—were improved. In short, Mary must know, he was fast becoming "a virtuous man." The one fear was that in the absence of Teresa he might relapse into vicious courses again—in fact, Byron said that he was sure he would. All the more reason for getting him out of Ravenna and sending him back to Teresa—if possible, some place where Shelley could keep an eye on him. From her letters it would seem that Teresa was devoted, though, perhaps, sentimental. Another good point in her favour—Byron said she was fond of Allegra. Perhaps, then, it might be a good idea if she were to go on living with Byron, so that she be made responsible for the child's welfare. She was with her brother in Florence for the moment—Pietro, by the way, was a personal friend of Byron's and acquiesced perfectly in her connexion with him. They talked of going to Switzerland, merely from the novelty of travelling, Byron said peevishly. He preferred Lucca or Siena—any place but Florence.

So much in report to Mary. Byron objected to Switzerland because it was "a swinish country" and full of English tourists. Florence was less "swinish," but it, too, was full of tourists. What he required was a quiet backwater like Ravenna. Shelley had spent the spring in Pisa—what did he think of the town? Shelley replied that it was a humdrum place, not much visited by the English, but the climate was good, there was the sea close by and good riding in the woods.

---

return it. Elise later denied to Mrs Hoppner that she had ever told her the slander—a denial that only proves Elise a liar. Mrs Hoppner continued to believe the story and repeated it to Henry Crabb Robinson in August 1834. When, after some years, she met Mary Shelley again Mary cut her dead.

Good, said Byron, Pisa let it be—would Shelley write to Teresa and persuade her to that effect? An odd thing, thought Shelley, for a stranger to write to a man's mistress on a subject of such delicacy! He wrote Teresa a long letter in lame Italian setting forth the objections to the Swiss scheme. He had lived there with Byron in the past, and, he assured her, life had been rendered intolerable by the malevolent curiosity of English tourists. She, who knew only "the gentler manners" of Italy, would never understand how abominably the English could behave, once their moral fury was aroused. He, like her, was an exile—like her, his only thought was Byron's happiness—would she abandon the idea of going to Switzerland? He received a lyrical letter in reply, full of graceful compliments that made him think more highly of Teresa's intelligence. She would go wherever Lord Byron wanted to go—and so would her father and her brother. She closed with an appeal to this unknown friend. "Signore, your kindness makes me bold to ask you a favour—will you grant it? *Don't leave Ravenna without Milord.*"

Now, wrote Shelley to Mary, by all the laws of knighthood, I am captive to the lady's request—but to business. Byron was coming to Pisa. What about their own plans for the winter? Should it be Florence or Pisa? "Judge—I *know you like the job.*" The winters are cold at Florence. In Pisa we need not distil our water. The presence of Claire in Pisa would be a difficulty when Byron came—"gunpowder and fire should be kept at a respectable distance," he wrote with studied impartiality, but in every case something must be risked. Personally his one desire was to retire with Mary to a solitary island in the sea, "but this it does not appear that we shall do." So they must face the alternative. "Our roots never struck so deeply as at Pisa, and the transplanted tree flourishes not."

Now he must tackle the delicate matter of Allegra in the convent. He was pleased to find that Byron was not committed to Bagnacavallo—it was a temporary expedient only, dependent on his residence in Romagna. Shelley would not have been Shelley if he had not raised objections to a convent as a place of education. He confessed to Byron that there had been a Teresa in his life, too, last winter—the beautiful Teresa Viviani, called Emilia for purposes of romance. She had been imprisoned by harsh parents in the convent of Santa Anna in Pisa. He had visited her there with Mary. Evening walks had followed, eloquent letters, a generous use of the words *amor* and *amico*, *fratello* and *sorella*, in all their ripe implication—and Mary had been vexed and all Pisa talked. The business was now running down to an unromantic close, and Emilia was soon to leave her convent to marry a respectable lawyer. But out of it had blossomed a poem—*Epipsychidion*, or "Laying on of Souls." It was full of the most exalted sentiment, but for all its platonic fervours, Shelley confessed with unwonted humour that it had no deeper source than the mooning

M

of a housemaid with her sweetheart. But his intimacy with Emilia had taught him to disapprove of convent schools—for more reasons, perhaps, than Emilia herself realized.

Byron was pleased to hear that Shelley was human, but he was firm about the convent. Allegra was to be bred a Catholic, and the faults of Italian women must be blamed on a rotten social code, not convent schools. Shelley shifted his ground. With her father gone from Romagna —with the kind Countess Guiccioli gone—Allegra would be alone and friendless out there at Bagnacavallo. Byron bit his nails and frowned— very well, then, Allegra must come with him to Pisa. He would select from among his servants a maid to take care of her on the journey. In the meantime would Shelley find some good convent for the child to go to in Pisa?

Shelley's mission was accomplished. He wrote to Mary. Would she at once set about renting a large commodious palace for Byron at Pisa? At the same time, why not look out for more modest winter quarters for themselves? Williams and his wife had better come to Pisa, too. Would she make inquiries about a convent school for Allegra—any place but Santa Anna—perhaps Emilia might advise her on that point. Failing a good convent school there might be a private family willing to take the child in. Certainly she must not remain in her father's house—it was full of dissolute menservants who would do her nothing but mischief. A last charge—a maid for Allegra—the woman that Byron had chosen was "odious and unfit"—would Mary, or should he, find some one to take her place?

His instructions sent off, Shelley made a tour of the Palazzo Guiccioli, while Byron was in bed, and rapidly computed how many wagons he would have to send from Pisa to cart away the poet and his beasts, furniture, arms and ammunition. Then, when they went out riding to the pumpkin range, he took up another topic, that he had already broached —why should not his friend Leigh Hunt come out to Italy and collaborate with Byron in a Liberal quarterly? There would be room for him and his family in the large palace in Pisa.

A day or two before he left Ravenna, Shelley rode out to Bagnacavallo, bearing a gold chain as a sop for Allegra's vanity and a basket of sweetmeats. Allegra did not recognize this tall stranger with the stooping shoulders and untidy brown hair flecked with grey. At first she was shy, but she melted with the gift of the chain and prattled dreamily about Paradise and angels and the *Bambino*. She was paler, thought Shelley, her beauty more delicate and her temper less wilful, but, in his affectionate eyes, among those brown-skinned Italian children this fair-haired child with luminous dark-blue eyes was a creature of a finer and a higher order. Byron's daughter was still a handful. Soon she was flying through cloister and garden with Shelley in pursuit. Half the nuns were in *siesta*, and the others scuttled demurely out of sight of this lanky male heretic as he chased a wood-nymph. Allegra rang the convent bell till the pigeons flew out of the campanile in startled, wheeling flight, and it needed all the efforts of the Prioress to drive the nuns back to their beds. What message, asked Shelley, as he caught her in his arms, should he carry to *mammina?* "Tell her to send me a kiss and a beautiful dress." —"And what shall the dress be made of?"—"All of silk and gold." "And what message for Papa?"—"Tell him to come and see me and bring *mammina* with him." Loyally Shelley supposed that *mammina* was Claire, and, he told Mary, he refrained from delivering all that message. But Allegra had no memory of her real mother. For her *mammina* was the golden-haired lady who lived with "*Bon dì Papa*" and took her out driving in the coach.

As he drove away from Ravenna Shelley pondered. Of all men he knew he believed that Byron was the greatest poet, and he felt humble in his presence. He would gladly be his friend, but was that possible? He somehow felt that he liked Byron more than Byron liked him. In his own house, perforce, he had to listen to much evil spoken of him. Mary said he was "very nice," and, when he was present, she was susceptible to his charm, but she was prim about him behind his back. Claire hated him and scoffed. But away from the womenkind, all alone with him, Shelley felt in Byron all the enchanting folly of genius.

Yet there was something in him, too, that jarred—his false pride, his ribaldry, his coarseness. He was selfish with women and capricious, said Shelley to himself, forgetting the time when he had haled Elizabeth Hitchener into his house as "the Sister of his Soul," only to drive her forth three months later as an "ugly, hermaphroditical beast." Undoubtedly, too, Byron was harsh with women when he ceased to care for them, and this Italian Countess would have leisure to repent her sacrifice, said Shelley again to himself, without a thought of Harriet Westbrook lying dead at the bottom of the Serpentine. But a truce to these reflections—he was an idealist about women, Byron was a cynic—that was the difference, but, oh, he sighed, as his head nodded and his eyes closed, the difference it made to women!

On the whole, his business had gone well. Leigh Hunt was provided for—at Byron's expense. A palace would be found in Pisa, Byron would rejoin Teresa and be saved from relapsing into dissolute courses, and Teresa, no doubt, would be happy. But greatest boon of all—Allegra was coming to Pisa. Mary would find a family for her to board with away from her father's disorderly household. Claire would come to stay with him, or the Williamses, or her friends the Masons—and then—and then—Claire would see her child again and hold her in her arms. That was all that mattered—and Shelley fell asleep.

## CHAPTER VIII

# Autumn in Ravenna

THE Church in all its wisdom—with all its knowledge of that passion of the laity called love—had failed to dislodge Byron from Ravenna. But that atheist Shelley had succeeded where the Church had failed. Eight wagons drove up to the doors of the Palazzo Guiccioli and were loaded under the eyes of the police. The Cardinal was now reassured that Lord Byron would obey the call of love—don't bother about the arms and ammunition, he told the police, for God's sake let them go to Tuscany, too.

As he sat over his gin and water in the evening, Byron reflected glumly that—for a lazy man—he had promised a great deal. He would leave Ravenna, which he liked, and his luxurious quarters in the Palazzo Guiccioli, he would take Allegra away from Bagnacavallo, would go to Pisa, rejoin Teresa, and start life all over again. Also, it appeared, Leigh Hunt was going to live with him at Pisa with a wife and six children, and they would start a radical magazine. He had asked Shelley to write to Hunt on that matter, and the worst of it was that Shelley had written.

It was one thing to promise to leave Ravenna, but it was another thing to pack. At the beginning of September Shelley wrote from Pisa to say that he had rented the Palazzo Lanfranchi for four hundred crowns a year. The Contessa had already arrived and taken up residence in the town with her father and brother, and she was "especially delighted" with the house. He awaited instructions about furniture and stables. Two weeks later came another letter saying that the wagons were on the way. Pietro, too, had been infected with the spirit of management and on his own account dispatched another eight wagons to Ravenna; but these, Shelley said, he had turned back at Florence. Emilia Viviani—by the way, don't talk about her, please, as it annoys Mary—was about to be married, and that again made him think how undesirable convent schools were for all but very young children—"respectable private families," he believed, might be found to take charge of Allegra. Claire, he promised, would not be allowed to interfere. "I have seen the Countess frequently, and I pronounce you secure against any of my female friends here." Teresa, in other words, was beautiful beyond all rivalry in Pisa—you will have no cause for backsliding—you will remain "a virtuous man."

Shelley's wagons arrived, and Byron wrote crossly to Moore on September 19.

I am in all the sweat, dust, and blasphemy of an universal packing of all my things, furniture, etc., for Pisa, whither I go for the winter. The cause has been the exile of all my fellow Carbonics and, amongst them, of the whole family of Madame G; who, you know, was divorced from her husband last week [?] on account of P.P. clerk of this parish, and who is obliged to join her father and relatives now in exile there, to avoid being shut up in a monastery, because the Pope's decree of separation obliged her to reside in *casa paterna*, or else, for decorum's sake, in a convent. As I could not say with Hamlet, "Get thee to a nunnery," I am preparing to follow them.

It is awful work, this love, and prevents all a man's projects of good and glory. I wanted to go to Greece lately (as everything seems up here) with her brother, who is a very fine, brave fellow (I have seen him put to the proof), and wild about liberty. But the tears of a woman who has left her husband for a man, and the weakness of one's heart, are paramount to these projects, and I can hardly indulge them.

Perpetual flight! Never-ending pursuit! Pack and follow, pack and follow! That was life with Teresa. Once there had been a thrill in the pursuit, but now with every flight the thrill grew fainter. Once Brunello had added a spice of peril to the game, but that old mountebank had gone up in ludicrous smoke, and now, when he dropped down beside Teresa on their next branch, there stood white-haired Count Gamba with his watch in his hand! The hills rose more steeply, the world was closing round them. And still her letters—her incredible, her preposterous letters—poured in upon him, shouting, "Come." He fumed and fretted in his dismantled palace. He was lonely—all his friends were gone—banished—he was, he realized, as he lolled gloomily in his bath, "the last of the Carbonics."

Away with these low spirits! Out into the forest! The sea's voice rolled inland like a muffled omen. A young crescent moon rose above the pine-trees, and there, in the glade, a woman was walking alone. With the Wild Huntsman's faint, far halloo he cantered down the lane of yellowing trees and dismounted. The lady was a stranger, she was startled, but they walked together for an hour. She wanted him to make love and he tried. But he made only a few commonplace speeches, and she looked disappointed and then laughed mischievously. He left her with a word of simpering regret and walked back sadly to his horse. . . .

"Come!" whispered Teresa across the hills. . . . What had she done to him that made him know that he would go to her? His feeling for her now was bleak and sane—without illusion—nothing like what he had felt about those other women—Caro Lamb, Annabella, La Fornarina! "Come!" laughed Teresa through the leaves . . . she had changed her *Inglese*—Italian minx that she was! . . . She had stripped him bare of his self-consciousness, his ingrowing sentiment, his hereditary sense of sin, and left him feeling like a naked pagan, unashamed and free! . . . "Come," wailed Teresa, as the wind rose and the moon slipped behind a cloud . . . she had built a home for him in her husband's house, and there he reigned, a God beside his hearth, the centre of his dreams . . . she had given him a family, friends, her brother. . . . A chime ringing from the city yonder, suddenly, and ceasing as the wind veered and bore the sound away—the clap of the dinner-bell across the mist and darkness of a forgotten garden, and "Come!" called the voice, more sharply now—was it Annabella calling from the window?—"I'm coming," he shouted angrily . . . she had taken him away from other women. . . . Oh, no, he wasn't free nor unashamed . . . he couldn't make love any more! . . . No longer did he love his—Oh, he cried, laughing and groaning at the thought—in wonder—relief—despair—"I'm coming," . . . you might just as well be my wife!

He wrote to Augusta. It was a kind letter, but brotherly—a letter of farewell—with every now and then a flick. He had recovered his senses at last, and now she was safe—if that were any happiness to her. He enclosed a lock of grey hair—"has there been nothing to make it grey?" "You know," he said casually, "or you do not know, that Madame La Comtesse G. was separated from her husband last year (on account of P.P. clerk of this parish)." Since that time, he assured Augusta, they had been living "very quietly and decently"—the Countess "at her father's (as the Pope decided) and I at home" (in Teresa's former house). But her father had been exiled, she had gone with him, and he was off to join them at Pisa.

So there's a *romance* for you. I assure it was not my wish nor fault altogether. Her husband was old—rich—must have left her a large jointure in a few years; but he was jealous, and insisted, etc., and *she* like all the rest *would* have her own way. You know that all my loves go crazy, and make scenes—and so—"She is the sixteenth Mrs Shuffleton." Being very young —very romantic—and odd—and being contradicted by her husband besides . . . you are not to wonder much at it; she being too a beauty . . . and married not quite a year (at our first acquaintance) . . . It is very odd that all my *fairs* are such romantic people; and always daggering or divorcing —or making scenes.

But this is "positively the last time of performance" (as the play-bills say), or of my getting into such scrapes for the future. Indeed—I have had my share. But this is a finisher; for you know when a woman is separated from her husband for her *amant*, he is bound both by honour (and inclination —at least I am), to live with her all his days . . . So . . . *you* will probably never see me again as long as you live. Indeed you don't deserve it—for having behaved so coldly when I was ready to have sacrificed everything for you—and after [at this point some one has crossed out several lines and the letter proceeds] It is nearly three years that this *liaison* has lasted. I was dreadfully in love—and she blindly so—for she has sacrificed everything to this headlong passion. That comes of being romantic. I can say that, without being so *furiously* in love as at first, I am more attached to her than I thought it possible to be to any woman after three years [here comes another line erased "except one and who was she can You guess?" and the letter goes on] and have not the least wish nor prospect of separation from her . . . If Lady B. would but please to die, and the Countess G's husband . . . we should probably have to marry—though I would rather *not*—thinking it the way to hate each other . . . However you need not calculate upon seeing me again in a hurry, if ever . . . Yours.

Augusta felt jealous of the Countess G. and unfeignedly grateful to her. There was a postscript with another flick.

*You* ought to be a great admirer of the future Lady B. . . . she is a grand patroness of the present Lady B. and always says "that she has no doubt that" she was exceedingly ill-used by me . . . She is an admirer of yours, and I have had great difficulty in keeping her from writing to you eleven pages (for she is a grand scribe) and . . . she having read *Don Juan* in a *French* translation—made me promise to write *no more* of it, declaring that it was abominable, etc., etc., and that *Donna Inez* WAS meant for Lady B. and in short made me vow *not* to continue it. . . . Is this not altogether odd enough? She has a good deal of *us* too. I mean that turn for ridicule like Aunt Sophy and you and I and all the B's.

News travelled fast in Romagna, especially in religious circles. The story of the eight wagons reached the convent in Bagnacavallo. Now Allegra must needs write him a letter, asking for something, as women will. "*Caro il mio Papa,*" she wrote on September 28, in careful copper-plate on ruled lines, "*essendo tempo di fiera desiderei tanto una visita del mio Papa, che ho molte voglie da levarmi, non vorrà compiacere la sua Allegrina che lo ama tanto!*" ("My dear Papa, it being fair-time, I should so much like a visit from my Papa, as I have many wants to be seen to; won't you please your Allegrina who loves you so?")

The Prioress wrote a few words on the back of her pupil's composition. There was a note of reproach in her letter.

We have heard with sorrow of your approaching departure, which we have thought fit to keep a secret from my little lady. I cannot, however, conceal my more than common regret . . . not to have had the honour of meeting you personally, so that, if I did not feel that I was trespassing on your kindness, I would beg you to grant us that consolation and so satisfy the lively desire of your Allegrina, before you go, on which occasion you will have the opportunity of seeing where, and how, she is situated, and, let me say, too, how much she is loved for her good and unusual qualities.

"Sincere enough, but not very flattering," Byron wrote across the top of Allegrina's letter. "She wants to see me because it 'is the fair' to get

some paternal gingerbread—I suppose." The child reminded him of a
mare he once rode in Switzerland when her mother was with him—a
pretty little feminine quadruped, always neighing when she wanted
something, which was every five minutes. It looked as though he would
have trouble with the Prioress if he tried to take Allegra away from her.
Certainly he would not ride out to Bagnacavallo to face a scene with a
couple of women, shedding tears or looking at him with eyes big with
pained reproach.

And then there was Teresa. Shelley wrote again from Pisa—on
October 21. "Your house is ready and all the furniture arranged . . .
Hunt is coming out . . . by sea . . . The Countess G. is very patient,
though sometimes she seems apprehensive that you will *never* leave
Ravenna." More reproaches. Every week—from Florence, from Pisa—
Teresa's letters came—many of them—long letters—devoted letters—
loving letters. She was full of "*presentimenti*," of "*crudeli timori*," she
saw him surrounded by a "thousand dangers" in a town convulsed by
party spirit, and with every post she dreaded to hear that he was dead.
He was alone in that dreary house, and well she knew how bad solitude
was for him. He was not feeding himself properly—was drinking gin
and taking those everlasting doses of salts. But under all this solicitude
there ran one unchanging refrain—"Come!"

He wrote and scolded her. The Government dared not attack him,
the common people were on his side, he was safe, and he would be a
coward to run away. Didn't she understand that he was fighting to get
Count Gamba's banishment annulled? "If Papa is recalled, I go back
that instant to Ravenna, and if he is recalled *before* I go, *I won't leave.*"

If she had *presentimenti*, so had he. The wagons came and he packed,
but still he delayed. Ravenna somehow meant luck for him, the world
outside was nothing but unhappiness. "I am leaving here so much
against my will," he wrote in exasperated menace to Teresa, "for I see
so many evil consequences for all of you, and, most of all, for you—*you
will see.*"

It was one thing to pack, it was another thing to go. He clung obstinately to the thought that Ravenna was home, and outside his old gypsy
life awaited him and unhappiness and discontent. He remembered that
October was a month for ague and malaria. He had premonitions of a
fever coming on, and after his meeting with the lady in the wood it was
shaking through his bones in dead earnest. He felt a mountain of lead
lying on his heart. He grew savage and quarrelsome and suspected every
one of plotting against him—Teresa, the Gambas, Shelley, the Pope,
Fletcher—and because the others were out of reach he lavished all his
rage on Fletcher. He took a dose of salts—his unfailing remedy for
depression—and gradually his fever abated. But his "lemoncholy"

wouldn't go. He felt spiritual, his body was all gone, and he was nothing now but soul.

Murray had promised him the proofs of *Cain*, and he must wait for them. Murray, as usual, was dilatory—thank God!—and the proofs came several days late. Shelley wrote from Pisa on a tone of gentle reproach. Morosely Byron made up his mind to go. But he wouldn't toil out to Bagnacavallo—he wouldn't open that question again—Allegra must stay behind in Romagna. Shelley, with his talk of "private families"—eight wagons at his door was enough of *his* interference! He wrote to Teresa and told her Allegra was happy at the convent and he wouldn't, after all, bring her to Pisa—would she, please, tell Shelley that?

The day of departure came. His coach, carriages, wagons, horses, were drawn up in the narrow street outside the Palazzo Guiccioli. His 'ragamuffins' loaded them with furniture, pictures, papers, books, the menagerie of beasts, guns, cartridges, bayonets—all the accumulations of a year's sojourn in the house. He bade them take away his bed and linen and put it on a wagon, and sat up all night, waiting for the sun to rise. If he slipped between the sheets and fell asleep he knew he wouldn't go. Early on a fine, crisp autumnal morning (October 29) he drove away from Ravenna, looking back mournfully on Count Guiccioli's palace, where somehow he had found peace. The porter shut the doors to with a clang and spat contemptuously in the dust.

The sky grew brighter and the air was warmer as he slowly travelled south, but all the way he felt that he was going back—back into the past, back into the world from which he had lain so long hid with Teresa. On the road to Bologna he met his dearest friend of Harrow days—Lord Clare. They stood for five minutes only by the roadside, but, in that moment, all time slipped in a sheen of mock lightning into boyhood. The blood throbbed like thunder in his ears, he could scarcely speak, and Clare was yet more agitated. As they stood holding hands, they felt their hearts beating in their finger-tips.

At Bologna he found an acquaintance of London days—old Samuel Rogers, the banker-poet—who greeted him with his thin, cadaverous sneer. Byron loved him not and returned his greeting with a malicious smile. He carried him off to the Certosa graveyard and introduced him to his old friend the sexton. That worthy stared at Rogers "very hard," as though he would like to add his skull to his collection.

Together the two poets travelled on to Florence and there took leave of each other. Byron visited the picture-galleries and walked moodily beside the river, playing at ducks and drakes, and fell into talk with a young American whom he found busy at the same game. Then his caravan rolled away on the last lap of its journey.

Outside Empoli the public diligence coming from Pisa drew up to one side of the road to let the English milord's cavalcade go by. . . . He leaned forward to gaze from his window at the waiting coach. . . . From its roof a dark-haired woman with a sharp, startled face looked down at him—at the small head with the curling hair, the blunt, straight nose, the petulant underlip thrust forward in disdain. . . . His eyes met hers and travelled over her face carelessly with no glimmer of recognition. . . . He fell back lazily in his seat, tapping with his foot on the floor and murmuring to himself in a dreamy, mocking tone, "She *thought*—that I *was* —not un*worthy*—to *love* her" . . . and his caravan rumbled by.

That was the last time Claire Clairmont saw the father of her child.

# BOOK FOUR

# Melodrama

### CHAPTER I

## Reunion in Pisa

I AM leaving Ravenna so much against my will and so convinced that
my going can only lead from one sorrow to another yet worse that I
have not the heart to write more on that subject."

Thus Byron had announced his coming to Teresa. On the afternoon
of November 1, 1821, the good people of Pisa watched the mad English
Lord's caravan of coach and wagon rumble slowly along the Lung' Arno
to the Palazzo Lanfranchi. That accomplished spy of Prince Metternich
the Cavaliere Torelli was on duty to watch the unloading at the doors.
Lord Byron's coach was an impressive structure with a coat-of-arms on
the panels and the motto *Crede Byron*. Fourteen horses, noted the
Cavaliere in his diary, a groom, an English valet, and a horde of wild
servants from Romagna—a veritable "gang of murderers." Trouble
would certainly come in Pisa.

Byron called obediently on his lady and her father at their lodgings.
As he drove by Claire and the waiting coach he had been meditating a
poem—farewell to youth, farewell to fame, back again to love.

> Oh, talk not to me of a name great in story,
> The days of our youth are the days of our glory;
> And the myrtle and ivy of sweet two-and-twenty
> Are worth all your laurels, though ever so plenty.

> What are the garlands and crowns to the brow that is wrinkled?
> 'Tis but as a dead-flower with May-dew besprinkled.
> Then away with all such from the head that is hoary!
> What care I for the wreaths that can *only* give glory!

> Oh Fame!—if I e'er took delight in thy praises,
> 'Twas less for the sake of thy high-sounding phrases,
> Than to see the bright eyes of the dear one discover,
> She thought that I was not unworthy to love her.

He offered the poem to Teresa, and she was rewarded for her long
waiting. "*Mio Byron*," she chanted in delight, then with a frown—but,

*carissimo*, your hair is scarcely grey at all. She looked pensive as though she wanted more. He grinned and sat down to a table and wrote another stanza. Listen, he cried, and Teresa, who had been drowsing, looked up with a smile.

> *There* chiefly I sought thee, *there* only I found thee;
> Her glance was the best of the rays that surround thee;
> When it sparkled o'er aught that was bright in my story,
> I knew it was love, and I felt it was glory.

Dated "Pisa, November 6, 1821." Her pilgrim had returned—again—and Teresa was happy.

Pisa had been a dull town without Robin Adair. In memory it was always to remain a sad town for her—old and grey and tired. She had been an exile there, an outcast, and for a long time she had been lonely. Then happiness returned, then came doubt, a sense of change, and alarming *presentimenti*. Out of quietness life leapt suddenly into a whirlwind of farce, then ran rapidly downhill to death.

When Shelley's letter reached Florence Count Gamba applied to the authorities for permission to transfer himself and his family to Pisa. The *Buon Governo* of Tuscany no more desired the society of the Gambas than the Papal Legate in Romagna. Apart from wrong-headed activities in their home state the police of Florence looked with grave misgivings on the tribe of unruly servants that the Gambas had brought with them from Filetto. The household was placed under police supervision. Count Gamba was told that neither he nor his family would be allowed to leave Florence without special permit, and one or two of the servants were 'given the ticket,' which kept them indoors between the hours of sunset and sunrise. When Count Gamba applied for leave to go to Pisa his petition was granted with restrictions. He might reside there for two months only. If he or his son at any time engaged in political activity of an offensive kind, or if their servants brawled or stabbed in the streets, right of asylum would be withdrawn, and out of the state of Tuscany they and their lackeys would go.

The police of Pisa no more wanted the Gambas and their servants than the police in Florence. In time they noticed that the Countess Guiccioli and her brother were busy at the Palazzo Lanfranchi in the Lung' Arno, and the news was soon abroad that they were making the house ready for occupation by Lord Byron. The Pisa police wrote in alarm to Florence for instructions; if that turbulent nobleman arrived in Pisa they knew there would be the devil to pay. The authorities in Florence reassured them. It was well known, they said, that Lord Byron was going to Pisa "solely for the fair daughter of Count Gamba, so you may expect him." Privately they revealed to the Pisa police the domestic arrangements of the Countess Guiccioli, and intimated that when Lord Byron made himself obnoxious the fault should be laid upon the Gambas, who might then be expelled from Tuscany. It was a well-known fact that wheresoever the Countess Guiccioli went, Lord Byron was sure to go. In the meantime, pending an outbreak of the Byronic temper, which the Florentine police thought inevitable, the permit for the Gamba family to reside in Pisa should be renewed "at the proper time."

Teresa settled with her father and Pietro in modest lodgings, far away from the Lung' Arno under the shadow of the Cathedral, with a garden at the back adjoining the Campo Santo. There they lived very quietly until Byron came. Except for flying visits from the taciturn Vincenzo no one stayed with them, and they had few friends in the town. They were political refugees, poor and under police supervision, and it was not safe to know them. Pisa, too, was a bourgeois city, and the Countess Guiccioli was not looked upon with favour—a young wife separated with scandal from her husband and reputed to be the mistress of that notorious Lord Byron. Pietro and Vincenzo amused themselves with shooting at a *podere* outside the town. Teresa, with her more intellectual tastes, looked for society among the professors at the University. The famous surgeon Dr Andrea Vacca Berlinghieri visited their house and talked with her of England, where he had studied medicine. Giovanni Rosini, the Professor of Italian Literature, was another visitor. He was a bad poet and a writer of heavy romances, but he was a cautious liberal. Vacca was more outspoken, for he had helped storm the Bastille, and with both men the Gambas might talk politics.

Later came English friends. Shelley and Mary moved to Pisa from the baths close by and took up their residence in the Tre Palazzi di Chiesa, facing the Palazzo Lanfranchi on the opposite bank of the Arno. With them came Edward Elliker Williams and Jane Williams. Edward had been at Eton with Shelley and later was an officer in the dragoons. Jane had lived in St Helena and known Napoleon. The Williams passed for man and wife, and no one in Pisa supposed that they were anything else, but as a matter of fact Jane had an undesirable husband in India whom she had left for Ned Williams. Shelley's cousin, Tom Medwin, of the dragoons, joined the group. Claire Clairmont hovered restlessly in the background, but she and Teresa never met. As usual Pietro became a great friend with the English, and he and Teresa visited almost daily the Tre Palazzi. Shelley, like Byron, disbursed money anonymously among the poor, and Pietro served as his willing, if incompetent, agent.

The Cavaliere Torelli kept the Gamba family under his eye. They were busy at the Palazzo Lanfranchi with that disgraceful Englishman, Shelley, who called himself an atheist. Six months' rent had been paid down in advance, and furniture was moving into the bare and stately

rooms. From inquiries made Torelli was sure that the English nobleman was coming to Pisa for some political mischief, and certainly he
deserved the attention of the united police force of Europe. But then he
was a famous poet, it appeared, and, as was often the case with Englishmen of the upper classes, he was slightly cracked. Weeks went by, and
months; and it seemed that not all the charms of "Count Gamba's fair
daughter" would lure him to Pisa. The "odd creature" had changed his
mind and was not coming at all.

So, too, thought Teresa sometimes, as August came to an end and
September passed slowly by and October drew to its close. Not for her
sake did she want him to leave Ravenna, but for his own—thus she wrote
him every week. She imagined him alone there in that gloomy palace
that had been once her home. His friends were banished, he lived among
enemies, and one day he would be killed. His answers to her letters were
cross and impatient and full of dire forebodings—for her, for himself—
if ever he left Ravenna, and, against her will, she, too, was filled with
"*presentimenti*." But anything was better than absence with this constant
fear that the next news would be death.

Then that odd angel Shelley visited Ravenna for some purpose of his
own. He wrote her a letter out of a blue sky, giving her wise counsel,
and Byron had come back. She was grateful to Shelley, and in her gratitude she loved him. Yet when she told him that Allegra was not coming
to Pisa he had frowned and looked at her in a disapproving way. He
seemed to feel for that child almost as a father would. She gave him a
curious glance, for Byron had once told her in a bitter mood that Allegra
was Shelley's child—a lie for anyone who looked at Allegra and loved
Byron.

The old life of Ravenna was renewed. Sometimes in the afternoon
Teresa drove out with Mary Shelley in Byron's carriage to meet the
gentlemen as they returned from their shooting-match at the *podere*. In
the evening Byron paid his *devoirs* at the Gamba lodgings. He read
poetry, she sang to him; Count Gamba came in from the theatre, and
talk relapsed into polite generalities; Pietro came in from a lively session
at Don Beppo's *caffè*, and talk was all of constitutions in Spain or independence in Greece, for Pietro's enthusiasms now spread far beyond the
bounds of Italy. The other English dropped in—Shelley, Ned Williams,
Tom Medwin, whom Teresa found *seccatura*—that is, a bore—and
Edward John Trelawny, who brought with him an exciting atmosphere
of piracy and tropics. More politics—talk of poetry—religion—argument
round and about it in a language she didn't understand. Then Dr Vacca
came in, and Rosini, the bad poet, and 'Count' Taafe, another bad poet,
and the Canon of San Pierino. Teresa was proud, for in her poor house
she had now all the honours of a *salon*—a small *salon*, perhaps, yet even
in the eyes of critical Pisans a distinguished one. For whatever might

be thought of strange folk like Byron or Shelley, Dr Vacca and Professor Rosini and the Canon of San Pierino were great men indeed. At midnight the room emptied and Byron said good-night—and, if Count Gamba were not looking, embraced Teresa. Then home he went to the Palazzo Lanfranchi to write poetry into the small hours of the morning.

Why was it that in after-years she remembered her lover so vividly in the quiet garden by the Campo Santo—the way he looked and walked, the things he said and did? In Venice, at La Mira, in Ravenna, he had been a god, but now she was face to face with a *man*. Never had his conversation been more delightful, more amusing, more kind! Even the solemn Annabella in her honeymoon had fallen under the spell of her husband's conversation—"springs in deserts found," she called those all-too-brief moments of happiness in retrospect. There was, she confessed, a "language of nonsense between us . . . he would give play to his imagination and suddenly deliver the deepest reflections, then"— Annabella sighed as she remembered—"shrink from them in frolic and levity." The grace, said the poor woman, of *genius*—the only "grace" her "dearest duck" ever had! Teresa, too, as an old woman tried to remember that impalpable charm, but characteristically her mind worked the other way from Annabella's. He seemed to emerge for her out of deepest thought with a perplexing smile, then suddenly body and soul rocked together in a harmony of mirth. The air round him was radiant in a sunshine of laughter, and you were dazzled and caught up in his bliss and laughed aloud yourself. Then, with another smile and a quick turn of phrase, he switched you into dreams again.

Yet there was a subtle transformation in her Byron. He was not the man she had left in Ravenna, and even in her happiness she was distressed. Her own feelings, too, had changed. Somehow she felt more wifely about him. For his sake she must demand less for herself and more for him. She worried about his health and teased him to eat and drink more sensibly—less green tea, less gin and water, less unholy mishmashes of vegetables—more meat and wine. He must consult Dr Vacca and forgo his laudanum and everlasting doses of salts. Poetry was hard work. Solitude, he said, was essential for making it, yet those last months of loneliness in Ravenna had been bad for him spiritually. He must go out and see people. She herself was an exile and could not give him, as she had given him at Ravenna, the world of her own friends and family to live in. But he had his own house now. Why should he not entertain Shelley and Medwin and the other English there? Why didn't he ask Lord Clare to stay with him, and old Mr Rogers, the poet, and—who knows?—perhaps Mr Hobhouse, who seemed to symbolize all England for him, might pay him a visit one day!

To his friends in England Byron wrote that he was out of his low spirits. He was living in a fine old feudal *palazzo*, said to be built by

Michelangelo, and at night Fletcher flitted restlessly from room to room in search of a bed not occupied by a ghost. He liked the feeling of ownership. "I can walk down into my garden, and pluck my own oranges," he told Moore, "and, by the way, have got a diarrhoea in consequence of indulging in this meridian luxury of proprietorship."

He threw off his airs of misanthropy and went out riding with his new-found English acquaintance. Led by Pietro and Vincenzo, they frequented the *podere* outside the town and practised shooting. There was a pretty peasant girl there to whom Byron made love in the lordly style of young squire with a milkmaid. He loaded her arms with cheap bracelets, and there were kind friends enough to let Teresa know of these princely junketings.

On Wednesday nights he gave dinners to the English. Medwin was loud in his praise of the elegance of these repasts—they reminded him of the 'best houses' in London—all sorts of wine and all the delicacies of fish and game in season. Shelley deplored the melancholy spectacle of human beings turning themselves into "vats of claret." For years Byron had lived in Italy with the Italians, scornfully refusing to associate with the English, but now he found himself in England once more. His feelings were in a turmoil. English voices made him homesick—for English faces—for friends of old days—the sights and sounds of England—Harrow churchyard and the school-bell ringing in the distance. But he felt, too, that cold English eyes were upon him once more, spying out his frailties, listening sharply to every word he said. Under a mask of raillery he was on guard.

They were a strange crew—Shelley the 'atheist,' Trelawny the 'pirate,' 'Count' Taafe, the comic Irishman, who wrote bad poetry, Tom Medwin, the long-faced dragoon with literary ambitions, Captain Hay, the melancholy hunter of big game—only Elliker Williams, with his good-natured face and friendly laughter, seemed an ordinary human being. Shelley was the one man among them that Byron cared for, but Shelley, he was sure, disapproved of him. Trelawny burst upon the quiet community with a wild aura of passion and romance about him and a volley of sailor-going oaths, and Shelley and the women sat at his feet and listened eagerly to his stories. Yet, for all his airs of masculinity, Trelawny was as sentimental and, if crossed in his vanity, as malicious as a woman. His favourite hero was the Corsair, and he had scrambled across the Alps to meet the creator of the Corsair in real life. Good, Trelawny, then, must be 'bammed.' Instead of Childe Harold he found a "highly facetious personage" in the Don Juan vein. Like the women, he was disappointed and raged impotently under Byron's mockery when he essayed his more exotic airs of piracy. As for Medwin, Byron knew he was taking notes of every word he uttered with a view to a book later on. Medwin, too, was 'bammed,' and Teresa protested stormily—he must be careful what he said in Medwin's presence, otherwise he would be given to the world as a cynic and a rake. But Byron only laughed. Medwin, he said, so gullible—with his eyes popping and his mouth gaping—reminded him of his wife—recording likenesses that weren't like.

Teresa felt that she was being submerged. She had known practically no Englishmen until she came to Pisa—save Byron, and he transcended all nationality, he was God. These men intrigued her, they puzzled her; without their meaning it, they amused and, if the truth be known, often disappointed her. They were tall, good-looking, more virile than Italian men; yet passion with them was a mental process and lacked the graces of the body. They were more intellectual than Italian men and talked and argued a great deal. They were soft-voiced yet emphatic and, she thought, arrogant in stating their opinions. With her they were polite, but somehow every one of them, save Shelley, seemed to give her his left hand. They made her feel like a foreigner in her own country, for she knew that behind her back they called her ' *La Guiccioli*,' as though she were an opera singer, and laughed at her for being 'so Italian.' She was indifferent to most of them, but Tom Medwin, who treated her as a nice little woman, she cordially disliked. He was vulgar and sentimental —a combination of virtues that no Italian woman will tolerate—and he disgusted her by his leering talk of conquests among the 'sex.' But for Trelawny she had a real liking. He treated her with rough-and-ready kindness—she was vain, perhaps, he thought, and affected, but at heart she was 'a good fellow.' On her side, like the other women, she was fascinated by his tales of "antres vast and desarts idle." As he stood there, with his deep-sunk eyes, his hawk-like nose, his high Arabian shoulders, arms folded gloomily across his chest, he was the Corsair come true—the man her Byron might have been, the man she had once hoped he was. And yet—the Corsair in real life was a trifle unreal—a little pathetic—and with Byron she sometimes laughed.

There were only two other women in the circle. Jane Williams was a remarkably pretty Anglo-Indian flirt with an easy sex-appeal that she kept in check for Ned's sake and in good repair for her own. The Shelleys said she was perfect, and Shelley wrote her poems—she was Miranda, his "magnetic lady," who played charmingly on the guitar. Teresa thought her a little common—and so did Byron. But Jane gazed serenely over Teresa's head with the confident smile of a woman who wins and holds masculine admiration without allowing it to upset her nursery routine.

Mary Shelley attracted Teresa in the beginning because she was Shelley's wife, but later she made good on her own account. She was intellectual, she was capable. Slender almost to attenuation, with a small head and reddish gold hair round a sharp face, somehow she fell short of beauty. In repose her face was disconsolate, but whatever were her

N

cause of sorrow she hid it under a manner that was elaborately arch. Teresa knew her story—how she, too, had endured obloquy and exile for her poet's sake—and felt that they were sister-souls. Mary had expected something more formidable in Byron's mistress—at least a dark-haired siren, like Emilia Viviani, with a downward smile and a loud, emphatic voice. Instead she found a child with gold hair and blue eyes, musical voice and artless manner, who plainly wanted to be friends. "A nice, pretty girl, unassuming and amiable," said Mary and, with a touch of condescension, admitted her to friendship. They laughed together over the vagaries of their poets and, when Byron's carriage came, went out driving in the Cascine. After years of comfortless vagabonding, in Teresa's society Mary felt like a lady, the daughter-in-law, as in truth she was, of an English baronet.

But Shelley was different from the others. His affair with Emilia Viviani had come to a miserable end. The lady had tried to borrow money—had told him to be more careful in his letters—had married her lawyer, and was now leading him and her mother-in-law "the devil of a life." Shelley was ever kind and courteous, but he was shy with Teresa. She was pretty, sentimental, innocent, he thought, she had proved her devotion to Byron and cured him of his vices. But she was a dunce, and, with her effusive manner, her deep voice and carefully disordered ringlets, she was, like Emilia, an Italian—theatrical and, in all but love for Byron, superficial.

In her way Teresa loved Shelley, and Pietro adored him. He didn't belong to this earth, they said; he was an angel, a faun, a sprite, and they made fun of him—behind his back and to his face. Well she remembered that windy morning when he called at her house with the blood streaming down his face from a wound in his forehead. She inquired anxiously what had happened, thinking naturally of a fight in the street. Shelley clapped his hand to his forehead and, withdrawing it, stared dreamily at his own blood. Yes, he remembered, a flying tile had hit him on the head and sent him tumbling into the gutter—but he hadn't noticed it at the time, he was thinking of something else! Every one laughed at Shelley—falling off horses, capsizing in the Arno—and every one respected him. She looked up with a smile when he came into the room and listened with a fond countenance while he talked to her in that low, rapid voice of his, rising to a shriek as he thought of God. Why did he hate God so, if he didn't believe in His existence? Why did he call himself an atheist? A Calvinist like Byron she could understand, thanks to her training in theology. But an atheist was a man who believed in a vacuum!

One afternoon the 'gang,' as Trelawny called them, were in her small parlour. Byron told with some humour the story of a miracle that was said to have taken place in Lucca recently. Shelley's voice grew shrill

with scorn as he denounced all belief in miracles as a deplorable super-
stition. Tom Medwin solemnly dismissed them as impossible—they were
against the law of Nature. Teresa showed her displeasure by keeping
silence. Byron turned to her with a smile.

"Do you, then, believe in that miracle?" he inquired.

"I believe in miracles," she answered bravely, "because I believe in
God."

There were smiles round the room, and Shelley's jaw was thrust out
in defiance. But the fair theologian went her way. The law of Nature,
she said, staring haughtily at Medwin, was a law only and might be
amended or repealed. God had made the law of Nature, and in His wisdom He might change His own handiwork. Shelley was on his feet
muttering something about irresponsible despots, but she bore him down.
All these *signori* in her *salon* were lovers of liberty, for themselves and for
the human race—what right had they, even if they had the power, to
deny liberty to God? Was God alone to be stultified by His own works?
"I believe in miracles because I believe in God, and I could not believe
in God if I did not know Him to be omnipotent." "God!" cried Shelley,
"God! That—" but Byron tactfully closed the argument on Teresa's
side. "After all," said he, "common sense is the best philosophy, and
God Himself the first of miracles."

"Shelley's gone mad with metaphysics!" he told her when the company had gone, adding scornfully, "Metaphysics! What trash in all
these systems!" Teresa could not in those days read Shelley's poems, but
some years later she read them and deeply felt their beauty of phrase and
thought. But never could she feel or think as Shelley felt and thought.
All was abstraction here—no touch of common humanity—no Haidée
nor Juan, not even Cain, for Shelley never doubted, he always was sure.
She couldn't swoon that way nor float in such cold mountain ecstasy
through this life or the life to come. She would never faint upon a wild
west wind or dissolve in a skylark's song; nor, when she entered Paradise,
had she any intention of fading into insubstantial rainbow round the
Godhead. All this was paganism, perhaps it was pantheism—God not
only in His Heaven but immanent in trees and flowers—nay, was there
not a touch of mysticism in it, too—not the mysticism of the *Paradiso*
—so jubilant, so personal—but of St Francis of Assisi, perhaps, or
Pascal?

Many years later she went to the Protestant cemetery at Rome to lay
flowers on Shelley's tomb. The grass was growing rank over the grave,
and it looked forlorn and neglected. She brooded mournfully over the
fate of this man who had called himself an atheist, who had been a poet,
like her lover, and an exile from the same strange country. A woman
cannot live her life with poets without catching something of their spirit.
She wrote an elegy for Shelley.

A quella tomba che negletta vedi
Fra i tumuli superbi e incoronati
Di funebri cipressi e di verdura,
Arresta, amico, riverente il piede.

Pause, friend, reverently a while by this neglected grave amid proud monuments wreathed in verdure and sad cypress. The handful of dust that lies here once was wedded to a gentle spirit, to a wounded heart, a soul for ever homeless on this earth. Trailing echoes of the spirit-voices in *Prometheus Unbound* filled her ears.

Quella infinita immagin si pingea
E illuminava d' innefabili luce,
Per te i deserti, i flutti, il firmamento
Avean voci sublimi e ti chiamavano
Tutte all' eterna vita in seno a Dio.

O dead poet, for thee the world was bathed in light infinite beyond all power of words; for thee the solitudes, the waves, the sky, were filled with heavenly voices that called thee to life eternal in the heart of God. England, this poet of thine was no atheist! God loved him, and God spoke to him, and in his life he was a man tender and unwise.

Discussion was not always on the high plane of religion and poetry. There were moments more frivolous, and sometimes there was misunderstanding. Once they had been discussing *Othello*. "Why not let us act *Othello*?" cried Byron gaily. "All Pisa shall be our audience!" Mischievously he cast the actors for their parts. Our friend Trelawny, with his wild Arab look and his Arab stories, shall be Othello. For Cassio we pick cheerful Ned Williams, for the gullible Roderigo, Tom Medwin. Jane Williams shall be Emilia, with that underlying streak of commonness in her. And for Desdemona to Trelawny's Othello—Mary Shelley shall be Desdemona. That indeed was a wicked stroke on Byron's part, for Mary Shelley was perplexed and disturbed by Trelawny and remained under his spell all her life. And Iago, the scoffer, the cynic, the manipulator of poor human nature—*he* would play Iago to Trelawny's Othello.

Teresa was furious. It mattered not that the only part left for her among this troupe of English folk was that of Bianca, the harlot. But why should her Byron deliberately choose for himself the part of Iago—why must he always want to play the cynic? He must be the hero, Othello, and if he were Othello, *she* must be Desdemona. She laid her veto on the performance. The others gave in with a laugh—after all, they had only been fooling with the idea. The Countess Guiccioli was jealous—she had no sense of humour—and, oh, how tiresome she was, and how Italian!

After Ravenna, with its plots and pogroms, this was a dull provincial life. The Cavaliere Torelli kept his eye on the comings and goings of these odd English folk. They held aloof from the Italians—save for such suspicious types as Dr Vacca, the surgeon, and Rosini, the poet. They visited one another, dining at the Palazzo Lanfranchi one night, calling on the Countess Guiccioli another. In the daytime they went shooting at the *podere*, and Lord Byron evidently had designs on the *contadina* there.

But under this quiet exterior there was trouble brewing. Count Gamba was homesick and melancholy. Teresa was sad on his account and often felt lonely. Pietro alone was happy, dreaming of revolution. The servants were daily growing more difficult, for they, too, wanted to go home. In Byron there was a fury of suppressed restlessness. Suddenly it exploded, and, as the Cavaliere Torelli had prophesied, he and his "gang of murderers" at last gave Pisa a taste of their true temper.

## CHAPTER II

# *"Shiloh" goes*

ONE Sunday evening in March (1822) the 'gang'—Byron, Shelley, Pietro, Trelawny, Captain Hay, and 'Count' Taafe—were riding home from an outing in the country. Teresa followed the shambling cavalcade of horsemen with Mary in the carriage. As they drew near the Porta alla Piazza a tipsy, red-haired hussar galloped through their midst, jostling Taafe and knocking his hat off.

"Shall we endure this man's insolence?" roared Taafe.

"No," shouted Byron, "we will bring him to account."

"As you will," shrieked Shelley, and set spurs to his horse.

With that the hunt was up. All the party—save Taafe—galloped down the road after Shelley and the red-haired hussar. The coachman whipped up his horses, and Mary and Teresa followed in the carriage. Shelley overtook the hussar by the city-gate and resolutely barred his way into town. The others rode up, and Byron, mistaking the fellow for an officer, threw him his card and asked him what he meant by his insolence. Pietro, knowing better, slashed at him scornfully with his whip. The hussar—Sergeant Masi was his rank and name—belched and blustered with his hand on his sabre-hilt and tried to ride them down.

"Why don't you arrest them!" cried the soldiers at the gate. "Tell us to arrest them!"

"Arrest me if you can!" shouted Byron with a laugh, and with Pietro he galloped through the gate to fetch arms from the Palazzo Lanfranchi. Roaring that the others were under arrest, Sergeant Masi drew his sabre and laid about him wildly. The soldiers ran out from the gate and beat Trelawny about the thighs with the flats of their swords. The ladies drove up as the scrimmage began. Shelley rode the soldiers down and spurred his horse at the hussar. He was hit over the head by the whirling sabre and fell sprawling in the dust.

"O Heaven! Have pity! Have pity!" shrieked Teresa, as she saw Shelley fall. Mary was silent, but her eyes shone with pride.

Captain Hay rode to Shelley's defence and was sliced across the nose, and away galloped the sergeant with the honours of the field.

The citizens of Pisa scuttled to the walls as the red-haired hussar thundered past them, roaring in his triumph. At long and sorry intervals after him rode three angry Englishmen—dusty, bleeding, dishevelled—brandishing riding-crops and canes. Byron came galloping back from his *palazzo*, and Sergeant Masi charged at him, shouting "*Siete soddis-fatto?*" ("Are you satisfied?")

"No," said Byron, laying his hand on his sword-stick. "I'm not. Give me your card!"

Tita ran with blazing eyes to his master's side and clutched the bridle of the sergeant's horse. Byron told him angrily to let go. With an oath Masi turned his horse and galloped away. Dusk was falling, and as by magic a crowd had gathered before the Palazzo Lanfranchi. A servant ran out from the palace, wild-eyed and furious, as Masi rode by, and stabbed him in the ribs with a pitchfork and vanished with a triumphant yell. Reeling in his saddle, Masi rode on a hundred paces and tumbled off his horse in front of Don Beppo's *caffè*. His helmet rolled clattering into the gutter. His red hair blazed round his white, puzzled face. "I'm killed!" he cried, and fainted.

Ned Williams and Jane were sitting patiently in the Shelleys' lodgings, waiting for them to return home for dinner, when Trelawny burst in with the news of the affray by the gate. They hastened across the street to the Palazzo Lanfranchi. A few minutes later Byron came in with Teresa on his arm, followed by Pietro and Shelley, Captain Hay and Mary. All was noise and excitement. Byron was wild with anger and, as always happened when he was excited, was laughing. Shelley was puking, and Captain Hay was holding his bloody nose. Pietro was shouting furiously at the servants, and Trelawny thundered that he would beat the bones out of Taafe's body. Teresa was on the verge of fainting. Mary Shelley looked philosophically on. A surgeon was summoned to attend to Teresa and the wounded Captain. Finally Byron left to take Teresa home, and Captain Hay went back to his lodgings with his nose bandaged.

The council of war moved across the street to the Tre Palazzi. Byron and Trelawny hurried off to be the first in lodging a complaint with the police. Taafe looked in with a brave tale of his own doings and left for the police station, too, where he deposed that he was looking for his hat at the time of the scrimmage by the gate. He returned with a long face to say that the hussar was dying and vanished, uneasily, leaving behind him a crop of rumours. Trelawny, it appeared, had been left dead at the gate, and Byron was mortally wounded. Byron and Trelawny returned, and over their brandy and water they all discussed "how the attack ought to have been conducted" in the best style of military strategists. The general opinion was that the business had been "bungled." Shelley thought something should be done about the hussar—an apology, a pension, or doctor's bill paid—and Byron swore that never would he shake Taafe by the hand again.

Without the town was in an uproar. Turn the *maladetti Inglesi* out! some were crying. No, shouted others, hats off to brave men! Then came a sobering sight. Every Englishman in the city from lord to groom was

walking, arrogantly and sedately, towards the Palazzo Lanfranchi, with
pistol, cane, or riding-crop in his hand. Lord Byron's morals might be
disgraceful, but, by God, he was an Englishman for all that! He had
been insulted—he was in danger—if there was to be a row, he might
command their services!

And, last of all, the touch of enchantment. A ghostly Oriental horse-
man galloped through the dusk, with a blackamoor running before his
horse, and vanished like a streak of lightning. Darkness and quiet fell
upon the tumult.

Sergeant Masi did not die, though rumour killed him a hundred times.
He left the army and settled down at Pisa in a tobacconist's shop. In old
age, when suitably encouraged, he told tourists the story of his fight with
Byron, and how he—alone and strictly sober—had sent the famous poet
—aye, and a dozen other English, too—toppling in the dust. "The devil!
The devil!" they cried, as one by one they fell.

The police instituted an official inquiry into the outbreak. The business was felt to be sufficiently serious for the Grand Duke of Tuscany
to come to town, and a special magistrate was sent from Florence to conduct the inquiry. It was long and thorough. All the leading participants
in the fray were courteously examined and acquitted of ill-doing. Mary
and Teresa had to bear their share in catechism. Mary was patient and
superior and dismissed the examining magistrate as "a talkative buffoon."
Teresa darkened counsel by declaring that the man who had stabbed the
hussar was Mr Taafe. The servants were examined more roughly and
made a bad impression by appearing in court with pistols and stilettos in
their sashes. Tita and Teresa's footman, Antonio, were banished from
town on general principle. The actual wielder of the pitchfork, carefully,
was not discovered. The verdict was that the assault had been committed
by the Gamba servants—who lived far away from the scene of battle, out
at the Campo Santo. Count Gamba and his sons were accordingly notified that they and their lackeys must now leave Pisa. In protest Byron
rented the Villa Dupuy at Montenero, outside Leghorn, for himself and
the Gambas and made ready to leave town, too.

While the magistrate was taking depositions on the Masi affair Claire
Clairmont arrived in Pisa (April 15). She went to stay with the Shelleys
at the Tre Palazzi, facing the Palazzo Lanfranchi. Gunpowder and fire
were now in close proximity!

When she learned from Shelley that Allegra was not coming to Pisa
she had left in despair to stay with friends in Florence. There she had
come to a wise resolution. She must leave Italy. There was nothing for
her there but unhappiness and frustration. She was idle and, though
Shelley was infinitely kind and hospitable, she had outworn Mary's

patience. She would go to Vienna, where her brother Charles had set up shop as a teacher of English, and earn her living as a governess—a dreary ending to all her dreams of emancipation, when she had thrown herself at Byron's head.

But before she left she must see Allegra. Unknown to Byron or Shelley, she sent her own scout, Mr Tighe, to Bagnacavallo. He came back with an alarming report. The Capuchin sisters were poor and austere, the building was dark, the food meagre, and in the winter there was no fire before which the children might warm their hands and feet. In the marshes below the town there lurked a fever which from time to time ravaged the whole countryside. Claire was made no happier by meeting Allegra's former nurse. Elise impudently denied the slander that she had told Mrs Hoppner and wrote to that lady to rebuke her for spreading "*des horreurs*" about Mlle Clairmont. But she maliciously substituted for one *horreur* others more calculated to make Claire unhappy. All that winter she brooded over her daughter, helpless in a cruel father's hands, forlorn and shivering in that cold convent on the hill. Nightly she woke from dreams that the child was dead. At last she wrote to Byron, begging him to let her see Allegra before she left Italy. For once she forgot to scold and wrote with dignity. "I can no longer resist the internal inexplicable feeling which haunts me that I shall never see her any more. . . . My dear friend, do not make the world dark to me, as if my Allegra were dead."

Byron did not answer that letter, and Claire became desperate. Her first thought was to appeal to Teresa for help, and it is a pity that she did not put the thought into action. Without knowing her, Teresa was harsh; but, seeing Claire, she would have been kind, and in the upshot she alone could persuade Byron to change his mind. But it was Teresa who had chosen the convent, and people told Claire that she was jealous of Allegra. So Teresa as an ally was discarded, and Claire fell back on wilder schemes. Shelley was to forge a letter to the convent, and Allegra must be kidnapped.

Both Mary and Shelley protested against this plan, Mary with a battery of muddled argument, Shelley in anger. Claire never forgave Mary for her arguments. She returned to Pisa, still nourishing schemes of kidnapping. In the meantime Shelley was exercising all his powers of persuasion on Byron to induce him to let Claire see Allegra. He was in a difficult position. Leigh Hunt had been kept in England by a chapter of mishaps, and Byron was already repenting his bargain there. But Hunt was at last on the way, and until he arrived Shelley realized that he must not break with Byron. What with fighting Hunt's battles and Claire's, he was exhausted and sad. Byron only sneered and exclaimed impatiently that women must always be making scenes when he told him how Claire was tortured with the fear that Allegra would die before she could see her.

My friendship with Byron is at an end, he said angrily; I must break away from him and his "detestable intimacy." Thank God he was going to Leghorn! In the meantime they must find a summer residence elsewhere and take Claire away with them. Ned Williams was dispatched to Lerici to look for a house by the sea, and Claire went with him. They found only one house available—the Casa Magni—a derelict villa, solitary and unfurnished, standing in wild country on the very edge of the sea. They returned to Pisa in two days to report their poor success. Williams met Shelley in the street. His face was white and furious. Allegra was dead.

The fever that Claire dreaded had broken out in the convent, and Allegra fell sick. The Prioress sent bulletins to Teresa Guiccioli to tell her how the child was faring. Byron was alarmed and full of remorse—were Claire's dreams to come true? He bade Teresa tell no one and remained within his palace, not caring to go out and meet Shelley's inquiring eyes. Special messengers were dispatched across the mountains, and for a while it seemed that the child would recover. Then a messenger came back to Teresa with the news that Allegra had died.

She went to the Palazzo Lanfranchi. Byron looked at her anxiously when she met him on the terrace and asked, had the messenger come back from Bagnacavallo? Teresa stammered and was silent. "I understand," he said, "it is enough. Say no more." His face was pale. He sank into a chair and remained there immovable for an hour. Teresa had been fond of the dead child in a kind, good-humoured way, and she grieved for her death as she would have grieved over the extinction of any life young and beautiful. But she loved the child's father so much more, and all her sorrow for Allegra was swallowed up in tender pity for him. She sat at his feet and tried to comfort him, and as she looked up into his face it seemed to her that in its grief, "so helpless, so profound, so sublime," it revealed him as "a being of a nature superior to humanity."

He told her crossly to leave him. The next morning he met her with "an expression of religious resignation on his features." "She is happier than us," he said; "besides, her position in the world wouldn't have allowed her much happiness. It is God's will—let us say no more." He never mentioned Allegra's name again to Teresa, but he talked to her more and more of his other daughter, Ada, in England.

He left the matter of the child's burial in Teresa's hands. At his command she sent a lock of hair and a miniature to Claire and arranged for the small body to be shipped back to England. For, asserting his authority to the last, Byron decreed that Allegra must be buried in Harrow Church, where once he had dreamed in happy schooldays of being buried himself. After all, he said, the baby had died a Protestant, and Protestants were not allowed burial in consecrated ground in Italy. While Teresa superintended the shipping of the coffin he solaced himself by drawing up an epitaph to be raised in Harrow Church to the memory of "Allegra, Daughter of G. G. Lord Byron." He had never once gone to see her when she was in the convent at Bagnacavallo, but his epitaph closed with David's words of mourning for his dead child of sin by Bathsheba:

I shall go to her, but she shall not return to me.

The Prioress and the sisters of Bagnacavallo mourned the fair-haired English child who had lived so short a while among them and died. They made a small statue in her likeness and placed it in their chapel, arrayed in one of her dolls' gorgeous frocks with atheist Shelley's gold chain hanging round its neck.

Annabella was living close by Harrow and sometimes came to the church. The vicar and churchwardens would have none of the poet's epitaph and refused to allow his child to be buried in the church. She may well have died a Protestant, but she was a bastard for all that. She was buried in the churchyard outside in a corner under the trees. When, many years later, Teresa visited Harrow churchyard, she found no stone or memorial to mark Allegra's grave—only a rose-bush, dropping white petals on the grass.

Shelley was on the rampage again, sweeping every one before him like a torrent hurrying to its close. With Byron across the street he dared not break the news to Claire. Mary, who was expecting a child, must leave for Lerici at once and take the Casa Magni. Claire would go with her, and Trelawny must be their escort. He and Ned Williams and Jane would follow with the nurse, the children, and the furniture.

After six bewildered days they found themselves all huddled together in the comfortless squalor of the Casa Magni. Jane mourned the loss of pots and pans, and Mary was exhausted. Claire was impatient and wanted to be gone. The wind rose in the evening and the waves broke with a dirge-like sound on the rocks outside. Claire noticed that the others avoided her. She followed them into Jane's bedroom, where she found them all whispering together. They looked up at her with white, startled faces, and she guessed the truth.

In the first delirium of grief they thought that she would go mad. She wrote a wild letter to Byron, sneering, snarling, taunting him in bitter triumph, and cursing him. Byron sent it to Shelley, pleading by implication for his sympathy. Shelley tore the letter up and humbly apologized to Byron for its contents. Then suddenly Claire was resigned. In a few days she was vivacious as in old times. She nursed Mary, who came near to dying at Casa Magni from a miscarriage, and teased Shelley, as she had teased him long ago in their London lodgings. Trelawny had fallen in love with her, thunderbolt-fashion, and she teased him, too—

coquettishly and ironically—and taught him the lesson he had little need to learn—to despise Byron, to love Shelley. But life was over for her. She had closed the door upon youth, thanking God that she would never be young again, nor be a fool again, and suffer. With resolute eyes she turned to look down the future—into middle age, to bleak years of poverty and spinsterhood in foreign lands.

After grief and trouble a strange peace descended on Shelley. At Casa Magni, standing in utter loneliness on the margin of the sea, he had found the desert island for which he so long had yearned.

> Love still has something of the sea
> From whence his mother rose—

and the sea called him with a bright premonition of peace and eternal quiet. With Ned Williams he went sailing every day in their small boat, the *Don Juan*, and as he gazed down into the water he pondered the solemn mystery of death. His face was tanned with sunlight and brine, and for all his thoughts of death he was happy as he had never before been in his life. In the evening, while he lay back in peace, voluptuously weary with the day's sailing, Jane played music to him. "Like Faust," he said, "I could cry to the passing moment 'Oh, stay, thou art too fair!'" Only Mary was sick and fretful and full of dark forebodings that their one child, Percy Florence, would die.

One evening he was walking with Ned Williams on the terrace before the Casa Magni. A cloudless spring day had set in cold, clear moonlight, and the waves broke like small white spaniels on the shore at their feet. Out of the foam—white and naked—Allegra rose, clapping her hands in glee and beckoning to him. He stopped dead in his walk and grasped Williams by the arm and stood there in silence, staring intently out to sea.

"Are you in pain?" asked Williams anxiously.

Shelley's hand tightened on his arm. "Look," he whispered, "there it is again—there!"

But Ned Williams saw nothing. . . . With a faint, shrill laugh that seemed to come from a long way, down long, pale streams of time, Allegra vanished into moonlight and surf.

The ground floor of the Palazzo Lanfranchi stood ready furnished—at Shelley's expense—and awaited occupation by Leigh Hunt. But the Gambas were gone from Pisa, the Shelleys were gone, Trelawny, the Williamses—every one was gone, as though whirled away by an enchanted tempest. In May Byron packed up and left for the Villa Dupuy, outside Leghorn. The Palazzo Lanfranchi was empty.

A child had died. The curtain fell for a moment on bleak tragedy. Tiredness held the stage. All the big characters had vanished, and the moment was come for the clowns again. Enter the Gamba servants with daggers in their belts, and life slipped back into farce.

With the 'gang' dispersed and the Palazzo Lanfranchi deserted, this was the moment that Leigh Hunt picked for arriving in Italy with an ailing wife, six children, and no money. It were useless to describe the misadventures of storm and sickness that kept him the best part of a year beating his way out to Italy after receiving his sailing-orders from Shelley. It is enough to say that his boat sailed into Leghorn harbour on July 1, 1822. He was greeted by Trelawny, looking very much the knight-errant, who told him that Byron was staying at the Villa Dupuy close by. Marianne Hunt and the children were deposited at an inn, and, ever blithe and optimistic, Hunt climbed the hill to the Villa Dupuy. The day was hot, the road was dusty, the house was painted salmon pink —never, said the perspiring Hunt, had he seen a hotter-looking house!

A lean scarecrow was standing under the portico, gaunt and unshaven, with a red 'sans-culotte' cap on his head. He glared savagely at the visitor, but Hunt pushed haughtily by him and was admitted into the house by a trembling servant. Byron met him in the hall, dressed in a loose nankeen jacket and white duck trousers. Hunt was shocked, for Byron was fat and his hair hung down in stringy ringlets round his throat. If the house were hot Byron's greeting was cool. He led Hunt into an inner room and presented him to a lady there—the Countess Guiccioli. Her hair was lying in dishevelled curls over her shoulders, her face was flushed, her eyes were sparkling with anger, and altogether she had an uplifted, spiritual look. She scarcely deigned to notice Signor Hunt and turned to Byron and spoke to him with great animation, using the word *scellerato* (wretch) every now and then. Byron whistled, hummed a song, lounged about the room, looking peevish. A young man came in with his arm in a sling and was introduced as the lady's brother—the Count Pietro Gamba. He, too, turned from Hunt and spoke to Byron with angry volubility. Byron drew a mazarine coat over his nankeen jacket, clapped a velvet cap on his head, and moved to the door with a lordly air. The lady clutched him by the arm and held him back with loud protests, but Byron answered her in cool tones and "with an air of voluptuous indolence." He drew Hunt to a window and pointed to the scarecrow in the red cap, who glared up at them both with a fierce and bloodshot eye. A row had broken out among the servants that afternoon, explained Byron; Count Pietro had tried to restore order and been stabbed in the arm for his pains. Fletcher had gone to fetch the police, and in the meantime Count Pietro's assailant had established himself in the portico with the avowed intention of stabbing any man who left the house.

A perplexing country, thought Hunt, so different from Hampstead Heath! But the carriage was at the door, the horses were waiting, and Byron would be kept no longer from his afternoon's exercise. The whole party moved in a group towards the portico, with Teresa earnestly pleading to "Bairon" to keep back and Pietro elbowing his way valiantly to the fore. Together they erupted through the door, all squabbling and scuffling for pride of place, and turned anxiously to face the enemy.

That monster pushed his cap over his eyes and fell on a bench and burst into tears. There he sprawled, weeping and wailing, and begged Milord to pardon him. He jumped to his feet and, with tears streaming down his unshaven face, spread his arms out in a wild gesture of entreaty, then laid the tips of his fingers on his chest and begged Milord to kiss him.

Byron rejected the kiss of peace with a pale, astonished glare. He told the fellow sternly that he was forgiven but must leave his service. The blessed creature then fell on his knees and kissed Milord's hands. He held out a humble hand to the young Count. Pietro ran to him, clapped him on the back, and shook him joyfully by the hand. The Countess Guiccioli found it hard to subside all at once from her state of indignant exaltation, but she looked relenting, her eyes filled with tears, and at last, because Byron had forgiven the sobbing scarecrow, she gave him her hand to kiss.

This was not the first time there had been trouble with servants at the Villa Dupuy. A short while before the Gamba servants had quarrelled with Byron's 'ragamuffins' in the garden, and both sides had drawn their knives. Byron rushed out on the balcony with a pistol in his hand and threatened to fire unless all knives were dropped. As it was, the police had been called in to quell the riot, and here they were coming back again with an ominous glitter in their eyes.

When, a day or two later, Hunt took his ailing Marianne to call at the Villa Dupuy, Byron gave her a curt nod and walked away without a word. The Gambas had been banished from the state of Tuscany and were off to Lucca, and he was going to follow them. Hunt felt anxious for a moment and wondered what would happen to him and his family in this sun-dazzled, exciting land of Italy. But Shelley, his good angel, came sailing into Leghorn harbour with Ned Williams, and he spent two blessed days in his society. Shelley, too, had changed since Hunt had last seen him, but whereas Byron had grown fat, Shelley looked robust. His hair was turning grey and his face was sad. He was not sanguine about Hunt's prospects, but he promised his best help. His talk was melancholy, and he spoke of Mary with a touch of bitterness. But Hunt's spirits revived in his company. Byron changed his mind. Let the Gambas go to Genoa, he said, he would return to the Palazzo Lanfranchi, and Hunt and his family must come with him. But, he declared firmly, all those ragamuffins from Romagna—his own, the Gamba servants, and Teresa's—every one of them was discharged. And since Teresa would not go with her father and brother to Genoa, she must come with him to Pisa—and live with him in the Palazzo Lanfranchi!

Shelley lay behind this change in plan. He accompanied Hunt to Pisa and helped settle him and his family in their quarters in the Palazzo Lanfranchi. With grateful heart Hunt wrung him by the hand when he left for Leghorn. There Ned Williams waited impatiently. His Jane was calling—things were not going well at Casa Magni—Mary was ill and difficult—she had clung to Shelley when they left, had wept, didn't want him to go. It was fine weather for sailing—the priests were praying for rain, "but the gods are either angry," Williams wrote in his diary, "or nature is too powerful." For God's sake, let them put to sea!

Trelawny watched the *Don Juan* leave the harbour with a doubtful mind. A short while after the boat reached the open sea, the sky darkened and there came a sudden rattle of wind with sharp claps of thunder and a driving cloud of rain. The prayers of the priests were answered! The storm lifted soon into watery sunshine. Trelawny looked out to sea. The *Don Juan* had vanished from view. Miles away at Pisa Hunt, still marvelling at the comic violence with which all things happened in Italy, gazed with awe at the "horrid lightnings" of a meridian squall.

Alone with Byron! Thanks to Shelley, she was alone with Byron, as in the good days of La Mira! The Hunts on the ground floor didn't count.

The third night after their arrival there came a loud rapping on the door of the Palazzo Lanfranchi.

"*Chi è?* [Who's there]" cried Teresa's maid from the window.

Signora Shelley was below in a carriage with Signora Williams. She must speak to Signor Hunt at once.

Signor Hunt was asleep, his lady was sick—would Signora Shelley speak with Lord Byron?

Teresa threw a mantle over her nightdress and ran with a happy smile to greet her friend. Mary looked like a ghost. Her face was white as marble, and a pale phosphorescence seemed to emanate from it in the candlelight.

"Where is he?" she gasped. "*Sapete alcuna cosa di Shelley* [Do you know anything of Shelley]?"

Byron had followed Teresa into the room. Mary told him her story. Six days ago Shelley had sailed with Ned Williams from the Casa Magni to meet Hunt at Leghorn. He was to bring him and his family to Pisa and settle them in the Palazzo Lanfranchi, then he would return to Williams and they would sail home. They had not returned. On Monday night a storm had beaten on the rocks outside the Casa Magni. She had come with Jane Williams to Pisa for news—where was Shelley?

Byron and Teresa knew nothing. Shelley had left Pisa on Sunday for Leghorn. On Monday there had been a sharp storm out to sea. That was all.

The body was washed up by the sea not far from Viareggio. It was burned on the beach where it was found. Trelawny, who had been tireless in the search, took charge of the funeral ceremony. Byron and Leigh Hunt, who in different ways had both loved the man who was now only a mass of bones and putrid flesh, drove out together from Pisa to pay their last tribute of affection. Hunt lay back in the coach, exhausted with sorrow, and looked on from a distance. Byron stood on the beach and watched the body burn.

The day was intensely hot. The sea, now radiant and smiling, fawned lazily on the shore as though to make peace with it. The flames leaped up in limpid beauty, and cliff and beach and island shook and trembled in a brittle haze. A seagull flew backward and forward above the steady column of smoke.

Byron felt sick and disgusted as he watched his lost friend's body smoulder and break apart. He left the pyre, stripped naked, and swam out to sea and vomited. As evening fell, hot and breathless, he drove with Hunt through the woods back to Pisa. They laughed, they shrieked and called the echoes with wild halloos, they sang, they drank long life to each other in wine, and the coachman—a good-natured Italian—joined in their mirth.

## CHAPTER III

# The Voice of England

WHAT do you think, Mrs Hunt?" said Byron one day. "Trelawny has been speaking against my morals! What do you think of that?"

He found conversation with Mrs Hunt difficult work. He was nervous with her and flustered, but she was always self-possessed and provoking. This opening gambit was a poor thing; it was naive and self-conscious and left him exposed to a slap from anyone who was in the slapping mood.

Mrs Hunt tossed her head. She threw her husband a meaning look and turned towards Lord Byron to take him up on the subject of his morals.

"It is the first time," she said deliberately, "that I ever heard of them."

Leigh Hunt was lost in admiration of his Marianne's spirit in retort. Lord Byron was a man of wit—now, if ever, he had been put upon his mettle—he should come back with some graceful rejoinder. But no, as Hunt observed with glee, his lordship looked "completely dashed" and never said a word.

When Hunt was annoyed with his host, which was every day and almost every time they conversed, he would regale him with further specimens of Marianne's irony. One morning Byron was speaking with more humour than charity of the personal appearance of some of Hunt's friends, so—"What do you think Marianne said of *your* portrait by Harlow?—why, that it makes you look like a great big schoolboy who has had a plain bun given him instead of a plum one." Shelley (whose sense of humour was uncertain) had nearly died of laughter over this neat stroke of portraiture—"it was so like!" But even at second-hand Marianne Hunt daunted Byron. This time he looked "as blank as possible" and turned the conversation.

When Shelley was drowned Byron told Hunt that he wished to take his place as friend and benefactor. Hunt heard him without enthusiasm. No one could take Shelley's place. Besides, he knew by now that Byron was sick of the *Liberal* before the first number was printed.

Hobhouse and Tom Moore and the London cronies had from the first protested against the partnership. Hunt was a cockney, a newspaper Radical, a fifth-rate, Rimini-Pimini poet—in every possible way he was most certainly not a *gentleman*. From such an association would only come loss of prestige for Byron and a quick decline in the sale of his own poems. Byron was shaken by their warnings, but he argued stoutly on

Hunt's behalf. Hunt, he said temperately, was a good man—an honest man—an industrious man—he was a legacy from Shelley—here he was with ailing wife and six children, penniless in a foreign country—it would be arrant treachery to desert him now! At least, he pleaded, let the *Liberal* have a fair chance—perhaps with the *Vision of Judgment* and more cantos of *Don Juan* the thing would sell—and, after that, they would see. But the protests of his friends lingered in his mind, and his comments on the *Liberal* (particularly when it didn't pay) grew more bitter with every letter he wrote. In exasperation he declared that helping Hunt was like pulling a suicide out of the water who immediately flung himself back into it again. So Hunt was suspicious and Byron was impatient, and there grew a coolness between the two men that ripened into cordial dislike.

"My dear Byron, I must trouble you for another cool hundred of your crowns."

That was Hunt's way of asking for a remittance, for loan it could scarcely be called. Hunt had, as he freely confessed, "peculiar notions" about the give-and-take of money. Where one man gave of his surplus to another for his labour, gratitude was not "an essential refinement." On the contrary, it was the duty of the beneficiary (or by whatever name he should go) to rid his benefactor of all sense of conferring a favour. So you asked for money on a light tone, as for something which, though of little importance in itself, you had a right to expect, and you held out your left hand nonchalantly to take it. Yet Byron had all a patron's itch for—well, if he might not look for gratitude, he could at least expect deference from a man to whom he gave money—a certain modesty in asking for it and a polite contrition in taking it. Deference, however, was a favour that Hunt, on principle, would not grant him, so these airy demands for money were referred to Lega Zambelli, the steward. Lega, said Hunt wrathfully, counted out the crowns one by one as though they were "so many of my disgraces." To suspicion and impatience now was added resentfulness on money matters. Byron hadn't been cajoled and Hunt had been insulted. The *Liberal* was doomed to failure from the very start.

Hunt was poor—always a crime—he was improvident, and his mild literary achievements had made him sensitive and vain; but against these faults may be scored greater virtues. He was honest and hard-working, as Byron said, whimsical, kindly, a shrewd judge of other men's poetry, a good fellow at heart, who would share his last sixpence with a friend in need, even though he begged that sixpence of him to share it. His gravest fault was, perhaps, that he was an affectionate husband in whose eyes his Marianne could do and say no wrong. Marianne was a poor house-keeper and not a wise mother. After years of matrimony and child-birth she had still a strong dose of the spinster left in her veins. She was for ever on guard against being 'bossed' by men and looked on the whole breed with disapproval and suspicion. Privately she thought her husband was too meek with his men-friends and made good his deficiencies by having what is known in her sex as a 'mind of her own.'

At the Palazzo Lanfranchi she declared war on Byron and set to work to make him feel uncomfortable in his own house, and it mattered little that her husband suffered in the process. She had never wanted to come to Italy, to begin with, and by temper and seasickness and coughing and spitting blood she had made the voyage as long and tedious as possible. She arrived in the detested country in a commendable state of physical collapse with a sturdy refugee complex thrown in. Then again, years ago, Lord Byron had driven out with his bride to call on her at Hampstead. His lordship had graciously come indoors and sat astride the children's rocking-horse as he chatted with her. But Lady Byron remained disdain-fully in the carriage outside. A woman could not hope for a better reason for disliking a man than that. Add to this old offence the fact that her husband was now dependent on Byron and they were living in his house, and her case for full-blown malice was complete.

Here in Pisa she was given the 'basement' of the palace to live in, and, as every one knew, only servants slept in the 'basement'! The furniture —which Shelley had paid for—was shoddy. The servants—whom Mary had hired—were impudent sluts. There were iron bars across the win-dows and they were overgrown with ivy, the rooms in the 'basement' were dark, and if by chance you caught a glimpse of the garden there, if you please, stood orange-trees! Italian wines were sickly stuff, and when she thought of England with its beer and its gin and its brandy-and-water, desolate tears rose to Marianne's eyes! She took to an invalid couch, and Dr Vacca was summoned to her side. Less shrewd than Dr Aglietti, he diagnosed from her coughing and spitting of blood a rapid decline and death within the year. But Marianne was sharp, as her hus-band tells us, and he records with pride in his *Autobiography* that she out-lived her physician by many years. In the meantime she languished on her couch and dreamed crossly that Shelley was peeping at her from behind a cloud with luminous eyes and a commiserating smile.

In her general disapproval of the domestic arrangements at the Palazzo Lanfranchi the Countess Guiccioli took pride of offence. As she put it to Hunt, she was not a narrow-minded woman and foreigners might do what they chose in their own countries, but Hampstead ways and the English language were good enough for her. She had no intention of learning Italian if it involved her in acquaintance with "that woman." The two ladies were presented to each other in form, and from Hunt's embarrassed allusion to the encounter we can guess what happened. Teresa greeted Mrs Hunt with a pretty speech of compliment and a wel-come to Italy. Marianne replied not in words, but she gave her would-be

hostess a lurid glance which said plainer than words, "Good gracious!"
This was Teresa's first encounter with a British matron. She beheld an
untidy woman with sleek black hair who looked cross and sickly and
certainly did not want to know her. She accepted the situation with her
usual smile and swept the speechless lady a curtsy. Mrs Hunt returned
her obeisance with a crisp nod and snapping of the lips, and the two
ladies parted. Teresa did not visit the ground floor, and Marianne told
her Hunt angrily that if there was one thing that she despised more than
aristocratic looseness in morals, it was aristocratic insolence.

But all "feminie" was avenged—Caro Lamb, Annabella, Claire!
Byron was routed in his own house by Marianne Hunt, and not a woman
but must rejoice in her victory. Women had thrown him scenes ere now,
had raged at him, hated him, but never yet had he met that type who is
known to herself and her gossips as 'a woman of spirit.' Marianne let
him know, daily and frankly, by shrill titter and loud snort, that she disliked him with all his looks and ways. He was afraid to meet her—
couldn't talk to her—dared not retort to her—even behind her back.
He wrote to his friends in London and remarked mildly that Mrs Hunt
was "no great things."

Count Guiccioli, too, was avenged. Byron's house was no longer his
own! As he climbed the stairs, there the Hunt children sprawled and
slobbered—Thornton and Johnny and Mary Florimel, Swinburne and
Sylvan and Percy—teasing the monkey, baiting the bulldog, and hugging
their own addition to the menagerie—a dilapidated goat that Marianne
had brought from England because she had no opinion of Italian milk.
"Don't let the cockneys come this way," he shouted to Moretto, the
bulldog, in a voice that could be heard in the 'basement,' and went into
his library and slammed the door. . . . A sound of wailing rose from the
stairs. Moretto was tired of being baited by the 'cockneys.' He had
flown at the goat in a fury and bitten off its ear.

Was there ever, Byron exclaimed in disgust to Mary Shelley, such a
pack of mischievous little Yahoos, such a *kraal* out of the Hottentot
country! He had thought sometimes that he liked children, but the
children he had known were Allegra—pretty and clean and vivacious—
or Carluccio, or Harry Fox of Holland House—well-behaved little some-
bodies who, at least, treated their elders with the deference they demanded for themselves. But these children! Hunt said they were brought
up on a new principle of 'Nature.' They were encouraged to be themselves and must not be checked for fear of disastrous consequences in
later life. That was all very fine in their parents' house, but it was a
nuisance in other people's houses! In their calico shifts and drawers they
exuded themselves all over the palace, romping on the stairs, breaking
the orange-trees in the garden, digging their dirty finger-nails into the
furniture, and squealing all the time about the "good joy" that they

were having! Byron did not know how to deal with children who
behaved like this.

One and all they shared their mother's ability to 'dash' him. Handsome, dark-eyed Thornton engaged him in conversation on what was
meant for equal terms, and threw him a 'My lord' every now and then

LORD BYRON,
*as he appeared after his daily ride at Pisa & Genoa.*

*From a silhouette made by Mrs Leigh Hunt*

as a concession to his vanity, as though, said his proud father, "he had
always lived in the world instead of out of it." Such self-possession in a
lad of twelve put "his lordship out of his reckoning." The second boy—
"little ranting Johnny" his parents called him in fun—had "vivacity of
temperament," which sometimes took the form of exploring the baby's
cranium with the scissors. He believed in saying what he thought about
people to their faces, which was usually what his mother said about them

behind their backs. "Take care," Byron told him after listening to one of these home-truths, "how you get odd notions about sincerity and truthfulness into your head—they may hinder you in making your way in later life." Marianne said she wasn't going to have her children encouraged to tell lies and forbade them to speak to their host for fear their morals should be corrupted.

None of these people—not even the children—were bad, but the Palazzo Lanfranchi was not a congenial household. Byron wished to be generous, but he was not accustomed to bearing with other people's follies gladly. Hunt was good-natured, but in this unaccountable land of Italy he was anxious, overworked, and resentful. Marianne was sick and in a short while showed signs of bearing another Huntling. When the Countess Guiccioli walked in the garden the children scuttled out of her path like rabbits, and then peeped at her curiously through the bushes. And when they met their host in the courtyard they looked at him with eyes of sly disapproval, and Mary Florimel walked past him with her nose in the air.

Teresa was amiable and kind, and on her shoulders we lay, if you will, full blame for discord in the Palazzo Lanfranchi. She was Italian, and though that is not always a vice in itself, we must regret that she did not remember that Mrs Hunt was a stranger in her country and a guest in her lover's house. She ought to have visited the ground floor and borne her snubbing meekly. Mrs Hunt, too, was ill, and Teresa should have shown more sympathy for a woman who coughed and spat blood when the world went contrary. But she was so engrossed in her "Bairon" that she would not notice Marianne Hunt and passed her children by with an absent smile. So far as she was concerned none of them was there.

But she was punished for her sins. The Hunts *did* count. Still she must spend her love-time under the scrutiny of prying eyes. Still other people's children filled her house. Carluccio had been hostile and Allegra sometimes made her jealous, but these children were ubiquitous, and she wasn't sure they didn't laugh and stick their tongues out behind her back. From the ground floor there welled an atmosphere of spite and discontent that permeated the whole house like a nagging voice.

Like all Shelley's experiments in other people's lives this one, too, had failed. A few years later, when Byron was dead, Hunt committed his rancour to a book. Cleverly and spitefully he stripped Byron of romance and left him sitting, like a fat pasha just issued from his bath, on his terrace behind the Palazzo Lanfranchi, toying with the rings on his plump hands, picking his teeth and pushing back stray locks of greying hair.

"Leontius!" he shouted, and, quivering with irritation, Hunt went out to join him on the terrace. Conversation with Hunt soon became as difficult as with his wife, and in desperation Byron struck the facetious note. "Why, sir," he would reply to Hunt, and roll his head at him in the manner of Dr Johnson. Hunt stared morosely at the 'baby-work' on his patron's shirt and saw nothing amusing in this trick of speech. But he replied in kind—"Why, sir, Lord Byron is lacteolous—he is milky, sir—he loves a pretty girl!" or with some merriment to that effect. . . .

The Countess Guiccioli came downstairs, her "sleek tresses" fresh from the maid's brush, and walked with self-conscious elegance in the garden, plucking flowers. At a distance she made a pretty picture in the style of Fragonard, and Hunt rummaged among the poets for appropriate imagery. She was the fair Emelye of Chaucer's poem.

> Y-clothed she was fresh, for to devise,
> Her yellow hair was braided in a tress
> Behind her back, a yardé long, I guess,
> And in the garden (as the sun uprist)
> She walketh up and down, whereas she list.

"Sun uprist" was good, for neither Byron nor his Countess rose till noon —but to close in the more mannered style of Dryden—

> At every turn she made a little stand
> And thrust among the thorns her lily hand.

The lady came to sit with the gentlemen on the terrace. Hunt gazed at her now with a more surly eye and catalogued her charms bleakly, one by one—as, *item*, "blonde" hair with an "inclination" to yellow and "within the limits of the poetical"; *item*, a nose "one of the handsomest of its kind"; *item*, regular features "of the order called handsome," large but not coarse, "more harmonious than interesting." Her head and shoulders and bust were well enough, but thereafter—Hunt could lay his hand upon his heart and swear she was squat. Her manners were "ladylike and agreeable," and for an Italian her voice was gentle. "None of her graces," he decided, as he eyed her sourly, "were free from art," though they combined in an effect of sincerity and good humour—doubtless deceptive. Certainly she was not an intelligent woman, although—a malicious stroke, this—she could look intelligent and indeed smile very sweetly when Byron threw her a kind word. Calculating, theatrical, a flattered beauty—Hunt ran through the damaging epithets in his mind, searching for the phrase that should crystallize his dislike—ah, that was it!—thank God for Marianne's landlady turn of wit!—the Countess Guiccioli was no more than "a buxom parlour-boarder, compressing herself artificially into dignity and elegance and fancying she walked in the eyes of the whole world, a heroine by the side of a poet."

Teresa's deep voice was booming all this while in the drowsy air under the orange-trees. Byron had not yet recovered from Marianne's witticism about the poet and the plum bun. He had been absent in replying to Hunt, and his foot beat nervously on the ground. Suddenly he turned upon Teresa with a glower and cut across her eloquence with a few sharp words in Italian. She exclaimed and "wondered at him," but on he went with a savage smile. The lady's face flushed with mortification, her eyes glittered, her plump bosom heaved. The fan snapped between tense fingers, and, with animated gesture of shoulder and arm, her voice rose and drowned out her lover's in a reproachful bellow. Abruptly Byron rose from his chair and limped away into the courtyard. Hunt was left to console the angry beauty with laboured compliments in the style of Ariosto. But she broke in upon his flatteries with vehement complaints of her "Bairon's" brutal language. She prodded him with a thousand questions about the girl at the *podere*. On her lover's want of generosity in money matters, says Hunt, "I will not repeat what was said and lamented"—by Teresa, we are to understand, not Hunt.

As he watched the poet and his lady day by day in their garden—with Marianne at his shoulder, lending acid to his thoughts—the scales fell from Hunt's eyes. Here were two people, he declared, who had been tricked into a *liaison* by their own vanity. Byron could never love a woman for herself. All he cared for in Teresa was her body and her physical graces, and now that he was tired of those he made no pretence at tenderness or affection. Her jealousy alternately gratified and fatigued him, and it amused him to goad her into displays of vanity natural in a spoilt beauty. Teresa on her side was, no doubt, capable of genuine attachment and would have loved Byron if he had allowed her to. But she was frivolous and vain, and what she really deplored in her "Bairon" was not his lack of affection but his lack of gallantry.

Marianne Hunt's presence in his house at least galvanized Byron into activity. He had done little work in Pisa, but now, for the *Liberal's* sake, he must get back to "poeshie." Teresa, too, was restless. She was anxious about her father and wished to settle in Genoa to be near him in his exile. Byron hated this perpetual packing that Teresa always called for, but he wanted to leave Pisa, too. Mary Shelley was dispatched to Genoa. Her instructions were to find a large, comfortable villa for Byron with a wing in which Count Gamba and Pietro might live. A smaller villa was to be found for Hunt and Marianne and their brood—at a mile's distance, at least, from the other house.

Another shadow rose to cloud Teresa's happiness—that irrepressible poem *Don Juan* that would never die. With a considerate humility that brooked no denial Byron begged that the ban upon the poem be lifted. Most unwillingly did his 'dictatress' grant his request—but there again the Hunts had counted. The new cantos of *Don Juan* were to be written to pop bread into the Huntlings' mouths—they would be printed in the

*Liberal* and help to sell it, and Leigh Hunt might keep the royalties. But the ban was raised with conditions and under protest. There must be no more attacks upon Lady Byron—why, for Heaven's sake, couldn't he forget that unfortunate woman! No attacks on anyone—Wellington, Castlereagh, or Robert Southey. No scoffing at love. No cynicism and, above all, no indecency—why couldn't he just tell a story? Why not let Juan really fall in love? It makes me unhappy, she told him, to think that you are writing coarse and ribald things in the house in which I am living. Somehow an atmosphere of naughtiness filled the palace, and she felt soiled and bedraggled.

Byron promised that he would do his best to be a good boy—he could promise no more. I'll send Juan to England, he said, and he shall turn Methodist—what could be safer than that! Nay, if Teresa demanded it, Juan should, meekly and virtuously, fall in love with a good girl—more beautiful than Haidée—and, he added roguishly, better, too, in one respect—she shall be a Catholic with some knowledge of divinity—in the higher meaning of that word.

The Palazzo Lanfranchi was slowly dismantled for the flitting to Genoa in the autumn. In odd corners of the house and at chance tables he scribbled away at his poem. Juan was clear of the harem now with one pledge to the past in a tiny bastard daughter. He was a soldier and had been blooded in the Russian wars. He had reached the court of the Northern Semiramis—Catherine the Great—he was a royal favourite, a man *à bonnes fortunes*. Away with him to Germany and let him be a sad-faced Werther-man—to France and be Chevalier Faublas to a *duchesse* and turn revolutionary in the game. But before all that should come to pass—to England with him, to London, to Newstead Abbey— to country squires and lordly politicians and their wives—so beautiful, so stately—and so bored—and amorous!

Love—pooh! It was a shadow, a bubble—at its best something "pinnacled dim in the Intense Inane," as Shelley wrote about it—too dim and far away for the human race with its leg-o'-mutton appetites.

> Love is Vanity,
> Selfish in its beginning as its end,
> Except where't is a mere insanity,
> A maddening spirit which would strive to blend
> Itself with Beauty's frail inanity
> On which the Passion's self seems to depend.

Back—back—backward galloped the story—up the Rhine, past the castled Drachenfels, across the flats of Holland, over the white-capped sea until "at length they rose, like a white wall along the blue sea's border"—the cliffs of England! Then Dover—"*dear* Dover," with "thy waiters running mucks at every bell . . . and thy long, long bills."

On with the horses!  Off to Canterbury!
    Tramp, tramp, o'er pebble, and splash, splash through puddle;
Hurrah! how swiftly speeds the post . . .

On! On! Through the meadows, managed like a garden, a paradise of
hops—"and when I think upon a pot of beer—but I won't weep"—on,
postilions!—and at last—

    A mighty mass of brick, and smoke, and shipping,
        Dirty and dusky, but as wide as eye
    Could reach, with here and there a sail just skipping
        In sight, then lost amid the forestry
    Of masts; a wilderness of steeples peeping
        On tiptoe through their sea-coal canopy;
    A huge dun cupola, like a foolscap crown
        On a fool's head—

and there is London Town!

Oh, that incomprehensible island! Those incomprehensible people,
who had kicked him out so arrogantly and came marching soberly to his
rescue at Pisa! Damn them always, damn their women most of all—so
hard—and so sensitive! Italy! Greece! America! What were they to
England? He must go home. But he would not slink home like a shame-
faced beggar by the back door—Annabella's repentant husband. No, he
would show them what he could do, and they would welcome him home
with guns firing and pealing bells!

Teresa feared that Juan would lead her Byron astray, down imaginary
paths of naughtiness into the arms of other women. But now she knew
that her "nice boy" was luring her lover farther from her side—he was
taking him home.

One morning they were walking in the garden. Timidly she encouraged him to speak of England. He told her of his life in London, of his
political ambitions and his many friendships—how animated life had
been in those days, how varied, how full of interest and occupation!

She asked him—did he not sometimes grow tired of his life in Italy
—so solitary, so concentrated, so lost in writing poetry? Had he not,
perhaps, sacrificed too much—she fumbled for the words and looked up
shyly into his face—on the altar of affection?

"Oh, no," he replied, "I regret nothing belonging to the great world,
where everything is artificial. A man can't live to himself there; every
one is much too busy there with what others think and not busy enough
with what he ought to think himself. What should I have done there?
Made some opposition speeches in the House of Lords, which would
have done no good . . . been obliged to frequent, without pleasure or
profit, a society that doesn't suit me, have had more trouble in holding

and expressing my own opinions, I shouldn't have known you . . . Ah well, I'm better pleased to know you. What is there in the world worth true affection? Nothing. If I had to begin all over again, I would still do what I have done."

She was silent, waiting to hear more that would have made "earth a paradise" for her . . .

A sound of footsteps hurrying along the terrace . . . a cheery laugh . . . a stout man, packed tightly into a frock coat . . . waving a beaver hat . . . hooked, Jewish nose . . . large, dark eyes and sleekly curling, dark hair. . . . "Ha, ha, my dear fellow, at last I've found you!"

Byron's face, turned down to hers a moment since so mournfully, was irradiated with a lightning flash of joy. It vanished, leaving his cheeks ashen pale. His eyes, she saw, filled with tears.

"*Hobhouse!*" he whispered, and sank into a chair.

Hobhouse was hurt by the formality with which his old friend received his affectionate advances. He looked at him critically. Fat, fat, he sighed, far fatter than in those Venice days, and his expression was injured. As he bowed over "the Romagnuola Countess's" hand, he stared at her boldly. Pretty—well, yes, perhaps—good bust, white throat, delicate skin, gold hair—a lady, yes—then, with a respectful drop of his eyes to earth—bad ankles, though—a large foot—like Annabella—must be good. But what the deuce did Byron mean by writing about her as though she were a woman of the world? She was a child!

Leigh Hunt was approaching from the house, looking suspicious. Hobhouse gave him a nod and held out his hand with a gracious smile. With a few hurried words of politeness Teresa left the gentlemen to themselves.

She sat by the open window alone, gazing into the night. The willows drooped noiseless on the quiet air. Over the wall drifted the dull murmur of the sleeping city. Below her two voices in the garden . . . a burst of laughter, and the voices grew clearer, the words sharper and clearer . . . but what they said, why they laughed, she did not know. . . . A bat flew with an angry squeak across the garden and was gone. . . . The voices lowered again to a confidential murmur. . . . A shrill wail from a window on the ground floor, and a woman's voice rose fretfully into the night . . . always this unknown English language round her . . . the sound of an infant buttock smacked . . . a louder wail. . . . "Oh, Mamma!" . . . and the window closed with a snap, stifling the sound. . . . "Oh, damn," from the garden, and then in a mocking tone—"*Buona Notte, Byron!*"

The main purpose, apart from affection, of Hobhouse's descent on the Palazzo Lanfranchi was to put an end to this damned nonsense of the

*Liberal.* But he preached to a man already converted. The magazine was a bad business, Byron confessed. Hunt was a good man—but feckless—and he wasn't a congenial companion—and his children were, well —"not very tractable." But there it was—Hunt was penniless in a strange land, his wife was sick, and he had promised Shelley—he couldn't and wouldn't desert Hunt now—afterwards, well—don't let's talk about it any more.

Hobhouse found his friend indolent and melancholy. Allegra's death had disturbed him more than he was free to own. And then, so soon afterwards, Shelley's death—his thoughts seemed to run on death. They went out riding together every day, and—"Oh, Hobhouse, why don't you come with me to Genoa? The Hunts are going by felucca, Count Gamba is coming to fetch the Countess Guiccioli because he won't let her travel with me as in the good old La Mira days. You and I could go in the *berlina* and argue and squabble as we used to when we went Childe-Harolding together." But Hobhouse had a mother and sisters in the offing and declined the invitation. They visited the *podere*, and Byron told him that the peasant girl with the silver bracelets on her arms was his mistress. That, at any rate, was a spice of the "dear fellow" in old days, for then every pretty girl he ogled was his mistress—he had told Rogers that the sexton's daughter in the Certosa cemetery was his mistress, too. Still Hobhouse was shocked by the goings-on at the *podere*—these Italians were frank in speech and coarse in gesture, and the girl's mother was a wicked old hag.

In the evenings they sat up late in the garden, talking. Byron told his friend the story of conspiracy in Ravenna. The Romagnuoli, he declared bitterly, were a testy, shabby people. They shot round corners, they stabbed in the dark, they brawled in the streets, but they didn't care for honest fighting and would never make good soldiers. The way the Italian people were, there was little hope that they would ever achieve independence. Hobhouse thoroughly agreed with him—he had reached the same opinion yet more decisively without the labour of living among the Italians. "And what are your plans now?" he asked. "You may expect me," Byron replied, "in England—next spring."

"We had some talk of his *liaison*," wrote Hobhouse in his diary. Apparently at the Villa Dupuy the Countess Guiccioli, her father, and her brother had all lived with Byron in the same house. For the moment the Countess was living alone with him at the Palazzo Lanfranchi, but when they reached Genoa old Count Gamba and his son would share a house again with Byron and his mistress. Hobhouse whistled under his breath. "This," he confided austerely to his diary, "is Italian morality!" Byron declared that he had lost all capacity for strong feeling, but he spoke of Count Pietro Gamba with affection. His *liaison* had brought him that friendship, at any rate, and through Pietro he had been lured into *Carbonari* plots. But it seemed to Hobhouse that the "dear fellow" wanted to bring his love-affair to an end.

Day after day Hobhouse bustled in and out of the Palazzo Lanfranchi, cheerful, loquacious, and possessive. Teresa left him alone with his friend, which argued more tact in her than Byron had credited her with. She made every effort to please Hobhouse, and he found her gentle, more intelligent than he had expected, and—yes, prettier on second sight than first.

"Hobhouse," said Byron, as they shook hands for the last time, "you should never have come—or you should never go."

Tom Medwin paid a flying visit to Pisa to gather more notes for his book. The Palazzo Lanfranchi was empty of furniture, but he found Byron and Teresa sitting companionably under the orange-trees at the back. They looked very affectionate together, and Byron patted Teresa's hand and called her *piccinina*.

Medwin jotted mentally for his book. Byron was thinner—but indolent—better spirits, perhaps, but sad when he talked of Shelley. And he must sketch in Teresa, too—interesting type, dark auburn hair, dark eyes, beautiful teeth, face mournful—worries about her old father—too much *embonpoint*.

"I have Hunt with me," Byron told Medwin—a good fellow, Hunt —might have been a good poet, but educated at the Bluecoat School! In a day or two they all would be gone to Genoa. After that—well—"I am thinking seriously of going to America," he said, "to live with the Yankees." He tapped Teresa's hand and she smiled, not knowing what he said.

Medwin looked back at them, sitting under the trees, and he wondered if the business would last. Byron might be managed, but no woman could drive him. The Countess Guiccioli certainly had done well by him—a nice, sensible woman, said Medwin to himself as he gave her a farewell wave of his hat. Byron was grateful to her, tender, fond, and in his book Medwin would call her "lovely" and "young for her years" and all that —but, as he placed his hat on his head and turned his back on her—*entre nous*, her looks weren't holding up—she was plain—almost as plain as his cousin, Shelley's widow, Mary, had turned these last few months.

## CHAPTER IV

# Exiles in Genoa

THE exodus to Genoa was a calvary. As Shelley was dead and Mary was gone before, Trelawny took command of the caravan. The Hunts left in one felucca and the servants in another with the furniture, menagerie, and accumulated trash of the Palazzo Lanfranchi, for Byron could never bear to throw away anything, not even unanswered love-letters from unknown women. Trelawny sailed in the yacht, the *Bolivar*, carrying plate, books, and guns and ammunition of Ravenna days. Byron travelled with Teresa by coach. The party met at Lerici, not far from Shelley's last home at Casa Magni, and rashly Byron went swimming with Trelawny. On returning ashore he was seized with spasms and for four days lay sick on a bed in the worst room of the world's worst inn. Teresa insisted that he should send for a doctor, and a mild young man called and talked learnedly of Hippocrates and Byron dismissed him. Trelawny despised the prostrate poet for a weakling. "How do you feel?" he jeered.

"Feel!" roared Byron. "Why, just as that damned obstreperous fellow felt chained to a rock, the vultures gnawing my midriff, and vitals, too, for I have no liver." Then, as the spasms shook him again, "I don't care for dying, but I cannot bear this! It's past joking. Call Fletcher—give me something that will end it—or me. I can't stand it much longer."

Fletcher came bearing ether and laudanum and hot towels for the suffering Prometheus, but Teresa clamoured loudly for the doctor again. He returned and diagnosed inflammation of the bowels and, with the aid of clysters and formidable concoctions, coaxed his patient back to health. Byron loved to think of himself as an elemental force—a thunderstorm, the ocean beating on the shore—and at Lerici Nature heard his groans and responded to his convulsions. One night the town was shaken by earthquake, and people ran out in terror into the streets. But our poet slept peacefully through the cataclysm and scuttled out of bed as soon as he could and rowed twelve hours by nightfall to Sestri. He arrived in Genoa, with skin shed in one long brine-blister and sunburn, feeling like a snake in a glossy new suit. He was thin and emaciated, and his clothes hung round him like a scarecrow.

The Casa Saluzzo stood in the hills of Albaro, above the city—a spacious house with sixty rooms, a garden, a terrace, balconies, ilex-trees,

and a fine view out to sea. Mr Hill, the British Minister, who had taken
a liking to the Gambas, father and son, urged that Byron should take
them into his house, for only under the protection of a well-known
English nobleman would they be safe from persecution by the Government of Sardinia. Pietro greeted his sister and her lover with a cheerful
laugh when they arrived, but Count Gamba was sad and silent. Teresa
once more fell under her father's protection. He told Byron that he must
live in a separate wing with his own servants and take his meals apart, and
he would of his poverty pay his way. And on this point Count Gamba
insisted almost angrily; Teresa must live with him on his side of the house,
otherwise, immunity from political persecution or not, he would not stay
in Lord Byron's house. Byron yielded, and Teresa sighed as a mistress
once more, but obeyed as a daughter. She went to live with her father
and brother and keep house for them in a separate wing of the Casa
Saluzzo.

At the Casa Negroto, a mile or two away—another spacious villa of
forty rooms, with one good fireplace for the winter—lived Hunt and
Marianne with their six children. Mary Shelley and her small son lodged
with them. Marianne no longer hoped for early death. She was waiting
for summer to come, with another Huntling. Mary divided her time
between housekeeping for Marianne and transcribing *Don Juan* for Byron.
Hunt toiled away disconsolately at the *Liberal*, which eventually landed
his brother John in gaol—thanks to Byron's *Vision of Judgment*—but
obstinately refused to make money. His severance from Byron was now
complete. Twice or thrice a month he walked over to the Casa Saluzzo
with his children whooping behind him. Sometimes he talked with
Byron, whom he liked better now that they did not share a house together.
But his business now was with Lega Zambelli. Byron refused to set
foot inside the Casa Negroto, and social intercourse between the houses
was carried on by Mary Shelley and Teresa. Mary carried her transcrip-
tions to the Casa Saluzzo and called on Teresa in the Gamba wing.
Teresa, on horseback or in carriage, would go by the Casa Negroto and
look in upon Mary. Marianne still remained virtuously aloof, and
Teresa took no manner of interest in her cause of ill-health. As relations
between the two houses grew more strained, Mary and Teresa were
made messengers of complaint and explanation, and their friendship
cooled.

Never was there a more disgruntled colony of exiles. At the Casa
Saluzzo only Pietro was cheerful, with his dreams of fighting in Greece.
Count Gamba was homesick for Filetto, and Teresa pined under his
mute, disapproving eyes. At the Casa Negroto Hunt was pessimistic for
the first time in his life. He was cross with Mary because, from words
dropped by Shelley at their last meeting, he was sure that she had been
a poor wife. Marianne, of course, was sick and more peevish than ever,

and the children were troublesome, particularly "little ranting Johnny," who had now developed a talent for homicide. Mary Shelley wept and moaned for her dead Shelley every night in her diary and blamed herself for never loving him enough. She had become a "poor, lone creature" who felt things more than others, whom nobody liked. Hunt didn't like her—and he monopolized the only fireplace in the house. Byron—"dear, capricious, fascinating Albé"—didn't like her—and he was mean to her in money matters and unkind about Shelley. Teresa, silly woman, was jealous—of her who had loved Shelley, a mere skeleton of a woman now—and, she was sure, held Byron back from being as kind as he wished. Byron (in his lazy way) was fighting her battles with her husband's family, but she needs must fight Hunt's battles with Byron— because Hunt to her, as to Byron, was a legacy from Shelley. But Mary had neither her husband's patience nor his tact. She argued and fell into that trick of other women in dealing with Byron—she reproached him. More misery—impatience—misunderstanding, culminating in an open breach.

Byron was exasperated. His mother-in-law had died while he was in Pisa, and in right of Annabella he was now a wealthy man. But just at the moment when he would like to feel rich, here he was in Genoa, surrounded by dependants. True, Teresa, as he always took care to say, never cost him a penny and the Gambas paid their way, but they hung like a millstone round his neck—filling up room in his house—and, oh, what a helpless breed they were, with their plots and cut-throat servants! Mary and the Hunts always wanted help, and they took his help and his money, and in repayment he got sour looks and pained argument. In desperation he offered to pay for them all to go home. They took him at his word, then he shilly-shallied and repented of his promise. Mary wrote letters, and Teresa rode over to the Casa Negroto to explain or inquire and returned in a bad temper.

One thing he had decided: he must leave Italy. It was an enervating country; he had done no good there, he was simply the slave of women —all of them in different ways plaintive and demanding. Besides, he knew now that Teresa was not to blame for the life of pack-and-follow that he had led these past few years. Grand Dukes were anxious to make his acquaintance, Papal Legates were affable, magistrates courteous, the police always smiled—but, one and all, they moved him on—from Ravenna to Pisa and thence to Genoa—another outbreak of Gamba folly, and he would be over the Alps next! Always in the eyes of the mocking world gallivanting after "Count Gamba's fair daughter!"

In the past he had been impatient when people hoped to find in him the hero of his poems, or believed that all the things his heroes did were actualities in his own life. But nowadays, though he turned a mocking face to Trelawny and Hobhouse, in his heart he knew that "poeshie"

BYRON AT GENOA, 1824

*From the drawing by Alfred, Count d'Orsay*

ALPHONSE DE LAMARTINE
*From a drawing by Théodore Chassériau*

was stuff of his own life. Poetry was experience, after all—experience tumultuously felt, transmuted in imagination, boiling over like lava down the side of a volcano. He had lived his poems before he wrote them. He would live them again—intensely, more deliberately—as a man of action, a soldier, a statesman, not a dreamer by his desolate fireside. After that, let him write all the "poeshie" he would. Of course, he must take the centre of the stage, but this time the stage must be the world. The thought of Greece had long been simmering in his mind, and here was Pietro at his elbow, clamouring to go there and fight. *Mashallah*, it was God's will. He was going home to England—the soldier-poet who had made Greece free.

He drifted away from Teresa. He turned his back upon Italians. He wanted his countrymen now. He dined with Mr Hill, the British Minister. He made friends with Mr Barry, the banker. He called upon Dr Alexander to make him well, and that practical Scotsman banned laudanum and salts and made him live sternly like an anchorite.

A ghost from that far-off English past rose in the shadowy form of Lady Frances Webster—the unhappy wife who had shrunk from his caresses in hopeless tears. She had left her husband now and was living in Paris with her children. Bouncible James, her egregious spouse, came to Genoa and pestered Byron with his confidences. In the name of friendship—as a fellow-poet—as the godfather of his son—he begged the one-time wooer of his wife to write to her—plead with her—to come back to her husband's longing arms. Life was running downhill, it was repeating itself, for this was La Mira, reflected Byron, with Count Guiccioli begging in tears to have his wife again! At least Jimmy Webster had beaten the Count to the post in two respects. By a miracle of last-minute virtue he had not lost his wife—then—that was left for the Duke of Wellington to accomplish—and he had obtained a thousand pounds from her lover. . . . He wrote to Lady Frances, and she answered, gratefully and tenderly —if he bade her return to her husband, she would obey.

To urge him on in the good cause Webster sent his intermediary a miniature of his wife. The timorous child that Byron had known was a woman now, long-nosed, handsome, with smiling lips and mournful eyes. A sad remembrance, he told Webster when he sent the token back, and he wrote to Lady Frances again. She gave him a thousand reasons why she never would go back to her husband—beginning with his cruelty and ending with her own infidelity. Be my friend, she implored, but not in friendship as the world understands that feeling—"No, that lovely passion which Byron alone can understand—Byron alone can feel."

Before Webster left Genoa, Byron suggested that he should pay at least the interest on that loan of a thousand pounds. Webster scratched

P

his black wig and looked dubiously into his friend's face—would it be convenient, he mumbled, if he left all arrangements about that loan for his 'heirs' to settle?

Always backward, ever since he left Ravenna! England with its memories, grave and gay, was calling.

Juan was at Newstead Abbey now with Lord Henry and Lady Adeline and her frolic Grace Fitz-Fulke. By night and day there were strange doings in the old house, but was it possible that Juan was falling seriously in love, and for the last time? His eyes rested in reverence on Aurora Raby. She was young, a Catholic—

> . . . sincere, austere,
> As far as her own gentle heart allow'd.

She came of a noble race that "had never bent or bowed to novel power."

> She gazed upon a world she scarcely knew,
> As seeking not to know it; silent, lone,
> As grows a flower, thus quietly she grew,
> And kept her heart serene within its zone.
>
> There was awe in the homage which she drew;
> Her spirit seem'd as seated on a throne
> Apart from the surrounding world, and strong
> In its own strength—most strange in one so young!

Mary Shelley made a fair copy of these lines and sent them back to Byron. "Is Aurora a portrait?" she asked in her most roguish manner. Then, purring softly, "Poor Juan," she added, "I long to know how he gets out—or, rather, into—the net."

In the spring of 1823 the Greek Committee was formed in London. Trelawny got in touch with one of the members and put up Byron's name. The committee elected him unanimously, and Byron's mind was made up. He would go to Greece. He wrote back to the Greek Committee and offered his services and money. Hobhouse, too, was informed of this latest resolution—and laughed in his proprietary fashion—Venezuela one day, the Yankees the next, and now it was Greece! The "dear fellow's" health wouldn't stand the strain of politics and war! But Pietro was delighted. He drew up involved plans of campaign, opening with his beloved word *Considerando*, and filed them carefully away. He ran about the harbour, looking at ships and talking to sailors, and then, galvanized into action by affection, wrote to Dr Vacca and asked him to recommend a physician for the voyage. "Poor" Byron was in bad physical condition and must have some one to look after him—some one young for choice and not too expensive—for Byron, it appeared, was as poor in pocket as in health.

Mary Shelley wrote sardonically to Trelawny. "Do you come to Greece? Lord Byron is in the same mind. The Guiccioli is an obstacle and certainly her situation is rather a difficult one. But he does not seem disposed to make a mountain of her resistance and he is far more able to take a decided than a petty step in contradiction to those about him."

Trelawny was vagabonding gloomily about Italy and shooting in the Maremna. Claire Clairmont had gone to Vienna, and he wrote her turbulent love-letters which she answered coolly. At last, on June 22, came the summons from Byron, who had engaged a "collier-built tub" called the *Hercules*.

Trelawny called at the Casa Saluzzo in the evening. All the doors and windows stood wide open in the loitering daylight, but silence brooded over the house like a tired dream. There were no servants, no living creature, to be seen, and he wandered about the Sleeping Beauty rooms, looking for the poet. He found him at last, seated at his desk, pen in hand and papers before him. A plate of salad and sardines and a bottle of hock lay beside him on a table. He was so lost in work that he did not notice his visitor's approach. There was upon his face a shadow of painful thought and brooding ecstasy, as of a Pythoness on her tripod.

When at length he saw Trelawny he shook off his absorption, jumped to his feet, and wrung him heartily by the hand. Then, dropping back into his chair, he picked up a sheet of manuscript.

"My tottle don't square with Lega," he remarked dreamily. "The amount of this bill is only one hundred and forty-three lire, which is not six pounds."

Every arrangement that Byron had made for his expedition, Trelawny told him, was wrong—the wrong ship, the wrong captain, the wrong doctor. He had designed a uniform and helmet for them to wear when they landed in Greece, but Trelawny bluffly told him that he would wear neither. "Blind chance"—that was Byron's only principle of action. Trelawny himself did not know why he was going to Greece, or what he would do when he got there, but at least he could criticize what Byron had done. Teresa was nowhere in sight, and he strolled over to the Casa Negroto. He found Hunt tired and bitter. Marianne was suckling and cantankerous, and the children were noisy. Mary Shelley's face lighted up when she saw him, but she, too, was cross. She railed at Byron for niggardliness, and her old friend Teresa was included in the general jeremiad—she cost her lover nothing—her one claim upon his affection —she was cheap! A poor lot, thought Trelawny, without Shelley to hold them together! He told Mary not to worry—he would pay her passage back to England—and gratefully she accepted his offer.

Byron had been annoyed by the refusal of his friends to take him seriously on the matter of Greece. In April he had written to Hobhouse, insisting that this was business, and complained of the difficulties he had to face in his own house. He enclosed a letter from the Greek Committee to prove that his services were accepted.

> There is no obstacle to my going up, but the "absurd womankind," and how absurd they are, as well as those under their dominion, thou knowest by all tale and history, and the experience of several of your friends. . . . However, I *will* go ("d—n my eye I *will* go ashore") an't be possible, or do all I can in the cause, go or not. . . . I presume the Committee would give me some regular instructions. . . . I will serve them as humbly as they please.

The difficulty was—not that he was forbidden to go, but that he was not to go alone. "I am doing all I can to get away," he wrote to Kinnaird (May 21) in exasperation,

> but I have all kinds of obstacles thrown in my way by the "absurd woman-kind," who seems determined on sacrificing herself in every way, and preventing me from doing any good, and all without reason. . . . She wants to go up to Greece too! forsooth, a precious place to go at present! Of course the idea is ridiculous, as everything must there be sacrificed to seeing her out of harm's way. It is a case, too, in which interest does not enter, and therefore hard to deal with; for I have no kind of control in that way, and if she makes a scene (and she has a turn that way) we shall have another romance, and tale of illusage, and abandonment, and Lady Carolining, and Lady Byroning, and Glenarvoning, all cut and dry. There never was a man who gave up so much to women, and all I have gained by it has been the character of treating them harshly. However I shall do what I can, and have hopes. . . . If I left a woman for another woman, she might have cause to complain, but really when a man merely wishes to go on a great duty, for a good cause, this selfishness on the part of the "feminie" is rather too much.

Grandfather Gamba had been petitioning the Vatican that his son and his grandchildren should be allowed to return to Romagna. Pietro's misdoings were beyond all pardon, but the Pope was willing to show mercy to his old friend Count Ruggiero Gamba. In April 1823 Teresa's father was told that he might go back home.

But His Holiness in his clemency wished also to serve the cause of morals. In the rescript dissolving the union of the Count and Countess Guiccioli no mention had been made of Lord Byron. If that nobleman continued to serve the Countess Guiccioli as her *amico*—well and good, no harm was done to morals in such a *relazione*—indeed, the Church in its charity had presumed upon its existence in seeking to persuade his lordship to leave Romagna. But it had been ordained that, for her better protection, the Countess Guiccioli should live henceforth in her father's house. Sorrowfully the Church must state that Count Ruggiero Gamba had not lived up to his bond. Had not the Countess Guiccioli lived alone in the same house with Lord Byron at Pisa? Was she not still living under Lord Byron's roof at Genoa? Omission in the past to acknowledge Lord Byron's existence did not mean that the Church was blind to the charges that Count Guiccioli had made in seeking to discipline his wife. The presence of Count Gamba in the Casa Saluzzo did not mitigate the grave reality that the Countess Guiccioli was now living in her lover's, not her father's house. If Count Gamba were allowed to return to Romagna, his daughter must return with him to the paternal abode. If, in contumacious pride, she refused to accompany him, the Church must in all sorrow consider whether it were not fitting that she should select a convent for her residence. Her father, in that case, would remain an exile.

"Is Aurora Raby a portrait?" Mary Shelley asked.

A portrait—perhaps! An idealized portrait of some one who was now dead—and loved by the dead.

As he looked at Teresa, then at himself in the mirror, he realized that —very quickly—they had both grown old.

He was a meagre skeleton with grey hair. His face—shaven now of whiskers—was drawn, white, there were shadows under his eyes and under his cheekbones.

Teresa's face had lost its look of youth, of eagerness, of happiness. She was haggard, the roses had shuddered out of her cheeks, there were sharp corners round her eyes. Her mouth was drawn down in a mournful droop. The years had rolled backward and left her old. She was lean and pale, as she had been on her sickbed at Ravenna—when he had come to heal her—and she had closed her arms round his neck.

# BOOK FIVE

# *Merry-go-round*

## CHAPTER I

# *Enter the Circus*

ON the evening of March 30, 1823, the Earl and Countess of Blessington drove into Genoa and put up at the Albergo Imperiale. The Countess, after bathing and dining, withdrew to her bedroom and gazed at the lights in the harbour. She posted her diary for the day.

"And am I indeed in the same town with Byron? And to-morrow I may perhaps behold him. I never felt before the same impatient longing to see anyone known to me only by his works. I hope he may not be fat, as Moore described him at Venice, for a *fat poet* is an anomaly in my opinion. Well, well, to-morrow I may know what he is like: and now to bed to sleep away the fatigues of my journey."

Margaret (Marguerite) Power had left youth behind her and was entering on the age of charm. She was thirty-four and beautiful. Her life had once been troubled and in early days ran much the same course as Teresa's. But she was prosperous now.

Her father, 'Beau' Power, was an Irish squireen, a Catholic once, who had sold out for the dubious patronage of the 'Castle Party' in Dublin. Margaret was the eldest of his good-looking, sprightly daughters. He was a bully and a drunkard, and forced her at the age of fifteen to marry one of his bottle-companions, Captain Farmer of the Forty-seventh Foot, an Englishman with private means and many years older than his bride.

Captain Farmer, too, was a drunkard and a brute yet worse than her father. After three months of marriage, which left her with health permanently damaged, she returned to her father's house. From a miserable life there she escaped with another English officer, Captain Jenkins, a kindly man for a change, who took her to England and set her up in a house in Hampshire. There Margaret recovered her spirits and flowered into grace and gaiety. She had intellectual tastes, read books, taught herself to play with the things of the mind, and developed an ambition to write. Captain Jenkins was content with a mistress who daily grew more delightful under his indolent hands, and made few physical demands upon her. After several years of this tranquil life of sin he brought to his house Lord Mountjoy, an old friend of Irish days, and Margaret Power's fortunes took another upward turn.

Lord Mountjoy was an Irish peer of recent nobility with a vacuous eye and a cheerful donkey laugh. His leading virtue was good nature, and in the end good nature was the vice that killed him. As a schoolboy he had inherited the family title with an estate that yielded him thirty thousand pounds a year. Henceforth life for him was one long picnic. He cut a dash in magnificent clothes in London, collected snuff-boxes, and lavished the resources of limited brain and wealth that seemed without end on elaborate private theatricals. A man so rich and amiable would not remain without wife or woman long. His friend, Major Browne, on sailing from Ireland for service overseas, left behind him a pretty wife, whom the good-natured nobleman took under his protection out of sheer kindness of heart. Mrs Browne could only requite his kindness by bearing him a son and a daughter. Then, as the Major had long ceased to communicate with her, she presumed that he was dead. She urged upon her protector the desirability of marriage so that a legitimate heir be born to inherit his estates. He saw the force of her reasoning and married her out of hand. A few weeks later Major Browne returned to take his lady home from the protection of his genial friend. He withdrew discreetly, however, upon learning how matters stood, with, we may be sure, a generous compensation for his broken life. Lord Mountjoy was mildly disturbed by this episode and, to ease his conscience, went through the ceremony of marriage a second time with Mrs Browne. Then news came that Major Browne was indubitably dead. There was nothing for it but for Lord Mountjoy to lead Mrs Browne to the altar a third time. This much-married lady bore him two legitimate children, a son and a daughter, and died. Her husband was overwhelmed with grief and gave her the finest funeral that Dublin had seen in many years. Still disconsolate he came to stay with Captain Jenkins in Hampshire, and was captivated at sight by the charm of his friend's mistress. After affable discussion Captain Jenkins resigned his rights in Margaret Power to Lord Mountjoy, who, in a transport of good will, made him a present of ten thousand pounds. For some years Margaret lived happily with her new protector. Then the good news came, so often desired and so necessary to Lord Mountjoy's peace of mind when he took another man's wife to his heart. Captain Farmer had fallen out of a window in a drunken frolic at a debtors' prison, his neck had incontestably been broken, and Margaret was free. Like Mrs Browne before her, she suggested to Lord Mountjoy the propriety of marriage. He was delighted to comply with her wishes, and they were married at the church in Bryanston Square, in London.

Lord Mountjoy's private virtues had long called for public recognition, and a grateful Government made him Earl of Blessington. Margaret Power, therefore, embarked upon her social career as a countess—with her portrait painted by Lawrence, a fine house in Seamore Place, and a rich and uxorious husband in the background. Her ambition was to be a great London hostess. She had beauty, wit, tact, the best cook in London, perfectly trained servants, and soon clever and intelligent men were thronging her house. Unfortunately her life had not been spent among women of the world. Clever and intelligent men, like bridegrooms at a wedding, are essential to 'good society,' if it is not to perish of boredom; but it is clever and disagreeable women who rule 'good society.' The hostesses in power tacitly agreed among themselves that Lady Blessington must be stopped short in her career. Her past had nothing to do with the matter, for her worst enemy, Lady Holland, of Holland House, had in her day gone further with less excuse than Margaret Power. Lady Blessington's offences were threefold—she was beautiful, she was amusing, she was nobody—the widow of one Jenkins—or was the man's name Farmer? The clever and intelligent men continued to visit Seamore Place. With infinite good nature their wives and mothers watched them go, but they did not call at Seamore Place themselves. Countess though she was and rich, Lady Blessington failed to find her place in 'good society.'

She lost heart in the baffling struggle. Why not leave London for a while, with its crowded ballrooms and insolent hostesses, and live abroad more easily and luxuriously among people who cared nothing for the snobberies of England? Lord Blessington acquiesced gladly. He was annoyed because people would not take his beautiful wife on her own terms. Apart from that, he was bored and had long ago voted that 'good society' in London was dull. But, if they travelled, they must travel in the grand tradition of the English milord. *Barouches, calèches*, every kind of vehicle was pressed into service. Troupes of footmen and maids, beds, sheets, wardrobes, a whole *batterie de cuisine* under charge of a chef who had stood fire in an emperor's kitchen—a small army with commissariat department—followed the Earl and his lady into the jungle of Continental life. Lady Blessington supplied herself with gorgeously bound notebooks, for she intended writing a book about the expedition when they returned. Twelve days in Paris for clothes, couriers, and other impedimenta, and the 'Blessington circus' rolled southward across France, armed with a letter of introduction to Byron from Tom Moore.

At Avignon Alfred Count d'Orsay attached himself to the expedition. This was a most beautiful young man of ancestry as dubious as Lady Blessington's past. His father was a Napoleonic general of doubtful background, but handsome as the day was long. His mother was beautiful and witty, the illegitimate daughter of a German princeling. His grandmother was an Italian actress, who, after the German princeling left her, found her way to India, where she made a name for herself as 'la belle Sullivan' in right of her new protector. She left the amorous Sullivan for the millionaire Quintin Crawford and came with him to Paris. There with her Nabob—who eventually became her husband—she kept magnificent house from the days of Marie Antoinette through consulate and empire to Waterloo.

With so much beauty and opulence in his background Count d'Orsay was born to shine expensively in society. He was tall and slender, with broad shoulders and tapered waist; his features, with straight nose, Cupid's-bow mouth, round chin, and luxuriant curly hair, were classic in their perfection. He dressed with daring simplicity, was a skilful rider, a connoisseur in a dozen arts—painting, fencing, theatricals, furnishing houses, gloves, boots, waistcoats, horses, cards, champagne, epigrams, and the *cuisine*. Yet with all these accomplishments he had the disarming manner of a high-spirited boy—friendly, genial, mischievous, turn and turn-about—always with a touch of conquering impudence. Naturally he made enemies in life, but his friends and admirers were legion, and they were more often men than women. And some of the men who liked him were no fools—Carlyle, the Duke of Wellington, Disraeli, and Lamartine.

At twenty-one he visited London, carried 'society' by storm, snubbed Lady Holland in her own house, and drifted into the Blessington *salon* in Seamore Place. Lord Blessington was delighted with him, and his cup brimmed over when he found that his wife took delight, too, in the society of this amusing youth. Alfred left England for France, threw up his commission in the Royal Guards, and thenceforth devoted his life to the consolation of the childless Countess of Blessington and her susceptible lord.

Never in history were there travelling companions more splendid, more good-tempered, more free from care and vulgar responsibility, or more eager to enjoy life, than this trio—the beauty, the dandy, and the millionaire! From Avignon they made their leisurely way down the Rhône along the Riviera to Nice, and there they paused before they descended on Italy.

Lady Holland's son, Henry Fox, was staying at Nice. He was a slender, good-looking youth about d'Orsay's age, with a cross, sensitive face and walked with a slight limp. He was travelling abroad by consent of his parents to recover from an unhappy love-affair. He, too, was heading for Genoa, for he had known Byron as a boy and loved him because he had been kind, and he wanted to see him again.

Expansive as ever, Lord Blessington invited this sad young man to dine with his Countess and his beautiful youth. Henry Fox went to the dinner with some curiosity. As his mother's son he was prepared to disapprove of Lady Blessington and Count d'Orsay, individually and together; but if it would annoy his mother to learn that he had dined with the Blessingtons the evening would not be wasted. On the whole he was not disappointed in Lady Blessington. "She is not at all pleasant," he wrote in his diary (Sunday, March 23, 1823), "very vulgar and very abusive." She bantered too much, bragged, and, with it all, was a prude. She told him how she had snubbed Lord Grey when he made love to her—"ridiculous to any woman, but to me it was insolent!" Henry's eyes strayed quizzically from hers and dwelt on Count d'Orsay with an inquiring look. Lady Blessington explained his presence. He is to marry Lord Blessington's daughter, she said airily. "This, I suppose," Henry noted cynically in his diary, "is only a blind." The girl was thirteen years old, and d'Orsay had never seen her.

The Blessingtons would have been glad if Lady Holland's son had travelled with them to Genoa, but Henry was a severe young man and fastidious in his choice of associates. The Blessingtons were *mauvais ton*, and he left them and pushed on to Genoa by himself. He arrived there on Good Friday (March 28, 1823). The next day he called at the Casa Saluzzo, but Byron was out. The following day, Easter Sunday, a letter came from Byron, bidding him with every expression of affection call at two the next afternoon.

The day was dull with lowering clouds, and as Henry Fox drove up the hill to Albaro the rain fell in a fine drizzle. Great was his disgust on reaching the Casa Saluzzo to find the Blessington carriage standing before the door. In it were seated the Countess and her sister. Lord Blessington and Count d'Orsay had already made their entrance into the house and had been there some time. The Countess and Miss Power drooped forlornly in the rain.

Suddenly Byron appeared from the house, hatless and dishevelled, limping painfully. As he stood bowing by the Blessington carriage he seemed nervous and shy. "You may have thought me," he said with elaborate politeness, "quite as ill bred and *sauvage* as fame reports, in having permitted Your Ladyship to remain a quarter of an hour at my gate; but my old friend Lord Blessington is to blame; for I only heard a minute ago that I was so highly honoured. I shall think you do not pardon this apparent rudeness unless you enter my abode, which I entreat you will do."

Together the party moved within doors, Byron stiffly apologizing, Lady Blessington affably conversing, Miss Power smiling, and Henry Fox limping and sulking in the rear. Upstairs in the library they sat by the open window, and for two hours the Blessington party chattered and laughed. Byron was still nervous, said little, and seemed annoyed. At last his overpowering visitors departed, and Henry Fox was left alone with Byron.

Henry looked at his old friend with affectionate eyes. The face was as beautiful as ever, only, he noticed with sorrow, grey locks were now mingled in the hair that once had been so romantically dark. Still the same musical low voice that he had so loved as a boy. Only one disappointment—"his figure is shorter than I recollected"—but even that disappointment Henry loyally explained away. "I was a boy," he reminded himself, "when I last saw him, and I have grown a lot since then." Byron's manner towards him was frank and cordial as ever, and he talked openly about a hundred matters and people—about Lord and Lady Holland, about Caro Lamb, Rogers, *Don Juan*, *Cain*, conspiracy in Ravenna, and brawl in Pisa. He even talked about his wife and said he did not yet know why she had left him. As for Ada, he had no memory of what she looked like, and if he were to meet her now he wouldn't know her. And then with a drop into present time he said that he was sorry he couldn't talk French, for he would have gladly conversed with Count d'Orsay.

Henry had a pretty wit of his own, and he delighted Byron with his stories of London life, told with a deft and charming malice. How could Lady Holland, with her caustic mind, bear to let this son of hers live away from her? But Henry's face darkened when the talk fell upon his mother. Heigh-ho, thought Byron, a bit like me with *my* poor mother, who, God knows, was never fun! He looked at Henry again, and in this slight, handsome boy with dog-like eyes and sensual mouth, who limped and spoke in a low, soft voice, he saw his own lost youth. He felt sentimental and sad and terribly affectionate, and his affection made him critical. The boy was clever, humorous, unhappy, but frail, and he was far too self-conscious. He had been reared by women in a hothouse atmosphere, and there was an old-maid sharpness in his wit. He needed the society of men, more of the rough-and-tumble of life, he must grow kinder and less fastidious—it would do him a world of good if in Italy he fell in love with a frank and passionate Italian woman.

Henry Fox said good-bye to Byron. He never saw Teresa Guiccioli at the Casa Saluzzo. Byron remarked casually at his going that he was tired of Italy, must "cut cables" there, and evidently was homesick for England.

Four years had closed to the day upon Byron's *liaison* when Henry Fox called at the Casa Saluzzo and left it without seeing Teresa Guiccioli. He never met Byron again.

The next morning Byron wrote to Moore to tell him that the Blessingtons had presented their credentials. "Mountjoy seems very good-natured," he said, "but is much tamed since I recollect him in all the glory of gems and snuff-boxes." Milady seemed "highly literary," to which he attributed the honour of her calling upon him. "She is also very pretty even in a morning—a species of beauty on which the sun of Italy does not shine so frequently as the chandelier." As for "the French Count," he had "all the air of a *Cupidon déchaîné*." But it was Henry Fox whom he wished to write about most.

## CHAPTER II

# Conversation Piece

IN the meantime Lady Blessington was posting her diary at the Albergo Imperiale. If Byron had shown himself politely indifferent to her charms, she, on her side, was taken aback. "I have seen Lyrd Byron," she wrote, "and am disappointed."

Certainly he was not fat. He was ludicrously thin, and his odd Italian clothes hung upon his body like rags. She, too, like Henry Fox, had imagined him taller—a dignified, commanding air—"a hero-looking sort of person." He should have been melancholy and scornful, and she found him on first meeting only "gentleman-like." Then even that illusion faded, and she thought him *gauche* and ill at ease and altogether wanting in that self-possession that characterizes a man of birth and education. As the days went by and their intimacy grew, his shyness fell away and the "highly facetious personage" crept into sight—that mocking creature who had shocked Annabella and exasperated Trelawny. Flippancy—that, noted Lady Blessington with surprise and disapproval, was the prevailing, the tedious, note in all his conversation, and in his flippancy he was often frank beyond the limits of decorum. His taste, too, was bad; his clothes were garish, the appointments in his house vulgar and ostentatious, and he was, for a gentleman and a liberal, distressingly conscious of his noble birth. Then behind this flippant, tawdry creature another man loomed, dangerously tender and sentimental, and Lady Blessington found herself writing "poor Byron" again and again in her journal.

With women and with most dull men Margaret Power never had success, but with clever men she knew that her charm would find a way. She had come to Genoa to talk with Byron, and she stayed there two months, taking copious notes of his conversation. Luckily for the success of her reporting, she was heart-free for him. Yet he challenged her pride as a woman, and she responded to his danger as a man. She must hold him at her finger-tips in an intellectual minuet, and he must dance to the tune she called. Like all good female conversationalists, she was a ready listener. She wooed him, she lured him on, she let him talk, she checked him, reproved him, then flew with gay inconsequence to another topic, then once more relapsed into beckoning silence.

After that embarrassed visit she never went to the Casa Saluzzo again. But Byron called at the inn, he dined, he went out riding with the Blessington party and showed them the sights of the town. Soon the Earl and the French Count dropped into the background, and the poet and the beauty went out riding alone.

A few days after their arrival in Genoa Lord Blessington received news from Ireland that his only legitimate son was dead. The loss left him tottering on the verge of thought for the first time in his life. All things on earth, he concluded, were uncertain, and he spent the time drawing up his will—an extraordinary document in which he practically disinherited his wife and remaining (illegitimate) son and left the bulk of his fortune to his second (and legitimate) daughter on condition that she married Count d'Orsay. Thus, in his blundering way, he planned to leave all the people he cared for happy and united after his death. D'Orsay, in the meantime, put the finishing touches to a cheerful document—his *Memoirs* to the age of twenty-one, when, under the law, he had achieved years of discretion. When Milady returned from her ride with Byron he greeted her with a gay and quizzical glance, and Milady tapped him on the cheek and smiled very kindly.

Byron brought Pietro Gamba to call upon the Blessingtons, and they took to him at once. He was, they were told, very like his sister in disposition and looks. In that case, Lady Blessington decided, the Countess Guiccioli must be a handsome woman, animated and kindly, and, for an Italian, surprisingly fair-haired. She was never able to judge for herself, for during the whole of her two months' stay in Genoa Teresa remained aloof and unseen in the Casa Saluzzo.

She made inquiries about the Countess Guiccioli of Mr Barry, the banker. Mr Barry spoke of Teresa in the highest terms of praise—in fact, he was quite sentimental about her. Certainly, he said, she was beautiful, and she was intellectual, too. But she worried about her father's exile and lived the life of a recluse in the Casa Saluzzo, devoting her time to music and books and the comfort of the poor old Count. She seldom left the gardens of her villa, but now and then she went to call on Mrs Shelley or that annoying Mr Hunt at the Casa Negroto. Sometimes, too, she went for solitary walks on the seashore, but she never descended into the city. Sad had been her life, said Mr Barry—married at sixteen to a man old enough to be her grandfather—long had conscience fought in her heart against passion, but when Byron followed her to Ravenna she could fight against the call of love no more. She had left her husband, abandoned wealth, position, friends—willing to forget the world, by the world to be disowned. Behind her veneer of brittle worldliness Margaret Power had a warm Irish soul. She was touched by this story. In many ways it reminded her of her own unhappy marriage as a child, only Teresa Guiccioli, perhaps, had been more fortunate in that she had found a lover whom she could respect as a man, and that Margaret Power had never yet found and, she knew now, never would find.

Delicately she hinted to Byron that she had not yet seen the Countess

Guiccioli. "Oh," he replied with a blush and an uneasy laugh, "she has a fine red head of her own and don't care to show it."

Lady Blessington knew that she had been snubbed—by Teresa Guiccioli—and her pity turned to malice.

To another woman friend, Lady Hardy, Byron wrote the truth. With her cool, sarcastic humour she reminded him of old Lady Melbourne, and they exchanged sprightly letters. "My coz," he called her, and "cold Calypso." She told him about James Webster, who was laying noisy siege to her virtue pending reconciliation with his wife. Byron scolded her for tormenting the poor man and regaled her with his own domestic trials and a great deal more about Webster's in the past than he had a right to tell.

> There be here [he wrote] and have been for some time past the Earl and Lady Blessington and a Parisian *ami* of the family's . . . The Parisian is very young and a beauty, of which last advantage he is fully aware, but he is not at all disagreeable and I suspect that the women find him more formidable than dreadful. Miladi is the Miladi of whom Lawrence made a picture that set all London raving . . . She is also an authoress, hath written three books and will I suppose write thirty in due course of time and tide . . . I could not easily (in my usual way) escape being occasionally with them, especially as they are equestrians, and I met them frequently in my rides about Genoa; but this has plunged me into a bit of dramatic trouble, for *la mia dama*, Mde la Comptesse G., was seized with a furious fit of Italian jealousy and was as unreasonable and perverse as well can be imagined. God He knows she paid me the greatest compliment . . . I have long come to years of discretion and would much rather fall into the sea than in love any day of the week. Her Ladyship was extremely well guaranteed from any presumed observation of my inclination by her Parisian appendage and would only have changed for the worse, which would have neither suited her or me.
>
> Madame Gi (who never saw her) won't allow her to be pretty and *will* allow her to be not young. I dared not form a judgement on the subject before one who argues with all the insolence of four and twenty. I send you this gossip that you may laugh at it, which is all that it is good for, if it is good for so much.

Don't be fatuous, Lady Hardy replied, about the Countess G., and she warned him against falling in love with Lady Blessington, adding, no doubt, to her warning some unkind truths about that lady's past. "Very right, my dear cousin," he replied,

> but you see there was no danger, for I have an awful dread both of new love and learning and besides, to say truth, thought that I was as well off at home . . . Besides my long foreign *liaison* of five years and my being exceedingly governed and kept tight in hand, I do not know how it is, but it would [be] difficult for me to fall in love again with an Englishwoman . . . I have laid down a rule never to have a feeling of that kind (that is a new one) after

thirty. My present attachment began before I had turned that awkward corner of existence, so that it was but just in time. Having begun, it will probably continue to the end of the chapter unless something out of the way stops it, as it does many things of that kind.

A forlorn picture! So much beauty—and high spirits—and potential danger—gathered together, and every one was safe—or tired.

As the weeks went by Margaret Power probed more deeply into Byron's heart and scribbled her discoveries in her notebook. How strange it was, she noted, that he talked about his wife so much! Womanlike, she must put her finger into that pie. She lectured him and defended Annabella and made herself intermediary for a letter of qualified peace-making. Naturally she disapproved of *Don Juan* and extorted from him a confession (oh, Byron!) that he was ashamed of that poem. He was strangely preoccupied with the thought of death, but when she tried to stir his ambition by talking about Greece a blank fog of levity fell between them. He was only going there, he told her, because Hobhouse said he never would. Then the fog lifted, and he talked of death again.

About Teresa Guiccioli Lady Blessington remained resentfully discreet. He wound his way to the topic through abstract discussion of love, friendship, marriage, and kindred themes. No beauty of the flesh, he said, could vie with the beauty of a poet's dream.

"I like to close my eyes," he said, playfully suiting the action to his words; "and fancy one of the creatures of my imagination with rose-tipped fingers playing with my hair . . . little snowy-dimpled hand on mine . . . the fairy foot, round and pulpy, but small to diminutiveness, peeping from beneath the drapery that half conceals it. I detest thin women," he said dreamily, then opened his eyes with a mournful stare; "unfortunately nearly all plump women have clumsy hands and feet." His eyes lit up with a smile and he leaned from his horse to speak more softly. "I can so well understand the lover leaving his mistress!—I should leave mine, not to write to, but to think of her, to dress her up as my ideal beauty and then I should adore the idol I had formed."

True love, he said, never dwindles into friendship—it dies. Margaret Power contradicted him with a stream of theory that washed Teresa out to sea. He changed his tone and sought to spur her on to further contradiction by hurting her pride in Teresa's name. "There is a frankness and simplicity about Italian women," he said; "when they love, they love without shame and with all their hearts. Beside them Englishwomen seem cold and calculating." Margaret Power was Irish, and she held her peace. "Women love with more purity and delicacy than men," he said, and flung out his hand to seal the rake's confession.

One evening he was sitting with her under the moonlight on the balcony of the Albergo Imperiale. From the ships in the harbour below

HENRY FOX, LORD HOLLAND

Henry Fox, like Lamartine, was said to look like Byron. Compare this with
the Prepiani miniature (facing p. 80).

*Engraved by C. H. Jeens from the portrait (lost) by G. F. Watts*                    240

LA MARQUISE DE BOISSY
Teresa, in her late fifties, as a *grande dame* of the Second Empire.
*From the oil-painting by Joseph Fagnani*

241

floated a bewildering medley of sea-chanties, sung in a hundred different tongues. Little by little the songs died away and there was silence. Then —final and triumphant—rose the words of *God Save the King* from a merchant ship by the pier. Tears filled Margaret Power's eyes, and she turned to look at her fellow-outcast and there were tears in his eyes, too. "O Big Ben, Big Ben," he murmured with a tragic smile, "you little know what loyal subjects you have here, and that I am among the number, too."

His levity fell away from him like a discarded cloak, and he spoke of Teresa—of her gentleness, her devotion, her unselfishness. Margaret Power recovered her equanimity at the sound of the name and listened sharply. "He represented La Contessa," she wrote briskly in her journal that night, "as a most amiable and lady-like person, perfectly disinterested and noble-minded, devotedly attached to him . . . He had been passionately in love with her and she had sacrificed everything for him . . . He dwelt with evident complacency on her noble birth (and her husband's wealth and the coach with the six black horses) . . . In his praises it is quite evident that he is sincere and I am persuaded that this is his last attachment . . . In short, he has said all that was possible to impress me with a favourable opinion of this lady and has convinced me"—Margaret Power held her pen, as she meditated how to close her sentence—"that he entertains a very high one of her himself."

After that he found it easier to talk of Teresa, and Lady Blessington listened with an air of polite constraint. "There is no real happiness," he said, "outside the pale of marriage . . . *Liaisons* that are not cemented by marriage must produce unhappiness, when there is refinement of mind and that honourable pride which accompanies it. The humiliations and vexations a woman, under such circumstances, is exposed to, cannot fail to have a certain effect on her temper and spirits, which robs her of the charms that won affection. It renders her susceptible and suspicious; her self-esteem being diminished, she becomes doubly jealous of that for whom she lost it, and on whom she depends; and if he has a feeling to conciliate her, he must submit to a slavery much more severe than that of marriage, without its respectability."

He recited to her the lines he had written when Teresa had gone back to her husband—"Could love for ever, run like a river"—but Lady Blessington dismissed them as doggerel and said they belied all that he had said about marriage. She had heard enough and had no doubt that, when the time came, "poor Byron" would have difficulty in saying good-bye to Teresa. He still harped on the theme of matrimony and said that if he and the Countess Guiccioli continued to live together, people would point to them as the ideal married couple. And yet, Lady Blessington remarked mischievously, "La Contessa Guiccioli has, perhaps, little reason to be satisfied with her lot."

Q

Byron had the grace to look remorseful, but he still held himself to the centre of the stage and asked for pity.

"Perhaps you are right. Yet she must know that I am sincerely attached to her. But, the truth is, my habits are not those requisite to form the happiness of any woman . . .

"I am worn out in feelings—less capable than ever of those nameless attentions that all women, but, above all, Italian women, require. I like solitude . . . and when with the person I like, am often *distrait* and gloomy." He was off now on the Childe Harold horse. "There is something in the poetical temperament that precludes happiness, not only to the person who has it, but to those connected with him. Our imaginations are warmer than our hearts. This is our misfortune but not our fault, and dearly do we expiate it. We are rendered incapable of sympathy and cannot lighten by sharing the pain we inflict. We are not so unfeeling as not to be grieved by the unhappiness we cause, but imagination transports our thoughts to other scenes, and we are always so much more occupied by the ideal than the present that we forget all that is actual."

He paused a moment, then continued gloomily, "But let the object of affection be snatched away by death, and how is all the pain inflicted on them avenged!

> " Oh! what are a thousand living loves
> To that which cannot quit the dead!

How did I feel this when my daughter Allegra died! How much more severely would Teresa's death afflict me! To think that while I had been soaring into the fields of romance and fancy, I had left her to weep over my coldness or infidelities of imagination!"

But this was holiday-time. Greece was calling, and the quest of pleasure made it essential that the Blessington circus should leave Genoa. On the night of June 2 Byron came to say good-bye at the inn. He was nervous, and for a while his tone was flippant and sarcastic. But his voice became inarticulate and he sank down upon a sofa and they saw that the tears were running down his face. "This is our last meeting," he said; "I am not coming back from Greece."

"*Poor* Byron," wrote My Lady in her diary before she went to bed that night. "*Poor* Byron! The very idea that I shall not see him again overpowers me with sadness and makes me forget many defects that had often disenchanted me with him." She closed the book, smiling absently at the thought. To-morrow to Florence, and to Rome and Naples, and pastures new of indolence and pleasure.

# Good-bye, Juan

BUT, *piccinina*, as the Santissimo says, you must not live naughtily with a heretic and a *Carbonaro* and a foreigner like Lord Byron."

Teresa was past laughing with her lover and past struggling, too. The cards were stacked against her. Her father said nothing, but he looked at her hopefully and reproachfully. Pietro clamoured every day that she had no right to keep her father living in exile or her lover from going to the wars. The Pope was all kindness and did not insist on her returning to her husband. Her mother was dead, and some one must look after the little sisters at Filetto, when they grew up and wanted husbands. And Byron was resolute to go to Greece—without her. When things were safer, he promised, he would send for her. Very well, she told him, I will go to a convent and wait for you.

He made his will and in it left Teresa five thousand pounds. She burst into angry tears when he told her. What she had given him, she gave him free and for love—she was not to be paid off like a discarded mistress! Byron kicked himself for a clumsy fool. This was the sum, he pleaded, that he had meant to leave Allegra—she had been good to Allegra—wouldn't she take the money for the child's sake? Teresa was mollified but adamant—she would not take the money. The gold ring that he had given her at Bologna was all the reward she craved. Some women are disinterested, mused Byron, and wrote and told his friends that solemn truth.

The last days were tranquil, only Teresa wanted always to be alone with him. One very hot day she begged him to come with her for a solitary walk by the sea in a little cove that she had found for herself. They scrambled down the cliff and over the rocks and walked up and down together by the sea. Then they climbed the cliff again. His face was drawn and white with pain, and he leaned heavily on her arm as they walked. She was sick with shame and anger against herself—she had no tact—she had forgotten his foot. But, as ever, he was noble and forgiving. As she bathed his foot on their return to the house, he laughed about it and told her with delightful frankness what a curse it had been to him all his life—how it had always made him feel sorry for himself, but he wasn't feeling sorry now. In his frankness and his laughter somehow she found consolation and swore to herself that never again would she say or do anything that would make him feel sad.

She stifled her *presentimenti* and talked philosophically of the convent. But in her heart she knew that she never was going to a convent—and so did he. She knew—far better than Lady Blessington—that he never would return from Greece. As she looked into his white, tired face—at his meagre skeleton frame—she knew that he was unfit for the hardship and disappointment of war. But she must never let him know that she knew that. She mustn't let him feel that way himself. So she talked gaily and ironically of life in the convent and of the good days to come when she would rejoin him on one of the Ionian islands—like Haidée with Juan, and they would laugh over his adventures. But the bright day was done and she was for the dark—the drab, domestic dark.

The day of sailing arrived—Friday, July 13—surely a date of evil omen. Byron went to say good-bye to Teresa. "Laugh, *piccinina*, laugh," he groaned; "you always used to laugh!" Teresa smiled bravely, and he pulled out his handkerchief to wipe away her tears. But he dropped into a chair and sobbed convulsively into the handkerchief himself. She laid her hand on his shoulder and gave him words of good luck. She kneeled beside him and pulled the handkerchief away. With a laugh she showed him her scissors and cut away a lock of his hair—a dark lock with no grey in it. She cut away one of her own long gold tresses and laid it on his knee and he clenched it fiercely in his hand. Then they cried into the handkerchief together. . . .

He sprang to his feet and with one sharp kiss hobbled from the room. Back to his library for the last odds and ends of business at his desk! Pietro was waiting for him. Together they rode down the hill to the harbour, where the brig *Hercules* lay moored, with Trelawny scowling disdainfully on board.

Teresa sat alone with the dark lock of hair twisted between her fingers. The damp handkerchief lay at her feet. She picked it up and laid it next her heart. Six weeks she wore it there, then she sent it to the wash. She had a small wooden chest made and into it she dropped the manuscript of poems, love-letters from other women, the handkerchief, the lock of hair.

The brig *Hercules* tossed restlessly at its moorings, and Pietro moaned and vomited all the long night. The next morning there was a dead calm. In the evening Byron rode up the hill with the wan Pietro to Albaro. The Casa Saluzzo was deserted, the windows closed, a ghost of a house from which the ghost had fled. Teresa had driven away that morning to Bologna.

He sat under an ilex-tree in the garden, munching cheese and brooding. He would give a kingdom now not to be going to Greece. His health was injured beyond repair, and he was right when he told Lady Blessington he would never come back. Faces rose up before him in the twilight, as before the eyes of a drowning man—Hobhouse's face, laughing and saying, "I told you so, I knew you would never go!"—his schoolfellow, Clare's face as they stood clasping hands by the roadside—Lady Blessington's face, as she leaned forward in her chair with a mocking smile. But always one face dominated all the others, ever changing, ever the same, like a face in an opium dream—clear and pale, moody, laughing, petulant, sarcastic, defiant . . . cloud and drifting mist, and now he stared at darkness blank as eternity . . . in the silver shadows of the cypress-trees a phantom stood before him—a small boy, mute and tense with humiliation. . . . "You little, lame brat!" . . . a poker whizzed past his head . . . then the bellows and the tongs . . . the boy's lips curled in scorn and anguish. . . . "I was born so—Mother!" . . . and merciful blind tears shut out the vision. . . .

The calm lasted two days. On the sixteenth Mr Barry, who had been indefatigable in making all arrangements for the poet, rushed down to the dock to ask what he should do about the geese he had left behind him at the Casa Saluzzo. But the brig *Hercules* was gone.

Mr Barry climbed the hill to Albaro and walked through the empty rooms of the Casa Saluzzo. He felt sad as he thought of Byron and the Countess Guiccioli. He came to the poet's study and sat down by the desk. He frowned at his thoughts and drummed restlessly with his fingers on the arms of the chair; then, with an impatient sigh, he turned and pulled open one of the drawers and stared into it absently.

There, among a litter of papers hastily torn up, lay a long tress of golden hair.

# BOOK SIX

# Comedy

CHAPTER I

## *Back to the House*

LIFE had gone hard with Count Guiccioli since Teresa left him in July of 1820. He withdrew to one of his smaller houses in the neighbourhood of Ravenna and there meditated gloomily on the folly of human nature. His wealth had brought him no peace in his old age, only a host of enemies and critics. Romagna was a lawless state in which neither a man's honour nor his property was safe. 'Rule by theocracy,' in his opinion, had always been a mistake, and now he was proved right. The Papal Government was incredibly weak—slipshod and easy-going one minute, aimless and savage the next. In the matter of his wife's *relazione* with this acquisitive English poet the Pope had shown himself an outright partisan of the Gamba family and handed down a judgment that was an affront to the manly state of husband. Romagna was no state for him, and he weighed the alternatives of life in the more peaceable Grand Duchy of Tuscany, with Florence for headquarters, or under the severer discipline of the Austrians in Venice. In either state he would find firm rule, some respect for property, and freedom from the interference of priests. In the meantime he lay low and kept a sharp eye on the comings and goings of his wife and her lover. If it were possible he meant to get Teresa back, and at every wayward turn in her love-affair he reached out his coils, like the old boa in the wood, to draw her home.

Two months after Teresa's flight to Filetto Carluccio died. This was a real grief for his father. He had not been happy in his relations with his son, but upon him the old Count had concentrated all his ambitions. Carluccio was to play a distinguished rôle in the political life of an Italy at once unified and divorced from priestly rule. Because he expected so much for his elder son he had heaped all his powers of affection upon him. Unfortunately even in affection old Brunello was despotic, and Carluccio had been rebellious and perverse.

Teresa heard the news—through Byron's steward, Lega—at Filetto. At once she wrote to her husband (September 15, 1820). "My dear Alessandro," she said, "if you think I am only slightly afflicted by your loss, you are wrong, as you would be wrong in thinking anyone in the world could wish to see you happy more than I do." With her usual frankness she went on, "I had no reason to love your son, perhaps some reason to hate him, but I couldn't be so harsh nor so soft as to feel for him one way or the other. I chose to look upon him as your one comfort, and that was enough to make his life dear to me and, now that he is dead, to make me mourn his loss."

She had been so short a time away from Count Guiccioli as his wife that, in wishing him better luck for the future, she could not forbear from lecturing him. At Filetto the *Carbonari* were holding meetings and plotting the liberation of Italy. Knowing that her Alessandro was interested in the plans of the *Carbonari*, she sought to rally him to the good cause. Only, she insinuated, by taking the right side in politics would he win that place in society which she knew he desired. She wished him not only to enjoy the compensations of wealth when he was an old man, but to prove that he was worthy to enjoy them. A rumour had reached her that he was going to Milan on secret business. As evidence of her good will she sent him a warning—"I should be very glad if you would give up that journey. I don't enter further into discussion . . . perhaps it would be needless, because you have probably guessed what I am thinking about."

Now that Carluccio was dead Count Guiccioli turned all his ambition upon his one surviving son, Ignazio. In many ways Ignazio repaid affection more than Carluccio. At fifteen he was a very handsome boy, and he shared one enthusiasm with his father in his love of the theatre. But Ignazio was lively and turbulent, and his imagination ran away with his powers of reason. He was going to be a poet and write plays like his father's old friend Alfieri. He read Schiller's *Robbers* and was filled with a vague ambition for a life of banditry. He did not endear himself to his father by reading *Childe Harold* and *Manfred*, nor by assuming poses of world-weary sorrow in the home. Above all, he disliked the dull, classical routine and heavy monastic discipline of his school in Ravenna and clamoured to be taken away and allowed to wander round the world in quest of nature and romance and all the pleasures of a gypsy life.

Count Guiccioli stubbornly refused to remove his son from school. Ignazio, therefore, snatched the key to the meadow for himself. In the summer of 1821 he was spending the holidays with a schoolfellow at his father's house, San Michele, near Ravenna. The two boys disguised themselves from a discarded theatrical wardrobe in the habiliments of eighteenth-century *abbés* and ran away. As their disguise drew amused and curious glances they kept off the main roads and wandered by side lanes and across open fields. They slept in barns and vineyards, lit fires in the woods, and lived plenteously upon fruit. In short, they had a glorious time and imagined themselves every kind of outlaw from Fra Diavolo to Friar Tuck. Then they grew sated with a life of adventure, and Ignazio from his hiding-place in the woods wrote a homesick letter to his father.

Old Brunello had been ill with alarm. Romagna was simmering with plots after the abortive *Carbonari* insurrection, and he feared that his runaway son might be killed or, worse still, kidnapped and held to ransom. Ignazio in his letter humbly asked pardon for running away. His father freely forgave him if only he would come home. But Ignazio held out for his own terms of surrender—he wouldn't go back to school. That point, too, his father conceded, and Ignazio returned. His father kept his word about the school and looked about him for a tutor for his son. His choice, in the circumstances, was an odd one, for he engaged Professor Costa, of the University of Bologna. Professor Costa had been Teresa's tutor and must be held responsible in part for her perverse notions about love and poetry and freedom.

Under Professor Costa's hand Ignazio did not lose his passion for romance. More than ever he was bent on writing poetry, and at sixteen he became a rapt 'Liberty boy,' like Pietro Gamba. With several of his former schoolmates he joined the *Carbonari* in Ravenna. By now his ambition had expanded beyond the life of Robin Hood, and he was soon neck deep in plots to assassinate cardinal and legate and all other minions of theocracy in Romagna. Count Guiccioli still knew not peace in his own house. Teresa had been a romantic rebel. His one and only son, the heir to his fortune, was undeniably a romantic pickle.

One might have supposed that, with Ignazio giving trouble at home, the Count would not risk his peace of mind by trying to make his wife come home, too. But old Brunello did not suffer defeat gladly, nor was he willing to give up anything that once had belonged to him. Now that Lord Byron had gone to Greece he was determined to get his wife back. The Pope was indifferent to his pleas as a wronged but forgiving husband—nay, with celibate perversity he seemed to disapprove of Teresa's return to the state of married life. Count Guiccioli, therefore, trained his guns upon his old friend Grandfather Gamba. Teresa, he reminded him, was entitled as his wife to handsome jointure when he died—but only as a wife who had lived conformably with him in his own house. Grandfather Gamba still had many granddaughters to marry—it would not help their chances of matrimony to have their elder sister living disreputably apart from her husband. Lord Byron had gone from Italy, and it was not likely that he would return, so that obstacle to reconciliation was out of the way. Teresa had come back obediently to Romagna with her father. She was young—only twenty-one—and would soon recover from her misplaced attachment for that troublesome foreigner, who had as good as deserted her. The Pope deserved some gratitude from the Gamba family for his unfailing kindness towards them in all their troubles, domestic and political—why should they not repay the Holy Father by signing

articles of general amnesty and patching up the marriage? Grandfather
Gamba, in his joy at recovering his son and granddaughter, was ready to
sign any treaty of peace. Count Guiccioli's arguments seemed to him not
only reasonable but Christian in their forgiving spirit, and he promised
to use every persuasion in inducing Teresa to return to her husband.

Apart from the solid advantages of reconciliation, Grandfather Gamba,
as an honourable Italian gentleman, was angry with Lord Byron on
Teresa's account. He had accepted him as his granddaughter's *cavaliere
servente*, and Lord Byron had repaid his *amicizia* with gross ingratitude
and ill-breeding. He had abducted Teresa into his own house at Pisa,
and then, in defiance of the law that no *cavaliere servente* should leave his
*dama*, had left her and gone to Greece. No amount of argument, no talk
of crusade and noble cause, could displace a sense of deep injury in Grandfather Gamba's mind. For all her devotion Teresa had been 'planted.'
The sooner she, and every one else, forgot her *relazione* with this English
barbarian the better.

Teresa left the Casa Saluzzo a few hours before Byron returned there
to mourn under the ilex-tree. She was carried half unconscious to the
carriage, and all the journey she remained in a daze. When she came to
herself she was with her father in a house in Bologna. Then followed
weeks of dolorous day-dream.

Life was over at twenty-one. Byron would never come back from
Greece, and she would never love again. "Woman wailing for her demon
lover"—that was all that the future held for her now. But, if life was
over, the business of living still went on. She had talked of waiting for
him in a convent, but she knew herself too well to believe she could find
rest for a wounded heart in the sterile tranquillity of convent-life. Besides,
what was the good of waiting there for a man who would never return?
The devotion that comes with love was gone with her lover and with his
death would soon be dead, but she still had devotion to give. All her
affection she now lavished on her father.

Count Gamba was home again. He was happy, he was grateful to his
daughter. He would not leave her while she was unhappy, and by a
thousand gentle wiles he tried to lure her into an interest in living. Soon
he was immersed in fresh plans for Italian freedom and mildly sought to
rekindle in her heart the old dreams. But Teresa remained indifferent.
She was not interested even in the freedom of the Greeks for whom her
lover was fighting.

Letters came from Greece—brief and hasty scrawls—from Byron and
Pietro, and she answered them. Pietro was all hopefulness for the cause,
but he was not reassuring when he wrote of Byron. *Povero Byron* was his
perpetual refrain. "Poor Byron!" he wrote in October. "He has been
terribly upset because of the news he got a fortnight ago of some head

ailment of his darling Ada's. You can imagine what gloomy ideas his
fancy conjured up before him! And to all that he added the fear that he
would have to pass several months before he could get further news and
the *suspicion* that people wanted to hide or disguise the truth from him."
Still, thought Teresa sadly, he thinks of England, not Italy, of that
woman, not me, and a deep bitterness welled up in her heart against
Annabella, part jealousy, yet more anger that she should torture her
husband with delays and deceptions. "Luckily," Pietro went on, "he has
got another bulletin that says she is out of danger, and then yet another,
assuring him that the general health of the child is already good, except
for trouble with her eyes. His melancholy is lightened but it hasn't
altogether gone." So Annabella had behaved like a woman, after all, and
Teresa liked her none the better.

Byron no longer wrote in Italian but in English, which she could now
understand. Perhaps because they were written in English, his letters no
longer seemed love-letters—they were more like the letters of a busy
man to his wife. He tried to make out that life was going easily and he
was in no danger, but he seemed nervous and depressed. "I was a fool
to come here," he wrote impatiently in October, and then again, "I shall
fulfill the object of my mission from the Committee, and then return into
Italy; for it does not seem likely that, as an individual, I can be of use
to them. . . . Pray be as cheerful and tranquil as you can," he added
bluffly, as though he were Pietro writing to his sister, "and be assured
that there is nothing here that can excite anything but a wish to be with
you again." By 'anything' I suppose he means 'another woman,' thought
Teresa, and warns me, as of old, against the sin of jealousy. Finally,
before he left Cephalonia for Missolonghi, he wrote, "You may be sure
that the moment I can join you again will be as welcome to me as at any
period of our recollection." Both he and Pietro had had a host of amusing
adventures, especially Pietro, he told her, "but I reserve them, in the hope
that we may laugh over them together at no very distant period."

When he left for Missolonghi he had not the heart to write to her.
He asked Barry at Genoa to break the news. "You had better write to
Countess Guici to state that her brother and I are going (or gone) to
Missolonghi, and that everything is *quite pacific*, as well as the *business*
we are upon. This perhaps is not the exact or entire truth, but it is as
much as needs to be stated to one who will naturally be anxious about
her brother"—and he added lamely—"etcetera."

Teresa kept only a few of his letters. Before they parted, she had
arranged a mode of correspondence that held in it the spice of secrecy
and romance. When one of his letters came, written in English and in
black ink, she wrote her answer in Italian and in red ink between his
lines. Sometimes the same sheets of paper went backward and forward
two or three times with message and counter-message. "How," she

wrote desperately between the lines of one of his scrawls, "oh, how shall I persuade you that I love you?" He answered, "By never yielding to my madness, never yielding that which I only crave in hours of extravagance, so that our love may remain for ever beautiful and out of reach of human frailty." Had it, then, all sunk to that—all life gone backward to those far-off days in April when he had wooed her playfully and she had talked to him of platonic love?

By the end of December 1823 Byron was at Missolonghi. At last he was in the roll and tide of war. His diffidence and his melancholy left him. Physically he suffered from his lameness and old bouts of fever, but with delight he found that his mind was clear and vigorous. He could make rapid decisions and inspired loyalty among the wild hillsmen with whom he lived. His letters to his friends in England were sharp and practical, and with it all he kept a lucid mind, noting without bitterness or undue optimism the weakness and the virtues of his associates. He found himself a man well able to hold his own with other men.

From Missolonghi no letters came to Teresa, and she wrote no letters.

All this while from the doubtful, troubled look in her father's eyes she knew that he was plotting some mischief for her happiness. She needed not to be told what he was hoping. Gently and severely the pressure came—from her father, from Grandfather Gamba, from aunts and uncles and friends. Her love-affair was over; she now had a duty to perform for her family. She must return to her husband. Count Guiccioli wrote himself—kindly and with a near approach to penitence.

What did it matter whether she went back to him or not? At least she might look at the question from the point of view of common sense. She could not remain for ever waiting for a silent, unreturning lover—silent, she knew, because he was dead or dying. She could serve her family and make her father happy. She would look after the old Count's house, help him rear his children, nurse him into his tomb. But she could not love him nor would she bear him children. . . . She wrote to him saying that she would come home and, in all things but one, try to be a good wife.

She found him chastened by misfortune and grief. He was as arbitrary as ever in his own house. He still bullied his stewards and roared at his servants. His talk was still of *ordine* and *economia*. But he had learned his lesson with Teresa. He could not break her will by open war, so he sought patiently to master her by diplomacy. All those rules and regulations for her subjection that he had drawn up in La Mira days went by the board. Teresa lay in bed to a late hour in the morning, she splashed in cold baths, she sat alone for hours and read books. Chairs and tables changed places in the *salone* and pictures came down from the walls, and the Count set his teeth and bore it patiently. She slept alone, and beside her bed stood a wooden chest, filled with letters and poems and relics of the vanished lover—the sacred handkerchief, the lock of hair. She sat for hours beside this chest, rummaging through its contents, and the Count bore that patiently, too. One thing only he demanded—she must not write to Byron. Teresa gave him that promise.

There were flowers in the Palazzo Guiccioli once more, but no music. Once more she went back to school and studied under her old friend, Professor Costa. She tried to write poetry. With Ignazio she formed a friendship. He told her of his poetical ambitions, and she encouraged him to write.

One day she pulled down by chance from the bookshelf in her palace in Bologna the *Jacopo Ortis* of Ugo Foscolo. On the fly-leaf, in her lover's handwriting, she read "*Coelum, non animam mutant qui trans mare currunt*"—"They that cross the sea find a change of sky but not of heart." Was that an omen for what was happening now? He had added in English, "Most men bewail not having obtained the object of their desires. I had oftener to deplore obtaining mine, for I cannot love moderately nor quiet my heart with mere fruition." Words written five years ago, when she was absent—discovered now—the last message from her lover? She laid the book away in the wooden chest.

She was lying in bed late one morning in April, the month when all things happened for her. Ignazio entered the room. He was pale and embarrassed. His father had charged him with a message. She dropped her book languidly. Ignazio blurted out the news. Byron was dead.

He stared at her in terror. She stared back at him, quietly and steadily. Then she turned her face away to the wall. She neither spoke nor wept.

CHAPTER II

# Death of a Hero

PIETRO, as usual, had got into all sorts of comic scrapes in Greece. At one time he had been almost taken prisoner by pirates, and altogether, Byron told his sister, he had been his dear old silly self. But when his hero was lying sick at Missolonghi, Pietro was there, tearful and faithful, to watch him die. Dutifully he packed up all relics of the dead poet, including his sister's letters, and then with dog-like devotion followed the body back to England. He called on Augusta Leigh, who welcomed him with a mournful smile, and for her sake he wrote a modest, straightforward account of her brother's last days in Greece.

Byron died, as he would have wished, in a thunderstorm, clasping Tita's hand. Pietro and Fletcher stood beside the bed, crying. "Forward!" he shouted in his delirium. "Courage! Don't be afraid!" He turned to Fletcher. "It is now nearly over, I must tell you all without losing a moment . . . Now pay attention . . . You will be provided for." . . . "Oh, my Lord," sobbed Fletcher, "think of things of more consequence than that!" The dying man went on—"Oh, my poor dear child! My dear Ada! . . . My dear sister Augusta . . . You will go to Lady Byron and say—tell her everything!"

His voice died away in a mumble, then he looked into Fletcher's frightened face with the old mocking smile. "If you do not execute every order I have given you, I will torment you if possible hereafter."

Fletcher bent his head to listen. He heard only the names "Ada! Augusta!" gasped—then "Hobhouse! Kinnaird!" then something that sounded like "Clare!" His master opened his eyes. "Now I have told you all," he said.

"Oh, my Lord, I haven't understood a word," groaned Fletcher.

"Oh, my God! Then all is lost, for it is now too late!" Once more the dying voice trailed away into inarticulate murmurs—"My wife! My child! My sister!" slowly upward to the present hour—"Poor Greece! Poor town! My poor servants! . . . My hour is come! I do not care for death—but why did I not go home before I came here?" He was silent for a while, then murmured in Italian, "*Io lascio qualche cosa di caro nel mondo!*"

The doctor loosened the bandage round his head. "Good night," he said faintly and fell asleep . . . At sunrise he awoke for a moment only to whisper, "I must sleep now," and closed his eyes again . . . Night

253

fell with thunder and lightning and rain pelting against the windows.
He opened his eyes at the sound and closed them at once.

"I fear," said the 'learned' Fletcher, "his lordship is gone."

Ada! Augusta! My child! My sister! And my *wife*! Hobhouse!
And Kinnaird! And—could it be?—even Claire! No other names? No
other memories? What did he mean when he murmured in Italian, "I am
leaving something dear behind me in the world." Was he thinking of his
friends, or his daughter, or of his own memory?

Pietro found a brooch with hair entwined in it against the dead poet's
heart. Piously he gave it to Augusta Leigh. Augusta examined it
curiously, with its strands of faded golden hair. Then she had a very
happy notion. She packed it up and sent it to the Countess Guiccioli.

Hobhouse called on Augusta, bringing her Fletcher's account of her
brother's dying hours. He wept as she read it aloud to him. Augusta
shed tears, too. "Poor, dear Byron!" she sighed. "He has been snatched
away from us to spare him future trials and temptations."

Fletcher told the story to Annabella himself. She walked up and
down the room, racked with dry sobs. "Remember," she said hoarsely,
"try to remember what he said!"

Once more the Pope intervened. The Count and Countess Guiccioli
had decided that they no longer wished to live together. Mutual incom-
patibility of temper was the cause of their parting, and though at first
the Count had insisted upon a convent for his wife, they now took leave
of each other with mutual respect. Once more, upon instructions from
the Pope, the Count made his wife an allowance of one hundred *scudi* a
month. Teresa returned to the protection of her family and, at the Pope's
suggestion, went to live in Rome, where he could keep an eye upon her.
Count Gamba did not wish to leave home again, so Vincenzo took upon
himself the duties of chaperon. With her brother and one maid Teresa
left Romagna and lodged in the garret of an old palace in Rome.

All this had come to pass by the end of the year 1824. The following
year Cardinal Rivarola was sent to Romagna to reduce that turbulent
state to some semblance of order. His efforts at government were resented. Besides his virtues as a policeman the Cardinal boasted a handsome pair of legs which he was fond of displaying in their spiritual red
stockings to the ladies. Ignazio Guiccioli and his cronies formed a plot
to blow those legs off as His Eminence drove to a *conversazione* one
evening. The Cardinal escaped without a scratch, but a canon was killed
in the *mêlée*. The old Count whisked Ignazio away from Romagna, but
many of his friends were executed.

Count Gamba, who was not concerned in the plot, was arrested on
general principle as an old revolutionary. He was condemned to thirty

years' service in the galleys. His sentence, however, was commuted to imprisonment. He was sent to Ferrara and immured in the citadel there. And there he remained for six years.

Pietro was condemned *in absentia* to twenty years in the galleys. In London he won golden opinions from Hobhouse and the group of Byron's friends. They liked him for his good looks, his gaiety, and, above all, his single-minded devotion to Byron's memory. A fine island was England, Pierino told Mary Shelley, but he wished it wouldn't rain so much! With an old *Carbonaro*, Giuseppe Pecchio, he returned to Greece in charge of a loan of sixty thousand pounds and took service under General Fabvier. Two years later he died in Metana, a small peninsula in the Morea opposite Ægina. Characteristically he did not die in battle nor of wounds, but of a chill caught after a hunting-expedition. On his deathbed he gave his friend Antonio Morandi, the *Carbonaro* General, a packet of letters, begging him to take them to his sister, the Countess Guiccioli. Morandi was some time in making his way back to Italy, and in the interval he read the letters. They were the red-and-black-ink letters that Byron and Teresa exchanged. When at last he arrived in Italy Morandi spent most of his time hiding from the police. In escaping one night by the window from an inn at Ancona he forgot the letters, and presumably they fell into the hands of the police.

Count Guiccioli could endure Romagna no longer. He withdrew to Venice, where he bought the Palazzo Malipiero. In that city he soon became a well-known figure, lean and tall, erect in bearing and walking stiffly, with his cloak wrapped closely round him to hide his knightly orders, and a green shade over his eyes. In 1827 he suffered from a cataract in the right eye, and six years later the sight of the other eye went, too, and he had to be led about by a young man. He now had two bug-bears—death and the doctors. Death he looked upon as an impertinence, and contemptuously he repelled its familiar advances. When he heard that a contemporary was dead he rejoiced grimly that he was not as other men were. Doctors were death's pompous lackeys, a profession of knaves and noodles, who battened on other men's sickness. He trusted neither their skill nor their honesty. He corresponded with Teresa on friendly terms and sent her long, matter-of-fact accounts of his ailments and the means he took to cure them. She, on her side, consulted with eye-specialists in Paris and London and supplied him with their dissertations and advice—free of cost.

In his old age his interest in the theatre revived. He made the round of opera-house and theatre every week, and when theatres failed him he attended the puppet-shows in the Piazza dei Schiavoni. His young man accompanied him on these expeditions and described for his master what he could not see for himself. In due course of time the old gentleman discovered that his pleasures were costing him too much. He suggested to a theatre impresario that, as his young man attended the play for duty and not for pleasure, he should not be charged the price of his seat in the box. Rashly the impresario rejected this demand. Old Brunello quietly made inquiries and, finding that his opponent was in financial trouble, bought up all his notes of hand. The impresario then gave in, and the Count's young man henceforth took his seat in the box free of cost. It would have been cheaper in the long run to pay for the young man's seat, but no matter! To put down a fool old Brunello was willing to spend his money.

Life in the Palazzo Malipiero was tempestuous. The blind old man would fly into furious rages. His servants, at least, could leave when his temper became ungovernable, and few of them stayed long at the Palazzo Malipiero, although they were paid richly for their servitude. But his daughters, when they came home from the convent, were at his mercy. He hated the very presence of the useless creatures. He roared and lashed out at them with his stick if they came within his reach. Ignazio, who alone was not afraid of his father, often had to intervene in these distressing scenes. The girls shrieked and wailed, and one of them—Alessandra—died laughing in an hysteric fit. Ignazio insisted that his father should find husbands for his sisters to put an end to the nervous uproar in the Palazzo Malipiero. With a growl the old man consented, but he warned his son, "You will be the loser by your advice." He corresponded industriously with lawyers and with parents with sons to marry. He wrote of his prospective sons-in-law as though they were so many pigs offered for sale in a cattle-market. Eventually, after long haggling, he procured a couple of the beasts at a reasonable price. Attilia married the Count Carranti, of Imola, and her husband had reason to repent his bargain, for she was blue-eyed and stern like her father, and every bit as fiery and eccentric. Argentina married the Count Zinanni, of Ravenna, and lived robustly until the last years of the nineteenth century.

Thus—in death and flight, in exile and imprisonment—ended the Romagna phase of Teresa's life. Henceforth she was a vagabond, roaming Europe, from Italy to France, from France to England, hunting for happiness again—looking to find her dead lover in this world of living men.

# Roman Winter

TERESA was not a woman of the world. She was well born, well educated, polite and kind, and in all things had the generous instincts of a lady. But Filetto was not a school for worldly wisdom, and she came to the business of social life with a wide-eyed innocence that never left her. She was, too, something of a hermit by nature. She was scholarly, she liked reading books and writing poetry, was fond of solitude. Life with Byron had not hardened her in the ways of the world. It had been a life remote from the common interests of men—solitary, intellectual, concentrated. It had been, too, a thrilling, an exhausting experience. Most women had not been able to live with him for more than a week or a month, but she had lived with him for four years. Those years had left their mark upon her. Always prone to see the world through a haze of poetry, she was henceforth to search for happiness only in romance.

She was serenely unaware of what the world had thought about her during those four years. She had known something of the ill-natured gossip of Venice, but it had left her untouched because she knew it was false. Honestly for a while she had believed that she was playing the game of *dama* with her *cicisbeo* and never realized that, in her innocence, she had given that stale institution its *coup de grâce*. In this new, more virile age of romance women were going to demand love, not gallantry, and men for lovers, not fan-carriers, and there was to be no nonsense of acquiescent husbands in the background. Her love had carried her far beyond the game of *serventismo*, because the man she loved had brains. In imagination and in deed she had been his Beatrice, inspiring him to work and checking him when he made mistakes. But she did not know that in the eyes of the world she was simply his paramour—'the mistress of Lord Byron'—the last of a long line of women to hold that title. In England, where they only knew her by name, she was the successor of Caro Lamb. In Italy she had followed after La Fornarina. Least of all did she know—as yet—those ribald letters that Byron had written to Hoppner and his male friends in England in which, in his desire to pose as a cynic, he had turned his love-affair into a merry tale of Faublas.

By birth and breeding she was entitled to move in the most princely circles in Rome, but some doors were closed against her as a wife living apart from her husband. Persons less austere, however, were glad to welcome to their *salons* the mistress of Lord Byron, for Byron's name in

257

R

Rome was as great as Bonaparte's. He had been a foreigner, too, and it is easier to be tolerant of the peccadilloes of a foreigner than a compatriot. But apart from the old native aristocracy there was in Rome a large foreign colony of exiles and pleasure-seekers, and here people were not inhibited by the restraints of public opinion. They were glad to meet the mistress of Lord Byron and to stare at her. Well-bred English people who had stoned Byron out of England for the badness of his morals made much of the Countess Guiccioli in Rome. When, however, she visited them some years later in London their doors were virtuously closed against her.

Teresa began to find a humble place in society. There was another lady from Romagna who spent her winters in Rome—Mme Martinetti, the wife of an archæologist from Bologna. In the far-off days when Napoleon Bonaparte first came to Italy she had been his mistress. She was still a beautiful woman. It became 'the thing' in circles where intellect was combined with fashion to invite Mme Martinetti and the Countess Guiccioli out together—Bonaparte's mistress side by side with Byron's mistress. The elder woman was the more beautiful. Teresa's face in repose was pensive, but when she spoke she was animated and she smiled. Mme Martinetti was always in repose, she spoke seldom and listened long, and there was about her face a radiant peacefulness.

It was natural that Teresa should gravitate towards the foreign colony. In theory she disapproved of Austrians, but her kindest protectors in Rome were the Austrian ambassador and his wife. She could salve her conscience by remembering that the Count and Countess Apponyi were Hungarians and, indeed, in some sort kin of hers, and they were not unfriendly towards Italian hopes for independence. Then, too, she was on visiting terms with the large clan of Bonaparte then settled in Rome. First there was Madame Mère, a handsome, big-boned old peasant woman who spoke French and Italian with a broad Corsican accent. Then there was Napoleon's Jacobin brother, Lucien, Prince of Canino, who solaced his exile with archæology and writing dull books. Lucien had a large family. His eldest daughter, Charlotte, was married to Prince Gabrielli in Rome, and with her lived her sister, Christine, Countess Possé. Then there was the florid Jerome, ex-King of Westphalia, with his patient German princess. And, last of all, there was Hortense de Beauharnais, former Queen of Holland, and her youngest son, Louis Napoleon.

With Hortense de Beauharnais Teresa was on a more intimate footing than with the others. They were alike in one thing—they were both living apart from their husbands. For some reason, too, Hortense lived in a twilight of mild romance. She was the daughter of the ill-fated Josephine. Napoleon had dearly loved her, yet at heart she had always been a royalist. She had been a Queen and she was an exile, she was unhappily unmarried, and she had once had a lover. There was about her an atmosphere of remembered prettiness, the fragrance of a gentle sorrow that could never be told. She had inherited something of her mother's creole nonchalance, but upon that Mme Campan had grafted the brittle elegance of a Trianon shepherdess. When she spoke or when she moved this *pot-pourri* charm evaporated. She was a plump, kindly woman, playful and a little childish, fond of picnics and parlour-games, a diligent and untidy housekeeper, a doting mother, a gossip, a sentimental soul who hunted moths by moonlight.

Her son, Louis, was a hobbledehoy—a short-legged, bony youth with an ugly face. But his eyes were dreamy, and, Teresa observed, his face every now and then lighted up with a strangely attractive smile, all humour and gay intelligence. He had not yet started dreaming of himself as 'the man of destiny.' He cared only for horses and galloped about the streets of Rome at breakneck speed. In politics he declared himself a Liberal, and he was an ardent supporter of the *Carbonari*.

Hortense was hospitable, and it was a joke in Rome that all the lady conspirators for revolution met in her house and discussed their plans for overthrowing the Government at her luncheon table. Foremost among these fair conspirators was Cristina Trivulzio, Princess Belgiojoso, with whom Teresa formed a strained acquaintance that lasted thirty years. Cristina came from Milan and had been reared in an atmosphere of political martyrdom. She was frail and vivid and attenuated to the point of emaciation. Her small, well-shaped head was balanced on a long white throat in which the bones stood out like slender columns. Her hair was raven-black and cut closely to the head, and she twined ox-eye daisies and water-lilies through it. Her face was thin and angular, with a long, sharp nose, high cheek-bones, and a pointed chin. It was white like water seen in moonlight with a glimmer of green about it. Her eyes were large and dark and sombre, and they glowed with a steady Sibylline fire. She was intellectual and wrote terribly learned books. Rich and incredibly well born even for an Italian—"*Si, sono un vermo*," she said as she lay dying, "*ma Trivulzio*"[1]—she had married, for love, at the age of seventeen, Prince Emilio Belgiojoso. Emilio was good-tempered and improbably beautiful for a man—a tall, blond-haired Apollo with a straight Greek nose and soft, caressing eyes. One other physical grace he had—the most wonderful tenor voice in all Italy. A couple more striking than this blond Apollo and his dark-haired Sibyl could not well be imagined. There lacked not one fairy gift to make the marriage happy— love, beauty, wealth, talent, and a community of tastes.

Emilio was voluptuous and Cristina was epileptic. The marriage collapsed dismally during the honeymoon. Thenceforth husband and wife went their separate ways. Cristina plotted and read deep books. Emilio

---

[1] "Yes, I am a worm, but a Trivulzio."

made love and studied music with his friend Rossini. He was a kind
man and kept an eye upon his sick wife from afar. Sometimes he rejoined
her in her house. At least they shared two interests in common—a love
of music and a devotion to the cause of Italian liberty. But Emilio was
indolent and Cristina was earnest, and over their enthusiasms they clashed
in silence. On his rare visits to his wife's house in Rome Emilio's eyes
rested languidly on Teresa Guiccioli's face, so fair and so different from
Cristina's, and Teresa found in him a flavour of Byronic charm.

More glorious even than the old Roman princes or the Pope and his
cardinals was the English winter colony in Rome. They came along the
Riviera, luxuriously fleeing from the rain and snow of Paris, in their own
armorial coaches, bringing with them their servants, their bed-linen, their
china, their silver, and their cooking-pans and kettles. They rented
palaces and entertained sumptuously with balls and dinner-parties every
week. They rode their own pack of hounds in the Maremna and visited
the studios of their compatriots in the city and ordered statues and huge
paintings of the more impressive moments in English history. They
visited the native picture-galleries, too, and the churches, picnicked at
famous beauty-spots, and made excavations in the Forum. In the evening
their carriages took right of way along the Pincian, and when silence fell
upon the Roman crowd with the ringing of the angelus, quiet English
voices rose upon the dusk, calling to one another in delighted recognition,
and low, musical laughter beat upon the air.

Teresa was drawn towards this glorious crowd because among Englishmen she hoped to find some one who would remind her of Byron.
Lady Davy, the wife of her old acquaintance Sir Humphry, was living
in Rome. A woman with blue-stocking tastes who was anxious to make
her way in society, she operated a mild *salon* where 'gentlemen' were
encouraged to hobnob with 'intellectuals' on equal terms. The Countess
Guiccioli was one of her 'lions,' and thus Teresa managed to make
acquaintance in the English colony.

The Marchioness of Bute was spending the winter in Rome with her
son and daughter. A banker's daughter, proud of the position that she
had achieved by marriage, it was Lady Bute's foible to be hard to please,
and obstinately she sacrificed her own amusement to the duty of boring
every one who lived with her. When her victims grew restive she put on
the flat, coaxing manner of a beauty which she had never been. Needless
to say, she was a fond mother and showed her affection by domineering
her children. For the moment she was busy shepherding her plain
daughter into marriage with an eligible young man of wealth and title.
But she had an eye left for her son, Dudley, too. He had been brought
abroad to polish his manners, but with the help of a pert, obsequious
tutor his mother kept fearful watch and ward over him, lest he should
get into mischief with the women.

Lord Dudley Stuart was the same age as Teresa—twenty-two. He was one of the breed of 'sad young men' that Byron had made fashionable. Slender, melancholy, handsome, he wore his collar open at the throat. He sat mournfully in the ruins of the Colosseum with *Childe Harold* open upon his knees and laid flowers on the graves of Keats and Shelley. He chafed resentfully against his mother's domination and cordially detested his tutor. He was an 'Eleutherarch,' and now that his idol was dead he wanted to go to Greece and fight for independence and, if possible, die there, too. In the meantime he took walks with Teresa Guiccioli and asked her questions about Byron and talked about himself. He read aloud his favourite passages from the poems and, looking up, saw a soft look in Teresa's eyes. They clasped hands across the page.

But it was too late. Dudley was in love—with a woman older than himself, and another man's wife. His *innamorata* was Christine Bonaparte, Countess Possé, daughter of Lucien. She had been married as a child to a Swedish nobleman, who turned out to be a drunkard and a madman. She left him and came to live with her sister in Rome. She was a diminutive woman with tiny hands and feet, a wild Corsican at heart, a small, fiery bundle of energy, sharp of tongue and unconventional, who had no intention of remaining a grass-widow all her life. She meant to love, to find a man with whom she could live happily, and the melancholy Dudley was her choice. She loved him furiously, and one day, marriage or no marriage, she meant to bear him a child.

Dudley confided his secret to his friend Henry Fox, and told him, too, with some contrition, of his momentary *passade* with Teresa Guiccioli. Henry hoped that Dudley would one day marry his sister, Mary, but now, without knowing either woman, he loyally gave Christine Bonaparte his blessing as his friend's mistress and whistled Teresa Guiccioli scornfully down the wind. Dudley told Teresa, too, of his love for Christine, and without a murmur she made way.

It was against Teresa's will that she was known everywhere in Rome as 'Lord Byron's mistress.' To one or two people she tried to explain how that expression profaned the nature of her relationship with the dead poet. But they smiled patiently and wouldn't understand, and she gave it up. A year after Byron's death she was lifted into notoriety as 'the cunning whore of Venice' who had held her poet prisoner by her venal charms.

By his death Byron had set a new fashion for poets. It was not enough for them to write poetry and make love. They must be men of action, too, leaders of causes, statesmen, ambassadors, and moulders of a people's destiny. On no poet had this consciousness of a poet's mission fallen with greater impact than on Alphonse de Lamartine in France; in July 1825 he published his *Dernier Chant du Pèlerinage d'Harold*. In that poem he described how the poet had broken loose from the chains of voluptuous pleasure to go and live among a wild mountain people, to rule them, to inspire them, and finally to die fighting in their behalf.

The poem opens in majestic gloom. Genoa—the silence of night— a palace all in darkness . . . a solitary light glances from window to window within the palace . . . it ceases to move and shines out steadily into the night . . .

Harold stands beside an alcove, smiling in sorrowful disdain as he holds up his lamp. Upon the bed there a woman lies asleep. Her golden hair ripples voluptuously over the pillows to the ground. Chaplets and necklaces, tossed carelessly aside, lie upon the floor among broken flowers. One white arm hangs down beside the bed as though the sleeper in her dreams would clutch at flowers and jewels. Her features are angelic in their beauty, but, alas! there is no innocence in them, even while she dreams. There is a furrow of care and thought between her brows, and her lips are twisted in a troubled smile.

"Sleep," Harold intones in a voice of suppressed love and scorn, "thou that I loved and who loved me—perhaps!—thou whose siren wiles lulled my heart, at least, with a phantom dream of love"—and onward rolls the poem in long alexandrines of stately contempt—"farewell to light pleasure of the sense and perfume of flowers trampled underfoot . . . in the cup from which we drank there were always dregs . . . I pour the last dreg out, a libation at thy feet . . . I love thee still, I go—good-bye."

The following September Lamartine, in pursuance of a poet's duty to be a man of action, took office as secretary under the French Minister to the Court of Florence. On New Year's Eve he was at Rome and went to a ball at Prince Torlonia's—but he must tell the rest of the story.

As he entered the ballroom with a party of other young Frenchmen a murmur rose and swelled on all sides. . . . "*Lamartine . . . Lamartine . . .*" and modestly he shrank behind his companions from curious eyes. Across the room he saw a woman seated in a chair alone, "radiant in beauty . . . a living poem." At the murmur of his name she half rose from her chair, her lips parted in suspense, and gazed at his group as though she were looking for some one. . . . A soft wail of violins, and she sank back in her chair. . . . The dancers moved out to the waltz . . . and she was hidden from his view.

Abashed by the attention he had attracted he stood cowering against the wall by the entrance to the ballroom. The waltz came to an end, the floor emptied, and once more he beheld the woman. She rose from her chair and, laying her hand on the arm of a young man who looked like her brother, slowly made her way through the crowd towards him. As she came her eyes stared steadily and earnestly into his.

There follows a long description of the fair unknown. She was, says

Lamartine with a strange certainty, twenty years old or, at most, twenty-two. Her hair was bright gold and caught the gleam from the chandeliers in a metallic shimmer. Her body served "as a pedestal to a majestic bust and to a throat and shoulders richly formed"—which is a gentle way of saying her legs were short. Her small head was held proudly as La Fornarina's—Raphael's Fornarina, not the gutter-girl of Venice with whom Byron had made love. A broad brow, blue eyes, sometimes vague as though they sought a ghost, sometimes disdainful in their stare, lips that opened in a deep respiration, an oval face, and cheeks in which there vibrated a warm current of youth, though sorrow had faded their bloom—ah, well, she moved as in a nimbus of reflected sunshine, with mournful gaze unflinching, towards him. Lamartine crouched against the wall "like a bird caught by a serpent's eye." At last she stood before him and said, in a voice quivering with anger and forgiveness, "*Monsieur*, I should hate you."

Lamartine stammered a few words, but she cut him short.

"Make no excuses," she said; "yes, I should hate you." Then, with a softened expression, she continued, "But I cannot, no, I cannot. You have chanted too well the praise of one to whom I gave my soul and for whom I would give my life a thousand times."

At this point the unfortunate poet realized that he was speaking with the Countess Guiccioli, and he blushed for what he had said about her in his book. Like Byron before him, he would have gladly avoided meeting her. But she gave him no time to speak.

"Let us talk no more," she went on in a deep, harmonious voice, "of the past—you to explain or me to protest. You are pardoned. Since chance has brought us together, let us lose no more time in misunderstanding or avoiding each other. I am happy to know you. Let us see each other, if you will, during your stay in Rome"—she paused, then, with a disdainful gesture towards the crowd that pressed and chattered round them, she added—"like two aliens speaking the same tongue in a world that understands them not."

Bravo, Lamartine! The stage has been set most effectively for your meeting! The poet enters . . . his name is carried in a whisper round the room . . . soft music of violins as he moves to the centre of the crowded scene . . . and across the careless throng of revellers the beloved of a dead poet approaches—*la femme fatale*.

Art thou demon? Art thou angel? Byron's spirit long had brooded over Lamartine. It was the great disappointment of his life that he had never met his master. Yet, as the years went by, he persuaded himself that once he had surely seen his face—in a flash of lightning—during a thunderstorm on the Lake of Geneva—the year of Waterloo—when Byron was in England, trying to be Annabella Milbanke's husband.

Every day of that winter in Rome, he says, he met Teresa Guiccioli. He visited her in her attic—or *salon*, as he more grandly calls it—and when the days grew longer and warmer they went for solitary strolls in the gardens of the Villa Pamphili-Doria. Teresa was quick in claiming his friendship, she was cordial and frank; yet, he felt, she was sincere and, when once she had given her affections, would endure much and long for the sake of one she loved. He was himself married to a good and devoted English wife, and though he would not say that Teresa was blind to his charm, of love in one sense, he is careful to state, there was nothing in their meetings. "There was always a third between us—a ghost," and he knew that in her heart she listened for a footstep limping painfully across the floor.

She brought him very close to Byron. He asked her a thousand questions and lured her on to speak of her dead poet as a man whom she had known more intimately than all the world beside. "Tell me," he said in his most impressive manner, "as your fair and deathless compatriot Francesca da Rimini told Dante, how you were drawn to love, and, in the poet's sad phrase, what was the day when he avowed his passion?"

Teresa hesitated, but he reassured her. "Be sure that what you care to tell me shall never issue from my lips nor from my pen without your consent. The secrets of a man," he said sonorously, "are sacred. But to violate the secrets of a woman, and of a woman young, beautiful, and confiding, is to profane the sanctuary of the heart. Such an indiscretion is no longer a crime—it is a sacrilege."

He meant what he said—for the moment—and Teresa trusted him and, little by little, told him everything. He was a poet and he would understand.

She told him of their first meeting—of the conversation she had overheard, the sound of the poet's foot beating on the floor. She told him about their rides in the Pine Forest. . . . Lamartine's attention wandered. . . . Ah, yes, that forest—he, too, had roamed it in his time, and once more he saw the face of a beautiful woman against the setting sun. When he listened again Teresa was telling him of the Countess Benzoni and her *cicisbeo* at the inn in Padua, and then—La Mira—it seemed to her now that those days of solitude and happiness had never been.

One thing she wanted him to understand. She hadn't been Byron's 'mistress' in the common sense of that term. "We never saw each other alone," she said, "when my father lived with me." Lamartine dared not hope that this was true, but she insisted—people had said hard things about her father and her brother, and she must defend their memory.

Lamartine's attention wandered again. With a contrite start he turned to her—was she telling him that her husband was dead? "I am a ghost only at whom you look—with whom you speak. But he is not all dead. The letters that he wrote remain with me. To them I give my tears."

She was silent. There were no tears in her eyes as she gazed at the snow on distant Soracte. She threw back her head with a sudden smile, and with parted lips inhaled the first warm promise of spring into her lungs.

He leaned towards her in his most tender fashion. His voice trembled slightly. "Those letters," he murmured, "will you trust me with them?"

She turned to him with a look of swift surprise. He stammered but continued, "Let me take from them something that"—with a jerk he recovered his Olympian air—"something that might reward the scrutiny of one—those that admired him."

She looked at him doubtfully. He was in a way like Byron—a cold, unsmiling Byron—a Jove that never nodded—with his strong, clear profile and resolute chin. He was a poet—why shouldn't he one day write the life of her poet—with the knowledge only she could impart?

"You only in the world," she answered slowly. "Take them, read them—without thinking of me. If you find me guilty, look for no excuse for me, for there is only one. I was myself—and he was himself." But she wouldn't give him the letters—yet. . . .

Night fell upon their parley, and they walked slowly back to the city past the fountain that foamed and murmured by the gate of the Pamphili-Doria gardens. . . .

The Frenchman doffed his hat as they stood for a moment before the palace where she lodged. He raised her hand to his lips and kissed her knuckles with a long, slow look into her eyes. Thoughtfully Teresa climbed the stairs to her garret.

The lamp was lighted. By the window a young man sat reading, dark-haired and pale of face. He rose as she entered and came forward to greet her. He limped on one leg as he walked across the room. With a laugh she laid her hands upon his shoulders and kissed him. But he was frowning.

"You have kept me waiting," he said in English—sharply.

## CHAPTER IV

# *Halting Angel*

ON Thursday, December 30, 1824, Lady Davy gave a small dinner-party at her apartment in Rome. Her guest of honour was Henry Fox. He was one of the young men who frequented her *salon* in London—a terribly fastidious young man, and he had a sharp tongue and said severe things. To meet him she invited that ornamental friend of hostesses Mme Martinetti. Henry Fox had already met this fair relict of Napoleon under Lady Davy's auspices and graciously admired her, for Napoleon's sake, and approved her mature charms. The other guest, said Lady Davy, would be the Countess Guiccioli.

Henry had never yet seen Teresa. He accepted the invitation gladly, for he would like to meet the 'mistress' of his old friend and judge her for himself. Lady Davy dropped a hint to Mme Martinetti before the other guests arrived that her party for Henry Fox was given by request and not with a view to serving his pleasure only. Mme Martinetti smiled into her fan and prepared herself for her favourite rôle of sympathetic silence.

So Henry Fox—

> com to diner in his pleyne entente,
> But God and Lady Davy wiste al what this mente.

Before going to bed that night he entered his impressions in his diary.

> Dined with Lady Davy to meet the Guiccioli, Lord Byron's mistress. She is coarse and far from being, to my taste, the least attractive. Her hair is nearly red, her figure squat, and her eyes have no expression but what with study and affectation she contrives to throw into them. Her manner of articulating English is agreeable, and those who know her say she is no fool, although she looks so. The Martinetti, who was there also, is a fine contrast.

Two weeks later Henry had exhausted the pleasures of Rome and left for Naples. There he found an old friend, Charles Percy, but, though they explored the country together, they did not 'suit.' Percy was "refined, aristocratic, discontented, fastidious"—faults that Henry did not brook lightly in other people. He paid a call on the old Margravine of Anspach and tells us in his diary that she was no better than "an old, wild harridan, with her face painted white and red and her eyebrows greasy with dye . . . I think I never saw any woman so entirely corrupt."

He renewed acquaintance with the Blessingtons at the Villa Gallo above
the town—"splendid view" but, he complained, "the whole family
bore me to extinction." My Lady had gone learned and "writes on life
and manners. I wish she would acquire some of the latter before she
criticizes." Count d'Orsay was a coxcomb, and the pair of them were too
fond, in Henry's opinion, of making unkind remarks about the people
they met.

One pleasure only came his way at Naples. Dudley Stuart arrived
there on a flying visit. "His manners, his feelings, his disposition, delight
me," Henry wrote in his diary, "and I feel quite an affection for him."
For two days they went riding together and exchanged sad confidences.
"He told me of his *succès* with the G[uiccioli] and his *embarras* about the
other."

Christine Possé was going to have a baby in the summer. Sooner or
later Lady Bute must be told. After Dudley left, Naples lost its charm
and Henry set sail on a sentimental voyage to Missolonghi.

Henry Fox was Lord Holland's heir and prospective owner of Holland
House. He was not, however, his father's eldest son. His parents had
married under difficulties. Elizabeth Vassall was heiress of a large slave-
plantation in Jamaica, and at the age of fifteen she made a 'grand marriage'
in England. Her husband was Sir Godfrey Webster, of Battle Abbey,
in Sussex. He was a morose man, overbearing and difficult of temper,
and his young wife sought refuge from the discomforts of her marriage
in frequent journeys in France and Italy. She met Lord Holland on her
travels, they fell in love and lived together quietly in Florence for two
years. In 1796 they returned to England, and after financial bickerings
with Sir Godfrey and the usual delays of law, a divorce was procured
and Elizabeth Vassall married Lord Holland. But life had moved too
quickly for the law. Before marriage a son had been born—Charles
Richard Fox. As he was illegitimate he could inherit neither the Holland
title nor the house and the estates that went with it. A second son, born
after the marriage, died young. By the time Henry was born his parents
were a respectable married couple of some years' standing. He was their
third son, and heir to title and estates only by luck and the modesty of
the law.

Henry was a disappointment to his parents. He was a delicate child,
and early in life developed a disease of the hip that left him with a limp.
He was not strong enough to go to school and was brought up by adoring
great-aunts and tutors at home. His childhood was unhappy. His father
was the kindest man alive, and Henry was devoted to him. But Lord
Holland secretly regretted that his sturdy elder son was not to be his
heir, and he was laying plans to leave his unentailed property to Charles.
Henry was too bright not to notice his father's preference, and it speaks

well for his temper and Charles's that they were affectionate brothers in spite of every temptation to be jealous of each other. His younger sister, Mary—a quiet girl with a bent for religion—Henry adored, but for his mother he had little love.

Elizabeth Vassall was a masterful woman, clever, arrogant, and caustic of tongue. In public she loved to show her power by bullying her good-natured husband. She would order him to leave her carriage and beat footman's knocks upon the doors of houses they visited and, in his own house, told the servants to take away his crutches so that he could not leave the dinner-table. In private Lord Holland was well able to deal with her ladyship, and if she were too outrageous in public he brought her to heel with a sharp crack of the Fox wit. But her children, naturally, were more helpless in her hands. Her favourite was Charles. He was strong and well built, good-tempered like his father, careless and casual, and lazily defied his mother. She liked him the better for being a rebel and felt bitterly on his account because he was not to be his father's heir. Charles had no wish to be ruled by his mother, so he joined the Navy when he was thirteen. Duty carried him to the Cape of Good Hope, and he continued to defy her ladyship humorously from afar. But Mary and Henry stayed at home and were made to cringe under the lash of their mother's tongue. Mary was humoured in her religious tendencies only that Lady Holland might exercise her wit at the expense of God and Christianity. As for Henry, she was cross with him for his good looks and cleverness, wherein he far surpassed her favourite, Charles. She resented the fact that this frail boy was to be her husband's heir, sneered at him for being lame, scolded him in public, and called him 'Hoppity' before her guests.

Lord and Lady Holland both admired intellectual distinction, and the best company in the world met at Holland House—statesmen, men of business, artists, poets, scholars—and there, too, was the best conversation in the world. Byron was one of their visitors, and husband and wife both made him their friend—and they were wise and staunch friends in his triumph as in his eclipse. Byron's liking for the parents spread to their children, and he looked very kindly on the quiet, lame little boy at Holland House. His face darkened when his mother scolded him and called him 'Hoppity.' He was not afraid of Lady Holland, and one day took her gravely to task. He told her how his own childhood had been made miserable by his mother calling him "a lame brat." Lady Holland smiled and thought the better of him for championing her son. There-after she took pains to be kind to 'Hoppity' in his presence and threw the child as much his way as possible—after all, the brat needed males in his life and would be none the worse for the society of a clever man. Henceforth Henry was under Byron's especial wing. Byron took him to the theatre, they went out riding together, and Henry learned to box and swim. This was the boy's first male friendship, and he was grateful to adoration. "The gentleman with the beautiful voice," he called the poet to the servants at Holland House, and when he was grown up he meant to speak that way, too.

Holland House held for Henry an oppression and a charm. It was his home—one day it was to be his own house—yet in memory it was linked to unhappiness. He liked it most when his parents were gone and the house was closed. Then he slipped back by a small gate in the wall and wandered in the park alone—under avenues of beeches, past cattle grazing in the long grass, past summer-house and dairy, up the steps into the garden, with its statues and flowers and trim yew-hedges. Within the house was full of stately memories, of high-ceilinged rooms and long, panelled galleries, of pictures and beautiful furniture and books. Grace was there, and solitude and tranquillity—and at night beyond the green bastion of trees that yellow glimmer in the sky, that faint, dull roar that was London with its crowds and ships and slums.

It was not a good school for a growing boy. Too long was his education left in the hands of women. Then followed an interlude of tutors and a brief sojourn in a country parsonage. While he was yet a boy he won the freedom of his mother's drawing-room. Great ladies like Lady Melbourne—charming women like Lady Bessborough—society beauties like Caro Lamb—caressed him and made much of him. Great men like Lord Grey unbent to him with heavy consideration. He listened to Sheridan talk, to Sidney Smith make jokes. He heard grave discussion of politics with Henry Brougham, of art from Thomas Lawrence, of history from Henry Hallam. Tom Moore warbled songs gracefully in the evening, and royalty fell asleep in its chair and snored. Conversation—unending conversation—profound, gay, witty—conversation was a passion at Holland House—anecdote and pun, monologue and epigram, and always that steady reign of Olympian humour—that power to praise or demolish character in one crisp sentence. Henry had changed the nursery and the schoolroom only for the society of his elders—of brilliant men and women of the world. At sixteen he was a precocious young man, well able to hold his own in elegant banter with great ladies and men of wit. He had a bitter tongue and a gift for the polished phrase. He was quick in spying out the *ridicules* in others, and harsh and youthful in his judgments. His sharp-tongued mother scolded him; sarcasm in the young, she warned him, was the quick road to making enemies. His father reasoned with him, more wisely but none the less severely, and told him that he was too critical for his own happiness.

As Lord Holland's heir it was his duty to enter Parliament and carry on the Whig tradition of his great-uncle, Charles James Fox. But Henry hated "politicks." They were the ruin of all human intercourse, he declared, and mightily he resented his great-uncle's ghost. They were always talking of him in reverent tones at Holland House, but Great-uncle Charles, so far as he could make out, had seldom held office, and then with little success, and left behind a powerful lot of lovelorn ladies and debts. He hated, too, that concomitant of "politicks" in England—country life—with its hunting and field-sports, its dreary tavern dinners and speeches to beer-sodden yokels. His tastes were mildly artistic. He liked books and paintings, old furniture and gardening—in a word, the things that gave Holland House its dignity and grace. A year's residence at Oxford did not fit him for public life. His studies failed to interest him, the dons were wine-bibbers and drones, and the undergraduates, for the most part, barbarians. Yet he shyly made friends there—with Henry Greville and Anthony Ashley Cooper, afterwards Earl of Shaftesbury and champion of factory children. Of another friend, John Stuart-Wortley, he wrote in his diary, "I hope he *does* like me, for I am so sincerely fond of him that I really deserve it." But he was new to the game of masculine friendship. He was possessive, like a girl, demanded open professions of liking, and too often his friends were discarded for inconstancy and baseness.

For a while he fluttered round the drawing-rooms of London. He was popular there because he was good-looking and Lord Holland's son and, in the eyes of scheming matrons, an eligible *parti*. People were a little afraid of him, for he was so very worldly-wise and wielded his mother's caustic tongue. But the drawing-rooms of Mayfair were too crowded for Henry's style of wit. He preferred humbler and more precious coteries where he was listened to with respect, and began to frequent the less fashionable and more intellectual drawing-rooms of London—Lady Davy's, or old Lydia White's, the blue-stocking, or the *salon* of Mrs Tighe.

Lady Caroline Lamb had long fallen from grace in the great world—not for her notorious love-affair with Byron, nor for the distressing scenes that she made in public afterwards, but for the novel she had written about it—*Glenarvon*. As the great houses of London would tolerate her no more, she took her comfort in queening it in the intellectual *salons*. The Hollands had cast her off, ostensibly because she had lampooned Lady Holland in *Glenarvon*, but really because they were loyal friends to Byron. Henry shared their disapproval and refused to speak to her when they met. But Caro Lamb, it appeared, was determined to make trouble. At Miss Berry's one evening she turned at the sound of his voice and stared at him earnestly. At Mrs Tighe's again she had entered, all gush and patronage, but at once fell silent at the sight of him and followed him all round the room with inquisitive eyes. She destroyed his pleasure in the party. "Why on earth does the little viper stare at me like that?" he said angrily to himself, as he limped his way out of the room.

Yet Henry was very susceptible among girls of his own age. His first love was 'Georgy,' or 'G-L,' as he called her for short in his diary. Lady Georgiana Lennox was one of the many poorly dowered daughters of the Duchess of Richmond who gave the ball before Waterloo. If her mother had not been beautiful Lady 'Georgy' would have passed for a pretty girl. As it was her looks were marred by frequent migraines and colds in the head. But she was sweet-tempered and patient. Henry longed to marry her, but there was talk that her hand was sought by the Earl of Worcester, who had made a fool of himself about Harriette Wilson a few years ago. Also a wealthy Mr Brinxman hovered in the background, and Henry began to doubt the steadiness of her affection. Then, too, he was distracted, as he put it, by her age and her family. She was twenty-six, and her family was Tory. He knew, as heir-apparent of the Whig royal family of Fox, that he would never be allowed to contract a *mésalliance* with the elderly daughter of a Tory duke.

Lady Georgy was a candid soul and introduced her suitor to pretty girls of her own acquaintance. Among them two stood out pre-eminent —Miss Harriet Canning, daughter of the great George Canning, and Miss Theresa Villiers, generally known in society as the daughter of the Honourable Mrs Villiers. Henry thought that Miss Villiers was a clever girl, and she diverted him exceedingly on their first meeting by her observations on a certain vulgarity that one notices in one's own family. But for Miss Canning he soon felt all the pangs of "the little god's darts." Manfully he confessed his change of soul to Lady Georgy. She was all kindness and wished him luck in his new adventure. A few days later she ordered Mr Brinxman to her side, listened to his declaration of love, and rejected it flat. She had already sent the Earl of Worcester about his business, and that susceptible nobleman contracted himself to Miss Smith on the rebound.[1]

The affair with Harriet Canning was brief, troubled, and painful. The Cannings were cold and unsympathetic, and Lord Holland, kindly but succinctly, told Henry that the marriage wouldn't do. Life at Holland House was expensive, contributions to the Whig Party were heavy, and the income from the Jamaica estates was dwindling. Charles, too, must be provided for, and Henry would not be a rich man when he became Lord Holland. He must, for his own good, marry money. None the less Henry wrote to Miss Canning and asked her to be his wife. He sent the letter to his friend George Howard and asked him to deliver it. He was in high spirits after writing, but when no answer came he fell to the depths of despair. Then George Howard wrote to say that he had not delivered the letter "as it wouldn't do any good and might do harm."

[1] Lady Georgy eventually married Lord De Ros and lived to be a handsome old lady of over ninety. As a child and a married woman she was a great favourite of the Duke of Wellington and corresponded with him assiduously.

Henry's spirits rose, and he felt a strange sense of liberty and relief. But his spirits were dashed again when he learned that Henry Greville and "the Copley girls" were saying all round Yorkshire that Harriet Canning had turned him down. George Howard had blabbed, and Henry was furious. Howard was dismissed as a friend, and Greville he denounced for treachery in high and haughty terms. When he returned to London Harriet Canning greeted him with a baffling mixture of reserve and expectation, and, puzzled and infuriated by the ways of women, he let her go by default as "a cold coquette."[1]

To recover from his disappointment he travelled on the Continent. He met the Blessingtons at Nice, visited Byron at Albaro, came home, and fell head over heels in love with Lady Georgy's other friend—Miss Villiers.

She was impeccable so far as birth was concerned, and also the politics of her family. The only daughter of the Hon. Thomas Villiers and niece of the Earl of Clarendon, she came of a breed in which florid good looks were hereditary and had in their day been notorious. But the Villiers looks were tempered in her with something that seemed like beauty. Golden hair with a gleam of bronze, dark-blue eyes, a brilliant complexion, small, delicate features—if Miss Villiers were not beautiful, said one of her admirers—a poet—then there be no pretty women. To beauty Theresa Villiers added that elusive gift of charm. She was graceful and vivacious, and conversation for her was, turn and turn about, a pretty toy that she tossed gaily into the air or a musical instrument upon which she played divinely. Yet though she was witty she was never unkind, and there were moments when she spoke thoughtfully and with a strange and poignant humour, and then her lovers were helpless before her. An only sister among many brothers, her brothers were the first of her admirers. "I wish," said George, the eldest (afterwards Lord Clarendon, and a handsome Foreign Secretary)—"I wish you weren't my sister, I wish you were my cousin, and then I could marry you, for I never met a woman that I thought so beautiful or for whom I felt a greater sympathy."

George Villiers scolded his sister for being melancholy. She was not at heart content with her triumphant progress in society. In her first season, when she was a shy and pretty girl, she had fallen deeply in love with a man who had wooed her for his vanity and thrown her aside. Ardent in all her feelings, she collapsed under the blow and for long she could not speak or walk. She was sincerely religious, and in her retirement she read the Bible and pondered it. She developed intellectual interests and wanted to withdraw from the world to write and study, but her family ordered her back to the social game. She returned with a will to conquer—a girl who, in bitterness and solitude, had become a beautiful

[1] Harriet Canning married the Earl of Clanricarde and was a successful ambassador's wife.

woman, armed with every weapon in the battery of charm. She hid her aloofness of spirit under a lively manner, and lovers multiplied round her. Many men were enslaved by her nimble wit and worldly grace and asked her to marry them, but, as season followed season, Miss Villiers was still without a husband, and still the men adored her.

Henry Fox, like others before him, fell in love with this brilliant creature without hoping that his love would be requited. In his diary we watch the passion bloom. When first he met her he was struck by her cleverness only. At subsequent meetings he quotes her witticisms, and the sad truth is they have lost their edge with time. He finds her less malicious than "the Copley girls"—for long his standard of high spirits. Then one day he notes shrewdly "she has not naturally all the gaiety she assumes. . . . I think she is not a happy person." That, he thought, was a fault, for it "keeps her in a constant state of effort to those with whom she is slightly acquainted." But he began to suspect that she had "a warm heart," and certainly "she is the pleasantest girl in London." One day in a burst of frankness she told him that she was nothing better than an actress—always circumspect, for all her wit, in what she said. That, said Henry, "I do not quite like because it leads one to imagine that she is always acting a part and that rarely, if ever, you can get to the bottom of her true feelings." Thereafter parties were dull if he did not meet Miss Villiers. And then—"God only knows if she ever will be mine. If loving can make me worthy of her, she ought." He took his fate in his hands and, not daring to hope that he—so lame and weak—would succeed where stronger men had failed, asked her to marry him. O bliss! O rapture! She consented, and Henry never drew a quiet breath again.

Lord and Lady Holland, without laying their veto on the marriage, frowned upon it and interposed every obstacle they could. Lord Holland still counselled prudence and a bride with money. Lady Holland's objection to Theresa Villiers was the same that held good for Georgy Lennox and Harriet Canning—she was the girl that Henry wanted to marry. Miss Villiers, however, was more offensive than the others, for she was beautiful, she was clever, and she had a will and a way of her own. Lady Holland brooked no rivals at Holland House.

A more insidious complication was Theresa's mother. Mrs Villiers was a type that grew more common in Queen Victoria's reign. She was handsome in a grave, repressed style of beauty. She was a woman of the world, yet she was, in her own stern way, religious; she was a passionate woman, yet she was a strict moralist. But, having great strength of will, she controlled these conflicting elements in her nature and made them serve her purpose. Mr Villiers was Paymaster of the Marines, Clerk of the Privy Council, Ranger of Cranborne Chase, and Registrar of the Duchy of Lancaster, but in all other respects he was a feckless gentleman who wasted the emoluments of a sinecure in sad experiments in making

S

hay and cheese. Him Mrs Villiers thrust to one side—"the Governor" she called him jocosely to her children—and resolutely set to work to manage her six handsome, clever sons without his aid and counsel and push them on in life. Her only daughter lay outside her schemes. Like other poor but well-born girls, she must marry young—if possible, a husband with money. Theresa was groomed like a horse for the game and emerged from the stables a most enchanting filly. But when she grew to lovely womanhood her mother was jealous. To one she deplored that her daughter was worldly, to another that she had odd notions in religion. She was, of course, devoted to her, but when one eligible suitor after another was dismissed, Mrs Villiers shrugged her shoulders and told her friends that her poor 'Tweezy' was at heart an old maid.

Mrs Villiers was greatly respected in society. She was a good woman, people said, yet tolerant and broad-minded for all her virtues. She gradually became Society's favourite confidante. Princess Amelia, youngest daughter of George III, confided her unhappy love-affair with Colonel Fitzroy to her. The princess died of erysipelas, and then her friend, Augusta Leigh, confided her troubles to Mrs Villiers. This intimacy led to one more impressive yet, for, as a result of her discoveries, Mrs Villiers switched her allegiance to Lady Byron. She and Annabella corresponded, and now there started an exciting game of spiritual blackmail. Augusta must be led to ways of repentance for having allowed her brother to love her too well, perhaps—by moral suasion and gentle reproof sometimes, but with vague threat of exposure always. Augusta was but a poor sinner. Repentance she oft and gladly swore, but somehow she never fell to the decent miseries of remorse. The two fair inquisitors often despaired, yet held meekly to their task. Mrs Villiers was in her element. She listened to Augusta with folded hands and the placid countenance of one who knows not sin herself but understands its attraction for others. Then she held grave counsel with Annabella and bore down again on Augusta, like an angel of the Lord, with uplifted finger and a warning. It was noticed in society that, when 'the Byron mystery' was discussed, Mrs Villiers was silent but looked sad folios deep of wisdom.

It was an axiom with Henry Fox that no man had a right to marry unless he were prepared to love his mother-in-law. He tried his best to love Mrs Villiers but he failed. She did not seem to care for him, yet she tolerated him. She lured him into confidences and wrote him wise and sorrowful letters. If he jibbed now and then at scraping his soul before her, she played the confidential tune herself. She told him that, *entre nous*, he was well rid of Georgy Lennox—she was a designing little fortune-hunter, and his parents would never have allowed him to marry her. Her own poor 'Tweezy' was different, but—she had so many suitors, was fond of admiration, and—Mrs Villiers shook her head sadly —so hard to please. Then, too, her reckless tongue—her mother sighed and sometimes thought she had no heart to give—if only she could settle down with Henry but—Mrs Villiers sighed again.

Henry found himself entangled in a delicate sipder's web of maternal innuendo. He somehow felt that he was a simpleton. He looked at Theresa with changed eyes. Her mother was right. Lovers and admirers never failed her, she was always gay in company—was she an actress, as she said she was? Did she really care for him, or had she taken him because he was the heir of Holland House and would be an easy husband? Was it possible that she and her mother were dangling him along until they could find some one better?

He was miserable and went abroad again. He went to Rome and made friends with Dudley Stuart. He dined with Teresa Guiccioli at Lady Davy's. With her gold hair and bright complexion and intellectual talk she reminded him of the other Theresa. But the likeness distressed him. It was a caricature. The Italian woman's features were large, and for that sweet earnestness that he hoped he sometimes saw in Theresa Villiers' face, in the face that Teresa Guiccioli turned to him he saw nothing but a bold concern.

From Naples he sailed to Missolonghi to visit the house where Byron had died. He wandered sadly about the dirty little town, thinking of his old friend. With him dead who was there left to withstand the tide of cant and hypocrisy that was engulfing the whole world? By July he was back again in Naples, still restless and unhappy.

On July 21, 1825, he made a round of visits. He called on Dudley Stuart and found him bright-eyed and flushed and in a high fever. Any day now he expected the news from Rome that Christine Possé had borne him a child.

He comforted Dudley and then went to call on Lady Mary Deerhurst. She was a grass-widow living apart from her husband, the unpleasant Lord Deerhurst who figures malodorously (in every sense of the word) in Harriette Wilson's *Memoirs*. Lady Mary, like Christine Possé, was a tiny, lively woman, and Henry liked her in a mild way. But he disapproved of her profoundly, too. She rattled away like a housemaid, and her conversation was full of "veiled indecency." She had a tiny daughter, of whom Henry disapproved, because she rode astride.

From Lady Mary's he went for a stroll in the gardens of the Villa Reale. Whom should he meet there, fresh from Rome, but the Countess Guiccioli? With Dudley's confidence tingling in his ears, he greeted her with ill-disguised merriment.

She is "full of sentiment and absurdity," he wrote in his diary that night . . . "she is in search of an adventure, and wants to fix herself upon some handsome and illustrious man."

## CHAPTER V

# Moonshine in Naples

HENRY made no entry in his diary after meeting Teresa Guiccioli in the garden for close upon three weeks. On the morning of August 9 he opened the book, read the last words he had written there, and added a few lines.

"Strange as it may seem after having written the above paragraph I find myself now ... when taking up my pen to continue this diary to have to record that though neither *handsome* nor *illustrious* I am strange to say become the object of T[eresa] G[uiccioli]'s affection."

A breathless entry—without punctuation. It was all very bewildering, and he didn't know whether to laugh or cry. It had happened last night ...

Life, for a change, had gone very pleasantly at Naples, and he had been cheerful and gay. In the first place there was the society of Dudley Stuart. Henry forgot his own sorrows in commiserating with the anxieties of his friend. On the very day—July 21—that he had gone to visit him and found him ill, Christine Possé had borne him a son in Rome. Thank Heaven, things were going well! Lady Bute had behaved like a Trojan. For all her tiresome airs she was a practical woman. She went to Rome and brought the baby back to a villa in a healthy spot above Naples. The next thing to be done, she decided, was for Dudley and Christine to marry. That entailed divorce for Christine from her lunatic Swedish husband. Christine was a Catholic, and the Bonapartes, as a family in which divorce had not been unknown in the past, chose now to take a high Catholic tone against divorce. But Lady Bute was a resolute woman. She adopted the great Napoleon's tactics and approached the Vatican personally for the dissolution of Christine's union with Count Possé.

In the meantime Dudley and Henry went sailing together in the Bay of Naples and took long rides round the heights of Vomero and Capo di Monte. Henry still hoped faintly that the affair with Christine Possé was a *passade* and that Dudley might yet marry his sister, Mary. But Dudley convinced him of the strength of his attachment to Christine, and loyally Henry made up his mind to love her for his friend's sake. Dudley had no disguise from him and told him all his life. "He is a most amiable, noble, fine-spirited character," wrote Henry affectionately in his diary, "and I quite love him."

He kept his cynicism alive by calling again upon the old Margravine of Anspach. It was a sobering experience to contemplate the ruins of a once-famous beauty. Then, in sheer boredom, he had acquired the habit of calling at the Villa Gallo. With Lady Blessington he was still on guard, but at least there was gaiety in her house, and he was fast yielding to Count d'Orsay's charm and wondered whether he might not admit him into the exclusive band of friends. There was delightful sense of mischief about Alfred, and between them they had great fun in making bores and vulgarians look ridiculous at the Villa Gallo.

Then almost every day he took *déjeuner* with Lady Mary Deerhurst. He flirted with her outrageously, and the little Baron von Haugwitz was furious. Lady Mary was a harum-scarum creature, but she was sound at heart. She was a good mother and was bringing up her daughter in a sensible manner to be a poor man's wife by making her learn all about housework, from scrubbing floors to cooking. Henry still disapproved of that riding astride, but, in the intervals of flirting with her mother, he played with little Mary Coventry. She was a tiny, spirited creature with a quick, friendly charm learnt in Italy—pretty now—and Henry wondered idly what she would be like when she was a woman.

Then he made a new friendship—a valuable friendship—with Lady Compton. When he met her first he had, as usual, disapproved. She was a big, raw-boned Scotswoman, a 'blue,' provincial, superstitious, not well born, and so forth. But Lady Compton took this supercilious, sad young man under her motherly wing. In her wholesome way she told him many things that were good for his soul, and Henry was grateful. She had "a kind, warm heart," he discovered, though with it went "many twists and fancies. . . . I hope never to offend or wound any of these twists, as I really value her friendship." In short, Henry was ceasing to be a clever boy with a sharp tongue and was gradually becoming a man.

And by night there was moonshine. He went for long walks with Teresa Guiccioli, and their conversation was sentimental. He told her about Byron and his "beautiful voice," and she hung upon his arm and listened with upturned, enraptured face. He "proffered her civilities," to use his own decorous phrase, and she seemed rather to seek than shrink from them. She had little worldly address, and he wished impatiently that she wouldn't call attention to his lameness by begging him to rest when they were walking together. They sat on Serrazoro's terrace and gazed out upon the starlit summer sea. Playfully in his new-found cheerfulness he made love to her, and she responded gaily. But he was growing up, and sentiment was not enough.

"There is nothing like the moon for mischief," he confided ruefully to his diary. "It was on Sunday evening, the 7th of August, that she listened and consented at her balcony as we were gazing at Dian's chaste beams."

But not for Sunday night. "Sentiment or caprice would not permit her to yield then." On Monday night Henry kept his tryst. "She received me as those females receive one, who make such occupations not their pleasure but their trade.

"I was not prepared," he confessed, "for the extreme facility of the conquest, which (such is the perverseness of one's nature) scarcely gave me pleasure. She is too gross and carnal."

It was his first experience, and he was disillusioned. He had been false to Theresa Villiers and he was angry with himself. His bitterness overflowed against Teresa Guiccioli. Yet the moon still shone and the nights were happy. He went sailing in the evening with Teresa. They landed at a lonely little cove near Nisida and wandered along the shore. The moon shone more splendidly and mischievously than ever that night, and summer lightning played about the sky.

It was love by starlight. In the daytime Dudley must never know, nor Lady Mary, nor his new friend, Lady Compton. Least of all must Lady Blessington and Count d'Orsay know, for there would be no end to their raillery. Vincenzo, the chaperon, was sent away to Aversa, and Henry and Teresa took refuge in a solitary villa at Sorrento. There they spent several days together. Sorrento was a lovely spot and the villa "quite heavenly," and Henry was fain to admit that the time passed "rather agreeably." Teresa "amused" him, he admitted, "though I felt rather ashamed of affecting sentiment I did not feel and professing unalterable attachment."

There was a shadow between them—a teasing, mocking shadow. One morning she gave him her copy of Caro Lamb's *Glenarvon* and begged him to read it. He read the book under protest and, when he handed it back, told her the truth about Caro Lamb. Her portrait of Byron, he said, was a caricature. Never was there a kinder man nor one more gay nor less like the gloomy Childe Harold of his poems. Women had never understood him—they couldn't—as a sex they lacked all humour, particularly when they imagined themselves in love.

Yet there were alarming symptoms at Sorrento. Henry wanted secrecy, but Teresa demanded absolute solitude. Henry was grateful for a merry interlude, but Teresa talked of a five years' constancy, at the very least, and wished him to give up all society for her sake. Once he had prided himself on being a misanthrope, but now, as he gazed sulkily out to sea from their hiding-place, he felt differently. "Society is necessary to me," he said; "I am sorry to own it, as I once thought and always wished otherwise."

Teresa dropped his arm and walked away to the end of the terrace and pulled a flower to pieces angrily.

He looked after her crossly. "Her sentiment is ridiculous," he thought, "especially to me, knowing as I do all her history within these few months." She came back to him and talked to him in broken English. She was badly dressed, and he was affronted by her poverty and her lack of worldly aplomb. "Her manners are bad," he told himself, and he harked back to Theresa Villiers—"she is an instance of those who, from living with clever people, think it their duty to be clever, too. She has a pretty voice, pretty eyes, white skin, and strong, not to say turbulent, passion. She has no other attraction." He sighed wearily and kissed her hand. "Poor Lord Byron!" he thought. "I do not wonder at his going to Greece."

So there were scenes and reconciliations at Sorrento. At first Henry was frightened by the scenes, but in the end he looked forward to them with some excitement. He was still self-conscious, and his timidity made him rude and *gauche*. Then Teresa laughed at him, and he was angry. Acutely aware of something lame and wanting in himself, he exuded upon her a dismal, superior laughter of his own—what he called his "English sense of humour." She understood nothing of that and retorted on him with flashing eyes and exasperated tears. Somehow it was exhilarating. "I grew to like her better," he admitted in his diary, "as I knew more of her." At least she was sincere, and, after a scene more lively than usual, he owned that she was "very true spoken." How was this truthfulness to be reconciled with her sham sentiment? Henry pondered that problem in his mind and resolved it to his own satisfaction. Her sentiment was assumed, but it was real while it lasted—at least, so she thought.

They moved from Sorrento back to Naples and took up separate abode again. By day Henry rode and sailed with Dudley, flirted with Lady Mary, and talked amusing nonsense with Count d'Orsay at the Villa Gallo. The nights he spent with Teresa. She was *exigeante* and suspicious now. She still nursed a grievance against Lady Blessington from Albaro days and wished Henry would not visit her house. She had other reasons for not wanting him to go riding with Dudley, and she resented his flirtation with Lady Mary Deerhurst. The scenes and quarrels became more frequent, and Henry grew impatient. Besides, in Naples, back among his worldly-wise friends, he was ashamed of his *liaison* with a woman who lived with one maid in a garret.

His parents were growing anxious in England. They wanted him to come home, and even dropped a hint in their letters that they would waive their objections to Theresa Villiers. Very reluctantly Henry began to make up his mind to leave Naples, where, for the first time in his life, he had been happy. But Dudley left at the end of September with his mother and his child to rejoin Christine in Rome. Lady Compton left soon afterwards. On October 15 Teresa said good-bye and returned with the silent Vincenzo to Rome. Henry promised to join her there in a few days, but as luck would have it his horse fell the very next day as he was riding up the hill to the Villa Gallo, and he bruised his ankle so severely that he was unable to travel.

Lady Blessington insisted that he should stay in her house until his ankle was well. Nothing could exceed her kindness, and Henry melted under her genial Irish warmth. Certainly there was no more pleasant house in all Europe than the Villa Gallo. It reminded him of Holland House, but many were the differences, and every difference was in favour of the Villa Gallo. A guest was a free man there with only two duties— to be present at the dinner-table at noon and at night. Otherwise you went your own way, lying late abed and reading books, rising slowly to write letters or lounge in the garden, talking lazily with your fellow-guests. The bell rang for *déjeuner*, and the guests assembled for a meal of light food exquisitely cooked and light wine carefully chosen by that connoisseur of food and drink Count d'Orsay. Lady Blessington was an admirable hostess. She steered the conversation skilfully at her table and drew every one of her guests into a friendly circle of repartee. The conversation never languished, and it was never pompous or profound. "Politicks" were shunned, and the talk was all of books and life and people. The afternoons were given to pleasure, every man according to his will—a *siesta*, if you would, or, if your ambitions were literary, you studied and wrote books. Count d'Orsay was ever willing to try his skill at fencing with his guests, and there were horses in abundance for rides and expeditions. The more unwary of the guests were lured by the Earl into a sail on his yacht—the *Bolivar*—that had once been Byron's. In the evening dinner—a more elaborate ritual than *déjeuner*—but still delightful food and wonderful wines and that quiet, friendly ripple of intellectual small-talk. And after dinner there were charades and dressing-up and amusing romps about the house, or, when the guests were tired with the day's excursion, music and cards.

Certainly Lady Blessington and Count d'Orsay had succeeded in creating for themselves and their guests a haven of gay and busy indo-lence, remote from all touch with the common world. One of its charms for Henry was that, except for Lady Blessington and her sister, there were no women there. It was a haven created especially for men—for one man, perhaps, by a clever woman—and from d'Orsay there emanated a perpetual radiance of masculine good will and happiness. Henry sank back with a sigh and rested from anxiety in this sprightly paradise. He accused himself of harshness in his first judgment of Lady Blessington and tried to talk with her without suspicion or reserve. She was a delightful conversationalist and drew him quietly into frankness. They spoke of Byron, and casually she asked him if he had met Teresa Guiccioli that day when they had both called upon the poet at Albaro. Henry replied that he had not met her. Lady Blessington, laughing lightly, told him that she, too, during all her stay at Genoa had not been honoured by the Countess's acquaintance. "Poor Byron!" she said, gazing with half-closed eyes out to sea—she had good reason to suppose that he was "tightly governed" in his own house. Henry remarked vaguely that the poet had said something to him about "cutting cables" in Italy—whatever that might mean—and Lady Blessington's smile grew more subtle. What with Mr Hunt and his wife and children and Mrs Shelley, she said, and, at the Casa Saluzzo, old Count Gamba and young Pietro, "poor Byron" had managed to collect a great many people round him to live upon his bounty. "Poor thing," she added briskly, "she feared him a great deal more than she loved him." Then, withdrawing her gaze from the sea, she told Henry that the Countess Guiccioli had spent the summer at Naples, but of course she had not met her.

Perhaps it was that tone of hers—condescending, malicious—impudent almost at times—but Henry discovered that he still did not like Lady Blessington, for all her charm. He veered away from intimacy, and under her effusive manner he felt something pretentious in her parade of wit and intellect. He was ashamed of himself for accepting her hospitality. "It rather hurt me," he wrote in his diary, "as I felt myself acting with duplicity . . . it hurt me not to be able to like Lady Blessington as I should wish to like her, but she has exactly the defects that . . . wound all my little peculiarities of opinion and disposition."

But with Count d'Orsay it was a different matter, and Henry rebuked himself sharply in his diary for jumping to hasty conclusions. Under that dandy exterior there beat "a warm and generous heart." In a hundred little ways Alfred had shown that he wanted to be his friend, and Henry, who had been wont to woo friends shyly, was delighted to be wooed in his turn. It was a friendship unlike all others, because, with all his affection, he was not blind to Alfred's faults. He had undoubted talents, good nature, generous impulses, but vanity, alas! had so disfigured his character that his virtues had almost turned to defects. Henry laid the blame on Lady Blessington. "The fatal *liaison* with such a woman . . . is calculated to do him a terrible deal of harm, living as he does the solitary life of an idol incensed by flattery all day long." But, disapprove as he might, he could not tear himself away from the Villa Gallo, and solely on Alfred's account he stayed there for over two months.

But his parents were nagging him from England. As he still loitered in Italy they meant to visit Paris in the spring, and he was ordered to join them there. Most unwillingly on December 13 he left Naples for Rome. His first thought there was for Dudley, whom he found happy and hopeful now that he was living close by his dear Christine again. For nine days he wandered restlessly about the city, calling on old acquaintances, and then at last made up his mind. He climbed the stairs slowly to the garret, half torn between excitement and depression. She greeted him with blazing eyes, with a torrent of reproaches. He stammered and expostulated—his ankle—a fall from his horse—but she turned from him in scorn. He lost his temper. "Well, this is the end," he shouted, "thank God!" She leaned her head against the window-pane and beckoned to him wildly with her hand to be gone. He slammed the door angrily and limped downstairs.

She was in bed, exhausted with fury, when he called upon her the next evening. He hovered unhappily round her, and suddenly she burst into tears. With an exclamation of concern he sat down upon the bed and would have taken her hand. She flung her arms round his neck and laughed for sheer happiness. When he left her he said good-bye tenderly, and she, yielding to his decree, said good-bye, too, but this time they parted friends.

For two months Henry lingered at Rome, postponing his departure for Paris day after day. He could not bear to leave Dudley Stuart, and all day long they walked and rode together, discussing plans and prospects. And in the evening Henry climbed the stairs to Teresa's garret.

For a while he pleaded gout and palpitations of the heart as an excuse for not leaving, but at the end of February he was obliged to set out on his journey. "My *séjour* at Rome has been delightful," he wrote sadly in his diary, ". . . the day with Dudley and the nights with T.G. . . . I never can be so happy again . . . I feel I behaved rather ill to T.G., but I do not think she will suffer more than a little momentary vexation and mortification."

Before he left Rome he wrote to Mrs Villiers. All the time that he had been in Italy she had written him letters, imparting hope and breathing doubt and calling upon him reproachfully for confidence. Curtly he informed her that the correspondence must cease. He further instructed her to tell her daughter from him that everything was now over between them. If he must return to England he would go there "unshackled and free."

CHAPTER VI

# A Scene from Fragonard

*In her first passion woman loves her lover,*
*In all the others all she loves is love.*

TERESA had protested when Byron read her those lines at La Mira.
But was he right? She went for walks with Lamartine in the Pamphili-
Doria gardens, and they talked deeply and profoundly of love—and
Byron. She would not have confided in him if he had not been a poet.
And upstairs in the garret was the lame boy. She would never have loved
him, had he not been lame. Oh, no, Byron was surely wrong. Always
she was looking for one man—her lover who was dead—and not dead.
It was the pity of life that he came back to her as two men. She walked
with him by daylight in the garden as Lamartine, the poet—who was
pompous and unsmiling—and she didn't altogether trust him. She made
love to him by night in her garret as Henry Fox, who was lame—and
sulky—and sometimes made her cross.

Henry wronged her when he said that only her vanity was hurt when
he left her. She grew tired of Rome and went back to Filetto. Life was
mournful there. Her mother was dead, Grandfather Gamba died, her
father was in prison, Pietro was dead in Greece, and she had never seen
him since he sailed away with Byron. Her younger sisters were still in
the convent. Only Grandmother Gamba, and her faithful watchdog,
Vincenzo, who seldom spoke, and their younger brother Ippolito, who,
at least, was lively. But Grandmother Gamba kept Ippolito on leash.
He, too, was all agog for Italian independence, and Grandmother Gamba
felt that the family had suffered enough and did not want to see another
grandson sent into exile. She received her granddaughter kindly but a
little grimly, for Teresa, in her way, had been the greatest disappointment of all the family.

Teresa helped her grandmother keep house. She visited her sisters
in the convent and went riding with Vincenzo and Ippolito in the Pine
Forest. She studied and wrote poetry and corresponded with Ignazio
in Venice about his literary ambitions. She drove over frequently to
Bologna to see her old friend Professor Costa. There, too, dwelt her
Roman acquaintance Madame Martinetti, the archæologist's wife. A
friendship grew between the two women, and they confided in each other.

But Teresa was restless and had to break away from the sadness of
Filetto. She went on poetical pilgrimages to Garda and the Lake of

283

Como, and there she met Emilio Belgiojoso. He took pity on the solitary little woman, travelling alone and stopping in cheap hotels, where English tourists stared at her and nudged one another and faded away in apoplectic silence if she ever dared speak to them. He persuaded her to visit him in his palace, the Villa Pliniana, on its all-but-island on the Lake of Como. Teresa had a weakness for solitary palaces in romantic settings, saw no harm in the invitation, and accepted this bachelor hospitality in all good faith. Cristina Belgiojoso was not so indifferent to Prince Emilio as she hoped to be. She dressed in black and mourned her husband's defection for all the world to see in her opera-box at Milan.

Sometimes Teresa stayed with her great-aunt, the Marchesa Sacrati, in Florence. Aunt Sacrati was fully ninety years old. She had been a beauty once and *amica* of a Pope, but now she was in disgrace and had been banished from Rome for plotting for Italian freedom. She was a delightful old lady with a fine, high spirit. In her dingy lodgings in Florence she still held a *salon* and, under the light of two poor candles, entertained *abbés* and poets and faithful cavaliers as ancient as herself. She had known every one in her day in Italy, and her memory reached back to Cardinal Alberoni when he lived in exile in Bologna. Among her acquaintances in her old age was Queen Caroline, and when that indiscreet woman went back to England to face an investigation about her life in Italy the Marchesa Sacrati scrambled across the Alps to bear witness in her favour. Every one in London loved the dear old lady with her white hair, black eyebrows, and sparkling eyes. Her wrath with "*ce mauvais sujet*, Broggam" for defending the Queen without believing in her innocence was comic. Yet she served the Queen's cause none too well by trying to explain the ethics of *cavalier serventismo* to the English. "Did that courier fellow Bergami behave himself towards Her Majesty as an English gentleman would?" asked one of her listeners severely. The old lady pondered her answer, and then, "No," she replied, "he certainly did not"—her interlocutor shrugged his shoulders and looked in triumph round the room—"no," said the Marchesa thoughtfully, "Signor Bergami did not behave to the Queen of England as an English gentleman would—he was always very gentle with her—and respectful—and considerate."

In the early winter of 1827 an acquaintance from old days arrived in Ravenna. Sir Humphry Davy, the scientist, was ill and he knew that he was dying. His doctors ordered him abroad to a warmer climate for the winter. He remembered Ravenna with fondness—its silence, the friendliness of its people, and the lovely rides round about it in the forest—and nothing would satisfy him but that he should spend the winter there. He arrived with his brother in February, and the Vice-Legate offered them the hospitality of the Apostolic Palace. Sir Humphry was still able to ride, and with gun and dogs he explored the Pine Forest, hunting for

strange breeds of snipe and *petzardone* or watching with a scientific eye
the flight of an eagle over the trees against a background of snow-clad
mountains. But he was in a melancholy frame of mind, and poetry and
religion interested him more nowadays than science. He had brought
with him all the works of Byron and fell to writing sad poems to Nature.

> . . . I still in vernal times
> May look on Nature with a poet's eye,
> Nursing those lofty thoughts that in the mind
> Spontaneous rise, blending their sacred powers
> With images from mountain and from flood.

"I am in utter quiet here," he wrote to his wife. Every one in Ravenna
was kind. The Vice-Legate treated him like a brother and played *écarté*
with him in the evening. Mme Martinetti came over from Bologna to
see him. But his favourite was the Countess Guiccioli. She listened to
his poems, she brewed his tea for him, she brought him from the forest
violets and acacia and juniper in blossom. Her bright laughter, the
never-ending ripple of her conversation, cheered his solitude. He had
liked her, and laughed at her a little, when he met her in the days of her
glory with Byron. Now that she was poor and not very happy he felt
for her the fondness of a father.

But Count Guiccioli was making himself a nuisance again. He agreed
to raise Teresa's allowance, but she must leave Romagna and live permanently at Florence. Teresa accepted his terms with a mental reserva-
tion to forget them when she could, and left Ravenna to stay with Aunt
Sacrati. Sir Humphry found Ravenna dismal without her and packed
up forlornly and set out for Rome. He was ill there, and Teresa left
Florence in defiance of her husband and returned to Rome to cheer her
old friend.

Henry Fox had promised himself nothing but sorrow and annoy-
ance when he rejoined his parents in Paris, and he was right. After two
years of being his own master he fell back into the old routine of subjection and dependence. The intrigues and plots that go on in a family
ruled by an absolute monarch disgusted him. He disliked his mother
more than ever, was peevish with his father, and thought his sister spoilt
by worldly vanity. Back in England he felt more miserable than ever.
He found he had no taste for 'society' in London—it was all "selfish-
ness, vanity, and frivolity," and his one wish was to marry the woman
he loved and retire from the world and live in a society of choice souls
of his own selection. As usual, Dudley Stuart was his one prop and consolation. He came home to London, bringing his son, with Christine as
his wife! Henry genuinely rejoiced in the happiness of his friend, but it
only made his own luck seem all the harder.

He had broken with Theresa Villiers because he wished to start all over again. He disliked and distrusted Mrs Villiers. She had made him feel that Theresa didn't care for him—worse still, she had made him feel that he didn't love Theresa. Now he would woo her again, cut free from all her mother's web of soft innuendo. But the bitter work had been done. "I feel," he wrote, "that Theresa is the person most calculated to make me happy." They met and tried to resume life on the old footing, and Theresa by every means in her power sought to convince him that she loved him, "but," he wrote miserably in his diary, "I have sad doubts." Mrs Villiers, perforce, must write letters, and then Lord and Lady Holland intervened—the marriage must not take place. Henry refused to accept their veto. On July 3, 1826, he said good-bye to Theresa and left for the Continent, vowing that he would never return until his parents gave consent to their marriage. Reluctantly in November they consented, but they warned Henry of the difficulties he would have to face if he persisted. A month later he wrote from Rome to say that he had broken off his engagement with Theresa Villiers.[1] In the spring of 1827 he requested the consent of his parents to his engagement to the Countess Nathalie Potocka, with whom he had been acquainted only a few weeks. The Countess Nathalie was a young Polish girl of noble ancestry, and she was an heiress. The Hollands gave their consent to the marriage, but the girl's mother, the Countess Wonsovicz, did not approve and took her daughter away from Rome. Nathalie fell into a suitable melancholy and wrote sad letters on the sly to Henry, which he was too lazy to answer. Upon mature reflection she broke off the engagement—a decision which Henry accepted with equanimity.[2]

At Rome he renewed his friendship with Lady Compton. He fell for his sins very much under the influence of that mature and overpowering beauty the Countess of Westmorland. He had found a new and very dear friend in Edward Cheney and visited his mother's, Mrs Cheney's, apartment. Finally he entered into cosy terms of intimacy with Hortense de Beauharnais and went to the Villa Paulina almost every day. Hortense made him sit for his portrait, but the paint-brush was dropped early in the sittings, and, with ever and anon a glance towards the mirror, she read him the story of her life that she was writing. From reading she

[1] Theresa Villiers would have made Henry Fox a good wife and was probably sincerely in love with him. She was slow in marrying and had many admirers after Henry, including the Duc de Morny. She made an unworldly marriage in 1830 with Thomas Henry Lister, the novelist (Granby, Herbert Lacy). She wrote or collaborated in novels herself. In 1844 she married for a second husband Sir George Cornewall Lewis, one-time Chancellor of the Exchequer, friend of Gladstone, Grote, and J. S. Mill, "a grave-looking man, cold-blooded as a fish." Theresa in later life wrote scholarly and historical works and died at Oxford in 1865. Sir William Harcourt was her son-in-law.

[2] The Countess Nathalie Potocka soon afterwards made the usual worldly marriage with a compatriot, Prince Sangusko, and died young.

fell to talking in a fond, reflective tone of the great days of Napoleon when she had been a Queen. From her *Memoirs* she prattled onwards to her tragedy, *Valérie*, and Henry was allowed to attend when Hortense read that important work aloud to old Madame Mère. He liked Hortense, but for a woman of her age he thought she was childish and too fond of flattery. He wished she would sometimes stop talking about herself and the splendours of her castle in Switzerland, and in her devotion to that ungainly son of hers she was morbid and hysterical. Frankly, Louis Napoleon was a lout and Henry ignored him in his mother's house.

On January 14, 1828, he received a long letter from his mother, finding fault with his way of life in Italy. He threw the letter impatiently aside and went to the Borghese gardens—where he met Teresa Guiccioli by appointment. They walked for a while in the gardens, and, says Henry, Teresa was "amiable and agreeable"—almost the first kind word he had spoken for her. He left her for the more regal society of Lady Westmorland, whom he found "in all the paraphernalia of her *toilette*" for a reception at the Austrian Ambassador's that evening. "I cannot dislike her," confessed Henry, "as much as my reason tells me I ought to do." He dined with Lady Compton, and—"I passed the evening with T.G."

They had met again under the friendly, flighty wing of Hortense de Beauharnais. Slowly Teresa came back into Henry's life—and into his diary. One evening he dined alone with her and admitted that she "looked very well." He had spent the day unhappily with Lady Compton, who had been disagreeable and, he felt, insincere. By contrast Teresa was "agreeable," and, said Henry in his diary, "her frankness and sincerity are unparalleled." He was still critical, for Teresa, although a countess, was not a fashionable woman. Every minute the former pupil of Professor Costa betrayed her lack of decent education. And still he must deplore her manners, but then, poor thing! he reflected kindly, she "has never had opportunities." She was poor, her family was poor, she came from a provincial city lying far away from the Great World. And her life with Byron—so solitary—spent in the company of poets and people like that—of moral outcasts like Shelley—a squalid, Bohemian world—yet distressingly bourgeois, for all that! No wonder that she had not the manners of Holland House. But "she has many merits." She might be ill-educated, but she was clever and "has read more than I could have believed. I was surprised at her knowing so much of *Hamlet* by heart."

The *liaison* was resumed, but it was a more tranquil business now. Teresa still pined for solitude, but the scenes were less frequent and she settled gradually into the rôle of listening in the evening to the saga of Henry's disappointments by day. He was still shocked by what he called her "total want of delicacy of manner or feeling," but her heart was good and "her talents very superior to what I first supposed them to be."

Certainly Henry was growing up. He was learning that his first harsh judgments were not always right. He noted, too, that in her way Teresa was growing up, too. Two years passed in good society had done her a world of good. "She is more like other people," he owned with a sigh of relief, and he rewarded her for her improvement by going about with her in the open light of day.

They went masked to the Carnival and pelted their fellow-maskers with sugar-plums. Teresa dragged him to the great ceremonial services at St Peter's, and Henry fell under the charm of Catholic ritual. In the springtime the waterfalls lured them to expeditions in the country, and they roamed the woods and hills on horseback or in chaise. They went to country fairs and watched displays of fireworks and took their rest in quaint little inns that were cheap but, to Henry's mind, primitive and unclean.

He had rented the Villa Muti, near Frascati, and there he lived in bookish solitude with his friend Edward Cheney, to whom he had transferred all the affection that he had once given Dudley Stuart. One spring day Hortense demanded a picnic and an 'expedition' to Tusculum. With Teresa Guiccioli she drove out to the point of rendezvous in an elegant *calèche* drawn by four horses. Apparently there had been some misunderstanding about the time of meeting, for, when Henry and Edward Cheney arrived an hour or so later, they found that Hortense and Teresa had driven off to inspect a neighbouring villa. They overtook them at the villa and there were presented to the other guests, M. Schnetz, the painter, and M. and Mme Boudain-Dufresne. They continued in a group on their way. A sharp sirocco was blowing and covered them all in a fine dry dust. They left their carriages and horses and mounted donkeys to climb the hill to the Villa Belvedere. The ladies screamed and said their saddles were wrong and wouldn't be left alone for two minutes. The sun shone more hotly every hour, and M. Schnetz and M. Dufresne were lost.

After a desultory tour of the Villa Belvedere the vote went for *déjeuner* now and Tusculum afterwards. Hortense insisted that every one must be "very rural," by which she meant that they should eat their food sitting on the grass. Henry declined politely to sit upon the grass and sent for a table. Hortense then produced from her donkey's back a pie —a large and greasy pie—and, as by miracle, M. Schnetz and M. Dufresne reappeared. Gaiety had flagged under the dust and sunlight, but cheerfulness and wit returned at the sight of the pie. There was a sad decline in hilarity after it had been consumed, but that resourceful picnicker Hortense then conjured sundry bottles of champagne from her hamper, and the woods rang with laughter. They did not go to Tusculum that day.

Henry was confined to bed with a bilious headache after that picnic.

His friends came to console him. Lady Westmorland burst in upon him and prayed beside his bed for three minutes, calling upon God to forgive her husband because she herself certainly would not! Lady Compton followed and ordered him briskly out of bed. The scientists had announced that Vesuvius was about to erupt, she had room for him in her chaise, and he must leave with her for Naples that night. Then Teresa came to cheer him up and nurse him. Harshly he broke the news to her —Vesuvius was erupting, and duty called him to Naples. "We had sad scenes about my departure, and this will probably put an end to a *liaison* which bores me and does not satisfy her. She requires such exclusive devotion that I have neither time nor love enough to bestow upon her."

So Teresa, who had come to the Villa Muti with such high hopes of sickness and devotion, went sadly back to Rome and Sir Humphry Davy, and Henry drove away that night to Naples. The heavens opened on him in their fury as he drove. Lightning crackled in his ears, thunder crashed above him and he was beaten and buffeted with hail. Never had he known such a tempest nor made a journey more uncomfortable! Lady Compton was enormous, and she squeezed him right out of the chaise. He was drenched to the skin and miserable when they reached Naples, and wished he had never come.

Vesuvius sent up plumes of calm, sarcastic smoke into a cloudless spring sky and nothing happened at Naples but the old, old moonlight. Lady Compton fell under its spell, and they went for long drives by night in the exiguous chaise—sentimental, said Henry, but chilling. "I eat, drink, sleep, and feel in a state of positive enjoyment as to physical existence, but I do so feel the void of my second half's society."

In her bluff way Lady Compton had been right. He was healed, in spirit as in body, of the picnic. But friends and affection were so dear, so real, to Henry in absence. He was homesick for the Villa Muti and Edward Cheney.

T

## CHAPTER VII

# *Sweet Sorrow*

HENRY was right. Teresa had lived too long in a small world of poetry. By temper and in manner she was not made for the great world of Howard and Colonna that Alfred Count d'Orsay so gracefully adorned. But the pair of them were caught up as very tiny cogs in the great world's wheels that grind exceeding small.

Henry had long been distressed by the course that his friend Count d'Orsay was pursuing. Lord Blessington had sent for his daughter, Lady Harriet Gardiner, from Ireland. A girl of fifteen, white-faced, apathetic, young for her years, she was bewildered and unhappy in her father's household. She had been brought up piously and strictly in Ireland by a grandmother and a spinster aunt, and the worldly gaiety of her father's palace in a foreign land shocked her. She had seen little of her father in her life and did not recognize him in this gross, bewhiskered man with the noisy laugh, who too often now was drunk in the evening. Her brilliant stepmother, with her graceful, coaxing manner, terrified her. The beautiful young man who was always at her stepmother's side fascinated yet filled her with a strange repulsion. She felt herself inadequate, and, one and all, this overwhelming trio took her in hand and did their best to rid her of her prim old-maid ways of thought and manner. Her father slapped her playfully on the back, her stepmother tricked her out in fine clothes and gently scolded her for clumsiness, the beautiful young man bowed over her hand and bantered her with pretty speeches. If she ventured a timid remark about home or the things that interested her, they looked at one another and smiled, and effusively her stepmother embraced her for a little, quaint goose.

Henry visited the Blessingtons and was sorry for the dull and frightened child. His dislike of Lady Blessington increased with every meeting, and it was only his enjoyment in Count d'Orsay's society that brought him to the house. Then one evening Alfred drew him aside and asked him to be a witness at his forthcoming marriage to Harriet Gardiner. The news did not take Henry by surprise. Lady Blessington had confided the plan to him several years ago; and it was common knowledge in Rome that the Blessingtons had applied to the British Minister at Florence for a licence. But Lord Burghersh had behaved in a manner so rude and insulting that they had left Florence in stately protest. Henry felt as strongly as Lord Burghersh on the marriage. Yet there was a strange charm about Count d'Orsay—an aura of the 'eternal boy'—and Henry remembered gratefully his many kind actions in the past wherein he had shown the delicacy almost of a woman. In his presence he could not refuse his request. But, whatever were his quirks and oddities, Henry was an honourable man, and with his friends he was honest. The next morning he wrote to Alfred and declined to be present at his wedding. He told him flatly his reason for declining; he hated the whole idea of this marriage and knew that it would be the ruin of Alfred's happiness and his good name. Alfred answered in the kindest, most friendly manner, assuring Henry that he bore him no ill-will. With ingenuous frankness he avowed his affection for Lady Blessington and admitted that he felt no affection for his bride, but what would you? It was too good a marriage to turn down, and it was essential for his own happiness. And, after all, Count d'Orsay's happiness was the most important thing in all the world.

When they met in public now, though Alfred almost humbly sought his eye, Henry coldly turned his face away. The Blessington circus left Rome for Naples, and there Count d'Orsay went through the form of marriage with Harriet Gardiner—a form it could only be called, for he would not consummate the marriage. Joyful and triumphant, the circus returned to Rome and rented the Palazzo Negroni for a gay season of dinner-parties and balls. Once more Lady Blessington and Count d'Orsay were seen everywhere together, radiating pleasure and good will, while the Earl drank himself into maudlin happiness in the evening and the child-wife moped sulkily at home.

But Henry's Egeria, Lady Westmorland, rose like an angel clad in wrath and cashmere against the Casa Blessington. She was a brilliant, tempestuous creature, vain and eccentric to the verge of madness, but she had a fine talent for managing other people's lives, and once her mind was made up on a course of action she spun round and round like Nature in a fury. The Blessingtons, she announced, were now beyond the pale of decent society. They must not be received by the English colony in Rome. Yet more—Roman society must not receive them, nor must they be entertained by the Ambassadors of foreign Courts. The great world called Society held its own views upon the marriage, and many people who had disdained the Blessingtons when they were considered merely vulgar were willing now to drop them as impossible. But Society is human. It had suffered in its day from Lady Westmorland's passion for interference. The Blessingtons, too, were undeniably rich, they were gay, friendly, and hospitable—and as long as Lord Blessington was content—Society shrugged its shoulders and decided that Lady Westmorland might be ignored. The first blow in the skirmish was struck by the French Ambassador—Prince Adrien de Laval-Montmorenci. On the night of January 29, 1828, he gave a costume-ball to all the great world, native and foreign, at Rome. The Blessingtons were there, gorgeously arrayed as Turks.

Lady Westmorland's wrath reached apocalyptic heights. The French Ambassador, she declared, had degraded the English nobility and was fomenting revolution in England. She would not rest now until he was driven out of Rome with the Blessingtons. She retired into the country to pray and fast and commune with God alone. She did penance for her own sins and held her tongue for seven days. She emerged from her retirement more voluble than ever. "God must manifest himself more plainly!" she cried. "I cannot fight His battle any more. There must be another Incarnation . . . I have done all I can for the cause of virtue. God must complete the work!"

But God was lazy, and, woman-like, she snatched the work of retribution from His hands. By exhortation and abuse and voluminous correspondence she carried on the crusade against the French Ambassador and the Blessingtons. Count d'Orsay dashed impulsively into the battle. He wrote her a letter, telling her every story ever told against her virtue, and threatened, if not to murder her, at least to insult her publicly when next they met. Lady Westmorland arrayed herself in mourning and handed the letter to the French Ambassador at a public reception. "*Cela, monsieur*," she said with a deep, sad curtsy, "*appartient à la France, pas à moi.*" She then demanded an audience of the Pope.

Prince Adrien was offered the embassy at Vienna by the French Government. He left Rome, and Chateaubriand took his place. God had lingered painfully on the way, but Lady Westmorland had shamed Him into action. The Blessingtons braved it gallantly for a while under the lightnings of her wrath. On the evening of April 29 Henry was brooding sorrowfully over his troubles in the Colosseum. All round him in the shadows he heard soft murmurs of "*Vi amero sempre*," and his heart was filled with regret. Suddenly there were loud cries, shouts of laughter, and a clapping of hands, and the echoes and the owls flew out from the ruins in startled protest. Lady Blessington and Count d'Orsay strode in revelry and splendour under the moonlight, and all other lovers vanished like moths before their triumphant entry. But it was their last great moment in Rome. A few days later Lady Blessington wrote in her journal with unwonted melancholy, "To-morrow we leave the Eternal City—perhaps to see it *no more*. This presentiment filled me with sadness when I this evening from the Monte Pincio saw the golden sun sink beneath his purple clouds . . . Yes, parting is a sad ceremony."

The Blessington circus rolled away majestically from Rome—to Ravenna, to Venice, to Milan—ever northward. But it never struck root in Italy again. At last it found its way to Paris, and there Lord Blessington fell off his horse and died. Lady Westmorland's will was done.

Willy-nilly Henry was dragged into this vortex of rage and diplomatic intrigue when he returned to Rome. His feelings were on the side of Lady Westmorland, but, unlike her, he was sick and sorry about the poor little Countess d'Orsay. Lady Westmorland literally made his head ache with her prayers and reproaches and hysterical violence. Then Alfred needs must look for some one upon whom to avenge his wounded honour. He chose the lame and nervous young man who had declined to attend his wedding. Henry had long ago given him a snuff-box for a present. He packed it up and sent it back with a letter. "I return you your souvenir, for I do not wish to keep anything that could remind me for an instant of one as false and ungrateful as you." Henry replied with spirit. "I am very glad that you have returned a souvenir the sight of which, I can well believe, must be painful to you. You know well enough that I have not been false or ungrateful. The gratitude that I owe you for past kindness makes me regret keenly your present conduct and candour obliges me to express my regret." The lie had been passed, and it was now matter for a duel.

Lady Westmorland forbade Henry to fight with Alfred—that would be doing him too much honour, she declared in a solemn fury—and in the end Society accepted her ruling. Duelling, it was ordained, was the privilege of gentlemen, and Count d'Orsay was recommended to find other means of restoring his self-respect. But it had been a terrible time. Henry was brave, but he had little stomach for duelling. He would never have forgiven himself if he had been killed by d'Orsay, and if he had killed him he would have been sorry. In the general turmoil of frayed tempers he quarrelled with Lady Westmorland for good, for she changed her mind and in another solemn fury denounced him for unmanliness in not fighting Alfred. Altogether she had shown herself "a most dreadful friend." Even Edward Cheney was found wanting, and in his need for consolation Henry turned to Teresa Guiccioli once more.

Rome became intolerable, and in September he left for Florence. Teresa had gone before him and was staying with the Marchesa Sacrati. Dudley Stuart had been in Florence, but he left two days before Henry arrived. Christine, however, was staying in the same inn, and she and Henry became fast friends. She introduced him to her quasi-aunt, Eliza Patterson, the first—"and before God the only"—wife of Jerome Bonaparte. Madame Bonaparte was an American—a handsome, middle-aged lady from Baltimore—voluble and, in Henry's opinion, too loud of voice. She was a great authority upon sex—a topic which does not interest Italians—and discussed the physical shortcomings of the husbands of her friends with a frankness that Henry mistook for knowledge. She had admitted Teresa to her confidence, and one evening at the theatre she abused her soundly and warned Henry against her. He told her sharply that he had come to hear Madame Vestris act.

The truth was that Henry was jealous. He attended the Marchesa Sacrati's *salon*. He couldn't help liking the old lady, sitting there upright in bedgown and nightcap and cracking aged jokes with her aged courtiers. Louis Bonaparte, husband of Hortense and former King of Holland, was her principal 'lion'—an ugly, fat man who wrote bad poetry and laid down the law in a loud, sonorous voice. He was pleased to think himself the victim of a *belle passion* for Teresa and wooed her, emphatically and stentoriously, to the exclusion of all other conversation in the room. Henry left the house crossly and went to the theatre, then drove back and crept upstairs to Teresa's room to have a word with her. She nearly fainted at the sight of him, and when he scolded her she fell on the sofa with her handkerchief to her eyes. The Marchesa, she wailed, must have heard his carriage drive up, and it would awake some *sospetto*. But Henry was irritated and masterful. Her tears would not flow, he said in his diary, "and as I showed but little interest at this theatrical exhibition, she dried her eyes."

He left Florence and went back to the Villa Muti. He left the Villa Muti and went to Naples. Lady Compton carried him off to Sicily for seven months. He left Sicily with Edward Cheney and sailed for Malta. On June 17, 1829, he was back in Naples. He was surprised and a little contrite when he received a letter from Teresa. She was in Naples and wished him to meet her that night on Serrazoro's terrace. That was the spot where four years ago he had first spoken words of love to her. Henry groaned in spirit and went.

It was a dark, moonless night, a cold wind blew from the sea, and rain fell with the morning. Henry could only describe the meeting as "painful and extraordinary." Teresa told him that, though she could only love him, in his absence events had occurred which must limit their intimacy. Great was the sentiment, he said sarcastically, in choosing Serrazoro's terrace for this particular scene. However, she must have her way, so "we each pretended to be taking an eternal farewell." He rejoined Edward Cheney later at a gambling-den.

Three days later he climbed the stairs, as of old, to Teresa's garret. He had hardly been there ten minutes when there came five sharp tugs at the bell, which announced that another visitor was mounting the stairs. In walked Lord Fitzharris. He looked daggers at Henry and Teresa. Henry glared back at him—the hatred of a young Whig for a young Tory. He had met Fitzharris in Sicily—a most insufferable young man, conceited about his good looks and his fine throat which he displayed, Byron-fashion, in an open collar. If there were anything else needed to make him offensive in Henry's eyes, it was this—Theresa Villiers was in Rome with her mother, and Fitzharris had been attentive. What business had he now in Teresa Guiccioli's attic?

Fitzharris restrained his temper and fell sulkily into a chair. Henry was all airy persiflage. He congratulated his enemy on his beauty and his talents and told him of the distress his friends at Palermo had felt when he denied himself to Society in favour of a hunting-trip. Fitzharris melted under his compliments and smiled upon him with great good humour. Henry made for the door and hobbled angrily downstairs.

Two days later Henry and Fitzharris met at dinner. Henry found the young man more offensive than ever—"extremely flattered by having obtained success with T.G.—a triumph he seems to suppose hitherto unheard of." But Fitzharris had some odd attraction for him. He called upon him the next morning, and, if possible, Fitzharris was duller and more affected than the day before. He was half naked and he was reading Teresa's copy of *Glenarvon*—which he seemed to think a rare privilege and a grave intellectual enterprise. "I do not think his manners are at all good," said Henry, and Teresa didn't like him either—she had told him that his temper was bad.

Henry wandered about Naples fretfully. A letter came from his parents saying that they wanted him to come home. He packed lugubriously for Rome and went to say good-bye to Teresa. Before he left for England, he promised, he would invite her to stay with him at the Villa Muti.

> We took a tender leave. I shall always feel excessive interest and regard for T.G., and I think she has shewn much generosity and nobleness of character in many occasions. Certainly her conduct to me has always been most admirable, considering my very unpardonable neglect of her; nor can I the least blame her for taking a fresh lover when I had deserted her in the manner I had done.

Henry managed to postpone his departure for England one way and another until September 1830. On the eve of sailing he reviewed the past few years sadly. "I look back . . . with much repentance," he wrote; "I have cruelly and wantonly played with the feelings of others and I have never believed anyone attracted to me." Lady Compton had died unexpectedly, and, alas! they had parted in displeasure before she died. He had been unkind to Theresa Villiers and Nathalie Potocka—though with Theresa Villiers he was sure there had been duplicity. And, saddest thought, his friendship with Edward Cheney could never again be what it had been—he was a bad counsellor, discontented, tart, and *difficile à vivre*.

Teresa paid her farewell visit to the Villa Muti in the spring, when Henry was feeling more than usually mournful at the thought of returning to England. She came with Vincenzo, and Henry sadly recorded the visit in his diary.

> *Sunday, March 28, Villa Muti.* I arranged with M^e Guiccioli about her coming over to Frascati, and I set off in the morning. I waited several hours for her arrival, her heavy carriage, her heavy brother and her own substantial person, fatiguing, I conclude, her rats of horses. At length she came. We

# BOOK SEVEN

# Aftermath

## CHAPTER I

## Cinderella's Palace

AS you see her now, so she has always been."

It was Monday evening, and the Marquise de Boissy was 'receiving' at her hotel in the Rue St Lazare. Young Mr Jerningham, of the British Embassy, turned at the sound of these words murmured over his shoulder. He had been staring across the crowded *salon* at his hostess as she held out her hand in greeting to that distinguished English diplomat and one-time Foreign Secretary Lord Malmesbury.

An old gentleman stood at Mr Jerningham's elbow. He recognized him as the Marquis de Flamarens—a well-preserved old gentleman, dressed with scrupulous neatness, who, they said, had been in his day the victim of more than one tender *liaison* and the Marquis de Flamarens, too, was staring at his hostess with a glint of pensive humour in his eye.

"In what way?" asked Mr Jerningham curiously. "As she is now, so she has always been?"

M. de Flamarens bent a faded yet quizzical eye upon the young man. "*Attachante et attachée,*" he replied briefly and, with a bow, turned to speak with Princess Walewski.

Worldly folk laughed at those 'receptions' at the Hôtel de Boissy. The Marquise was rich, but she was not fashionable, and she jumbled her worlds together with a fine simplicity. Bonapartist generals rubbed shoulders there with grim Royalist dowagers, bankers hobnobbed with painters, and an archbishop would find himself engaged in animated conversation with a *prima donna*. To season this *macédoine* of notabilities there were always many poor and simple people—country *curés*, ministerial clerks, young authors—to whom the Marquise wished to be kind, and a large assortment of English and American folk, wandering melancholy and tongue-tied from room to room.

If the company were mixed, the setting was magnificent. Everything that the Second Empire had dreamed in its vulgarity had been translated into gorgeous fact throughout the stately rooms to create an impression of boundless wealth and luxury. The walls were tapestried in crimson satin damask, with here a dubious Madonna of Murillo and there a huge Venetian mirror, framed in a golden riot of squabbling cupids. The curtains across the windows were wine-coloured velvet, stiff with dragons in gold brocade. The chairs, the tables, the cabinets were glorious in buhl and ormolu. Enormous crystal chandeliers drooped in rainbow splendour from the painted ceiling—for ornament only—for light was shed round the room in a milk-punch glow from a hundred shaded lamps, set on silver pedestals or sunk in vases, jade-green and sapphire-blue. A perfume of tropical flowers brooded like a weary thunderstorm on the air, and beyond the hot-house *patio* a fountain gushed noisily in the night. Tall, powdered footmen in the English style glided noiselessly among the guests, proffering chocolate and sherbet with aloof, impeccable devotion. On the face of many a lady and gentleman there rested a look of bliss recollected in satiety, for they had dined with the Marquise before her reception, and her *chef* was reckoned the best cook in Paris, and the vintages from the Boissy cellar were a *gourmet's* dream.

Cinderella's palace, thought Mr Jerningham; yet how incongruous Cinderella looked amid all this fantastic splendour! A sturdy little figure, dressed in white silk and foamy lace, she circulated among her guests, first on the arm of one cavalier, then another, and jockeyed the most unlikely people into talk. That great Royalist nobleman the Duc de Rohan first led her out. He served her as assistant host, for he was widower of the daughter of the Marquis de Boissy by his first wife. The Marquise with a smile surrendered him to the Countess Waldeck, a handsome cockney woman who once had been a cook.

The Duc de Persigny, faithful henchman of the Emperor, waylaid her with a polite leer, inquiring of her health. "*Hélas*, monsieur," she replied, "I am an old lady in these days—I need your arm." "Dare I ask, madame," said the Duc de Persigny boldly, as he gave her his arm, "dare I ask you—what is your age?" She tossed her head, shaking long ringlets at him. "Always, monsieur," she replied, "*j'ai l'âge de ma chevelure*," and presented him to Dr Sebastian Evans, the American dentist.

Count Waldeck trotted up to her, beaming through his spectacles. He had excavated Mayan temples in the jungles of Yucatan. He was over a hundred years old, had seen Mme Dubarry when he was a boy, visited Marie Antoinette in prison, spoken with Marat, and accompanied the great Napoleon to Egypt. "I must thank you, madame," he said, "for your efforts, and Miss Smith's, to find me a patron in America. I have great hopes that Mr Barnum will admit me to his establishment." The Marquise took his arm and presented him to Madame Adelina Patti, the great singer. "Monsieur Barnum," she said, "performed marvels for our divine Jenny Lind in America."

Lord Malmesbury—genial, handsome, sixty—with merry laugh and shrewd and cheerful eye—stood bowing before her and would have taken her hand to kiss it. But she took his hand in hers and gave it a friendly English squeeze.

They were standing under a portrait of Lord Byron. Mr Jerningham glanced at the portrait—so scornful, so flamboyant—and looked hard at the little woman in white who stood beneath it. Her face was unlined; there was still a rosy shimmer in her cheeks; her eyes were bright and very blue; her shoulders and bust were beautifully formed; she had plump, pretty arms and pretty, capable little hands. Greatest marvel of all, for Mr Jerningham knew that the Marquise was well over sixty— her hair was gold. But why did she wear it in that quaint, old-fashioned way—in corkscrew ringlets, drooping round her face? Had she ever been beautiful? Pretty—yes, perhaps—but beautiful? There was a quiet, patrician look to her features—she was always smiling, always kind and polite—sometimes, Mr Jerningham thought impatiently, I should like to penetrate behind that mask, for there is something in her more than kindness and politeness, I am sure. He looked at her again, and—yes, she was prettier than he thought the first time—there was a beauty in her face—placid, a little cow-like, perhaps—but steadfast and serene.

Miss Rebecca Smith—the lady from Philadelphia—bustled up on the arm of the *curé* from Luciennes, where the Marquis de Boissy had died. Like Mr Jerningham, she frequently visited the Hôtel de Boissy—an emphatic lady of rigid moral views whom he liked to tease. He nodded towards the portrait on the wall and their hostess standing under it with Lord Malmesbury.

"*On revient toujours à ses premiers amours*," he said, mischievously.

Miss Smith gave him a disapproving glower. "Why not?" she said sternly. "The king of poets—and the king of men, too. Besides—I know what you mean and it isn't true, and I won't have you laugh at her. She never loved anyone but him and she was engaged to be his wife. She loved him as Beatrice would have loved Dante, if she'd known. She was living with her father at the time, and he always approved of the connexion. Young people are too censorious these days."

Mr Jerningham assumed an expression of mock bewilderment. "You refer to the subject of the portrait, I perceive—not the gentleman standing under it. And the late Marquis de Boissy—I understand that he, too, approved that connexion."

"The Marquis," replied Miss Smith pointedly, "was a gentleman, a perfect Christian. His love for her 'made breath poor and speech unable,' if you know what I mean. Why, when he came home late in the evening, he would take his boots off in the vestibule and walk in his stockinged feet down the passage so as not to wake her—though sometimes, poor soul, he would forget to take the second boot off and go clip-clopping down the passage and wake her just the same."

"Yes, I've been told he was a very odd man," said Mr Jerningham, "and she was a martyr of amiability where he was concerned."

"A martyr, nonsense! She was devoted to him!" retorted Miss Smith. "Why, only the other day she said to me, 'I had the most perfect friendship with the Marquis de Boissy—the most perfect love for Lord Byron. I should be unhappy in Heaven without them both. They are together there now, they are the best of friends, and' "—Miss Smith's eyes brightened sentimentally—" 'I shall be with them ere long.' That's what she said, sir, so now, perhaps, you'll not be so smart. Why, she's a saint— the purest saint that ever breathed, and shame to them that talk rubbish about her!"

Miss Smith turned to the *curé* from Luciennes for corroboration. "There are many saints on earth," said that cleric sedately, "and Madame la Marquise may surely find a place among them. It is well, perhaps, that the custody of great wealth be given into hands such as hers. She never cared for it and has given it away generously—carelessly, perhaps, to unworthy persons who were ungrateful. Yet there are thousands, rich and poor, who bless her for help and simple deeds of kindness. I remember," continued the *curé*, smiling gently, "how she would stand with her sainted husband outside the toyshop windows at New Year's time, listening to the poor children talk. Then into the shop they went and came out with just the doll or trumpet every child had longed for."

"So like her," declared Miss Smith; "she hasn't a snobbish bone in her body. The other day she climbed four flights of stairs to dine with me and the Count and Countess Waldeck. Think of that, now—the Marquise de Boissy in my garret!"

Lord Malmesbury had said good-night to the Marquise. He joined the group round Miss Smith in time to catch her closing words and note her adoring glance at the plump little figure under the portrait of Byron.

"The Marquise de Boissy in a garret, ma'am," he said with a humorous, reminiscent smile. "She was at home there, you may be bound. I've known her these forty years, and, when I first met her, she was very poor, ma'am—dressed badly—and lived in a garret with one maid. I was introduced to her by the Countess Apponyi—she was laughing when I first set eyes on her. I don't know, but I think I like her better as she was in those days—very frank and good-humoured, kind, you know, and full of fun. This manner of the *grande dame*—it hides all that's real in her— her goodness and that natural gaiety of Italians."

"I can hardly associate Madame de Boissy with a fondness for anything remotely approaching fun, sir," said Miss Smith austerely.

"Oh, yes, to be sure!" said Lord Malmesbury. "Once when I was in Rome the police had put her under house-arrest—she was a famous rebel, you know—friend of Cristina Belgiojoso, and the Emperor's, too, when he was a *Carbonaro*—but he don't like to be reminded of those days.

Well, arrest or not, she was dead-set to spend the summer with her family in her old home outside Ravenna. 'Hop into my britchka,' I said, and away we scampered across Italy. When we got to her own state—Romagna—blessed if she didn't make me put up at every little inn in every little town and showed me the sights—just as though there were no police after us!"

"Did you go to Filetto, sir?" inquired Miss Smith with a note of incredulity in her voice, as of one who would say, "You'll tell me you've been to Mecca next."

"I stayed there two weeks, ma'am," said Lord Malmesbury. "Delightful place, falling into ruin. They tell me they've laid a railway down where it used to be. Slept in a great big bed there, as large as a small cottage. I went shooting snipe and quail in the Pine Forest with her brothers. They had only one old dog and shot with flintlocks. I gave her brother Vincenzo my double-barrelled Purdy when I left, and he fairly hugged me. Poor fellow, he died of consumption soon afterwards. Good-looking bunch they were, the Gambas—monstrous well educated, I should say, for Italians—always hunting and shooting and talking about poetry and liberty and that. Always laughing, too, though what they had to laugh about God only knows—father in gaol, brother dead in exile, police after sister—and Teresa, ma'am—Madame la Marquise, I mean—laughed the gayest of the lot. When I left Filetto, I felt quite sad. Blessed if I didn't scramble home across the Alps and half over England and propose to my dear wife—so she did me a good turn there."

"Did she ever tell you anything about Lord Byron?" asked Miss Smith, in a tone of awe against her better judgment.

"To be sure she did, ma'am," said Lord Malmesbury with a twinkle; "she was very proud of him. Told me she had to feed him hot-cross buns on Good Friday."

Miss Smith would have turned to go, but Lord Malmesbury hurried on, "Blessed if she didn't make me read a silly book about him—said she was sorry for the woman that wrote it—Lord Melbourne's wife, Lady Caroline Lamb, you know—said she could understand how she felt. According to her Byron wasn't much like the heroes in his own books—rather cold in temperament and said sarcastic things. We young fools in those days used to think the fellow was the personification of sin and beauty. Beauty our friend the Marquise allowed him—*O, mon Dieu!* she'd say, *qu'il était beau!*—but sin—no, he hadn't got a vice in his bones. She was too good for him, though—the man was what they call a bounder these days."

"I gather from your reminiscences that you were not on terms of intimacy with the Marquise," remarked Miss Smith acidly, as she gave her arm to Count Waldeck and walked away. "Lord Byron—yes?" said Count Waldeck, "I went swimming with him once in Scotland—I

think?" "Did I ever tell you," said Miss Smith loudly, "what President
Lincoln wrote in my album the day the Civil War broke out? Most
uncultivated, and in prose, too!"

Lord Malmesbury was looking thoughtful, then suddenly he smiled
—a little sadly. "Well, that was all a long time ago," he said to Mr
Jerningham, "at Naples—I was only twenty-two at the time—the days
when I was James Fitzharris, you know." He paused and then added
inconsequently, "You should have seen Henry Fox's face when I came
into the room—sour as the dickens!"

His listener looked curiously round the room in search of the face that
belonged to Mr Fox.

Mr Jerningham left the Hôtel de Boissy with M. Paul Breton. They
were, in one respect, sufferers together. They had collaborated with the
Marquise de Boissy in two works of biography. With immense difficulty,
with frequent counsel and loving dictation, M. Breton had completed a
two-volume life of the Marquis de Boissy. According to his widow,
M. de Boissy was a saint and a great statesman whom his fellow-country-
men had consistently flouted. The trouble was that M. de Boissy had
never held office, never done anything that was remarkable, nor said
anything that was remembered save for its inappropriateness. His letters
were few and written in a telegraphic style, reminiscent of Mr Jingle,
and his speeches, of which he made many, were impromptu, so that the
materials for a biography were meagre. When all was said, M. de Boissy
had been the second richest man in France, a good employer, a generous
landlord, and, in all other respects, a highly comical personage.

It had fallen to Mr Jerningham's lot to make the English translation
of a work written by the Marquise de Boissy—*Lord Byron, jugé par les
Témoins de sa Vie*. It was a terribly long work, written in two volumes,
in bad French, with, in its original edition, several pages in appendix of
misprints. Laboriously the Marquise had set forth to confute all other
biographers of Byron and reveal him to the world as she had known him
—a faultless monster, without vice or physical flaw. In its French edition
the book had been published anonymously, and long had Mr Jerningham
pleaded with the Marquise to put her name to the English translation.
What did her name matter? she said. If people knew that she had written
the book they would say she was prejudiced—which she wasn't—they
might even laugh—and nothing about Lord Byron was a laughing-
matter. She gave in at last because Mr Bentley, the London publisher,
said that without her name the book would have a poor sale, and Mr
Jerningham lose his hard-earned profits. But for her husband's sake she
would not let her name appear as the Marquise de Boissy; she would
take the name that had been hers when Byron lived—'the Countess
Guiccioli'—which was what Mr Bentley wanted.

Teresa—to allow her to resume her old name—had long meant to write her own account of Byron, and only the knowledge that she could never express herself in prose had kept her from her appointed task. At Mary Shelley's suggestion she contributed a brief *storia* of her life with the poet to Moore's *Life of Byron*. It was an odd production, at once lyrical and matter-of-fact, and John Murray was disturbed by the thinness of the ice she skated over—especially at La Mira. Moore made but partial use of her narrative, and in general his life of her poet disappointed her. He had printed many ribald letters—especially about La Fornarina—even a few that were jocose about her own love-affair. It was just that ribald streak in him that she had fought, because she knew it was the stupid, defiant pose of an over-sensitive spirit. Thirty years went by, and one day she read Leigh Hunt's book. Her indignation was great. His remarks about herself—"the buxom parlour-boarder"—she ignored —Mr Hunt was welcome to his opinion—but his ingratitude to Lord Byron—that she would never pardon! The book, too, was disfigured by a horrible caricature—a silhouette of the poet cut out by Marianne Hunt —that made him look like a dissipated cab-driver! She wrote to John Murray the younger, in London. Lord Broughton (as Hobhouse had now become) must at once write a life of his friend to refute the abominable Hunt. For her husband's sake—the Marquis de Boissy—she could not publish all she knew about Byron now, but when she was dead a book would appear, and she cared not what ill the world should think of her so long as "the great and good heart" of Lord Byron was revealed in the "light of day."

She turned to her old friend Lamartine to find a champion for Byron. Lamartine had fulfilled his poet's mission. The Revolution of 1848 had made him ruler of France; then came insurrection and discord, the *coup d'état*, and Lamartine collapsed into obscurity and debt. He was now giving a series of discourses on literature, and begged Teresa to help him with information about Byron. Teresa was only too glad to help, and hoped that she might induce him to write a life of Byron. She wrote for him yet another *storia* of her love-affair—franker and more detailed than for Moore. She sent him Byron's letters to her to read. She insisted on the platonic background of their love, but if he thought the episode at La Mira should be told, he alone must be the judge.

Lamartine built her simple narrative into grand romance, but she was not contented. "Your picture of me (at the Torlonia ball)," she wrote, "is worthy of your brush, but I am not worthy of it." It was his picture of Byron that she must criticize. Then Lamartine behaved very ill indeed. In his printed *Discours* he said, "if Byron had not been lame, he would not have written *Don Juan*, that revenge of a spirit perverted by pride against those who walk straight." Sometimes, when she pleaded with Byron about *Don Juan*, Teresa herself had thought that her poet's lameness may have had something to do with the bitterness and cynicism of his poem; but when she saw those words in print, she knew that the truth was not in Lamartine. He said, too, of the love-letters, "What interest is there in the eternal repetition of the same words expressing the same feeling?" They proved only "the sterility of the imagination when it is absorbed by the heart." Worse still—Lamartine needed ready cash and sold his *Vie de Byron* (with Teresa's *storia*) to a newspaper, *Le Constitutionnel*, and there it appeared as a *feuilleton* for *concierges* to read, full of mis-statements that Lamartine had the impudence to credit to the "Comtesse Thérèsa," as he called her. "Monsieur," wrote Teresa, "you have been poisoned by Leigh Hunt. If Byron was the man you paint him, his books should be burnt. I wish you a happy New Year and a rest from all your cares." Then she relented and signed herself, "Affectionately yours."

Her own book was a disappointment, for she alone of writers succeeded in making Byron as dull as the Prince Consort. But it was the cause of a literary sensation. In Byron's lifetime she had been indifferent to Lady Byron, but Moore's *Life* had taught her to hate Annabella as the reason of her lover's unhappiness. She devoted one chapter to the poor woman, and Annabella emerges as a horrible caricature, with *The Protestant Manual* in one hand and a dinner-bell in the other—reeking of rump-steak and green tea—ineffably bourgeois—the only lifelike character in the book. Annabella had been dead some years, but she found a champion in America. Mrs Beecher Stowe, quoting her dear friend Lady Byron as her authority, in the pages of the *Atlantic Monthly* charged Byron with an adulterous intrigue with his sister, Augusta Leigh. Her revelations nearly bankrupted the *Atlantic Monthly*. But when Mr Jerningham discreetly questioned Teresa about Augusta, she only smiled and sighed. "Oh, she was a perpetual anthem," she said.

Mr Jerningham was rewarded for his pains—how many hours had he sat by the wooden chest while Teresa lifted out the sacred relics and raised them reverently one by one to her lips! No less a person than the Emperor Napoleon asked for a copy of his translation, and Mr Jerningham presented himself at the Tuileries with his two volumes magnificently bound in morocco. The Emperor was a sick, tired man, but his face, too, lighted up with a friendly smile as they talked of the Marquise de Boissy. He remembered her in his mother's house in Rome; they had made a sentimental pilgrimage down the Rhine once—had been poor and shabby in London and 'lions' in Lady Blessington's *salon*. What purpose had the Marquise in writing her book? he inquired. "To prove that Lord Byron was perfect, sire," said Mr Jerningham. "*Tiens*," said the Emperor, "but here is a chapter called 'The Faults' of Lord Byron." "To prove that he had none, sire," replied Mr Jerningham. He told the Emperor that the Marquise was about to write a life of her husband.

His Majesty had not been fond of the Marquis de Boissy—he was a brusque fellow who once had told him that he looked more like a creole than a Corsican. "The Marquise manages well," he said; "first a book about the lover, then a book about the husband. The book about her lover she should call *Mes Folies*, the book about her husband *Mes Regrets*."

## CHAPTER II

# And Prince Charming

*EH BIEN, oui, moi je suis aristocrate.*" That was a favourite aphorism with Hilaire-Octave du Rouillé, Marquis de Boissy. The nobility of his family dated no further back than the regency of Orleans, and its importance had been achieved by law and finance rather than soldiering and politics. Octave's father and his uncle, the Marquis d'Aligre, had been the two richest men in France before the Revolution, and (with a discreet withdrawal to London after the Bastille fell) they doubled their fortunes under the Empire. To a hard head in business the elder Marquis de Boissy added miserliness. He was his own kitchen-gardener and cook, and Octave was reared to count his pennies one by one.

As a youth Octave was a dainty Cherubino with curly hair and turned-up nose. In middle age he dried out into a nervous, bilious little man with a strong cast of Pecksniff to his countenance. He had been a model young man about everything but money, and there he distressed his father by his gay empiricism. Like Teresa, he had a weakness for poets. After a brief career in the Royal Guards he enlisted under Chateaubriand as a diplomat and went with him as secretary to London, Verona, and Rome when Lady Westmorland drove Prince Adrien de Laval in disgrace from that city. His first diplomatic mission was the procuring of a blue dinner-service for the embassy in London. Chateaubriand felt that this dinner-service should be supplied gratis by King Louis XVIII from his works at Sèvres. The King so far concurred as to offer Chateaubriand an incomplete service. Octave was instructed to arrange this delicate matter, which he did with consummate tact, by purchasing a complete blue dinner-service from Sèvres and sending it to his master as a present from his King. His frugal Majesty had a sense of humour and laughed pleasantly when he heard the news. Chateaubriand could not speak too highly of the diplomatic finesse shown by the young Comte de Boissy, and Octave hoped that he would find honourable mention in the *Mémoires d'Outre-Tombe* that his master was writing. But he made one fatal mistake. He lent Chateaubriand money. Chateaubriand was a proud man and made a point of quarrelling with the men whose loans he did not repay. Some years later he blandly informed the Comte de Boissy that he had sold the dinner-service (which somehow had remained in his hands after he had retired from diplomacy), and a poor price it had fetched. In his *Mémoires* the Comte de Boissy was dismissed in a catalogue of *attachés* who had followed him to Verona. Octave was hurt, for, to do him justice, he had never asked, nor even wished, that his loan should be repaid.

Obediently he married an heiress to please his father and took her to Florence, where he was serving as secretary to the French Minister. His lady was an invalid, he was a patient husband and properly disconsolate when she died, leaving him with an only daughter. His diplomatic career terminated in a quarrel. He saw no reason why, as an *attaché*, he should not write direct to the Minister for Foreign Affairs in Paris, and resigned in protest when that functionary told him to desist. He returned to France and, under the patronage of Marshal Soult, embarked on a political career. His experiments in money-making nearly broke his father's heart. He speculated in railways, in the modern telegraph, in steamships; he developed iron and ore on his estates, he built model factories and model villages for his workers. He sunk millions in these unprofitable schemes, but he had the Midas touch and made ten millions out of them in the end. Every time he lost money he was merry, he said, and put on flesh, but every time he made it he had a violent migraine and grew thin again. He was always visiting his factories and wandering about his model villages. He called on his workers in their homes with his pockets bulging with sweetmeats for their children, and in fashionable *salons* ladies smiled shrewdly and said that he was eccentric.

When his father died he became a Peer of France, and heavy were the sufferings of the Upper Chamber under his eloquence. He affected the oratory of the House of Lords—without gesture, flat-voiced, practical, all passion spent—but a natural turn for pyrotechnics made him forget his stoicism. Untiringly he unmasked traitors and denounced villains. Always he opposed. Sometimes his colleagues heard him with undisguised yawns, then suddenly they were moved to shouts of angry protest, then as suddenly the Chamber exploded in a gale of merriment at "*quelque bonne malice.*" His duels with the President of the Chamber were famous. "Monsieur de Boissy," thundered the Duc Pasquier, "I recall you to the subject under discussion." "There is no subject for discussion," replied M. de Boissy amid roars of exasperated laughter, and took wing for a fresh flight of irrelevance. The Duc Pasquier was dyspeptic, too, and sometimes from the chair gave vent to what the French call an 'indiscreet noise.' One day, as he left the tribune after a speech, M. de Boissy stumbled and tobogganed down the steps. "*Comment!*" said the Duc Pasquier from his throne above the tribune. "Must we put up a gangway here?" and punctuated his irony with a majestic indiscretion. "A wind-break would be more to the point," retorted the Marquis de Boissy with graver irony yet from his seat on the floor.

Having made a grand marriage for his daughter with the heir to the Rohan dukedom, Octave turned his mind to love. He met the Countess

Guiccioli at the house of their common friend the Countess Apponyi, in Paris, and asked her to be his wife. "*Ma voisine*," he called her tenderly—my neighbour, my gossip. Count Guiccioli had died in Venice in 1840, and Teresa was not anxious to put her neck into the matrimonial yoke again. But Octave wooed her incessantly, and she gave in. Then her father died (in 1846), and she broke off the engagement and took refuge in Filetto. But Octave bombarded her with letters, telling her about his political activities. She begged him to write her a love-letter for a change.

"When France is falling," he replied, "when the tempest growls, when everything on the horizon forebodes a flash of lightning . . . what shall I talk but thunderclap and shipwreck? Would you have me talk of the dainty green lawn under my windows? of baskets of flowers, arranged in tasteful posies? . . . chirrup like a bird? . . . poetic silliness that I have never talked any more than I have turned those lovers' phrases that those who don't love turn so well and every fool in love turns so badly." There, as Byron said, was poetry for you—in the best thunderstorm style of *Childe Harold*. Octave followed his effusion to Italy, he invaded Filetto, and Teresa capitulated again. "I can promise you," she said, "only patience and toleration." "Remember," he replied, "I shall be your lord and master in law—and your slave in fact."

Still she hesitated. She fled to Florence, and Octave followed her. She drew up a table of conditions for their marriage, guaranteeing for herself the old freedom—the right to travel when and where she pleased. Octave put his name to the document without reading it. "I am an owl," he said, "I mope, I am dismal, I shall always be delighted when you leave me. I have no capacity for happiness in myself. Be you happy, and I shall be happy in your happiness. Travel where you will without me and remember—in spirit I am always at your side, trilling like a lark. . . ." She prayed for guidance . . . wealth with all its boredom was lowering over her again . . . life repeated itself . . . no one ever died—really . . . Brunello was reaching out his arms. . . . "No," she said to Octave— firmly, and for the last time.

They returned to Paris and were married in the chapel of the Luxembourg in December 1847. He was forty-nine and she was forty-five. Proudly Octave presented his bride to King Louis Philippe. "Madame la Marquise de Boissy, sire," he said, "my wife and formerly the mistress of Lord Byron." Teresa scolded him soundly for that *gaffe*—it was their first quarrel and their last. She had lived with Lord Byron and was no more ashamed of the fact than Octave, but she hadn't been his mistress —she had been his Beatrice, his Laura, his affianced wife.

The Revolution of 1848 burst almost upon their honeymoon, and Louis Philippe was bundled out of France. By his denunciations and his exposures of fraud in the Chamber of Peers no man had done more than

Octave to overthrow the Orleans monarchy. But he was appalled by the republic that took its place. Amid the babble of communists and utopians his occupation was gone—his voice was heard no more in a Chamber of his Peers. Crowds rioted, barricades were thrown up—there was nothing left but to die for vanished monarchy. Octave donned his shabby old uniform of the National Guard and, calling upon his coachman and footmen to follow him, ran down into the street.

Two days Teresa searched for his dead body—in deserted streets, by barricades, in hospitals, and at police stations. He returned in the night, laughing and excited. His face was black, his eyebrows were singed, from head to foot he was covered in filth and blood not his own. In Teresa's admiring eyes he seemed like Dante as he emerged from Hell, gasping for the dew of Heaven. He had found himself in a crowd, he told her—some one had thrust a gun into his hand—then he was standing behind a barricade firing at troops at the end of the street—a dead man had fallen upon him and knocked him down—another corpse fell upon him, and another, and another—then he was pulled out from under his load of corpses—he stood rocking on his feet, shouting hoarsely "*Vive le roi*" and, lo! grimy communists were slapping him on the back and shaking him by the hand! Ah, in that moment he had known what it was to be an aristocrat!

Teresa was able to help Octave in his political career. When Louis Napoleon came to France to stand as candidate for President she invited him to stay with her in their chalet at Enghien. Octave hated the name of Bonaparte, but he was reconciled to Louis Napoleon, and after the *coup d'état* became a Senator of France. Once more his voice was raised in objurgation, and the Emperor Napoleon fared no better at his hands than King Louis Philippe. "The Emperor is an exceptional prince," he cried, "and I bless him—in the morning, in the evening—at night, too—when I don't happen to be asleep. . . . There are only three wise princes in the world," he said, "the Emperor is one, the Pope is another, and the third is"—the Senators looked up in curiosity, but their colleague paused and added with a sneer—"messieurs, I perceive that you all know the third. . . . But," he declared, "I will not burn incense before the Emperor. As the Chinaman who smokes opium dies a brute, so the prince who snuffs incense dies an exile." He demanded constitutional government, public debate in the Senate so that his speeches might be heard, and freedom of the Press, subject to legitimate control by bribery.

Octave dressed and tried to talk and behave like an Englishman. His house was filled with English friends. And he hated England. "I hate that nation," he declared, "as only an ugly old hag can hate a beautiful young girl." Englishmen as individuals were *bons enfants*, but in the mass they were rogues and hypocrites. Always England selfishly sought her own interest at the expense of France, and his bitterest cause of complaint against the Emperor was that he was (now and then) a friend to England. "*Waterloo!*" he declaimed in sepulchral tones one day in the Senate, as they were debating some agreement with the hated country; "*et Waterloo encore et toujours Waterloo!* I pronounce that name of execration—Hudson Lowe! Messieurs, I recall you to an honourable hatred. . . ."

Politics brought him nothing but mockery, defeat, nervous indigestion. The Emperor grew weary of his ambiguous compliments, and Eugénie detested him. Teresa, too, was included in the imperial disfavour, for she embarrassed Napoleon by talking at the Tuileries in a deep, clear voice of the days when they had both been poor. Gently she sought to wean her Octave from politics by reading him poetry and pointing out the beauties of nature. But Octave only smiled and yawned. "I know nothing of sentiment," he told her; "I leave that to you." The smoke of factory chimneys, slag-heaps, and grimy miners—those he loved and understood—but trees and birds and clouds left him cold. Only water amused him—the ocean in tempest, a thunderstorm in the hills, tumbling cascades, quiet lakes, and goldfish in a bowl. In the gardens of his many houses he surrounded himself with tossing fountains and laid out long ornamental pools. "*Eh bien, oui,*" he was wont to say, "*moi je suis aquatique.*"

For nearly twenty years Teresa lived happily with her lean and bilious lord. To her, who had given so much for love, he gave utter devotion. For the 'mistress of Lord Byron' nothing less than the château of Mme Dubarry would suit, and he gave her Luciennes, and there she grew strawberries as large as young tomatoes. He gave her a magnificent villa at Sesto, outside Florence, and there she spent her summers with her Gamba nephews and nieces. Poor Octave, he had terrible headaches and felt lonely when they were not together. "I send you a long letter to-day, my spouse," he wrote.

That's a bit young-mannish, you will tell me, a bit lover-like, a bit turtle-dove. *Eh bien, oui*, you are right. A man is wrong to reveal his inmost heart. If he is bad, you despise him; if good, you don't appreciate him, till he is no longer there. It is the same for husbands as for pictures by dead painters. Death gives them both a value people didn't know they had. The world is made that way and we must resign ourselves, as I do. I will say no more but that I beg your pardon for tiring you with my dismal fancies—the boredom of being alone—which is what I want, but it's a bore. A truce to this philosophy that I make without meaning it, just as, my spouse, I sometimes make poetry without meaning it, too.

His beloved daughter died, and Octave fell ill, too, and began to die of the aristocratic disease of gout in the stomach. Very gently he broke the news to Teresa. He summoned her to his bedside. The village carpenter was there, showing him a drawing. With a smile Octave bade her look at it. It was the design for a coffin—name-plate and all. "Always wear white for me," he said and kissed her hand. . . . For long summer days he lay back, staring at the goldfish in the bowl, watching through the window the swans upon the pool, listening to the plashing fountains. "Tell the coachman to turn the fountains off," he said at last, like a god tired of his creation.

Teresa kneeled with two nuns beside his bed, reciting the prayers for the dying. In her agitation one of the nuns dropped a word. Octave opened one eye and glared at her sternly. Painfully he raised his hand and shook his forefinger. The nun corrected her mistake, and Octave closed his eye and died.

# Epilogue at Setimello

OCTAVE died in the late summer of 1866. Forlornly, because he had desired it, Teresa entertained magnificently in her dreadful palace in the Rue St Lazare. She had never cared for the life of opulence and fashion. "I live *in* Society," she told Miss Smith, "but I don't belong to it." Only because Octave wished it had she been a *grande dame*, as once she had tried to be a good *Hausfrau* for Alessandro. She turned her carriage aside from the fashionable *cortège* and drove into more secluded alleys of the Bois de Boulogne, and there plucked violets with Miss Smith, as once she had plucked them with Byron in the Pine Forest. In all the Hôtel de Boissy there was only one memory of nature, of springtime and forest—and Byron and Teresa—a bowl of violets on the table in her room.

Paris had been her spiritual home for many years. She first came there in 1832. Cristina Belgiojoso was there, too, a political exile, living in picturesque poverty in a garret under the paternal eye of old General Lafayette. At the general's bidding the beautiful Emilio left Teresa's side at Geneva, where they were making sentimental pilgrimages round the lake and visiting the Byron haunts, and rejoined his wife in Paris. Cristina embraced her friend Teresa with a tepid smile and admitted her to friendship again.

The Austrian Government restored their fortune to the Belgiojosos, and Cristina set up a *salon* in the Rue de Montparnasse—a grim catafalque, draped in black bespangled with silver stars. Teresa was allowed to sit in the background and serve as secondary hostess. Art, politics, music, literature—all were represented in the Belgiojoso *salon*. Liszt played music there, and Chopin, and Paganini. Théophile Gautier and Stendhal talked poetry and novels; Cavour, the architect of Italian unity, discussed pretty girls with Adolphe Thiers, future President of the French Republic, as in cook's apron in the kitchen he made an omelette. It was Teresa's privilege to watch Cristina's cold, intellectual flirtations with men of genius. She had seen Alfred de Musset act veritable 'scenes from Fragonard' in the bleak, star-spangled *salon* and remembered him always for his gaiety.

A disciple of Lamartine—Léon Bruys d'Ouilly—had fallen in love with her by name and wrote a melancholy poem—*Thérèse*. He fell in love with her in fact when she came to Paris and asked her to be his wife.

312

She promised him her hand when her old Brunello died. A most delightful companion was Léon—the happiest poet that ever lived—a merry country squire, whose life was a better poem than his poetry. He pulled down his château amid the woods and vineyards of Ouilly and built in its place a white marble *palazzo* for his bride. His old spinster cousin disinherited him in wrath, but what cared Léon? Life with Teresa was all golden honeymoon and solemn day-dream. Through wind-swept, whispering woods—over clouded hills—down into secluded valleys—to curious little inns where the beds were hard and the wine was sweet—they drove together, as sure as the swallows came, in a chaise behind two spanking horses—the thrill of everlasting escape in a chariot with golden wheels that illuminated the road they travelled along. . . .

Alessandro died in the Palazzo Malipiero . . . Léon sat across the table from Teresa. The notary sat between them with the marriage articles laid out before him. Teresa was pale and tense. Léon was frowning and drummed on his teeth with his knuckles. Alessandro had kept his promise about the jointure, more or less—almost generously, all things considered. Teresa now had a comfortable private income. But she was left dependent on Ignazio's bounty, and Ignazio was mean and made unfair prohibitions and stipulations in paying over the money. And Léon—well, he had spent his fortune—sold all his farms and vineyards—to build his beauty's palace. He could offer her only two rooms now in his old cousin's boarding-house—with sermons and repentance for their diet.

Teresa never saw the palace that love had built for her. It stood empty and slowly rotted away. "After all," said Léon, "after honeymoon, why should we risk marriage? We were so happy then, *m'amie*! Madam, I give you back your freedom." Teresa burst into tears of wounded pride and unutterable relief. She had been jilted, but Léon was right. It was better to be unattainable—to be wooed rather than caught.

She went home to Filetto and kept house for her father. The little sisters had married one by one, all save the youngest, who died of consumption. Not grand marriages like Teresa's—they found small country gentlemen and lawyers for husbands. Only Ippolito made a grand marriage—with a Gonzaga—and now he was an important man, a Senator in the new Italian kingdom. Ignazio Guiccioli kept the promise of his youth. He wrote a bad tragedy in Italian blank verse—*Gli Stati di Blois*—ferociously romantic in the style of his latest idol, Victor Hugo, and dedicated it to his stepmother—"my most beautiful countess," he called her. But wealth had been bad for Ignazio. He was a Marchese now and a Senator, like Ippolito—pompous and parsimonious—and his wife had taught him to disapprove of Teresa—until she married 'the second richest' man in France.

From Paris, in her days of freedom, she made several visits to England.

There she toured the Byron shrines piously. She prayed in his college rooms at Cambridge. She went to Harrow and talked with his old head-master, Dr Drury, and looked for Allegra's grave in the churchyard. She called at Newstead Abbey, only to be turned away sourly at the door by the housekeeper. Once she met Augusta Leigh, and they talked for hours about "poor Byron," as his sister called him. In her day Augusta had been suspicious of the Countess Guiccioli. She feared that Teresa would stake a claim to Byron's fortune after his death, but that had been a false alarm. Her brother left her his unsettled property—a hundred thousand pounds—which she frittered away in paying blackmail and the never-ending debts of useless husband and worthless sons. She looked curiously at the earnest, artless little woman from Italy who had stead-fastly refused to touch a penny of her brother's money—she was poor and shabbily dressed. Teresa, in her turn, looked wistfully at Augusta —untidy, gushing, her face ever wreathed in affable smiles, laughing brightly at nothing and chattering scraps of piety from the Bible. The two women met once and never met again.

England, on the whole, was a disappointing island. Smoke—fog—rain! Noisy streets, dreary hotels, dismal songs! Perpetual roast beef—buttered toast—tea! But there had been the countryside—and the waves beating on the shore at Brighton—and the common people of England —in London streets, in country lanes! Sometimes she saw Byron in a sunburnt yokel sitting on a stile with his sweetheart and blowing on a penny-whistle, sometimes saw Shelley's face on the urchin who sold her matches in the Strand. She cared little for fashionable people, or for rich and comfortable folk with their talk of charity and blankets. She knew that they laughed at her slyly for a simpleton—and sometimes, too, she shocked them. Once, in a fashionable drawing-room, she was asked to sing. She sat down to the piano, ran her hands over the keyboard, raised her head to sing, and no sound emerged but a—hiccup! "*Dio mio*," she said, laughing gaily, and laid her hand lightly to her heart, "I've eaten too much!" . . . She could still see the red, protesting faces of the women—hear strangled snorts of laughter from the men. Yet surely she had behaved as an Italian lady—gracefully, sincerely— in a startled moment!

The truth was that most respectable doors in Victorian London were closed against this foreign woman who had been Lord Byron's 'mistress.' She made matters no better by staying at Gore House, in Kensington, when she came to England. Lady Blessington and Count d'Orsay were now definitely out of bounds in good society. The Earl was dead, and Harriet d'Orsay lived in Paris, defiantly, as the mistress of the young Duc d'Orleans. There were now no chaperons to make the affair respect-able. But at Gore House Teresa met the company she needed—interest-ing men with no leaven of uninteresting womenkind—Bulwer Lytton and his far more fascinating brother, Henry Bulwer; the Duke of Wellington; her old friends Trelawny and Louis Napoleon; the young Mr Disraeli, the rising politician; Mr Thackeray, the novelist; Captain Marryat, and old 'wicked-shifts' Brougham.

Had she forgotten her jealousy of Lady Blessington when she came to Albaro? They first met at that fatal ball which led to the expulsion of Prince Adrien de Laval from Rome. Lady Blessington gushed over her, but in the battle that followed Teresa was on the side of Henry Fox. Lady Blessington tried to set her against Henry by repeating malicious things which (she said) he had told her about her and Byron; and Henry, like a gentleman, said that Lady Blessington lied. But when Teresa came to London and found doors closed against her, Margaret Power, the outcast, alone of all women welcomed her into her house. Loyally Teresa went back there every time she returned to England. The two women wrote each other letters for many years—playful, sentimental, loquacious—masterpieces of the gentle feminine art of conveying polite distrust with a graceful warmth of compliment. When Gore House crashed and Lady Blessington took refuge from her creditors with Alfred in Paris, Teresa (who was rich now) was kind in her turn and gave her former hostess the use of her carriage. Cristina Belgiojoso was kind, too, and with Lady Blessington laughed quietly over the Marquise de Boissy and her sentimental airs about Byron. When Lady Blessington died and Alfred went slowly mad, dying in a garret, Teresa visited him and petitioned her old friend, Louis Napoleon, to give him a post in his Government.

When she married Octave she heroically vowed that she would make no more pilgrimages to England. But when he was dead she made her last pilgrimage. . . . She asked the young don who lived in Byron's rooms in Trinity College if she might come in. Moved by some intuition, he left her alone and closed the door upon her. . . . When he returned he found his bed-maker sniffing wrathfully over a bunch of violets and a rosary. "I caught one of them papists at her prayers under that gentleman's picture," she said grimly, "but I soon had her out."

The Franco-Prussian War broke out. Teresa left Paris for her annual visit to the Villa Setimello, outside Florence. Her heart was heavy with foreboding, for Octave had known this war would come and he had foretold defeat for France. Her worst fears were fulfilled. The battle was fought and lost at Sédan, and Louis Napoleon was carried a prisoner to Germany. The Empire was overthrown, and Eugénie fled in disguise through a raving mob from the Tuileries. The German armies advanced into France, and Paris was besieged. Then a humiliating peace, and the fury of the Commune. Teresa came back to Paris just as the riots and shootings were drawing to a close. She went to Luciennes. The château had been occupied by Prussian soldiers. It was ravaged and filthy, and the gardens were laid waste and desolate. Her old friend Fagnani, the artist, came to see her. He found her suddenly grown old with whitening hair and a mournful, lined face. She was puzzled, distressed, and grieved for France in its sickness and humiliation, but she was too old now to endure tragedy. She went home to Setimello and never came back to France.

Her smile was set now, her eyes were tired, as she drove through the streets of Florence in her grand carriage with the Boissy arms on its panels. A woman was walking slowly along the pavement—a very old woman with masses of untidy, snow-white hair and very dark eyes. She glanced up at Teresa's face with a sharp look of mockery and resentment . . . Claire Clairmont . . . now a Catholic and living in a convent. . . . Teresa stared at her, smiling vaguely, and didn't see her.

She could not sleep at night. She sat alone in her room with books tumbled round her—her Dante and the poems of Byron, Alfred de Musset's poems and Victor Hugo's, the poems of Martin Tupper and Alfred Tennyson, of Nathaniel Parker Willis, greatest of all American poets (he said), whom she had met in Paris, and Edgar Allan Poe. Listlessly she opened Monte Cristo—Alexandre Dumas—she had walked with him in the Colosseum once—he worshipped her, strangely for him, as a divinity—did not forgive her for marrying Octave—had made good-humoured fun of her in his romance. She dropped Monte Cristo and picked up Nicholas Nickleby. Charles Dickens—he was the only man in England worthy to take the torch from Byron. Many things she did not understand in his books, but she understood Mr Micawber—and Mrs Micawber better still. How she and Cristina Belgiojoso had wept over the death of Smike! And how Octave had wept, too, when she read it to him on his deathbed!

. . . Clip-clop down the corridor—one boot on and one boot off . . . had Octave come home at last? . . .

A large book, bound in crimson with a gold cross on the cover, lay beside her on the table. She opened it—page after page of her own handwriting—the questions she had asked—the answers He had given her from Paradise! That strange young American Daniel Dunglas Home had brought her this consolation—to communicate with those whom the world calls dead. Obediently she asked Octave's leave to communicate with him—only with him. "Pray give ce cher mylord my best respects," Octave replied, "and tell him that I look forward to meeting him, if, as you say, he is in Paradise." He tapped her on the shoulder kindly. "How gratifying for you, ma voisine," he said, "that he is a Catholic at last!" Sometimes, to please her, he would submit a question to his cher mylord and profited on the stock-market as a consequence. Now, through him, he sent her friendly messages.

She crossed her brow and under her hand closed her eyes to pray.

But the prayers wouldn't come. Only voices—scenes and people—a jumble of faces—Shelley's earnest face with the stag-like eyes, Mary's face, so ghostly that night at the Palazzo Lanfranchi, Cristina's face, white and brooding against the dark, Dumas with his mulatto grin under the moon, Louis Napoleon, dreamy-eyed and quizzical, Eugénie, *triste et souriante*, Augusta with her insipid smile . . . so many dead now!

Emilio Belgiojoso . . . the perfect lover, had she known it, the voluptuary . . . dead. . . . He ran away from Cristina with the beautiful young Duchesse de Plaisance . . . to the Villa Pliniana. Eight years they lived there in solitude, never going beyond the gardens . . . and then the Duchesse was rowed across the lake to a villa on the opposite shore, where a young man took Emilio's place. The Villa Pliniana stood empty, unchanged as on the day she left it. Emilio went on a pilgrimage to the Holy Land and came home to die . . . slowly, painfully. . . .

Léon Bruys . . . dead . . . in a hovel on his old estate . . . dying, as he had always lived, happily. . . . His last penny was given to found a newspaper for Lamartine . . . and Lamartine held his hand, as he lay dying. . . .

. . . Clip-clop down the corridor . . . not Octave, surely . . . a young man, limping across the terrace at Sorrento to apologize for his clumsiness. . . .

Henry Fox . . . dead . . . in Naples . . . that dreary farewell visit to the Villa Muti . . . that gentle voice reciting pretty speeches all one day . . . so flat, so insincere! "Vincenzo, take me away by nine to-morrow morning, or I shall go crazy!" Poor Henry, he had come back, though, climbing the stairs to her garret in Paris. Poor Henry, she thought, as she said good-bye to him, he wants devotion but he will never find it, because he will never see it when it comes his way. He left her and went back to Naples and fell in love for the last time in his life—with dainty little Mary Coventry, the girl who rode astride. Poor Henry, he might not see devotion, but he gave it with both hands—to his wife. . . .

. . . Clip-clop down the corridor . . . sunrise at La Mira . . . drifting through the curtain on her bed. . . . *He* was coming—her poet—at last . . . through her fingers, through folded eyelids, radiance gleamed. . . . A presence filled the room . . . bending over her, soft, caressing. . . . "*Ma bonne Thérèse.* . . ." His voice speaking . . . in French, the tongue of Angels, that he had not spoken on earth . . . the wind stirred the curtains . . . the radiance darkened . . . the voice sounded far away. . . . *Je t'attends* . . . and suddenly was near again.

"You have kept me waiting," he said in English—sharply.

# *Appendices*

## I

## LAMARTINE'S "VIE DE BYRON"

*LA Vie de Byron* appeared as a *feuilleton* over Lamartine's name in *Le Constitutionnel* (September 26–December 6, 1865). It was never printed in book form nor included in any edition of Lamartine's works—presumably by his own desire—in his lifetime or after his death. So far as I know the work has not been reprinted nor included in any recent edition of the complete works of Lamartine.

The basis of the *Vie* is Moore's *Letters and Journals of Lord Byron*, which Lamartine follows closely for the facts and chronology of Byron's life. Critical views and reflections on Byron as man and poet—not always favourable—are added to the narrative and had already been adumbrated in Lamartine's *Cours Littéraire*, *Mémoires Politiques*, and other writings.

But Lamartine lays claim to private sources of information—*viz.*, Tom Medwin, with whom he went riding in Florence, Lady Blessington, Lady Hester Stanhope, Professor Rosini, of Pisa, and Faurel, the French antiquary at Smyrna and Djoun, in the Lebanon. There is no reason to suppose that Lamartine did not speak with these individuals about Byron, but it should be pointed out that not one of them—not even Lady Blessington—knew Byron intimately or for a long time. Medwin and Lady Blessington, however, may be trusted to have spoken to Lamartine about their poet possessively and with authority, and it is not likely that either of them was kind about Teresa Guiccioli.

His chief source of private information was, however (according to Lamartine), "la Comtese Thérèsa xxx"—*i.e.*, Teresa Guiccioli herself. In 1865 Teresa had been the Marquise de Boissy for eighteen years. Her second husband, Octave de Boissy, was still alive. He died nine months after the *Vie de Byron* had run its course in *Le Constitutionnel*, and possibly he read Lamartine's account of his wife's love-affair with Byron in the pages of a newspaper.

Lamartine asserts (or implies) in the *Vie* that his sources for his statements about the love-affair of Byron and Teresa were (1) notes made on conversations that he held with Teresa at Rome, January to March 182– (when Teresa, he says, was about twenty-two), a few months after the publication of his *Dernier Chant* of *Childe Harold* and his arrival in Italy as a diplomat; (2) the unpublished *Mémoires de la Comtesse Thérèsa* xxx, from which he prints a long extract; (3) the love-letters of Byron to Teresa Guiccioli, which she gave him to read in March of the aforesaid year 182–; and (4) other material loaned him by Teresa. He declares succinctly that Teresa is the authority for his statements about her love-affair. He adds that he promised to publish nothing of what she had told or shown him without her permission. He concludes by saying that he has kept that promise. In short, Teresa was responsible for the story as he had told it, and she had consented to its publication as a *feuilleton* in *Le Constitutionnel*.

There are many mis-statements of fact in the story that Teresa tells Lamartine in his *Vie de Byron*. She says, for example, that she met Byron one evening in April at the Countess Benzoni's *four days* after her marriage and fell in love with him at once. It is a recorded fact that she married Count Guiccioli in January 1818 and did not meet Byron at the Countess Benzoni's until April 1819. Byron's letters make those two points sufficiently clear. So, too, for that matter, does Teresa make them clear in the *storia* that she sent Moore in 1829 for his *Letters and Journals* of Byron. She further tells Lamartine that after Byron's death she retired to a convent "for several years" and only left it when Count Guiccioli died. In short, it would appear that Teresa lied to Lamartine in the year 182–, and some of her lies were blatant—*e.g.*, Lamartine would have had little difficulty in finding out that her husband was alive at the time that she spoke to him. Certainly she took one lie back promptly in her *storia* for Moore in 1829—*i.e.*, about the time of her meeting with Byron in the Countess Benzoni's palace at Venice. When we remember that Lamartine lays the responsibility for these—and other—mis-statements on Teresa's shoulders, we cannot help asking—why did she tell him lies so outrageous and useless—lies, too, that she renounced a few years later in favour of the truth? Another strange point. On July 12, 1835, Teresa was in London and met Nathaniel Parker Willis, the American poet and newspaperman, in Lady Blessington's *salon*. She had known him in Paris previously in 1832–33 and suspected (what, indeed, was the fact) that he was cultivating the acquaintance of celebrities in Europe in order to write them up in an intimate, disrespectful way in the *New York Mirror*. She told him, pointedly, that she disliked newspapers, never read them, nor wanted to be mentioned in them—she wanted, so far as the public Press was concerned, to be forgotten—journalists reported the evil but neglected the good. If that was the way Teresa felt about newspapers in 1835, why did she give Lamartine permission to publish her story as a *feuilleton* in *Le Constitutionnel* in 1865? Apparently we must score another mendacity against her. She lied to Willis as she had lied to Lamartine. She desired newspaper notoriety and—if we are to believe Lamartine—gave him permission to publish her love-story as a *feuilleton* in *Le Constitutionnel*. She was punished for her sins. The *Vie de Byron* fell flat and was forgotten at once.

2

When did Lamartine meet Teresa at Rome? He states the year, vaguely, as being 182–. In the *Vie* he fills in the details. He was, he says, accredited to the court of *Naples* as a diplomatic agent from France. His duties brought him to Rome, and there he met Teresa for the first time at a ball given by Prince Torlonia to the *corps diplomatique* on New Year's Eve. He had recently arrived in Italy as a diplomatist. He had a few months before published his *Dernier Chant du Pèlerinage d'Harold*. In that poem he had made some uncomplimentary reflections on the character of the Italian people. These reflections accounted for the subdued murmur with which his entry into the Torlonia ballroom was greeted. Eventually, in the spring of 1826, they led to a duel with the Neapolitan revolutionary General Pepe. In his *Dernier Chant* he had also described Teresa as a "venal Aspasia," and that slur accounts for her remark (see p. 263) on first meeting him that she ought to "hate him," but could not because of the noble portrait he had painted of her dead lover.

The *Dernier Chant* was published in Paris in July 1825. In September 1825 Lamartine proceeded to Florence as a member of the French diplomatic corps there. In September 1828 he returned to France.

His first meeting with Teresa, therefore, must have taken place on New Year's Eve, 1825. His statement that she was, at most, twenty-two years old at the time would corroborate that assumption. He goes on to say in his *Vie de Byron* that he met her almost daily in her '*salon*,' or the Pamphili-Doria gardens, for the next two or three months. In March 1826 (he implies) she gave him Byron's letters to her to read.

We may, then, state that Lamartine and Teresa first met on December 31, 1825, at which time Teresa was in full flight with Henry Fox for a lover. But after that assertion we have to record two mis-statements against Lamartine. First, he was never accredited to the court of Naples, as a diplomatist. He went to the court of Florence in September 1825 in that capacity and left it in 1828. Secondly, as we know from his correspondence in March of 1826, he was in Florence and not, as he implies in the *Vie de Byron*, in Rome.

If Teresa lied, then, to Lamartine about herself in 1826, Lamartine was inaccurate, too (by implication, perhaps, more often than by direct statement), in the *Vie de Byron* that appeared in *Le Constitutionnel* in 1865.

3

The *Vie de Byron* opens on September 26, 1865, in *Le Constitutionnel*. Lamartine says that he questioned the Comtesse Thérèsa about the memoirs that Byron had written at La Mira and given to Moore. (After Byron's death the manuscript was burnt on Murray's insistence.) The Comtesse could give him very little information. Byron was secretive about writing his memoirs and did not consult with her. She, on her side, had no desire to pry into the secrets of her lover's past—perhaps, too, there was a portrait of her in the memoirs that he did not wish her to see. In any case, she neither read them nor asked Byron to read them to her. They were written on odd scraps of paper with great rapidity. When finished, he put the manuscript in a package and sealed it up—the Comtesse could not be sure, but she thought there might be a hundred sheets of manuscript all told. Almost at once Byron handed the package to Moore, as they were standing together on the steps of Count Gamba's palace in Venice. (Count Gamba had no palace in Venice, and Byron gave Moore the manuscript at La Mira.)

The Comtesse Thérèsa drops out of the story, and the *Vie* follows Moore's *Letters and Journals of Lord Byron* fairly closely until November 15. The Comtesse Thérèsa then reappears. The time had come, says Lamartine, for a serious emotion to save Byron from "the versatility of heart" and "profanation of genius" that had befallen him at Venice. Suddenly this "electric commotion"

X

took place. He loved a beautiful young woman "then in her dawn and always poetic," worthy to be ranked with Beatrice, Eleanora, and Laura—women who have been "immortalized by the love and the frailties, often culpable, of immortal men." We will not name her, says Lamartine, out of respect to her first husband—and her second. She shall be "la Comtesse Thérèsa x x x," of a noble family in Romagna. From thoughts of Romagna Lamartine jumps to the Pine Forest outside Ravenna and drifts off into a reminiscent daydream of a love-interlude of his own in that forest with a beautiful woman (? Mme. de Larche).

He then describes his first meeting with the Comtesse Thérèsa at the Torlonia ball (see pp. 262–263 of this book). Every day of that winter in Rome—a beautiful spring-like winter—"cemented between us a drawing-room *liaison*." He found Teresa a delightful companion—friendly, frank, trustful, and very sincere. Her emotions, though quick, were lasting. They went for walks in the Pamphili-Doria gardens. But "love," he says, "was impossible. There was always a *third* between us and this third was a shade adored by her and respected by me." Lamartine obviously did not know that the 'shade' had been reincarnated in physical form at that very time in lame Henry Fox. He delicately implies, however, that the Comtesse Thérèsa was not unmoved by his own masculine charms. He took down notes of their conversation and some years later recast them. He will now reproduce these conversations—never before printed. "These pages of my memories," he says, "are pages of history"—that is why he publishes them—in *Le Constitutionnel*.

One fine day in March, as they were walking in the Pamphili-Doria gardens, he asked the Comtesse Thérèsa to tell him her love-story, promising that he would never publish anything that she told him without her permission. The Comtesse Thérèsa set promptly to work in the best style of a one-eyed Calender in the *Arabian Nights*. "O how the world is deceived in its judgments by its own malignity . . . I was the daughter of the Count Gxxx, of one of the most noble families of Ravenna. . . ."

The story that follows is told by the Comtesse in the first person. Removed from her convent before she was sixteen, she married the aged Count Guiccioli. Four days after her marriage she met Byron at the Countess Benzoni's in Venice and promptly fell in love with him (see pp. 38–41 of this book for the narrative). Then followed *un roman*. She and Byron met every day. Her husband carried her away to Ravenna. She was delirious and nearly died. Byron followed her to Ravenna, and she recovered. Count Guiccioli invited Byron to live on the second floor of the Palazzo Guiccioli. A year of bliss followed. "We never saw each other alone. I did not want, nor did he seem to want, a more intimate familiarity. Understanding without speech, is not that the language of angels and souls?"

The following spring a mischievous priest told tales to Count Guiccioli. He treated his wife to scenes of jealousy and violence. In anger Byron left the Palazzo Guiccioli. The Count left for Rome to get his marriage annulled. Her own family decided that she must be rescued from the clutches of the Count and appealed to the Pope. People in Ravenna sided with her, but (says the Comtesse Thérèsa) they were odiously cruel and unfair to—Count Guiccioli. He might be violent and despotic, but he was capable of great generosity of mind. (Strange—yet not unlike her—that the only kind word ever spoken for Count Guiccioli should come from Teresa!) The Pope decided in her favour, and she left the Palazzo Guiccioli to live in her father's house. Then came further troubles. For plot and conspiracy her father and two brothers were banished from Romagna. She followed them to Pisa, where Byron rejoined her. She met Medwin and Shelley in Pisa. She did not live in the same house as Byron. "Nothing in our relationship passed the limits of that assiduous friendship that Italian society authorizes without scruple between an illustrious foreigner, a guest in their country, and a young woman living in her father's house."

Political troubles drove them out of Pisa. They fled to Genoa, and thence Byron sailed for Greece. He was not tired of love when he left her, but her brother Pietro had been egging him on to go to Greece. The Comtesse Thérèsa returned sadly to Bologna with her father. The absence of letters from Greece prepared her for Byron's death. She returned to her husband. He was still violent and jealous, and life was unhappy. The Pope intervened again. She retired to a convent for several years. Then her husband died, and she returned to the world—a ghost.

The inaccuracies of this narrative are obvious, and some of them have already been pointed out. We may, however, add that the story of the 'elopement' of Byron and Teresa from Bologna and their love-interlude at La Mira has been omitted. That omission was necessary if the Comtesse Thérèsa were to prove her point that her relations with Byron were purely platonic.

When the Comtesse Thérèsa had finished her story Lamartine suggested that she should hand over to him her love-letters from Byron. She agreed at once to that transaction, but added in evident embarrassment, "Read them without thinking of me . . . I have neither the shame of my happiness nor the hypocrisy of my innocence . . . There are fires that tarnish as there are those that purify—praise me only for my tears. If I was guilty . . . seek not to make excuses for me." In other words the Comtesse Thérèsa realized that the love-letters would give the lie to her contention that her relations with Byron were strictly chaste.

As night fell they walked home together to the Comtesse Thérèsa's lodgings, and there, Lamartine implies, she gave him Byron's love-letters. He read them and was disappointed. They showed that Byron loved the Comtesse Thérèsa—otherwise they were monotonous.

Lamartine's story goes on. A short while after showing him the love-letters the Comtesse Thérèsa sent him her written *Souvenirs*. She wished to contradict "certain rumours" and set him right about mistakes that Moore had made about Byron in his *Letters and Journals*. (Moore's *Letters and Journals*, by the way, were, as yet, unpublished, in 1826.) As Moore had made use of the 'confidences' of the Comtesse Thérèsa, Lamartine declares that he, in his turn, is entitled to publish her *Souvenirs*. "Once the seal is broken by the very hand of the person interested in secrecy, such documents belong to history." Accordingly he prints an extract from the *Souvenirs* entitled *Pages des Mémoires de la Comtesse Thérèsa*.

Lamartine characterizes these *Souvenirs* as *naif*. So, fundamentally, they are. But we have to disentangle Teresa's *naif* style from Lamartine's more majestic diction, for it is apparent that he rewrote much of what she had written before he published it. The Bologna-La Mira episode had been omitted from the earlier narrative of the Comtesse Thérèsa in the Pamphili-Doria gardens. Now Teresa Guiccioli, under the weight of professorial editing by Lamartine, tells that story—with considerable frankness, simplicity, and characteristic matter-of-factness.

Thereafter the Comtesse Thérèsa drops out of Lamartine's narrative. He returns to Moore's *Letters and Journals*. He rebukes Byron for "lightness of expression and carelessness of heart" in writing about Teresa to Murray and other friends in London. "He was not entirely worthy of the passion of Thérèsa at the moment when she was ready to sacrifice even her life for him." But was this 'carelessness' sincere? he asks. Was it not the vanity of a sceptic who loves to make fun of his own best feelings? His love for Thérèsa was a good force in his life. The *Vie* closes on a note of moral reproof for Byron. He was blasphemous, loved ridicule, lacked sensibility, morality, reason, and truth. His poetry is "delirium, enthusiasm, melancholy—and emptiness—" because there is no God in it. "Reading Byron is a most poetic tipsiness, but it is tipsiness just the same."

Henry Fox, when he returned to England in 1830, warned Moore (who was fond of her) that he must not make a *héroïne de roman* of Teresa Guiccioli in his forthcoming life of Byron. That is what Lamartine has made of her. As the Comtesse Thérèsa she is the heroine of a bad French novel. And she does not suit the part.

4

So much for Lamartine's story in his *Vie de Byron*. Now for the story of the writing of the *Vie de Byron* as revealed by M. Henri Guillemin in his *Lamartine, Byron, et Mme Guiccioli*.

Lamartine returned to France in 1828. He made amends for his "venal Aspasia" portrait of Teresa Guiccioli in his *Dernier Chant* by preaching the 'Beatrice' doctrine about her to Alfred de Musset and other French poets. He sent his young friends Edgar Quinet and Léon Bruys to visit her in Italy. They both were prepared to fall in love with her. Quinet chanted her praises in his *Ahasuerus* (1833), but was deterred from falling in love by the size of her feet. Léon Bruys gave her name to a melancholy poem he wrote—*Thérèse* (1836)—and succeeded where Quinet had failed. He asked Teresa to be his wife, she consented and, pending Count Guiccioli's death, a honeymoon of some years' duration followed during which, unknown to her, Léon built Teresa an Italian *palazzo* amid his vineyards (see p. 313). Léon's friends, including Lamartine, were more embarrassed than amused by this 'honeymoon.' Lamartine, in particular, must have resented the expenditure on the *palazzo*, as Léon was one of his most faithful financial backers in his political ambitions.

In 1847 Teresa married Octave de Boissy. He, too, was a friend of Lamartine. They had been colleagues in diplomacy, and Octave had probably helped Lamartine with money. By the Revolution of 1848 Lamartine became one of the rulers of France. He offered Octave the embassy at Rome and then backed out of his promise. Octave expressed his displeasure, says Count Apponyi, with his usual brusqueness, and their friendship cooled. Under the Second Empire Lamartine lost all political importance and found himself in financial straits. He returned to literature to recoup his fortunes, and in 1856 launched his *Cours Familier de Littérature*. He wrote to Teresa (de Boissy, as she was now), asking her to help him with material about Byron.

Teresa responded kindly. She was glad to help Lamartine in his financial difficulties. She also hoped that she would persuade him to expand his articles on Byron ultimately into a biography, for she was dissatisfied with Moore's *Letters and Journals*. At Lamartine's request she wrote (anonymously) a *Portrait Physique* of Byron. In May-June of 1856 Lamartine contributed three articles on Byron to *Le Siècle* (*Notes sur mes Lectures*). In November he printed part of Teresa's *Portrait Physique*. "These lines," he said, "have been recently communicated by a person who was dear to him (Byron) and who sees his face again across time, across death." Then for several months nothing more appeared about Byron.

Lamartine had decided to write a *Vie de Byron*. He had written up the account of their walks in the Pamphili-Doria gardens and the story that she told him there, and sent it to Teresa and asked her to let him read Byron's love-letters. Teresa was delighted that Lamartine wished to write a life of Byron. "*Mon cher Monsieur Lamartine*," she wrote on March 21, 1856, "how delightful they were, our walks at that beautiful Villa Pamphili, and how beautiful and touching is your description! I would not change a word." *But* —he had put the story of her love-affair into her own mouth—and there were 'inexactitudes' in the narrative. Tactfully she blamed the 'inexactitudes' on herself. She had spoken to him in the Pamphili-Doria gardens in "too much of a hurry." In order that the *facts* might be "faithfully produced" and "certain circumstances too well known to be passed over in silence" be brought out, she was writing "a brief narrative" of her love-affair. "Then there will be little to take out of your beautiful tale but some facts to add to it." As for the love-letters, she has read them again and feels that they ought not to be published. Not even Lamartine's eloquence in translation could do justice to the platonic spirit that lies behind them. However, she has classified them methodically and is willing to let him see them. With the help of "such living proofs" Lamartine may be enabled to reveal "that great and beautiful soul of a poet, so little known," to the world.

Apparently Lamartine requested Teresa to send him her 'narrative' and still insisted on seeing the letters. A few days later Teresa wrote again—"I do not wish to fail in my word to you, and I send you a few pages of the narrative that I promised you. It is only the first part. I have not finished the other part, and I will give it you when it is. It is a simple narrative, very much abbreviated, of the story you asked me for. You will be indulgent, as you needs must be for everything in it, for the bad French it is written in." Lamartine's *récit* is "*si ravissante et si simple*" that she would not alter it, *but*—there are "*quelques phrases un peu brûlantes.*" Ought she to tell the whole story about La Mira? "For vulgar souls wouldn't the truth there be, perhaps, not like the truth?" But—"You are You . . . You must be the judge." She has sent him the love-letters in a portfolio (with the key). "*You* will feel in the

simplicity of the style all the greatness of the loving heart beating as it writes."
The letters are difficult to read. She would like to read them aloud to him
and "explain a thousand things that are . . . unintelligible."

Lamartine does not seem to have accepted Teresa's invitation to a reading
of the love-letters. He took the first half of her 'narrative,' rewrote some of
it, and grafted it on his own story. For example, the account of the conversation between Byron, Scott, and the Countess Benzoni is sheer Lamartine,
grafted on notes given him by Teresa. She also gave him a list of the topics
(remembered by her so well) that she discussed with Byron on that fateful
April evening, and these Lamartine reproduces baldly and flatly in Teresa's
matter-of-fact style. But for the most part he preferred his own *récit* and made
little or no use of Teresa's 'narrative' to correct its 'inexactitudes.'

On April 3, 1856, Teresa wrote again. She had finished her 'narrative.'
She had tackled the La Mira interlude—an episode that "has held so
important and so sorrowful a place in my life." Lamartine alone is worthy of her
confidences on "that cruel romance that is my story." She has tried only to tell
the truth. Her 'narrative' is only "a simple, rude canvas destined to receive
*your* magic colours." She will do everything she can to help him write a life of
Byron "for your sake and *his*. . . . A thousand and a thousand things such as
I can say *to* you and *of* you."

After that letter there seems to have been a lull in writing the life of Byron.
In the following year (1857) Lamartine printed the sixteenth *Entretien* of his
*Cours Familier* with its famous sneer at Byron—he would never have written
*Don Juan* if he hadn't been lame. It was the revenge of a cripple on men
"that walk straight." Teresa never forgave Lamartine that sneer, and she
ceased to co-operate with him in writing a life of Byron.

Three years later (1860) Lamartine, being still in financial difficulties, issued
a circular asking for support in the publication of his forthcoming works.
Among the works to be published was a *Vie de Byron*. Teresa issued an
anonymous pamphlet, *Lettre à M. le Comte de* xxx, on June 17, 1860, in which
she declared that by his own remarks about Byron Lamartine had shown himself incompetent to write his life.

In 1862 Lamartine, being in yet deeper financial waters, sold his rights in
the *Vie de Byron* to *Le Constitutionnel*—without telling Teresa. In 1863, in
his *Mémoires Politiques*, he sought to disarm her by calling her "the Beatrice
of Liberty." In September 1865 the *Vie de Byron* started running its course
in *Le Constitutionnel*.

Teresa was shocked, hurt, and sad. Lamartine had betrayed her confidence.
He had not even taken the trouble to correct the 'inexactitudes' in his story.
He had trailed her romance in the gutter. On November 19, 1865, she wrote to
him—"I am appealing to your loyalty and delicacy." His declaration that she
had authorized the story in *Le Constitutionnel* has hurt many people to whom
she is attached. When he publishes his *Vie de Byron* in book form, will he be
good enough to be more explicit on that point—will he also print T. for
Thérèsa and write of her as *elle*, not *je*? What happens about the *Vie de Byron*
after her death doesn't matter, but now she must think of the feelings of others.
"You have painted me," she wrote sadly and ironically, "in colours more
worthy of yourself than me. All your shadows, all your rigours, you have

kept for the great poet. As for your appreciation of him, so contrary to every-thing I think, I have nothing to ask of you, nor say to you, but that, if that appreciation is founded in truth, it will survive, but it will fall if it isn't." Teresa was right. The *Vie de Byron* fell—flat.

Apparently Lamartine gave her the desired promise about the *Vie de Byron* in book form and tried to make some alterations in the story as it ran in *Le Constitutionnel*. After the last number of the *feuilleton* had been printed Teresa wrote a final letter to Lamartine. "In acquiescing to my appeal you have done *me* a favour, not a duty to truth and justice." She hated being put into a newspaper. She had no fault to find with what he had said about her, but, alas! he was woefully mistaken about Byron. He was *not* heartless or selfish or a profligate, his wife was much to blame, etc., etc. "A Happy New Year to you and a relief from your worries—affectionately yours, Thérèse de Boissy."

## 5

Out of this story Teresa emerges, on the whole, with dignity. She was vain, sentimental, too careful of Lamartine's feelings in exposing his 'inexactitudes'; she was assuredly a nuisance in her insistence on his painting *her* portrait of Byron, not his own; she was, perhaps, gullible—but how could she foretell that Lamartine—of all men—would behave in so strange a fashion? But she honestly desired to tell the truth about herself and (as she saw it) about Byron. And, in the end, her anger was aroused, not by Lamartine's treatment of herself, but by what he had said about Byron.

Lamartine's offences are, perhaps, easy to explain. He was in desperate need of money, he was overworked, he grew tired of writing a pot-boiler life, he was jealous of Byron, Teresa annoyed him with her Hosanna attitude towards her dead lover, and he suspected (not altogether wrongly) that she hoped for a sentimental portrait of herself. Her first story in the Pamphili-Doria gardens, no doubt, was confused, and obviously he didn't listen very carefully. He misunderstood the purport of her insistence on 'platonism,' and anyhow didn't believe it any more than she did, *au fond*. Probably he did ask her to show him Byron's love-letters in 1826—he was not the only one to ask for that favour and be refused. His notes were hasty and his memory was poor. And so forth.

But when we have explained we have not excused. Why did he make mis-statements about himself? Why did he not correct his 'inexactitudes' about Teresa with the help of her 'narrative'? Why did he imply that she gave him the love-letters in 1826—not 1856? Why did he sell the whole story to a newspaper without telling Teresa? Why does he claim that she authorized his many mis-statements? Why does he alternately claim that she had allowed him to publish and that he had a right to publish without her permission, anyhow? Let Teresa have the last word. He was *worried*—old and tired. He died a few years later.

## "LORD BYRON, JUGÉ PAR LES TÉMOINS DE SA VIE"

TERESA'S own book about Byron is a tedious book, says John Drinkwater, but it was not written by a tedious woman. That is a shrewd observation. Teresa's reading is wide, particularly in French literature of the essay and aphoristic kind. On religious matters she writes with knowledge and tolerance. To all but the most rabid Shelleyolator, what she says about Shelley as poet and man shows sympathy and insight if not always approval. Every now and then she hits out a good, revealing phrase. The fault of the book is that she did not trust herself to speak about Byron from her own knowledge. In her matter-of-fact way she often admitted that she could be a fool on that topic, so she quotes other people—and far too many of them.

As John Drinkwater again says, the book is, on the whole, free from faults of jealousy and temper. The one exception is Lady Byron. Teresa was indifferent to that poor lady in Byron's lifetime. In fact—knowing her Byron's faults —she sometimes felt sorry for her. With her usual frankness—Byron called it tactlessness—she told him that he thought of Annabella with more kindness than he was willing to allow. Certainly she taught him to stop hating her.

But after reading Moore's *Letters and Journals* she herself learned to hate Annabella with a furious hatred—for Byron's sake. Poor Annabella, her fate was so normal! If a pompous and stupid woman breaks down in the first year of marriage with a brilliant and likable man, there is not much she can do, or say, about it. The world will admit that her husband was guilty—and lay all the blame on her.

But Byron's other 'ladies'? Claire Clairmont, it is true, is dismissed contemptuously—but without name—in a footnote—but then, from Teresa's point of view, Claire was an ill-bred vixen. Caro Lamb is treated kindly, on the whole, and her *Glenarvon* is quoted with approval. And Augusta Leigh? Teresa told Hubert Jerningham that, *entre nous*, she grew tired of hearing Byron sing the praises of his sister. She met Augusta once and did not trouble to meet her again. Nor did Augusta desire to prolong the acquaintance. Teresa was not 'respectable' in England. Nor, for that matter, was Augusta respectable, but she wanted to be. She was an amiable ass, a "moral idiot," as Annabella in one of her less pompous moments called her, and as her management of the lives of her daughters, Georgiana and Medora, proved her. But in her *Témoins* Teresa accepts loyally, if without enthusiasm, the legend that Augusta was an ennobling influence in her brother's life. If Byron told her anything about the nature of his relationship with his sister Teresa never said a word about it to anyone else—not even in the height of the Beecher Stowe controversy. To break silence, then, would have been, in her code, not only treacherous but, worse still, ill-bred. Besides—in her code—why shouldn't Byron love his half-sister? It was a folly, no doubt, but not a crime, and she had educated him out of it. Mrs Stowe's revelations were a moral Much Ado about Nothing—and so English—or, rather, American!

Among men Chateaubriand is treated consistently with acidity. He had behaved badly to Octave. He performed his charities 'on the balcony,' whereas Octave—and Byron—had performed theirs on the sly. Hoppner had tried to make mischief between her and Byron and, after the poet's death, wrote articles implying that Byron cared little enough for her. Teresa dismisses Hoppner with a kindness almost insulting. He was just the sort of man, she implies, from whom Byron would hide his real feelings—as witness the ribald letters that he wrote about her (and Hoppner allowed to be printed). Lamartine died shortly after the book came out. He is dealt with severely on Byron's account, but considerately Teresa makes no reference to his conduct about the *Vie de Byron*. Tom Medwin she detested, but when she rebukes him—always deservedly—she calls him *Monsieur M.*

There is a curious explosion of temper at the very end of the book. Teresa loved (or tried to love) England—for Byron's sake. She was fond of English men—but apparently not of English women. But she hated 'respectable' people in England. Unexpectedly she lashes out at their condescension, their smugness, their moral airs, their appalling 'charities.' What right had they to charge Byron with heartlessness and immorality?

There are two mysteries in the *Témoins*. Teresa frequently refers to a Miss Smith and quotes with approval her remarks on Byron's face, voice, manners, etc. This was not Miss Smith from Philadelphia. Apparently she was the niece of a mathematical don at Cambridge. Her family was poor and her mother tried to force her into an undesirable marriage. She wrote religious poetry. She fell in love with Byron by fame. She visited him in his rooms at the Albany—to solicit a subscription for her forthcoming volume of religious verse. Byron was superlatively kind and—explained that he was engaged to be married to Miss Milbanke. Miss Smith ultimately withdrew from the picture in a state of mingled adoration and despair. In her old age she wrote all the story to a Mme B. in Paris (? Mme Belloc ? Mme de Boissy). Eventually a small volume was published in French in Paris. It would seem to have contained letters from Byron to Miss Smith, and Miss Smith to Byron. I have never seen a copy of this work. It is easy to see how Miss Smith came by Byron's letters to her—she kept them. But how did she come by her own letters to Byron? Were they among the packages of love-letters from other women left by him with Teresa when he sailed for Greece? Did Teresa de Boissy return them to Miss Smith? Did she pay for Miss Smith's book in Paris? If she did she paid off a debt for her lover, who had apparently not paid for Miss Smith's volume of religious verse in London in 1814. But, who knows? Probably that volume was never published. I have looked for it in vain.

The other mystery is this. Teresa frequently refers in her *Témoins* to a book called *Byron en Italie*. The Comtesse d'Haussonville wrote a book on this subject. She was a granddaughter of Mme de Staël, and it was her chief sorrow in life that she was not a daughter of Byron as well. Naturally she and Teresa were friends, and Teresa helped Mme d'Haussonville in writing her book. But it is clear that in her *Témoins* Teresa does not refer to the work of Mme d'Haussonville.

In the *Allgemeine Zeitung* for April 16, 1873 (I think, but I have mislaid my reference), there is a notice of Teresa's death in the preceding March. The writer, who knew Teresa well, says that she had left behind the manuscript of, or the materials for, a book called *Byron en Italie*. Certainly in 1870 Hubert Jerningham told the Emperor Napoleon III that Teresa was writing, or intended to write, such a work. What has happened to the manuscript of Teresa Guiccioli's *Byron en Italie*?

# THOMAS JEFFERSON HOGG AND TERESA GUICCIOLI

IT was Hogg's fate always to be a camp-follower in Shelley's life. He was expelled from Oxford with the poet, and he lived to write the first authorized biography of Shelley—only to have the work taken out of his hands by the scandalized son and daughter-in-law of the poet. In between whiles he was always following meekly and reluctantly in Shelley's footsteps.

On Shelley's orders he tried his best to fall in love with his sister, Elizabeth Shelley, and acquiesced in plans for an elopement. He made love to Harriet Westbrook a very short while after her marriage to the poet. Shelley—inconsistently, if we consider his views on marriage and free love—discarded Hogg from his graces for this peccadillo. But after the elopement with Mary Godwin Hogg was admitted to the fold again. By the express sanction of Shelley he tried to cultivate a free-love *liaison* with Mary, who did her best to respond. But there was no will on either side, and the affair came to an end with no harm done. After Shelley's death his Miranda, Jane Williams, returned to England, and Hogg promptly fell in love with her. Marry her he could not, for Jane had a husband—one Johnson—in India whom she had left for Edward Williams and from whom she could not obtain a divorce. *Faute de mieux* Hogg cohabited with Jane, and in the eyes of the world they passed for a married couple.

Jane Williams was not a sensitive type. She made no bones about it that Shelley had been attracted by her charms just before he was drowned. She gossiped about Mary and implied that she had been a poor wife to Shelley. Her innuendoes eventually led to an estrangement with Mary Shelley.

She gossiped about Teresa Guiccioli, too. She had thick ankles, she told Hogg, and a bad temper. When she was cross she tore Byron's night-shirts to tatters. Perversely and humorously Hogg chose to be amused by this display of temperament and liked Teresa all the better for it. Why, he said, did Byron leave all his money to his "silly sister" and not a penny to the "poor Countess," who, at least, was a real "human being? . . . I'm afraid," he declared, "our poet had more head than heart." Hogg never lacked shrewdness in his judgment of human nature. But he didn't know—why should he?—that Teresa had refused to take a penny of Byron's money—by legacy or otherwise—when he sailed for Greece.

In August 1825 Hogg left England for a Shelley pilgrimage in Italy. Jane Williams gave him letters to the Countess Guiccioli. Apparently he first met her in Pisa. She questioned him "closely and slyly" about Jane Williams and soon learned the state of Hogg's affections. Whatever Jane may have said about her, Teresa was full of warm praise for Jane. In December 1825 Hogg was in Rome and met Teresa Guiccioli again. He visited her almost every day and talked about Shelley. Just at that time Teresa was pining for the absent and dilatory Henry Fox, but she found time to be kind and helpful to Hogg. "With the Guiccioli," he wrote to Jane in England, "I am much pleased. . . . I found her well informed, clever, amiable, and I think handsome." She embarrassed Hogg by introducing him to her friends as the Englishman who was going to marry the "beautiful Mrs Williams." He begged her to stop doing this and allay the rumour as best she could. Teresa complied with his request. She knew, however, from another quarter of the obstacle in the way of Jane really *marrying* Hogg and had held her tongue about it. She could sympathize, for she, too, had an undivorceable husband in the background. Hogg gave her to understand, however, that Jane was really free to marry him. Teresa accepted his statement, but obviously didn't believe it. She wrote Hogg cheerful letters about the ceremony pending in London, for 'married' she was sure Hogg and Jane would contrive to be.

Hogg was apparently much taken by Teresa. He called her 'Teresina' and told Jane that she was *lovely* and *charming*. She gave him a letter to a school-fellow and friend when he went to Bologna—Clementina degli Antoni, "who is," she says, "beautiful and witty above all in the world." Hogg arrived in Bologna in January 1826. It snowed all the time he was there. "But the Clementina is such a love! . . . full of goodness, wit and grace, more hand-some than the lovely Theresa was willing to allow."[1]

In finding Teresa Guiccioli charming, kind, amusing, and, in spite of Jane Williams's strictures, handsome, Hogg, for a change, followed in Byron's foot-steps. Apparently Teresa held an attraction for clever men with sharp, disillu-sioned minds—Byron, Henry Fox, and Hogg—presumably because she was by turns imperious and docile, amusing and boring, good-tempered, gay, and subject to tantrums.

It is disappointing to relate that when Teresa visited England on several occasions between 1832 and 1847 she did not keep up with Hogg and Jane and Mary Shelley, although to Mary Shelley, at any rate, she for long wrote letters. The fault for lapsed friendship lay with Hogg and Jane and Mary. Teresa was not a respectable person in England, and she stayed with Lady Blessington. Mary in Highgate was growing timid and conventional. She wrote to her friends in terror lest the Countess Guiccioli should call on her. And Hogg and Jane, though living in sin, passed for a married couple. Natu-rally they were too respectable to know Teresa.

[1] Sylva Norman, *After Shelley.*

# IV

## JOSEPH FAGNANI'S PORTRAIT OF THE MARQUISE DE BOISSY (1860) AND HIS IDEALIZED PORTRAIT OF BYRON (1860)

GIUSEPPE (JOSEPH) FAGNANI was born at Naples on December 24, 1819. From childhood he showed a bent for painting. In 1832 he was taken under the patronage of the Queen Mother, Maria-Isabella, of Naples, who gave him a stipend from her privy purse to study for five years at the Royal Bourbon Academy. In 1840 he set out upon what was to be a lifelong pilgrimage of painting portraits of the royal, the fashionable, the rich, and the famous all round the world from Constantinople to Washington. He went first to Milan, Vienna, and Trieste. From 1842 to 1849 he hovered between Naples, Madrid, and Paris, with flying visits to London. In Paris the Queen, Marie-Amélie, patronized him, and in Madrid the Queen Mother Cristina. In Madrid, too, he formed a lifelong friendship with Henry Bulwer, made acquaintance with Eugénie di Montijo, and painted a portrait of her sister, the Duchess of Berwick and Alva. Others of his portraits were Henry Bulwer, Richard Cobden, John Bright, Alexis de Tocqueville, and the Comte d'Etiolles, illegitimate child of Rachel, the actress, by Count Walewski, illegitimate son of Napoleon.

In October 1849 he sailed for America. For the next eight years he painted portraits industriously in Washington and New York—Henry Clay, Daniel Webster, Elisha Kent Kane, the Arctic explorer, old Mrs Alexander Hamilton, widow of the statesman, his compatriot, Garibaldi (then in exile in America), and sundry Van Rensselaers, Rhinelanders, and Vanderbilts. In 1851 he married an American wife—Emma Everett, daughter of Thomas J. Goodwin, of Charlestown, Mass. In 1858 he returned to Europe for a while and made Paris his headquarters. By the end of 1865 he was back in America again and finally domiciled himself in New York. He painted portraits of General Sheridan, Stephen Morse, and Commodore Vanderbilt, but his most famous work was "The Nine Muses" (1868)—a series of portraits of nine fashionable New York 'beauties.' These portraits were painted for exhibition in the Metropolitan Museum of New York. They are still in the possession of that museum and may be seen—in the basement. They are, I am told, frequently examined by the descendants of the original Nine Muses. There was a tenth picture—a "Cupid"—Master George Watts. Fagnani died in New York on May 22, 1873.

Fagnani painted three portraits of Teresa Guiccioli. The first he painted in 1849, soon after her marriage to the Marquis de Boissy. The second he painted in 1860 (reproduced in this book), and the third in 1865. He painted two portraits of the Marquis de Boissy. The first was painted in 1847, at the time of the marriage. The second (painted in 1865) showed the Marquis in the uniform of a Senator of the Second Empire—"my footman's livery," Octave was wont to call it to Fagnani—and the Emperor Napoleon III.

Fagnani and his wife were close friends of the Marquis and Marquise de Boissy and visited their house regularly. The Marquis they found amusing, witty (in a French way), eccentric, kind, and "a very happy husband." Teresa, said Fagnani, was still a beautiful woman—below middle height, dazzling fair complexion, regular features, dimpled shoulders, a child-like smile that revealed perfect teeth and an expression that showed "a sunny disposition" and a reflective, cultivated mind. In 1860 Teresa had still not got a single grey hair.

The costume she wears in the 1860 portrait was white satin and tulle, designed by Roger, the Paris dressmaker. It cost five hundred francs, and Teresa was remorseful for spending so much money on mere finery. The costume was designed for a fête given by the Emperor Napoleon III in honour of Princess Clothilde of Savoy, the bride of Prince Napoleon. Octave de Boissy gave a special reception for the installation of the portrait in the Hôtel de Boissy. He had bright calcium lights in the courtyard illuminating the fountain. They shone through the windows of the *salon* straight on the portrait, thus throwing it in high relief. Neither Teresa nor Fagnani approved of this experiment in high-lighting.

Teresa refused to sit to photographers, because they made her features look vacuous and heavy. But she had six photographic reproductions made by Bingham of this portrait. The Empress Eugénie (who disliked Teresa and disapproved of Fagnani for being anti-papal) asked for one, but Teresa refused her request. She tore all the photographs up—save one which Fagnani surreptitiously obtained. Later (after 1865) in New York Fagnani painted from this photograph a replica of the portrait—which was in 1930 in the possession of Mr Edward Clark, of Cooperstown, N.Y. Arsène Houssaye (who disliked the Marquis de Boissy) said of the portrait when it was first painted that it showed very skilfully the likeness of the Marquise de Boissy to the Countess Guiccioli, whom Byron had loved—almost, he implied, Fagnani had seen the Marquise de Boissy through Byron's eyes.

In 1860 Fagnani executed another commission for Teresa. She gave him a miniature of Byron, painted by Prepiani in Venice just about the time that she first met him (1819). It was, she said, the only good likeness and showed Byron as he looked on that April night in the Countess Benzoni's *salon*. She asked Fagnani to enlarge this miniature into a portrait, and she sat beside him and watched him at work. She gave him detailed instructions about Byron's physical perfections—his eyes, his hair, his throat, his skin, his fingernails, and, above all, his lips and his smile. No one, she said, with that smile looked *less* like Childe Harold or Manfred. And his lameness—it was only "one grace more," she stoutly declared. Fagnani's finished work is reproduced in this book—not for its artistic merits nor for its likeness—but because it shows Byron as Teresa always saw and remembered him.

The Gamba family own a miniature of Byron with the Mulberry Hawk whiskers, grown at Teresa's request and noted by Moore in his account of his visit to Venice in 1819. Teresa told Fagnani that her poet dropped the whiskers by the time he arrived in Pisa. When Mrs Beecher Stowe's article on Byron

and his sister appeared in the *Atlantic Monthly* Fagnani had his picture of
Byron reproduced as an answer to her charges.

The above information comes from *The Art Life of a XIXth Century Portrait
Painter, Joseph Fagnani*, by his widow, Emma Fagnani, written in 1873 and
privately printed in 1930. The volume is full of reminiscences of Teresa, as
Marquise de Boissy, some of which I have utilized in my narrative. I here
give the more interesting points.

(1) Teresa said that she was practically unacquainted with social usages
when she first met Byron.

(2) Count Guiccioli was tall, handsome, witty, with distinguished manners.
He had been dissipated in youth, was unfaithful to her, but she accepted the
situation as a matter of course.

(3) She longed to understand English when she heard Byron and Moore
frolicking like two schoolboys at La Mira.

(4) Knowing Byron's dislike of regular meals and dining in company, she
tried not to nag him, but conspired with his valet, Fletcher.

(5) Byron told her that the three things that made life with Lady Byron
impracticable were (1) her love of method and regular meals, (2) her confidential maid, Mrs Clermont, and (3) her complaints about bailiffs in the house.

(6) He also loved telling tall stories about himself, making himself out to
be half demon, half murderer. Teresa didn't believe him and laughed at his
stories.

(7) Richard Cobden knew Lady Byron and said she was a 'good' woman,
but, after meeting Teresa, he said he now knew why the marriage had broken
down.

(8) Shelley, said Teresa, never seemed like a creature of this world. She
loved him. So did Byron.

(9) Mary Shelley was practical. Shelley was very dependent on her good
sense and devoted to her.

(10) Lady Blessington was disappointed that Byron was not captivated by
her charms, even though she had Count d'Orsay with her.

(11) Teresa said that she encouraged Byron to cultivate Lady Blessington's
acquaintance. He was unwilling to do so, but finally went, because, he said,
the Blessington party would provide him with types for *Don Juan*.

(12) Teresa later knew the Countess d'Orsay in Paris, liked her, and said
she was beautiful.

(13) Count Guiccioli in his will settled 30,000 francs a year on Teresa.

(14) The Duc Pasquier asked, "Marquis, is the lady you are marrying any
relation to the one so admired by Byron?" "*Mon cher*," replied the Marquis
de Boissy with a radiant smile, "it is the lady herself."

(15) The Marquis de Boissy hated Garibaldi and the Prince of Wales (afterwards Edward VII). By shaking hands with Garibaldi, he said, the Prince of
Wales had sealed his fate—he would die on the scaffold.

(16) Octave de Boissy boasted that he belonged to no party. Teresa's *salon*,
as a result, was mixed—*e.g.*, Louis Napoleon (before he became Emperor),
Lamartine, Montalembert, Girardin, Marshal Canrobert, the Archbishop of
Paris, Mme Ristori, Mme Patti, Richard Cobden, Lord and Lady Gort,

Dr Sebastian Evans (the dentist), the Duc de Morny, the Rev. John Barlow, the eccentric Duke of Brunswick, etc.

(17) In Teresa's box of Byron relics were the manuscripts of *all* of *Don Juan*, one canto of *Childe Harold* (which she ultimately gave away), the *Prophecy of Dante*, *Beppo*, *Manfred*. Also several fugitive poems, including that beginning "River that rollest by the ancient walls." One poem was written on the back of a cobbler's memorandum. Also there were 300 letters written in Italian —"worthy of Petrarch." All this material was bequeathed to a Gamba great-nephew, aged two and a half. (Teresa had at one time intended to divide her Byron manuscripts between the British Museum and the Bibliothèque Nationale.)

(18) The copy of *Corinne* in which Byron wrote his love-letter was old-fashioned duodecimo, covered in purple velvet.

(19) Teresa's *Témoins* was written for French consumption only and to refute Lamartine. Her *Byron en Italie* was to be written for English and American consumption and would be more personal.

(20) Mrs Fagnani sent Teresa Mrs Stowe's articles in the *Atlantic Monthly*. Teresa was indignant and transferred her hatred of Lady Byron to Mrs Stowe. She was pestered with letters on the subject, but declined to comment in public. She told Mrs Fagnani that Mrs Stowe, like Lady Byron, was a humorless busybody who would believe any wild story that Byron told about himself. She was sure that Byron had told *her* all the truth about himself and his sister —and more than that Teresa would not say.

Mrs Fagnani quotes in an English translation an Italian letter written by Mary Shelley (Harrow, November 28, 1835) to Teresa Guiccioli on the death of her brother, Vincenzo. Outwardly affectionate—"dearest little Countess ... it seems a thousand years since I have seen you"—it politely conveys the intelligence—"please don't call."

We conclude by saying that Teresa Guiccioli was difficult to please about her own portraits. Count d'Orsay's sketch (frequently reproduced) she conceded to be a *likeness*. But for the more popular Brockedon portrait, used by Murray in his landscape and portrait illustrations of Byron's works, she had no use at all. "It is not resembling," she wrote to Murray, ... "not on account of the ugliness of the features (which is also remarkable) but ... for having an expression of *stupidity* and for its being *molto antipatico*. ... Perhaps it is the fault of the original and I am sorry for that. ... Towards such a creature nobody may feel inclined to be indulgent, and if she has faults and errors to be pardoned for, she will never be so on account of her *antipatica*. But pray don't say that to Mr Brockedon."[1]

[1] Samuel Smiles, *Memoir of John Murray*.

# V

# "TERESA GAMBA–GHISELLI, BENEFATTRICE"

THUS is Teresa Guiccioli recorded in Italian encyclopædias and books of biographical reference—under her maiden name—as a philanthropist.

Her second husband, the Marquis de Boissy, despite his wealth and his oddities, was an unobtrusive philanthropist—to hospitals, prisons, Magdalen homes, his own workers, poets like Chateaubriand, and innumerable friends in difficulty. Teresa shared unobtrusively in his philanthropies.

She earned her name as *benefattrice* in Italy in 1866—the year Octave de Boissy died. Her native state, Romagna, and her own city, Ravenna, were ravaged that year by cholera. Teresa was prodigal in help, financial, personal, and practical.

In Italian encyclopædias her second claim to fame is that she was the sister of Pietro Gamba, a hero of the War of Greek Independence, and Ippolito Gamba, a Senator of the new Italian Kingdom.

Her association with Byron is quoted as her third claim to fame.

The Guiccioli family also achieved power and position under the new Italian Kingdom. Garibaldi's wife, Anita, died in a farmhouse belonging to Ignazio Guiccioli in the uprising of 1849.

# Bibliography

BARBIERA, RAFFAELO: *La Principessa Belgiojoso* (Milan, 1930).

BEERS, H. A.: *Nathaniel Parker Willis* (New York, 1885).

BENSON, A. B.: *Catherine Porter Stith and her Meeting with Lord Byron* (*South Atlantic Quarterly*, vol. xxii, Durham, N.C., 1923).

BLESSINGTON, MARGUERITE GARDINER, COUNTESS OF: *Conversations of Lord Byron with Lady Blessington* (London, 1834).

—— *The Idler in Italy* (London, 1839–40).

BLUNDEN, EDMUND: *Leigh Hunt: a Biography* (London, 1930).

BOISSY, TERESA, MARQUISE DE: *Lettre à M. le Comte de ×××, Paris, ce 17 Juin 1860* (an anonymous pamphlet, written to protest against Lamartine's proposed *Vie de Byron*, afterwards incorporated in *Lord Byron, jugé par les Témoins de sa Vie* as *Lord Byron et Lamartine*).

—— *Lettre à M. le Vicomte d'Yzarn-Freissinet* (Paris, 1867). (Afterwards reprinted as a *Lettre-préface* to the *Mémoires du Marquis de Boissy*, by Paul Breton.)

—— *Le Portrait Physique de Lord Byron* (1856) (originally written for Lamartine for his *Concours Littéraire*, and later incorporated in *Lord Byron, jugé par les Témoins de sa Vie*).

BRETON, PAUL: *Mémoires du Marquis de Boissy, 1798–1866* (Paris, 1870).

BROUGHTON, LORD (J. C. HOBHOUSE): *Recollections of a Long Life* (London, 1909–11).

BRUNNER, K.: *Byron und die österreichische Polizei* (in *Archiv für das Studium der neueren Sprachen und Literaturen*; Braunschweig, 1925, Jahrg. 80).

BRUYS, LÉON: *Thérèse* (1836), with a prefatory *Épître* to the author by Lamartine, reprinted among Lamartine's poems.

BYRON, GEORGE GORDON, LORD: *Letters and Journals*, edited by Rowland E. Prothero (London, 1898–1901).

—— *The Letters and Journals of Lord Byron*, edited by Thomas Moore (London, 1830).

—— *Lord Byron's Correspondence, chiefly with Lady Melbourne, Mr Hobhouse, the Hon. Douglas Kinnaird, and P. B. Shelley*, edited by John Murray (London, 1922).

—— *Poetry*, edited by Ernest Hartley Coleridge (London, 1898–1904).

CAMP, MAXIME DU: *Souvenirs Littéraires* (Paris, 1882–83).

CANTONI, FULVIO: *Byron e la Guiccioli a Bologna* (Bologna, 1927).

CHEW, SAMUEL C.: *Byron in England* (London, 1924).

CHORLEY, H. F.: *Personal Reminiscences* (New York, 1874–76).

CLARKE, ISABEL C.: *Shelley and Byron: a Tragic Friendship* (London, 1934).

CRAWFORD, S. C.: an account of Teresa Guiccioli and the Duc de Persigny, quoted by E. C. Mayne in *Enchanters of Men*. I have not located the original article. It appeared in *The Reader* for December 1906.

DAVY, SIR HUMPHRY: *Collected Works*, edited by his brother, John Davy (London, 1839–40).

—— *Consolations in Travel* (London, 1831).

DOWDEN, EDWARD: *Life of Shelley* (London, 1886).

DRINKWATER, JOHN: *The Pilgrim of Eternity* (London, 1925).

EARLE, MRS C. W.: *Memoirs and Memories* (London, 1911).

ELZE, CARL: *Byron; a Biography* (London, 1872).

FAGNANI, EMMA: *The Art Life of a XIXth Century Portrait Painter, Joseph Fagnani* (Paris, 1930).

FOA, GIOVANNA: *Lord Byron, poeta e carbonaro* (Firenze, 1935).

FOX, HENRY (afterwards LORD HOLLAND): *Journal, 1818–30*, edited by the Earl of Ilchester (London, 1923).

GALT, JOHN: *Life of Lord Byron* (London, 1830).

GAMBA, PIETRO: *A Narrative of Lord Byron's Last Journey to Greece* (London, 1825).

GAY, H. N.: *Scritti sul risorgimento: raccolti e ordinati da Tomaso Sillani (la Rassegna Italiana)* (Rome, 1937).

GORDON, A. C.: *Allegra: the Story of Byron and Miss Clairmont* (New York, 1926).

GRABINSKI, COMTE JOSEPH DE: *Une Princesse Révolutionnaire (Correspondant, vol. 29. October–December, 1902).

GRANVILLE, HARRIET, COUNTESS: *Letters*, edited by the Hon. F. Leveson-Gower (London, 1894).

GRYLLS, R. GLYNN: *Claire Clairmont* (London, 1939).

—— *Mary Shelley: a Biography* (London, 1938).

GUICCIOLI, ALESSANDRO, MARCHESE DI: *Dal diario inedito* (in *La Nuova Antologia*, Rome, 1932–37–38; published in book form as *I Guiccioli—Memorie di una Famiglia patrizia*).

GUICCIOLI, IGNAZIO, MARCHESE: *Gli Stati di Blois: dramma storico* (Paris, 1835), published in *Rivista Italiana del dramma* (Rome, 1938).

GUICCIOLI, TERESA, COUNTESS: *Lord Byron, jugé par les Témoins de sa Vie* (Paris, 1868). English translation by H. E. H. Jerningham: *My Recollections of Lord Byron; and those of Eye-witnesses of his Life* (London, 1869).

—— selections from her poems, published for the most part in Italian periodicals, are given in Luigi Rava's volume (see below). The poem on Shelley is dated 1844.

GUILLEMIN, HENRI: *Lamartine, Byron, et Mme Guiccioli (Revue de Littérature Comparée*, 1939).

—— *Le Jocelyn de Lamartine: étude historique et critique* (Paris, 1936).

HAUSSONVILLE, LOUISE, COMTESSE D': *Les dernières Années de Byron* (Paris, 1874).

HAYWARD, ABRAHAM: *A Selection from the Correspondence of, with his Early Life* (New York, 1886).

HEYNEN, W.: *Teresa Guiccioli (Preussische Jahrbücher*, Berlin, 1934).

HILLEBRAND, K.: notice of death of Teresa, Marquise de Boissy, and Countess Guiccioli, in the *Allgemeine Zeitung*, April 16, 1873.

HOUSSAYE, ARSÈNE: *Les Confessions, Souvenirs d'un demi-siècle* (Paris, 1885). (Contains d'Orsay's reminiscences of Byron at Genoa.)

HUNT, LEIGH: *Autobiography* (new edition, London, 1903).

—— *Correspondence*, edited by his eldest son (London, 1862).

—— *Lord Byron and some of his Contemporaries* (London, 1828).

ILCHESTER, EARL OF: *Chronicles of Holland House, 1820–1900* (London, 1937).

—— *The Journal of the Honourable Henry Fox, 1818–1830* (London, 1923).

JEAFFRESON, JOHN CORDY: *The Real Lord Byron* (London, 1884).

JERNINGHAM, SIR HUBERT E. H.: *Reminiscences of an Attaché* (Edinburgh, 1886).

JOHNSON, R. BRIMLEY: *Shelley—Leigh Hunt; how a Friendship made History* (London, 1929).

LACRETELLE, HENRI DE: *Lamartine et ses Amis*, translated by Marie E. Odell as *Lamartine and his Friends* (New York, 1880).

LAMARTINE, ALPHONSE DE: *Cours Familier de Littérature, Entretien X—"Une Nuit de Souvenirs"—et Entretien XVI* (Paris, 1856–57).

—— *Le Dernier Chant du Pèlerinage d'Harold* (Paris, 1825).

—— *Épître à M. Léon Bruys d'Ouilly* (in his collected poems) (originally published 1836).

—— *Notes sur mes Lectures*. Three articles on Byron in *Le Siècle* (May 11, May 25, and June 9, 1856).

—— *La Vie de Byron* (in *Le Constitutionnel*, September–December, 1865).

LIECHTENSTEIN, PRINCESS MARIE: *Holland House* (London, 1874).

LOVELACE, MARY, COUNTESS OF: *Ralph, Earl of Lovelace: a Memoir* (London, 1920).

LOVELACE, RALPH, EARL OF: *Astarte* (London, 1921).

MADDEN, R. R.: *Literary Life and Correspondence of the Countess of Blessington* (London, 1855).

MALMESBURY, JAMES, EARL OF: *Memoirs of an ex-Minister* (London, 1884).

MALVEZZI DI MEDICI, ALDROBRANDINO, MARCHESE: *La Principessa Cristina Trivulzio di Belgiojoso* (Milan, 1936–37).

MARSHALL, MRS JULIAN: *Life and Letters of Mary Wollstonecraft Shelley* (London, 1889).

MASSINGHAM, H. J.: *The Friend of Shelley: a Memoir of Edward John Trelawny* (London, 1930).

MAUROIS, ANDRÉ: *Byron* (Paris, 1930).

MAXWELL, SIR HERBERT: *Life and Letters of George William Frederick, Fourth Earl of Clarendon* (London, 1913).

MAYNE, ETHEL C.: *Byron* (New York, 1924).

—— *Enchanters of Men* (Philadelphia, 1909).

—— *Life of Lady Byron* (London, 1930).

MEDWIN, THOMAS: *Journal of the Conversations of Lord Byron at Pisa* (London, 1824).

—— *Life of Shelley* (new edition, London, 1913).

MOORE, THOMAS (ed.): *The Letters and Journals of Lord Byron* (London, 1830).

NICOLSON, HON. HAROLD C.: *Byron: the Last Journey* (London, 1924).

NORMAN, SYLVA: *After Shelley* (Oxford, 1934).

ORIGO, IRIS, MARCHESA: *Allegra* (London, 1935).
—— *Conte Alessandro Guiccioli: a Husband* (*London Mercury*, vol. 32, London 1935).
PASTON, GEORGE, with PETER QUENNELL: *To Lord Byron* (London, 1939).
PATMORE, P. G.: *My Friends and Acquaintance* (London, 1854).
PECK, W. E.: *Shelley, his Life and Work* (Boston and New York, 1927).
QUENNELL, PETER: *Byron in Italy* (London, 1941).
—— (with GEORGE PASTON): *To Lord Byron* (London, 1939).
RAVA, LUIGI: *Lord Byron e Percy Bysshe Shelley a Ravenna e Teresa Gamba-Guiccioli a Roma* (Rome, 1929).
REEVE, HENRY: *Memoirs of Life and Correspondence* (London, 1898).
RODOCANACHI, E.: *Notes Secrètes de la Police Autrichienne de Venise sur Byron* (*Institut de France, Académie des Sciences Morales et Politiques*, January–June 1918).
SADLEIR, MICHAEL: *The Strange Life of Lady Blessington* (Boston, 1933).
SHEE, WILLIAM A.: *My Contemporaries, 1830–1870* (London, 1893).
SHELLEY, MARY W.: *Letters*, edited by Frederick L. Jones (University of Oklahoma, 1944).
SHELLEY, P. B.: *Letters*, collected and edited by Roger Ingpen (London, 1909).
SHORE, W. TEIGNMOUTH: *D'Orsay, or the Complete Dandy* (London, 1911).
SMILES, SAMUEL: *A Publisher and his Friends: Memoir and Correspondence of John Murray* (London, 1891).
SMITH, EARL C.: *Byron and the Countess Guiccioli* (*Publications of the Modern Language Association of America*, vol. xlvi, December 1931).
SMITH, MARY R. D.: *Recollections of Two Distinguished Persons, la Marquise de Boissy and the Count de Waldeck* (Philadelphia, 1878).
TAYLOR, SIR HENRY: *Autobiography, 1800–1870* (London, 1885).
TILLETT, N. S.: *The Unholy Alliance of Pisa* (*South Atlantic Quarterly*, vol. 28, Durham, N.C., 1929).
TRELAWNY, E. J.: *Letters*, edited by H. Buxton Forman (London, 1910).
—— *Recollections of the Last Days of Shelley and Byron* (London, 1858).
—— *Records of Shelley, Byron, and the Author* (London, 1878).
VARÉ, DANIELE: *Byron and the Guiccioli* (*Quarterly Review*, New York, 1934).
VIEL-CASTEL, COMTE HORACE DE: *Mémoires* (Paris, 1883–84).
WHITE, NEWMAN IVEY: *Shelley* (New York, 1940).
WHITEHOUSE, H. R.: *The Life of Lamartine* (Boston and New York, 1918).
—— *A Revolutionary Princess: Cristina Belgiojoso* (New York, 1906).
WILLIS, N. P.: *Pencillings by the Way* (originally published in the *New York Mirror*, 1832–33).

# Index